Lecture Notes in Computer Science 15913

The series Lecture Notes in Computer Science (LNCS), including its subseries Lecture Notes in Artificial Intelligence (LNAI) and Lecture Notes in Bioinformatics (LNBI), has established itself as a medium for the publication of new developments in computer science and information technology research, teaching, and education.

LNCS enjoys close cooperation with the computer science R & D community, the series counts many renowned academics among its volume editors and paper authors, and collaborates with prestigious societies. Its mission is to serve this international community by providing an invaluable service, mainly focused on the publication of conference and workshop proceedings and postproceedings. LNCS commenced publication in 1973.

Wei-Sheng Wang · Frode Eika Sandnes ·
Chin-Feng Lai · Tengel Aas Sandtrø ·
Yueh-Min Huang
Editors

Innovative Technologies and Learning

8th International Conference, ICITL 2025
Oslo, Norway, August 5–7, 2025
Proceedings, Part I

Springer

Editors
Wei-Sheng Wang
National Cheng-Kung University
Tainan City, Taiwan

Chin-Feng Lai
National Cheng-Kung University
Tainan City, Taiwan

Yueh-Min Huang
National Cheng-Kung University
Tainan City, Taiwan

Frode Eika Sandnes
Oslo Metropolitan University
Oslo, Norway

Tengel Aas Sandtrø
Oslo Metropolitan University
Oslo, Norway

ISSN 0302-9743 ISSN 1611-3349 (electronic)
Lecture Notes in Computer Science
ISBN 978-3-031-98184-5 ISBN 978-3-031-98185-2 (eBook)
https://doi.org/10.1007/978-3-031-98185-2

This Springer imprint is published by the registered company Springer Nature Switzerland AG
The registered company address is: Gewerbestrasse 11, 6330 Cham, Switzerland

Preface

The *International Conference of Innovative Technologies and Learning (ICITL 2025)* provides a platform for those in educational technology to exchange experiences. Benefiting from a wide range of emerging technologies, the e-learning environment has become increasingly diversified. These technologies have fueled the development of advanced learning environments through the adoption of appropriate pedagogies. Moreover, they not only facilitate learning but also help students achieve enhanced learning outcomes. However, due to the rapid evolution of new technologies, how to integrate them with sound pedagogies to create adaptive or intelligent learning environments remains a challenge. Therefore, this conference aims to offer a forum for researchers in education, computer science, and educational technology to share their experiences in applying cutting-edge technologies to learning and to inspire new directions in the field. It is hoped that the work presented at the conference will inform researchers and practitioners aiming to build more effective learning environments. ICITL remains committed to sharing these efforts with the broader community.

This year's conference was held at Oslo Metropolitan University, Oslo, Norway, from August 5 to 7, 2025. We received 214 submissions from 37 countries worldwide, with each submission reviewed by at least three experts. 82 papers were selected after a rigorous single-blind review process. The acceptance rate was 38%.The accepted contributions represent the latest research across seven major areas: 1) Artificial Intelligence in Education; 2) Computational Thinking in Education; 3) Design and Framework of Learning Systems; 4) Pedagogies to Innovative Technologies and Learning; 5) STEM/STEAM Education; 6) VR/AR/MR/XR in Education; and 7) Application and Design of Generative Artificial Intelligence in Education. As educational technologies evolve, this year's conference reflected a clear trend toward integrating intelligent systems—generative AI, immersive environments, and adaptive learning frameworks. These developments signal a growing focus on innovation, pedagogical alignment, and personalized learning. Moreover, ICITL 2025 featured two keynote presentations and one invited plenary presentation by renowned experts and scholars. Nian-Shing Chen and Wilfried Admiraal provided insights into the future of technology-enhanced education with their keynote topics: "Revolutionizing Education: Multi-Agent Pedagogical AI Ecosystems for Personalized and Creative Learning" and "Trends in Teaching with Technology: Research and Practice Connected." The plenary topic, "Converging Design Thinking and Project-Based Learning: An Interdisciplinary Model for Sustainable Development Education," was presented in detail by Tien-Chi Huang. In addition to the keynotes and plenary session, ICITL 2025 also featured a panel session titled "Generative AI for Education: Innovations and Responsibilities." This panel explored the dual nature of generative AI in education—its potential to personalize learning and automate content delivery, as well as the critical responsibilities it raises regarding academic integrity, equity, and ethical use. The panel is joined by Professor Gwo-Jen Hwang, Professor Wei-Tsong Wang,

Professor Helge Høivik, and Professor Nian-Shing Chen, who offer diverse perspectives on innovation, governance, and the future of generative AI-powered learning.

We would like to thank the Organizing Committee for their dedication and efforts in ensuring the success of the conference. We also express our sincere gratitude to the Program Committee members for their timely and constructive reviews. Last but not least, we thank all the authors for their contributions in maintaining the high academic quality of the conference – we look forward to your continued support in shaping the future of innovative technologies and learning.

August 2025

Yueh-Min Huang
Frode Eika Sandnes
Chin-Feng Lai
Wei-Sheng Wang
Tengel Aas Sandtrø

Organization

Kinshuk	University of North Texas, USA
Lisbet Ronningsbakk	UiT The Arctic University of Norway, Norway
Maiga Chang	Athabasca University, Canada
Margus Pedaste	University of Tartu, Estonia
Monika Frania	University of Silesia in Katowice, Poland
Mu-Yen Chen	National Cheng Kung University, Taiwan
Pao-Nan Chou	National Pingtung University of Science and Technology, Taiwan
Qing Tan	Athabasca University, Canada
Ru-Chu Shih	National Pingtung University of Science and Technology, Taiwan
Rustam Shadiev	Zhejiang University, China
Satu-Maarit Korte	University of Lapland, Finland
Shu-Chen Cheng	Southern Taiwan University of Science and Technology, Taiwan
Siri Sollied Madsen	UiT The Arctic University of Norway, Norway
Sumalee Chaijaroen	Khon Kaen University, Thailand
Synnøve Thomassen Andersen	UiT The Arctic University of Norway, Norway
Tacha Serif	Yeditepe University, Turkey
Tien-Chi Huang	National Taichung University of Science and Technology, Taiwan
Ting-Sheng Weng	National Chiayi University, Taiwan
Ting-Ting Wu	National Yunlin University of Science and Technology, Taiwan
Tor-Morten Grønli	Kristiania University College, Norway
Yu-Ju Lan	National Taiwan Normal University, Taiwan
Yu-Ping Cheng	National Chi Nan University, Taiwan
Yuping Wang	Griffith University, Australia

Organizers

Sponsored by

Contents – Part I

Computational Thinking in Education

Design and Framework of Learning Systems

VR/AR/MR/XR in Education

Contents – Part II

Application and Design of Generative Artificial Intelligence in Education

Artificial Intelligence in Education

AI Tools for English Proficiency Test Preparation: A Research Review

Rustam Shadiev[1](✉), Zhanerke Zhangereyeva[2], Madina Boltayeva[2], Olga Mikryakova[2], Adina Nashenova[2], and Zhanargul Beisembayeva[2]

[1] Zhejiang University, Hangzhou 310058, Zhejiang, China
rustamsh@gmail.com
[2] L.N. Gumilyov Eurasian National University, Astana 010000, Kazakhstan

Abstract. This study systematically reviews the application of artificial intelligence (AI) tools in language learning, with a focus on preparing students for standardized English proficiency tests such as IELTS, TOEFL, and TOEIC. Following the PRISMA framework, 24 studies published between 2018 and December, 2024 were selected and analyzed. The review examines four key aspects: (1) AI tools and the language skills they target, (2) AI integration in test preparation, (3) key findings, and (4) reported challenges. The results indicate that AI tools such as ChatGPT, Grammarly, and Andy are widely utilized for enhancing writing and speaking skills, while applications for listening and reading remain underexplored. AI provided personalized real-time feedback, enhancing style and phrasing, assisting with grammar, spelling, and vocabulary, fostering learner autonomy, guiding revisions, and assessing. Findings show that AI tools effectively enhance English proficiency by improving listening, speaking, writing, and grammar skills, boosting test performance, fostering learner confidence, and alleviating anxiety. Several challenges were also reported, including accessibility barriers, technological limitations, and a lack of research on diverse learner contexts. The study highlights the need for integrated AI solutions that support comprehensive language skill development.

Keywords: Artificial Intelligence · test · IELTS · TOEFL · TOEIC

1 Introduction

Artificial intelligence (AI) has revolutionized various fields, offering innovative solutions once deemed unattainable [1, 2]. In language learning and assessment, AI has become indispensable, addressing key challenges such as accessibility, personalization, and the creation of authentic learning environments [3–6]. The integration of AI tools into standardized English proficiency tests like IELTS, TOEFL, and TOEIC represents a major advancement in both test preparation and language skill development. These exams assess essential skills (listening, reading, writing, and speaking) critical for academic and professional purposes. AI's ability to analyze, predict, and adapt has reshaped how learners engage with these assessments.

W.-S. Wang et al. (Eds.): ICITL 2025, LNCS 15913, pp. 3–12, 2026.
https://doi.org/10.1007/978-3-031-98185-2_1

Recent research highlights AI's role in enhancing test preparation by simulating native speaker accents, adjusting audio pacing for listening tasks, and providing personalized vocabulary and grammar support for test examinees [7–9]. AI-driven tools such as Google Lens and Reader Pro have improved reading comprehension and speed, offering real-time feedback to reduce anxiety and foster autonomy [10, 11]. In writing, applications like Grammarly, Perplexity AI, and ChatGPT provide tailored feedback, enhance coherence and structure, and simulate test conditions to alleviate learner anxiety [4, 12]. Additionally, AI-powered speaking tools create low-stress environments for practicing pronunciation, fluency, and grammar, helping learners build confidence and independence [13].

Despite these advancements, significant gaps remain in understanding AI's applications in standardized English assessments. Notably, no systematic review has comprehensively examined AI tools for English proficiency test preparation [3, 4, 13]. Therefore, this study seeks to address these gaps by systematically reviewing AI's role in preparing for IELTS, TOEFL, and TOEIC. Specifically, it explores the following research questions: (1) What AI tools are used in test preparation, and which skills do they support? (2) How do these tools enhance language skills? (3) What findings have been reported in existing studies? and (4) What challenges have researchers identified?

By answering these questions, this study aims to provide a comprehensive understanding of AI's potential in transforming test preparation, highlighting current practices, and identifying pathways for optimizing AI's role in language learning and assessment.

2 Method

This systematic review examined peer-reviewed articles published between 2018 and December 2024, following the PRISMA framework (Fig. 1) to ensure a rigorous selection and analysis process. Relevant studies were identified through searches in Scopus, Web of Science, and ResearchGate, as these databases provide reliable citation indexing in social sciences and have been widely used in review studies globally. Boolean operators were applied to refine the search, using keywords such as AI, artificial intelligence, IELTS, TOEFL, TOEIC, language, learning, and test. Only peer-reviewed journal articles and conference papers were included, while books, review articles, opinion pieces, editorials, and summaries were excluded.

Studies were selected based on the following inclusion criteria: (1) Relevance to AI and English language testing; (2) Empirical evidence supporting AI applications; (3) Credibility of sources (peer-reviewed publications); (4) Methodological rigor; and (5) Publication date (2018–December 2024).

The systematic search process initially retrieved 540 papers across the three databases. After title and abstract screening, 490 articles were excluded for not meeting selection criteria. The remaining 50 articles underwent full-text review, leading to the exclusion of 16 studies. Following an eligibility assessment, 10 additional articles were removed, resulting in a final selection of 24 articles for analysis.

To systematically analyze the selected studies, an analytical framework was developed with five categories: *Tools* - AI tools and platforms used in language testing; *Skills*

- targeted competencies (listening, reading, writing, speaking); *AI applications* - integration of AI in test preparation; *Findings* - reported outcomes in reviewed studies; and *Challenges* – issues identified in AI-assisted test preparation.

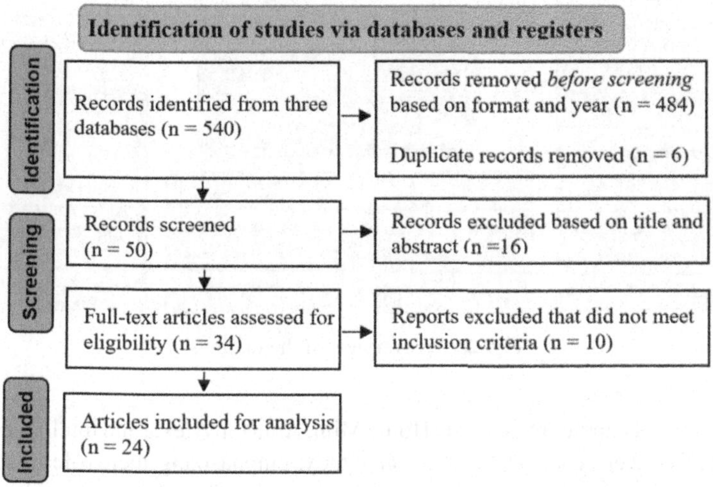

Fig. 1. The selection process of articles through PRISMA method

Five researchers participated in the analytical process. Each article was reviewed, coded according to the framework, and categorized. Discrepancies in coding were discussed until a consensus was reached, ensuring reliability in data interpretation.

3 Results and Discussion

A comprehensive summary of the review findings, including (1) AI tools and targeted language skills, (2) AI applications in English proficiency tests, (3) key findings, and (4) reported challenges, is shown in Fig. 2.

AI Tools and Skills: The AI tools analyzed in the reviewed studies are summarized in Appendix I and categorized based on their support for different language skills: (1) speaking, (2) reading, (3) listening, (4) writing, and (5) vocabulary and grammar.

Among writing tools, ChatGPT emerged as the most frequently utilized (n = 5), reflecting its popularity in interactive language learning, particularly for generating real-time feedback on grammar, structure, and coherence, which significantly improved writing proficiency [3]. In listening comprehension, NaturalReader (n = 1) was employed to convert text to speech, exposing learners to authentic accents and intonation patterns [7, 9]. For grammar and writing enhancement, Grammarly (n = 1) played a key role in refining written accuracy and fluency. In pronunciation training, Elsa Speak (n = 1) was specifically used to improve learners' pronunciation through AI-driven feedback.

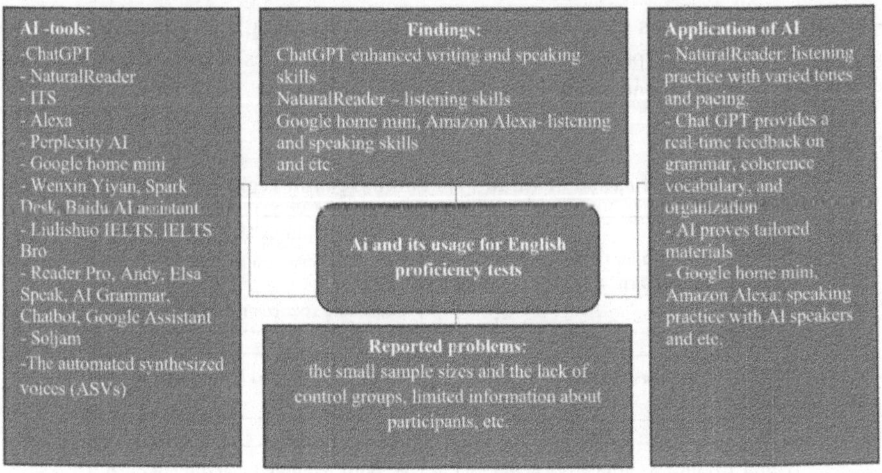

Fig. 2. An overview of the findings

Other AI tools, including Google Home Mini, Amazon Alexa, and intelligent tutoring systems (ITS), were each featured in one study, emphasizing their role in interactive speaking exercises and listening practice [14]. AI-powered reading tools such as Wenxin Yiyan, Spark Desk, and Baidu AI supported reading speed and vocabulary acquisition by offering access to curated content, improving learners' engagement with text-based materials [15]. Additionally, WordNet was highlighted for its effectiveness in enhancing reading comprehension and lexical knowledge, while Soljam (an AI tutor) demonstrated adaptability in supporting both listening and reading skills for TOEIC preparation [11, 16].

Writing was the most commonly addressed skill (n = 9), highlighting its central role in language acquisition, followed by speaking (n = 6), listening (n = 4), reading (n = 3), and vocabulary and grammar (n = 2 each). While some studies explored multiple skills, others focused on a single aspect of language learning. This variation underscores the versatility of AI tools in addressing different learning objectives.

The reviewed studies consistently demonstrate the effectiveness of AI-powered tools in enhancing writing, speaking, and pronunciation skills, with a smaller emphasis on reading and grammar-focused applications. However, while AI tools provide valuable learning opportunities, effective integration into pedagogical frameworks is essential to maximize their benefits. The findings suggest that AI should complement rather than replace human interaction to ensure well-rounded, sustainable language proficiency development.

Applications of AI Tools for Skill Development and Test Preparation: The application of AI tools in language learning and test preparation is summarized in Appendix II, covering seven key areas: (1) Listening, (2) Reading, (3) Writing, (4) Speaking, (5) Vocabulary and Grammar, (6) Overall Language Skills, and (7) Teaching.

Listening: AI was employed to simulate native speaker accents (n = 1), enhance pronunciation differentiation (n = 1), provide listening practice with varied tones and pacing (n = 2), and offer repeated practice for skill reinforcement and accessibility (n = 2). *Reading:* AI tools were utilized to analyze language levels (n = 1), enhance reading comprehension (n = 2), improve speed-reading (n = 1), generate context-related insights for reading passages (n = 1), provide immediate feedback (n = 2), simulate test environments to reduce anxiety (n = 1), and deliver tailored learning materials (n = 1). *Writing:* AI-assisted writing by providing personalized feedback on essays (n = 6), suggesting stylistic improvements and alternative phrasing (n = 4), enhancing vocabulary, grammar, and spelling accuracy (n = 4), fostering learner autonomy and reducing anxiety (n = 2), guiding focused revisions (n = 1), and scoring IELTS writing tasks (n = 1). *Speaking:* AI-supported speaking development through real-time feedback on fluency, coherence, pronunciation, and content (n = 2), immediate correction on pronunciation, grammar, and vocabulary (n = 2), confidence-building and learner autonomy (n = 3), simulating test environments with an AI examiner (n = 1), predicting scores (n = 1), creating low-pressure practice settings (n = 1), and evaluating pronunciation (n = 1). *Vocabulary and Grammar:* AI tools were applied to personalize vocabulary instruction based on individual needs (n = 1) and aid in vocabulary comprehension and sentence translation (n = 1). *Overall Language Skills:* AI facilitated daily language practice through AI speakers (n = 1), analyzed weak points and provided corrective feedback (n = 2), offered study materials (n = 1), and supported speaking and listening practice through exercises and conversations (n = 1). *Teaching Applications:* AI was integrated into teaching for lesson planning, instruction, and assessment, including brainstorming, generating session outlines, assisting in writing tasks, providing AI-based feedback, and simulating IELTS writing exams (n = 1).

The integration of AI tools in English proficiency test preparation has enhanced learning outcomes across multiple language skills, particularly in writing and speaking. However, AI remains limited in assessing higher-order skills such as argument development, critical thinking, and tone, which are essential for test essays. Future studies should focus on improving AI's contextual accuracy, ensuring that AI-generated feedback aligns with human evaluation standards. Additionally, comprehensive guidelines for AI integration in English proficiency test preparation should be developed to maximize its effectiveness. Finally, further research is needed on teachers' experiences, training, and familiarity with AI tools, as their effective implementation depends on educators' ability to integrate AI into instructional practices.

Findings: The reviewed studies provide strong evidence of the effectiveness of AI tools in enhancing language proficiency across various educational contexts. For example, NaturalReader significantly benefited non-EFL students by simulating native speaker accents and providing immediate feedback, thereby improving listening skills (N = 2). Additionally, intelligent tutoring systems (ITS) demonstrated notable improvements in vocabulary and grammar among university students (n = 3) by offering personalized instruction tailored to individual learning needs.

AI-powered voice assistants such as Google Home Mini and Amazon Alexa also showed a positive impact on overall English proficiency (n = 5) by facilitating daily conversational practice, which led to measurable improvements in speaking and listening skills, as reflected in higher test scores. Furthermore, experimental studies using pre-tests and post-tests consistently reported significant gains in essay writing (n = 4) when utilizing AI tools like Perplexity AI, which provided personalized feedback and enhanced writing structure and clarity.

In the context of language assessment testing, particularly IELTS, TOEFL, and TOEIC, multiple studies highlight the positive implications of AI in improving student competencies and experiences. For instance, [7] found that NaturalReader, a text-to-speech AI tool, enhanced TOEFL listening skills by exposing students to varied native speaker accents, tones, and speech paces, allowing them to practice pronunciation and intonation more effectively. Similarly, [11] reported significant TOEIC score improvements among students who used AI-driven support, with AI-assisted groups outperforming control groups.

Further evidence from [17] demonstrated that ITS systems successfully delivered personalized vocabulary and grammar instruction, leading to improved learning outcomes. Likewise, [18] found that integrating AI into IELTS writing courses enhanced students' peer assessment skills, writing clarity, and overall engagement.

Beyond skill development, AI tools were also shown to reduce test anxiety. For instance, [3] observed that using ChatGPT during TOEFL speaking tests boosted students' confidence and autonomy, leading to better speaking performance. Overall, participant feedback consistently reflects a high level of acceptance and appreciation for AI-assisted learning tools, with most learners considering them reliable and effective in improving language proficiency.

These findings collectively reinforce the potential of AI technologies in personalizing learning, enhancing skill acquisition, and optimizing test preparation, while also highlighting areas for further refinement in AI-assisted language assessment.

Reported Challenges: The reviewed studies identified several challenges in methodology, technology, and the learning process, which must be addressed to fully optimize AI tools in language learning and proficiency test preparation. *Methodological Limitations:* a common issue across studies was small sample sizes (n = 7), the absence of control groups (n = 4), and limited participant diversity. Some studies did not specify the academic proficiency levels of learners (n = 2). These limitations restrict the generalizability of findings and call for more robust experimental designs. For instance, [11] acknowledged that the absence of a control group made it difficult to draw definitive conclusions about AI tool effectiveness. *Technological Challenges:* issues related to technology were among the most significant barriers to AI integration. Some studies reported poor video quality (n = 2) and short video durations (n = 2), while others highlighted device limitations, such as inadequate tools (n = 1) and increased cognitive load experienced by learners (n = 1). Additionally, connectivity and device compatibility issues were frequently mentioned, with [11] demonstrating that mobile devices with small screens and low memory capacity negatively impacted AI-assisted learning. Several studies also reported physical discomfort, such as dizziness and fatigue, due to prolonged technology use, which detracted from the learning experience. *Learning Process Challenges:* the reviewed studies also highlighted difficulties related to instructional feedback, learner autonomy, and engagement. a key concern was insufficient instructor feedback (n = 2), often due to large class sizes and time constraints, making it harder for learners to identify and correct errors [18]. Additionally, students' unfamiliarity with AI technologies led to difficulties in understanding project instructions (N = 1) and challenges in pronunciation accuracy and unfamiliar vocabulary (n = 1). Some learners also struggled with distractions during tasks (n = 1), and the novelty effect of using new AI tools (n = 2) sometimes reduced sustained engagement.

Another major concern was the potential for overreliance on AI tools, which could hinder the development of critical thinking and problem-solving skills. While tools like ChatGPT provide instant feedback, they lack the contextual depth and pedagogical adaptability that human instructors offer. This raises concerns about students becoming dependent on AI-generated responses rather than actively developing their own linguistic competencies.

To overcome these challenges, future research should focus on larger sample sizes, controlled experimental designs, and improved data collection methods. Additionally, educators must receive adequate training to help students navigate technical issues independently while using AI for language learning without over-relying on automation.

Despite these limitations, AI remains a powerful tool in language education. Addressing the identified challenges is crucial for maximizing AI's potential in academic institutions. Further research and development should focus on enhancing AI-assisted language testing methodologies, improving technology implementation, and optimizing the overall learning experience for students.

Recommendations for Using AI Tools in Test Preparation: To maximize the effectiveness of AI tools in preparing for standardized English proficiency tests, students and teachers must adopt a strategic and informed approach. The following recommendations outline best practices for integrating AI into test preparation. *1. Familiarization with AI Tools and Their Functions:* both students and teachers should develop a strong understanding of AI tools and their capabilities. AI-powered applications, such as grammar checkers and pronunciation trainers, offer a range of features that can support different language skills. Understanding how these tools work enables learners to make informed decisions about when and how to use them effectively. *2. Recognizing Strengths and Limitations of AI Tools:* while AI provides valuable feedback on writing, pronunciation, and fluency, it may not fully grasp context, idiomatic expressions, or cultural nuances. Students must be trained to critically evaluate AI-generated feedback, rather than accepting it as absolute. Instructors should emphasize that AI tools are supplementary resources rather than definitive authorities on language accuracy. *3. Building a Strong Linguistic Foundation:* before relying on AI tools, students should develop a solid grasp of core language skills such as grammar, vocabulary, and sentence structure. This foundational knowledge allows learners to better interpret AI Feedback and distinguish between accurate corrections and misleading suggestions. For instance, understanding subject-verb agreement ensures that students identify and correct errors independently, rather than relying entirely on ai-generated recommendations. *4. integrating AI with Traditional Teaching Methods:* AI should be viewed as a complement to, rather than a replacement for, traditional instruction. While AI can provide instant feedback and personalized practice, human instructors remain essential for guiding students through complex language structures, answering nuanced questions, and providing tailored feedback. Teachers can use AI-generated data to personalize instruction, but direct student-teacher interaction remains crucial for developing critical thinking and problem-solving skills in language learning. *5. targeting exam-specific Skills:* students should prioritize AI-assisted learning based on their specific test preparation needs. For example: (a) IELTS Speaking Test: focus on fluency and pronunciation rather than minor grammatical errors; (b) TOEIC Preparation: prioritize listening comprehension and reading speed over writing accuracy; by taking a goal-oriented approach, students can allocate their time effectively and concentrate on high-impact areas that improve their test performance. *6. Encouraging Consistent Practice and Human Feedback:* while AI tools provide immediate feedback and create a low-pressure environment for practice, students should also seek regular feedback from teachers. Instructors play a critical role in validating AI-generated suggestions, helping students refine their skills, and ensuring that they are progressing towards their language learning goals.

We also propose some strategies for effective AI integration in test preparation. (a) Grammar and Writing Assistance: AI-powered grammar and spelling checkers (e.g., Grammarly) can identify common writing errors, but students must be aware of regional language variations (e.g., British vs. American English). They should also cross-check AI feedback with trusted grammar resources to ensure accuracy. (b) Writing Quality Improvement: AI tools help enhance clarity, coherence, and sentence structure, but students should not over-rely on AI-generated suggestions. Instead, they should review AI feedback alongside style guides or teacher recommendations to develop stronger self-editing skills. (c) Reading Comprehension Practice: AI-powered platforms can simulate exam-style reading tasks, helping students identify key information and analyze text structures. However, students should also practice summarizing passages and drawing inferences, rather than focusing solely on answering comprehension questions. (d) Personalized Learning Paths: AI tools can generate customized study plans based on a student's performance and weaknesses. While these tailored exercises are beneficial, students should also consult teachers to validate their progress and ensure that AI-generated tasks align with exam requirements.

By following these recommendations, students can effectively integrate AI tools into their test preparation for IELTS, TOEFL, and TOEIC. The key to success lies in understanding AI's strengths and limitations, using it as a supportive tool rather than a sole learning resource, and prioritizing targeted skill development. When combined with traditional teaching methods and instructor feedback, AI tools can significantly enhance test preparation, providing personalized learning experiences and helping students achieve their language proficiency goals.

4 Conclusion

This review study examined the impact of AI on preparing for English proficiency tests such as IELTS, TOEFL, and TOEIC, highlighting its transformative role in enhancing language proficiency and optimizing test preparation strategies. The findings demonstrate that AI-powered tools significantly improve learners' skills across listening, reading, writing, and speaking by providing personalized feedback, adaptive learning experiences, and real-time assessments.

Beyond skill development, AI was found to enhance learner autonomy, reduce test anxiety, and increase engagement, making language learning more accessible and interactive. The ability of AI to simulate authentic language environments, provide instant corrective feedback, and tailor learning pathways underscores its potential to revolutionize traditional test preparation methods. However, this review also highlights challenges such as technological limitations, overreliance on AI-generated feedback, and the need for educator involvement to ensure balanced learning approaches.

The significance of this study lies in its comprehensive insights into AI integration in language education, showcasing both its innovative potential and areas for refinement. As AI continues to evolve, future research should focus on optimizing AI-assisted learning methodologies, improving contextual accuracy, and developing structured guidelines for effective implementation in English proficiency test preparation. By strategically leveraging AI alongside traditional teaching methods and human feedback, learners can maximize their test performance and achieve sustainable language proficiency.

Acknowledgments. Blinded.

Disclosure of Interests. The authors have no competing interests to declare that are relevant to the content of this article.

Appendices

Appendices can be found from the following link: http://dx.doi.org/https://doi.org/10.13140/RG.2.2.16185.89440

References

1. Shadiev, R., Feng, Y., Zhussupova, R., Altinay, F.: Effects of speech-enabled corrective feedback technology on EFL speaking skills, anxiety and confidence. Computer Assisted Language Learning (2024)
2. Wang, L., Chen, X., Wang, C., Xu, L., Shadiev, R., Li, Y.: ChatGPT's capabilities in providing feedback on undergraduate students' argumentation: a case study. Thinking Skills and Creativity **51**, 101440 (2024)
3. Biju, N., Abdelrasheed, N.S.G., Bakiyeva, K., Prasad, K.D.V., Jember, B.: Which one? AI-assisted language assessment or paper format: An exploration of the impacts on foreign language anxiety, learning attitudes, motivation, and writing performance. Language Testing in Asia **14**, 45–55 (2024)
4. Ghafouri, M., Hassaskhah, J., Mahdavi-Zafarghandi, A.: From virtual assistant to writing mentor: Exploring the impact of a ChatGPT-based writing instruction protocol on EFL teachers' self-efficacy and learners' writing skill. Language Teaching Research 13621688241239764 (2024)
5. Shadiev, R., Wang, X., Chen, X., Gayevskaya, E., Borisov, N.: Research on the impact of the learning activity supported by 360-degree video and translation technologies on cross-cultural knowledge and attitudes development. Educ. Inf. Technol. **29**, 7759–7791 (2024)

6. Xu, J., Gao, J., Gong, X., Shadiev, R., Li, Y.: The impact of using ChatGPT on EFL students' writing. In: 2024 IEEE International Conference on Advanced Learning Technologies (ICALT), pp. 126–128. IEEE (2024)
7. Fitria, T.N.: Using Naturalreader: A free text-to-speech online with AI-powered voices in teaching listening TOEFL. ELTALL: English Language Teaching. Applied Linguistic and Literature **4**, 1–17 (2023)
8. Shadiev, R., Feng, Y., Zhussupova, R., Huang, Y.M.: Intercultural competence development through a tele-collaborative project supported by speech-enabled corrective feedback technology. J. Comput. Assist. Learn. **40**, 697–714 (2024)
9. Nakai, A.: Use and effects of an online text-to-speech resource to improve english listening for the TOEIC test. Journal of Tourism Studies **13** (2019)
10. Mohamed Haggag, H.: Implementing Artificial Intelligence-Powered Tools in Enhancing TOEFL-ITP Test Takers' Reading and Writing skills. Journal of the Faculty of Education **32**, 129–156 (2021)
11. Kim, N.Y.: AI-integrated mobile-assisted language learning: is it an effective way of preparing for the TOEIC test in classroom environments? English Teaching **77**, 79–102 (2022)
12. Wei, P., Wang, X., Dong, H.: The impact of automated writing evaluation on second language writing skills of Chinese EFL learners: a randomized controlled trial. Front. Psychol. **14**, 1249991 (2023)
13. Fathi, J., Rahimi, M., Derakhshan, A.: Improving EFL learners' speaking skills and willingness to communicate via artificial intelligence-mediated interactions. System **121**, 103254 (2024)
14. Bao, M.: Can home use of speech-enabled artificial intelligence mitigate foreign language anxiety – Investigation of a concept. Arab World English Journal **5**, 1–15 (2019)
15. He, X., Cao, X., Liu, J.: The Application and Effect of AIGC in IELTS Learning/Teaching. J. Higher Edu. Res. **5**, 133–137 (2024)
16. Kim, N.Y.: A Study on AI TOEIC Tutor: For English Learning by CEFR Proficiency Levels. Multimedia-Assisted Language Learning **27**, 23–45 (2024)
17. Kim, H.S., Kim, N.Y., Cha, Y.: A study on the use of AI-based learning programs by EFL students with different types of teacher support. Anglistics **22**, 355–376 (2022)
18. Asadi, M., Taheri, R.: Enhancing peer assessment and engagement in online IELTS writing courses through a teacher's multifaceted approach and AI integration. TALE: J. Langu. Teach. Res. **2**, 94–117 (2024)

Enhancing Social Adaptation in Young Learners Through a 2-Year Multimedia Program on Social-Emotional Learning

Fu-Rung Yang(✉)

Department of Social Science, National Open University, New Taipei City, Taiwan
yangfr928@mail.nou.edu.tw

Abstract. This study used multimedia videos and AI-generated images to design a two-year social-emotional learning (SEL) curriculum for lower elementary school students. A total of 158 students participated in the program. The curriculum was closely aligned with the students' life experiences and incorporated key SEL components, namely, self-awareness, social awareness, self-management, relationship skills, and responsible decision-making. The AI-generated images were flexibly adapted based on students' real-life situations and school-related events, offering personalized and relatable visual cues that deepened their understanding of SEL concepts. By discussing emotions and social interactions depicted in these images, students were guided to reflect on themselves and others, practice regulation strategies, and improve interpersonal relationships. The results indicate that the students exhibited better social adaptation the longer they participated in the program.

Keywords: Social-Emotional Learning (SEL) · Multimedia program in SEL · Affective Learning in SEL · Social Adaptation · Artificial Intelligence (AI)

1 Introduction

Social emotional learning (SEL) helps students become aware of their emotions, understand the causes of these emotions, and develop empathy for others, which can help them foster supportive interpersonal relationships [1]. CASEL (Collaborative for Academic, Social, and Emotional Learning) is a leading organization for SEL education in the United States. Many state education departments in the United States have used CASEL to establish learning standards and competencies for students from preschool through high school. CASEL provides a framework for SEL education with the goal of promoting equitable and continually improving educational environments through SEL.

CASEL's action framework centers on SEL and integrates efforts at the classroom, school, family, and community levels to enhance SEL learning outcomes. The framework involves an inner circle of five core competencies and an outer circle of four key settings. Together, these elements develop students' knowledge, skills, and attitudes, promoting adaptive and personalized learning and development. SEL programs have

W.-S. Wang et al. (Eds.): ICITL 2025, LNCS 15913, pp. 13–21, 2026.
https://doi.org/10.1007/978-3-031-98185-2_2

been implemented in the United States for 30 years, with research results indicating that SEL can enhance social skills, reduce problematic behaviors, and improve interpersonal interaction abilities in students[2–4].

The World Health Organization has designated October 10 as World Mental Health Day, and the 2023 theme is "Mental Health Is a Universal Human Right" [5]. Taiwan has increasingly emphasized the importance of individual mental health, and emotional education has been incorporated in curricula from the high school to the elementary school level. The Ministry of Education's 12-year Basic Education Curriculum Guidelines have incorporated emotion education into several subject areas. Emotion education curricula include topics such as emotional recognition, emotional understanding, and emotional regulation, and the focus of these curricula is to promote the development of positive interpersonal relationships. Emotional education courses have been incorporated in elementary schools to help students understand and recognize their own emotions, as well as those of others; enhance their emotional regulation abilities; and improve their mental health.

In Taiwan, emotional education at the elementary school level is often integrated into other activities, such as health and physical education or life skills education. Emotional education curricula in Taiwan generally focus on recognizing emotions, being aware of one's own and others' emotional states, exploring methods for regulating emotions, building positive interpersonal interactions, and setting goals. However, the curricula do not cover many aspects of the five dimensions of SEL. Thus, new SEL content should be designed for elementary school students in Taiwan.

The current study incorporated SEL into health education activities for lower-grade students. A 2-year SEL curriculum with a focus on learning SEL through issues was designed, and the effectiveness of the program in improving social adaptation behavior was investigated.

2 Literature Review

2.1 SEL

CASEL is an educational institution that promotes SEL and divides the core competencies of SEL into five dimensions, namely, self-awareness, self-management, social awareness, relationship skills, and responsible decision-making. These five components are interconnected, and they are described in the following [6]:

- Self-awareness:

Self-awareness refers to the ability to understand one's own emotions, thoughts, and values, as well as how they influence behavior in various situations. It involves recognizing personal strengths and areas for growth while maintaining an awareness of how different contexts shape individual actions.

- Self-management:

Self-management involves the ability to effectively regulate one's emotions, thoughts, and behaviors in a diverse range of situations while striving to achieve one's goals. It includes skills such as delaying gratification, managing stress, and maintaining the motivation to pursue both personal and collective objectives.

- Social awareness:

Social awareness refers to the ability to understand and empathize with others' perspectives, including exhibiting compassion for others and recognizing broader historical and societal norms to adapt behavior to different environments. It also includes identifying and utilizing resources from family, school, and the community.

- Relationship skills:

Relationship skills are the abilities to establish and maintain healthy, supportive relationships with a diverse range of individuals and groups. These skills include effectively communicating, actively listening, effectively collaborating, and constructively resolving conflicts. Relationship skills also involve the capacity to navigate social and cultural contexts, exhibit leadership, and seek or provide assistance when needed.

- Responsible decision-making:

Responsible decision-making entails making ethical, constructive, and socially responsible choices about personal and interpersonal behaviors. This includes evaluating the consequences of actions on oneself and others, considering the well-being of all involved, and making informed decisions aligned with both personal and collective values.

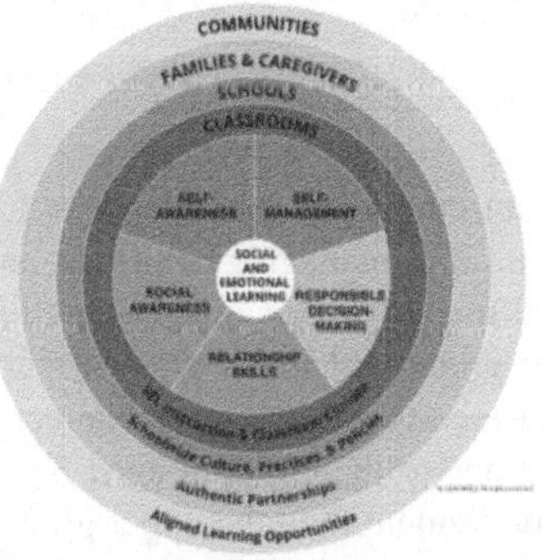

Fig. 1. CASEL(CASEL, https://drc.casel.org/what-is-sel%20%20/)

The aim of SEL is to encourage active student learning by connecting teaching activities with students' life experiences and interests (Fig. 1). Through experiential learning, SEL enhances students' awareness and ability to reflect, with SEL curricula providing opportunities for interpersonal interaction. Many states in the United States have implemented SEL programs, integrating SEL into various subjects, and studies have demonstrated that SEL enhances academic learning outcomes [6, 7].

Taylor et al. [3] conducted a meta-analysis of 82 studies involving 97,406 students from kindergarten to high school (average age: 11.09 years). The findings revealed that

SEL programs significantly improve students' social-emotional skills, learning attitudes, and positive emotions and reduce the likelihood that students will engage in substance abuse. These benefits were reported to be consistent across different racial and socioeconomic groups. The long-term promotion of SEL in the United States has been demonstrated to be remarkably effective, and the outcomes of such promotion can serve as a valuable reference for advancing emotional education in Taiwan.

2.2 Multimedia Learning

Multimedia learning through text, pictures, and videos enables students to understand concepts more deeply than learning through text alone does [8]. The cognitive theory of multimedia learning posits that the human information processing system comprises visual/pictorial and auditory/verbal channels (Fig. 2). These channels have limited processing capacity, and learning involves an active process of cognitive coordination. Multimedia stimuli should be presented that connect to students' prior knowledge and align with their cognitive processes to promote meaningful learning [8].

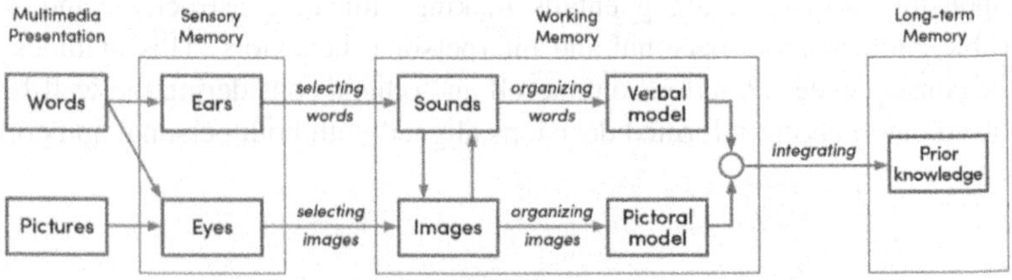

Fig. 2. Cognitive Theory of Multimedia Learning

D'Amico [9] designed an emotional intelligence software focused on perceiving emotions, understanding emotions, managing emotions, and using emotion to facilitate thought. The study assessed the software's effects on children aged 8 to 12, with the children divided into upper-grade and lower-grade groups on the basis of age. The results of the study demonstrated that the multimedia technology effectively enhanced emotional intelligence learning for the children aged 8 to 12; that is, the lower-grade group exhibited greater improvement than the upper grade did. A possible explanation for this finding is that in addition to individual software operation, the lower-grade group experienced more frequent discussions and interactions, which enhanced their learning outcomes.

Yang et al. [1] highlighted the advantages of multimedia teaching, noting that it can overcome the spatial limitations of traditional classrooms and provide a sense of immediacy similar to that of in-person teaching. Multimedia content clearly conveys nonverbal information, providing a medium for emotional learning and broadening the depth and scope of emotional learning. Incorporating questions into multimedia courses can help students better understand teaching content and more effectively recognize the connection between nonverbal cues and emotions. This can enhance students' ability to identify emotions, develop self-awareness, understand others' emotional states, and improve their emotional regulation skills.

This study utilized multimedia videos aligned with students' life experiences along with AI-generated images related to their learning experiences. Teacher-guided questions and explanations were provided that enabled the students to deepen their understanding of the learning content and grasp key concepts related to SEL.

2.3 Design of the SEL Multimedia Curriculum

Emotion charts can help students recognize their own emotions, name their feelings, and become more aware of others' emotions, thereby improving peer relationships [1]. Emotional responses involve both subjective cognition and the overall context [10]. Designing scenarios that reflect students' everyday experiences and illustrating how their thoughts about these events influence their emotions can help students better understand the causes of emotions. In this study, Canva and ChatGPT were used to generate images, including emotion charts, illustrations of real-life school situations, and illustrations of events. Teachers displayed these images and providing explanations, allowing students to connect their experiences with their thoughts and emotions and understand the relationship between emotions and various contexts.

Multimedia videos that depict school-based scenarios can be used to present dynamic storylines that closely resemble real-life school events. This study used multimedia videos from Taiwan's Da Ai Television series "Tang Dynasty Little Chestnut" to support SEL learning as follows:

- The curricular unit "Good Relationships Start with Kindness" [11] helped students develop social awareness by recognizing others' feelings and practicing positive interpersonal skills.
- The curricular unit "The Me I Like the Most" [12] guided students in practicing self-awareness by identifying their own emotions and making responsible decisions for self-care.

After watching the videos, teachers facilitated discussions to explain self-awareness, social awareness, self-management, relationship skills, and responsible decision-making, encouraging students to apply these skills in their everyday lives.

The SEL multimedia curriculum incorporated the four key elements of effective SEL instruction.

- Sequenced: The curriculum is structured in a progressive manner, teaching knowledge and skills step by step.
- Active: Engaging learning experiences are provided that encourage students to practice and apply new skills.
- Focused: The curriculum has clear learning objectives, emphasizing SEL skill development.
- Explicit: The targeted skills, attitudes, knowledge, and expected outcomes are clearly articulated.

By learning SEL concepts and strategies through multimedia resources, students can enhance their social-emotional intelligence, which can help them to develop improved interpersonal relationships and emotional regulation skills.

3 Methods

3.1 Participants

This study implemented a 2-year SEL program for lower-grade students at an elementary school in Taiwan, with a total of 158 students participating in the research.

This program was based on an issue-integrated formal curriculum designed by this study. The curriculum design was divided into two phases:

- Phase 1: The focus was on promoting harmony in group settings and fostering self-awareness of one's own emotions. The course content helped students understand that others' feelings may differ from their own. Real-life scenarios were designed to teach students about friendly behaviors in group settings and appropriate methods for calming their emotions.
- Phase 2: The focus was on self-awareness, encouraging students to recognize their positive traits and understand that other people are not necessarily like them. It also guided students in learning appropriate methods for seeking help, responding to others, and practicing self-care in daily life.

All students were randomly assigned to six classes, all instructed by the same teacher to reduce instructional variability that might influence the experimental outcomes. Weekly social-emotional learning (SEL) sessions were conducted, during which the teacher guided students to observe and discuss real-life incidents occurring within the school context. Based on the themes, characters, and emotions identified in these events, AI-generated images (Fig. 3) were created as learning materials for the students.

These AI-generated visuals served as concrete teaching materials, integrating students' lived experiences with social-emotional learning skills. Specifically, these images provided concrete and relatable representations, thereby solidifying abstract discussions about self-awareness, social awareness, and self-management. Through teaching activities utilizing these visual materials, the teacher encouraged students to identify and express their own emotions, recognize others' perspectives, and explore viable strategies for emotional regulation and interpersonal problem-solving.

The implementation of the curriculum involved embedding students' own daily experiences into dynamically generated, contextually relevant images. This personalized generation of visuals made the learning of social-emotional learning skills more vivid and actionable.

Fig. 3. AI-generated image

3.2 Procedures

The study adopted the Social Adaptation Checklist [13] and focused on the subscales of social-interpersonal and emotional behavior. It explored the interpersonal behaviors, emotional responses, and emotional stability of lower-grade students—as indicated by, for example, being "willing to actively help or care for others" and "…not (getting) upset over trivial matters."

The social adaptation scale was administered in two pretests: one was administered before the curriculum was implemented, when the students were starting first grade, and another was administered 1 year after the curriculum was implemented, when the students were finishing first grade (at the end of the second semester). A posttest was subsequently conducted, when the students were finishing second grade. The scale comprised 10 items rated on a 5-point Likert scale, where 1 indicated "never" and 5 indicated "always." Higher scores indicated better social adaptation.

4 Results

The social adaptation scale used in this study demonstrated good internal consistency reliability (Cronbach's $\alpha = 0.73$) and good reliability and validity (explaining 51.07% of the variance).

The students' mean social adaptation scores were 3.38 (standard deviation: 0.65) in the first pretest, 3.82 (standard deviation: 0.51) in the second pretest, and 4.02 (standard deviation: 0.64) in the posttest (Table 1). This indicates that the students had better social adaptation as they advanced through the curriculum.

Table 1. The effectiveness of social adaptation scores (N = 158)

Test stage	Mean	SD
Pre-test	3.38	.65
Second test	3.82	.51
Post-test	4.02	.64

A one-way analysis of variance and subsequent post hoc comparisons were conducted, and the results indicated that the change in social adaptation over time was significant (Table 2). Specifically, the students' social adaptation scores differed between the three time points ($F = 64.74$, $p < 0.001$), and the students had significantly higher social adaptation scores in the posttest than in the two pretests.

These findings indicate that the SEL curriculum helped students recognize their emotions, understand others' emotional states, effectively manage their own emotions, and improve their ability to interact with others. The findings also indicate that the curriculum should also be implemented over the long term, preferably for 2 years or longer.

Table 2. One-Way Analysis of Variance for Social Adaptation (N = 158)

Source of Variation	Sum of Squares (SS)	Degrees of Freedom (df)	Mean Square (MS)	F	Post Hoc Comparison
Between Subjects	90.33	157	.58		Curriculum (2 years) > Curriculum (1 year) > Before Curriculum
Within Subjects	115.54	316			
Treatment Effect	33.73	2	16.87	64.74***	
Residual	81.81	314	.26		
Total	205.87	473			

****$p < .001$.

5 Discussion and Conclusion

This study implemented a 2-year SEL curriculum to improve the social adaptation of students over time and observed the effects. According to the results from the emotional performance and interpersonal behavior subscales, the students demonstrated annual growth in emotional awareness and interpersonal skills as they participated in the curriculum. The students became more effective at recognizing their emotional states, practicing methods to calm themselves, sharing and collaborating with classmates, rejecting inappropriate contact, and seeking help from trusted adults to solve problems. The design of the SEL curriculum emphasized student interactions between themselves, which helped them practice their social adaptation skills in realistic, everyday settings. The use of multimedia teaching materials in the curriculum also helped students better understand the concepts of SEL.

In the United States, SEL education is administered from kindergarten to high school, and SEL education has been recommended to be administered early and consistently over the long term. In general, the findings of the current study can serve as a reference for implementing SEL curricula in Taiwan in the future.

6 Limitations and Directions for Future Research

The primary limitation of this study is the absence of a control group. Therefore, the observed improvements in social adaptation may be partially attributed to students' natural developmental maturation or influenced by external factors such as parental upbringing styles. Future research should incorporate a control group to clarify whether changes are specifically due to the intervention rather than maturation or parenting influences.

This study employed AI-generated images based on students' real-life experiences to facilitate the development of social-emotional learning (SEL) skills. Future research is encouraged to conduct a more in-depth investigation into the differential impacts of AI-generated imagery on elementary students' SEL skill acquisition and social adaptation. Such findings would offer valuable guidance for the effective integration of AI-generated materials into SEL interventions.

References

1. Yang, F.R., Wu, M.H., Tang, J.H., Wei, C.F.: Effectiveness of online multimedia courses for improving children's self-regulation through social-emotional learning. In: Huang, Y.M., Lai, C.F., Rocha, T. (eds.) CONFERENCE 2021, LNCS, vol. 13117, pp. 491–497. Springer, Cham (2021)
2. Durlak, J.A., Weissberg, R.P., Dymnicki, A.B., Taylor, R.D., Schellinger, K.B.: The impact of enhancing students' social and emotional learning: a meta-analysis of school-based universal interventions. Child Dev. **82**(1), 405–432 (2011)
3. Taylor, R.D., Oberle, E., Durlak, J.A., Weissberg, R.P.: Promoting positive youth development through school-based social and emotional learning interventions: A meta-analysis of follow-up effects. Child Dev. **88**(4), 1156–1171 (2017)
4. Crooks, C.V., Bax, K., Delaney, A., Kim, H., Shokoohi, M.: Impact of MindUP among young children: improvements in behavioral problems, adaptive skills, and executive functioning. Mindfulness **11**(10), 2433–2444 (2020)
5. Department of Mental Health, Ministry of Health and Welfare: World Mental Health Day: True Health Begins with Mental Well-being. https://www.mohw.gov.tw/cp-16-76196-1.html 2025/1/25
6. Collaborative for Academic, Social, and Emotional Learning (CASEL): SEL policy at the state level. https://casel.org/systemic-implementation/sel-policy-at-the-state-level/ 2025/1/25
7. Snyder, A.: Building social and emotional learning into the school day: Seven guiding principles. Mc Graw Hill Education, New York (2017)
8. Mayer, R.E.: Introduction to multimedia learning. In: Mayer, R.E. (ed.) The Cambridge handbook of multimedia learning, pp. 1–24. Cambridge University Press. Cambridge (2014)
9. D'Amico, A.: The use of technology in the promotion of Children's Emotional Intelligence: The multimedia program "Developing Emotional Intelligence." Int. J. Emot. Edu. **10**(1), 47–67 (2018)
10. Nolen-Hoeksema, S., Fredrickson, B., Loftus, G.R., Lutz, C.: Introduction to psychology. Cengage Learning, Washington (2014)
11. Da Ai Television: Good Relationships Start with Kindness. https://www.youtube.com/watch?v=bWy9xsaLP70 2025/1/25
12. Da Ai Television: The Favorite Me. https://www.youtube.com/watch?v=5PlC4iG7Mvg 2025/1/25
13. Lu, T.H., Cheng, H.C., Shih, H.L., Lin, Y.L.: Social Adaptation Performance Checklist. Psychological Publishing, Taipei (2003)

To Learn or Not to Learn Artificial Intelligence: An Anticipated Regret-Extended Expectancy-Value Theory

Hsiu-Hua Cheng(✉)

National Yunlin University of Science and Technology, Yunlin, R.O.C., Taiwan
chenghh@yuntech.edu.tw

Abstract. Artificial intelligence has significantly transformed the nature of work and altered the way people engage in it. University students who are about to enter the work-force face a future in which artificial intelligence may replace their jobs and threaten their careers. To mitigate this risk, it is crucial for universities to encourage students to study artificial intelligence and equip them with the necessary skills. Enrolling in artificial intelligence courses is an achievement-related decision, and future-oriented emotions can strongly influence students' choices. Although expectancy-value theory is widely used to explain academic motivation and behavior, it overlooks the influence of anticipated emotions. To fill this void, this study extends expectancy-value theory by incorporating anticipated regret to investigate the antecedents of artificial intelligence learning intention. Data were collected from 191 university students via an online questionnaire and analyzed using multiple regression analysis. The results reveal that self-efficacy positively influences intention to learn artificial intelligence. Intrinsic value and utility value have positive effects on intention to learn artificial intelligence, whereas effort cost hinders the intention. Anticipated regret plays a key role in shaping intention to learn artificial intelligence. This study provides valuable insights for universities and instructors and enriches literature on artificial intelligence learning intention.

Keywords: Artificial Intelligence · Learning Intention · Expectancy-Value Theory · Anticipated Regret

1 Introduction

Artificial intelligence (AI) has profoundly transformed the nature of work and the way individuals perform their jobs [26]. As AI continues to advance rapidly, university students preparing to enter the workforce face a future in which AI may replace their jobs and threaten their careers [4]. To help students prepare for this emerging challenge, it is important for universities to encourage them to study AI and equip them with the skills needed for an AI-driven job market and their future careers.

Enrolling in AI-related courses is an achievement-related choice and decision, and emotions, especially future-oriented ones, such as anticipated regret, could strongly influence decision-making, learning behaviors, and learning motivation [19, 22]. In the

W.-S. Wang et al. (Eds.): ICITL 2025, LNCS 15913, pp. 22–27, 2026.
https://doi.org/10.1007/978-3-031-98185-2_3

AI learning setting, the prospect of job replacement by AI may trigger anticipated regret among students. However, scant studies have investigated factors affecting university students' intention to learn AI, particularly considering anticipated regret. To fill this gap, this study proposes a research model of university students' AI learning intentions based on an extension of expectancy-value theory by incorporating anticipated regret.

Expectancy-value theory, highlighting the roles of expectancy for success and subjective task value in influencing achievement task choices and achievement motivation, serves as the theoretical foundation of this study [10]. While this theory is well-established, it does not incorporate future-oriented emotions. Therefore, this study extends expectancy-value theory by introducing anticipated regret to investigate key factors influencing AI learning intention.

2 Literature Review

2.1 AI in Education

Research on AI in education can be primarily categorized into four steams. The first stream focuses on the development of AI system [33]. The second steam explores how AI-enabled technologies facilitate and support learning [28]. The third stream addresses the design of AI-related courses [25], while the fourth stream examines factors influencing students' intention to learn AI [5–7, 27, 29].

2.2 Expectancy-Value Theory

Expectancy-value theory provides an important theoretical lens for understanding students' achievement-oriented choices and behaviors. Studies based on this theory have demonstrated that expectancy for success and subjective task value have direct impacts on achievement-oriented choices, behaviors and performance [12, 13]. Expectancy for success reflects students' beliefs about their competence. The predominant variable investigated regarding expectancy for success is self-efficacy [17], referring to individual beliefs in their abilities to successfully perform a specific task [2]. Subjective task value encompasses four components: intrinsic value (the perceived enjoyment derived from a task), attainment value (the relevance of task for self-identity), utility value (the usefulness of a task in goal achievement) and cost (the drawbacks of task participant). Given the high correlations among these components, Bong [3] identified a two-factor structure, combining attainment value and utility value into one factor and placing interest value in a separate factor. Bong named them as utility value and intrinsic value. Cost is further divided into three facets: effort cost (the effort required to complete the task), opportunity cost (foregone opportunities to engage in alternative activities) and emotional cost (the negative feelings associated to task engagement) [10].

2.3 Anticipated Regret

Regret is a negative emotion aroused from cognitive processes [16], typically experienced after realizing or anticipating that an alternative could have yielded a better outcome

[24]. Beyond the regret that arises from reflecting on past decisions [16], people can also anticipate to experience regret in the future if they make a particular choice [31]. This type of regret is known as anticipated regret [32]. Anticipated regret involves a cognitive expectation about future emotional responses [8].

3 Model and Hypotheses

Intention to learn is defined as the willingness to engage in AI learning activities in the future [5] and is considered an achievement-related decision. A higher intention to learn AI reflects a greater likelihood that individuals will choose to study AI in the future.

Self-efficacy refers the confidence that an individual has in his/her own ability to perform tasks, and it has a profound impact on individuals' achievement performance, choice, and persistence [1]. When individuals have confidence in their abilities to achieve success in subjects, they tend to adopt deeper cognitive strategies related academic success, enrollment in classes and persist in their academic goals [13]. In the AI learning context, students who believe that they can gain AI knowledge, polish AI skills and successfully complete AI-related tasks are more likely to invest greater effort to master AI-related material and persist in AI learning. Therefore, hypothesis 1 is proposed.

H1: Self-efficacy positively influences intention to learn AI.

Motivational beliefs, including value-related beliefs, play a significant role in shaping future academic course selection and sustaining motivation [11, 21]. Compared to expectancy for success, value-related beliefs are more influential in predicting choice behaviors [14]. Intrinsic value refers to the enjoyment an individual anticipates gaining from performing a task [12]. It reflects the pleasure students experience when engaging in the task. For instance, while studying AI, a student may find the subject interesting or expect to enjoy the classes. In this context, students view AI learning as having intrinsic value. On the other hand, utility value refers to the degree to which a specific task fits into an individual's short-term or long-term plans [12]. Students, who believe that studying AI will help them secure a good job or foster a successful career, perceive AI learning as having utility value. According to studies on expectancy-value theory [11, 21], these two motivational beliefs are key factors encouraging students to engage in AI learning activities continuously and take AI courses in the future. Therefore, hypotheses 2 and 3 are proposed.

H2: Intrinsic value positively influences intention to learn AI.

H3: Utility value positively influences intention to learn AI.

Effort cost refers to a perception of if the time and effort required to succeed in a task are considered worthwhile [10], and it affects the willingness to engage in a task and the decision to discontinue it [23]. Similarly, effort cost can serve as an inhibitor, discouraging students from enrolling in certain classes [10, 23]. According to the literature mentioned-above, it can be inferred that when students perceive the effort involved in AI-related learning tasks as not worthwhile, they are more likely to disengage in these learning activities or even tend to quit. This study, thus, proposes hypothesis 4.

H4: Effort cost negatively influences intention to learn AI.

Anticipated regret arises before making decisions, when individuals foresee feeling regret if they choose a particular option [30]. Zeelenberg [32] showed in uncertain circumstances, a connection exists between anticipated regret and decision-making. Individuals often opt for the choice that minimizes potential future regret [18]. University students are preparing to enter in AI-enabled workplace where the role of human workers is rapidly changing due to AI technologies. If students lack necessary AI skills and knowledge, they may not be well-equipped for a successful career. Given the uncertainty of human roles in the future AI-driven workplace, students are more likely to form a stronger intention to learn AI to minimize the regret they may feel later. Hence, hypothesis 5 is proposed.

H5: Anticipated regret positively influences intention to learn AI.

4 Method

An online survey questionnaire was developed to gather data from Taiwanese university students enrolled in AI-related courses. All measurements for the research model were adopted from prior studies [9, 20, 29]. A total of 191 valid responses were obtained. The demographic data indicated that the female participants (51.83%) outnumbered the male participants (48.17%).

5 Data Analysis and Results

The values of Cronbach's alpha for all constructs range from 0.83 to 0.93, with each value surpassing the 0.7 threshold, demonstrating good reliability [15]. The proposed model is tested using the multi-regression analysis with SPSS software. The regression analysis for the intention to learn AI is statistically significant ($F = 65.64$, $p < 0.001$), with an adjusted R-squared value of 0.63. The results show that self-efficacy ($\beta = 0.25$, $p < 0.001$), intrinsic value ($\beta = 0.29$, $p < 0.001$), utility value ($\beta = 0.36$, $p < 0.001$), and anticipated regret ($\beta = 0.19$, $p < 0.001$) positively affect intention to learn AI, whereas effort cost has a negative influence ($\beta = -0.08$, $p < 0.05$). As expected, all hypotheses are supported.

6 Conclusion

This study makes several contributions. First, this research contributes to the literature on anticipated regret by highlighting its new role in AI education. While studies have indicated that emotions are significant drivers of academic engagement [22], the findings of this study demonstrate that anticipated regret is an important predictor of intention to learn AI. Second, the classic expectancy-value theory has traditionally centered on expectancy for success and subjective task value, whereas it has not addressed anticipated regret. This study extends and supplements the expectancy-value theory. Furthermore, the significant effect of anticipated regret on intention to learn AI presents new opportunities for instructors in higher education who devote in preparing university students. By addressing future regret, educators can encourage students to thoughtfully whether the loss associated with not taking AI-related courses outweigh the benefits of studying them. Finally, the study suggests that minimizing perceived effort cost is essential for students, as it is found to negatively affect intention to learn AI.

Acknowledgments. This study was supported by the National Science and Technology Council of Taiwan (grant number 113-2410-H-224-029-).

References

1. Bandura, A.: Self-efficacy: The exercise of control. Freeman, New York (1997)
2. Bandura, A.: Social foundations of thought and action: A social cognitive theory. Prentice Hall, Englewood Cliffs, NJ (1986)
3. Bong, M.: Role of self-efficacy and task-value in predicting college students course performance and future enrollment intentions. Contemp. Educ. Psychol. **26**(4), 553–570 (2001)
4. Braganza, A., Chen, W., Canhoto, A., Sap, S.: Productive employment and decent work: The impact of AI adoption on psychological contracts, job engagement and employee trust. J. Bus. Res. **131**, 485–494 (2021)
5. Chai, C.S., Chiu, T.K.F., Wang, X., Jiang, F., Lin, X.F.: Modeling Chinese secondary school students' behavioral intentions to learn artificial intelligence with the theory of planned behavior and self-determination theory. Sustainability **15**(1), 605 (2023)
6. Chai, C.S., Lin, P.Y., Jong, M.S.Y., Dai, Y., Chiu, T.K., Qin, J.: Perceptions of and behavioral intentions towards learning artificial intelligence in primary school students. Educ. Technol. Soc. **24**(3), 89–101 (2021)
7. Chai, C.S., Wang, X., Xu, C.: An extended theory of planned behavior for the modelling of Chinese secondary school students' intention to learn artificial intelligence. Mathematics **8**(11), 2089 (2020)
8. Chun, H.H., Park, J., Thomas, M.: Cold anticipated regret versus hot experienced regret: Why consumers fail to regret unhealthy consumption. J. Ass. Cons. Res. **4**(2), 125–135 (2019)
9. Ding, Y.: Modelling continued use of information systems from a forward-looking perspective: Antecedents and consequences of hope and anticipated regret. Information & Management **55**(4), 461–471 (2018)
10. Eccles, J.S., et al.: Expectancies, values, and academic behaviors. In: Spence, J.T. (ed.) Achievement and achievement motivation, pp. 75–146. W.H. Freeman, San Francisco, CA (1983)
11. Eccles, J.S., Barber, B., Jozefowicz, D.: Linking gender to educational, occupational, and recreational choice: Applying the Eccles et al. model of achievement-related choices. In: Spence, J.T. (ed.) Sexism and stereotypes in modern society: The gender science of Janet Taylor Spence, pp. 153–191. APA, Washington, DC (1999)
12. Eccles, J.S., Wigfield, A.: From expectancy-value theory to situated expectancy value theory: a developmental, social cognitive, and sociocultural perspective on motivation. Contemp. Educ. Psychol. **61**, 101859 (2020)
13. Eccles, J.S., Wigfield, A.: Motivational beliefs, values, and goals. Annu. Rev. Psychol. **53**(1), 109–132 (2002)
14. Eccles, J.S.: Who am I and what am I going to do with my life? personal and collective identities as motivators of action. Educational Psychologist **44**(2), 78–89 (2009)
15. Fornell, C., Larcker, D.F.: Evaluating structural equation models with unobservable variables and measurement error. J. Mark. Res. **18**(1), 39–50 (1981)
16. Gilovich, T., Medvec, V.H.: The experience of regret: What, when, and why. Psychol. Rev. **102**(2), 379–395 (1995)
17. Jiang, Y., Rosenzweig, E.Q., Gaspard, H.: An expectancy-value-cost approach in predicting adolescent students' academic motivation and achievement. Contemp. Educ. Psychol. **54**, 139–152 (2018)

18. Krähmer, D., Stone, R.: Anticipated regret as an explanation of uncertainty aversion. Economic Theory **52**, 709–728 (2013)
19. Lazuras, L., Barkoukis, V., Mallia, L., Lucidi, F., Brand, R.: More than a feeling: the role of anticipated regret in predicting doping intentions in adolescent athletes. Psychol. Sport Exerc. **30**, 196–204 (2017)
20. Lee, S.Y., Friedman, S., Christiaans, E., Robinson, K.A.: Valuable but costly? University students' expectancy-value-cost profiles in introductory chemistry courses. Contemp. Educ. Psychol. **69**, 102056 (2022)
21. Meece, J.L., Wigfield, A., Eccles, J.S.: Predictors of math anxiety and its influence on young adolescents' course enrollment intentions and performance in mathematics. J. Educ. Psychol. **82**(1), 60–70 (1990)
22. Pekrun, R.: The control-value theory of achievement emotions: assumptions, corollaries, and implications for educational research and practice. Educ. Psychol. Rev. **18**(4), 315–341 (2006)
23. Perez, T., Cromley, J.G., Kaplan, A.: The role of identity development, values, and costs in college STEM retention. J. Educ. Psychol. **106**(1), 315–329 (2014)
24. Sagi, A., Friedland, N.: The cost of richness: The effect of the size and diversity of decision sets on post-decision regret. J. Pers. Soc. Psychol. **93**(4), 515–524 (2007)
25. Schleiss, J., Laupichler, M.C., Raupach, T., Stober, S.: AI course design planning framework: developing domain-specific AI education courses. Education Sciences **13**(9), 954 (2023)
26. Schwartz, J., Hagel, J., Wool, M., Monahan, K.: Reframing the future of work: future of work initiatives promise lots of noise and lots of activity, but to what end. MIT Sloan Management Review, 12–18 (2019)
27. Wang, F., King, R.B., Chai, C.S., Zhou, Y.: University students' intentions to learn artificial intelligence: The roles of supportive environments and expectancy–value beliefs. Int. J. Educ. Technol. High. Educ. **20**(1), 51 (2023)
28. Wang, Y., Xue, L.: Using AI-driven chatbots to foster Chinese EFL students' academic engagement: an intervention study. Comput. Hum. Behav. **159**, 108353 (2024)
29. Wang, Y.M., Wei, C.L., Lin, H.H., Wang, S.C., Wang, Y.S.: What drives students' AI learning behavior: A perspective of AI anxiety. Interact. Learn. Environ. **32**(6), 2584–2600 (2022)
30. Wong, K.F.E., Kwong, J.: The role of anticipated regret in escalation of commitment. J. Appl. Psychol. **92**(2), 545–554 (2007)
31. Zeelenberg, M., Beattie, J., van der Pligt, J., de Vries, N.K.: Consequences of regret aversion: Effects of expected feedback on risky decision making. Organ. Behav. Hum. Decis. Process. **65**(2), 148–158 (1996)
32. Zeelenberg, M.: Anticipated regret, expected feedback and behavioral decision making. J. Behav. Decis. Mak. **12**, 93–106 (1999)
33. Zhang, Y., Qin, G., Cheng, L., Marimuthu, K., Kumar, B.S.: Interactive smart educational system using ai for students in the higher education platform. J. Multiple-Valued Logic & Soft Comp. **36**, 83–98 (2021)

Improving Learning to Cross-Lingual Question Answering via Performance Enhancement with XLM-R+ model

Sudarshan Yerragunta[1], Paramveer Singh[1], Rajendra Prasath[1](✉), and G. N. Girish[2]

[1] Indian Institute of Information Technology Sri City, 630 Gnan Marg, Sri City 517646, Andhra Pradesh, India
{sudarshan.y,paramveer.s21,rajendra.prasath}@iiits.in

[2] Indian Institute of Information Technology Dharwad, Ittigatti Rd, near Sattur Colony, Dharwad, Karnataka, India
girish@iiitdwd.ac.in

Abstract. Recent advances in Question Answering (QA) have primarily centred on English, driven by the availability of large-scale, high-quality benchmark datasets. However, extending these advancements to other languages poses significant challenges due to the scarcity of annotated data. This motivates our research focus on enhancing Cross-Lingual QA (CLQA) by improving the performance of existing multilingual QA models. We propose XLM-R+, an extension of the XLM-R architecture that integrates sparse attention and enhanced regularization to improve CLQA performance. Evaluated on the MLQA benchmark, which includes seven languages - English, Hindi, Vietnamese, German, Arabic, Spanish, and Simplified Chinese our model demonstrates consistent improvements across language pairs. Our comprehensive experiments reveal effective strategies for extending QA capabilities to low-resource languages and highlight the broader utility of CLQA in real-world applications. In particular, XLM-R+ holds strong potential for multilingual educational platforms, such as language learning tools and intelligent tutoring systems, where content authored in one language can support question answering in another. Experimental results confirm that XLM-R+ outperforms existing SOTA CLQA approaches.

Keywords: Question Answering · Multi-lingual · Cross-lingual Question Answering

1 Introduction

Question Answering (QA) has become one of the comprehensively studied tasks in Natural Language Processing (NLP), powered by large-scale datasets such as MCTest [19], WikiQA [22], CNN/Daily Mail [8], SQuAD [18] and TriviaQA [10]. With the advances in transformer architectures, the performance of modern QA systems on several English benchmarks [5] is crucial. Despite this success, the significant progress

W.-S. Wang et al. (Eds.): ICITL 2025, LNCS 15913, pp. 28–37, 2026.
https://doi.org/10.1007/978-3-031-98185-2_4

is towards English-centric. Curating high-quality annotations in many languages is costly and logistically complex, leaving low-resource settings underserved [2]. Cross-lingual question answering (CLQA) mitigates this imbalance by letting users pose questions in one language while retrieving answers from documents in another. Early work exploited English-only data, for example, transferring knowledge from SQuAD to Korean [13], Chinese [12] and Bulgarian [7]-and demonstrated the regularizing effect of multilingual co-training [21]. Purpose-built resources have since emerged: bi-lingual Hindi-English MMQA [6], Japanese/French SQuAD subsets [2], nine-language XQA [16], ten-language XQuAD[1], and seven-language MLQA[14]. These corpora underpin aggregated multilingual benchmarks such as XTREME and XGLUE [9, 15].

Nevertheless, two core challenges remain. First, existing transformers incur quadratic cost, hindering long-context reasoning, crucial when answers reside in distant passages. Second, models trained on heterogeneous languages risk overfitting high-resource patterns and degrading on typologically distant languages. To address both issues, we propose XLM-R +, a sparse-attention architecture that couples (i) local and strided attention for efficient long-range dependency capture, with (ii) strong regularization-stochastic depth, layer normalization and variational dropout - to promote robust cross-lingual transfer. Our empirical study on MLQA shows that sparse attention and principled regularization are complementary, improving exact-match and F_1 in all seven languages, including the lowest-resource ones. Our model extends prior theoretical frameworks by demonstrating that sparse attention effectively addresses long-range dependencies critical in multilingual contexts. At the same time, robust regularization techniques provide stability across varying linguistic structures, thereby bridging theoretical gaps identified in earlier research.

2 Task Description

Given a context C_t and a question Que potentially in different languages, the objective of the cross-lingual QA task is to identify an answer Ans as a contiguous span within the context C_t. The context is defined as a sequence of tokens, $C_t = (c_1, c_2, \cdots, c_n)$, where n denotes the number of tokens in the context. Similarly, the question is represented as a sequence of tokens, $Que = (q_1, q_2, \cdots, q_m)$, where m is the length of the question. The answer Ans corresponds to a span in C_t that starts at position f and ends at position g, where $1 \leq f \leq g \leq n$.

3 Proposed Model

We employ XLM-RoBERTa [4] as the backbone of our CLQA system due to its strong cross-lingual transfer capabilities. This multilingual Transformer model has shown state-of-the-art performance across various benchmarks. At its core, XLM-RoBERTa uses a Transformer encoder with self-attention and feed-forward layers to capture long-range dependencies and generate contextual token embeddings, critical for accurate answer span detection in QA.

Our enhanced model, XLM-R+ (see Fig. 1), incorporates sparse attention to improve scalability and capture broader context, along with regularization modules (e.g., stochastic depth, variational dropout) for robust multilingual performance. For example, given a question in Hindi and context in English, the model predicts the answer span in English-demonstrating cross-lingual understanding.

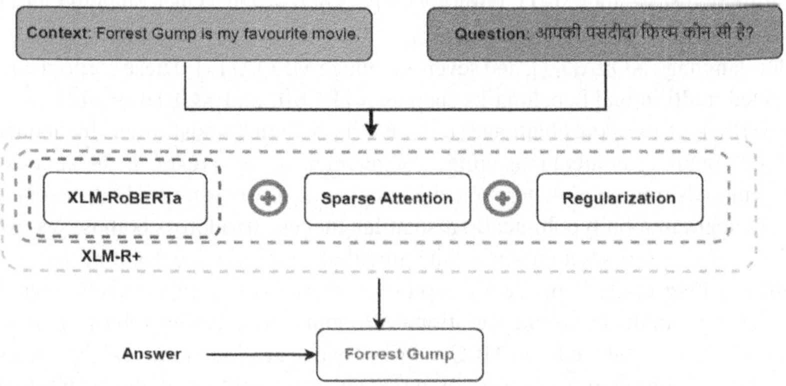

Fig. 1. Architecture of XLM-R +. For example, Context in English language, and Question in Hindi language. The answer in English language

3.1 Sparse Attention

We enhance the Transformer encoder with sparse attention by combining two patterns: *local attention* (LA) [20], where each token attends only to its neighbours, and *strided attention* (SA) [3], where tokens attend to others at fixed intervals. The final attention mask combines both to balance local context with global context. Figure 2 illustrates the unified sparse attention mechanism used in XLM-R +. For a window size w_i:

$$LA(Q, K, V) = softmax\left(\frac{QK^T \odot m_l}{\sqrt{d_k}}\right)V \tag{1}$$

where m_l is a mask such that:

$$m_{l,ij} = \begin{cases} 1 \text{ if} |i - j| \leq w \\ 0 \text{ otherwise} \end{cases} \tag{2}$$

$$SA(Q, K, V) = softmax\left(\frac{QK^T \odot m_s}{\sqrt{d_k}}\right)V \tag{3}$$

where m_s is a mask such that:

$$m_{s,ij} = \begin{cases} 1 \text{ if} j \bmod k = i \bmod k \\ 0 \text{ otherwise} \end{cases} \tag{4}$$

Combined Sparse Attention Combining local and strided attention:

$$SparseAtt(Q, K, V) = softmax\left(\frac{QK^T \odot (m_l + m_s)}{\sqrt{d_k}}\right)V \tag{5}$$

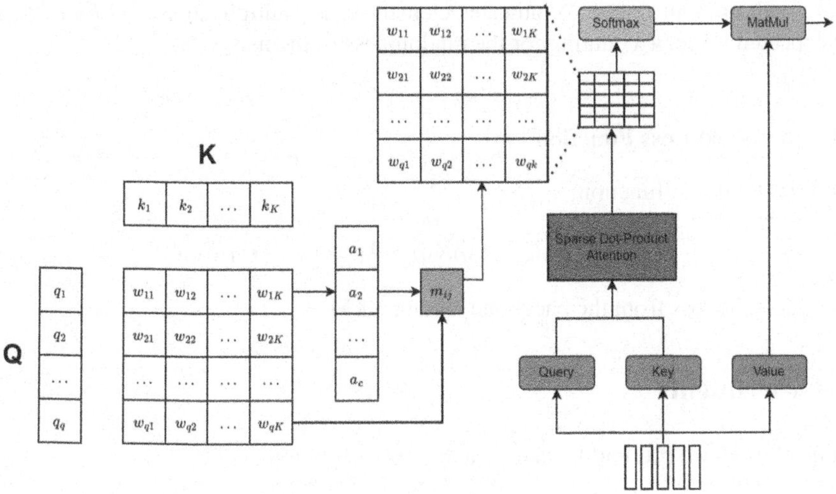

Fig. 2. Sparse Attention

3.2 Enhanced Regularization

Stochastic Depth Regularization: Stochastic depth is a regularization method that randomly skips entire layers during training, with each layer remaining active based on a survival probability p_l. The regularization term for Stochastic Depth is computed as follows:

$$R_{SD} = \sum_{l=1}^{L} p_l \left(L_{SD}(h_{ly}) - h_{ly}\right) \tag{6}$$

where p_l is the survival probability for layer l, $L_{SD}(h_{ly})$ is the transformation applied at layer l if the layer is not skipped, and h_{ly} is the output when the layer is skipped.

Layer Normalization Regularization: The regularization term for Layer Normalization R_{LN} is defined as:

$$R_{LN} = \sum_{l=1}^{L} \left(\frac{||h_{ly-1} - \mu||^2}{\sigma^2}\right) \tag{7}$$

where h_{ly-1} is the input to layer l, μ and σ are the mean and standard deviation of the activations, respectively.

Variational Dropout Regularization: The regularization term for Variational Dropout R_{VD} is computed as:

$$R_{VD} = \sum_{l=1}^{L} \left(E\left[||h_{ly} \odot m||^2 \right] - ||h_{ly}||^2 \right) \tag{8}$$

where h_{ly} is the output of the layer before dropout, $m \sim Bernoulli(1 - p)$ is the dropout mask, with dropout rate p, $\odot$ indicates element-wise multiplication, and $E[\cdot]$ denotes the expected value, accounting for the randomness of the mask.

3.3 Combined Loss Function

The Joint total loss function:

$$L_{total} = L_{task} + \lambda_{SD} R_{SD} + \lambda_{LN} R_{LN} + \lambda_{VD} R_{VD} \tag{9}$$

L_{task} is the loss from the backbone model, XLM-R.

4 Experiments

In this section, we present the dataset and implementation details.

4.1 Dataset

Our experiments cover two multilingual extractive QA datasets: SQuAD [18], MLQA [14], which focuses on twelve and seven languages, respectively. Each dataset offers unique features, and the idea is to experiment with all of them to obtain comprehensive results.

SQuAD[1] is a multilingual QA dataset consisting of 240 paragraphs and 1,190 QA pairs. It a collection of Wikipedia articles in English. Additionally, 11 more languages were added in XQuAD [1], including Hindi, German, Arabic, Thai, Turkish, Vietnamese, Russian, Greek, Chinese, Spanish, and Romanian.

MLQA[2] dataset is also a multilingual QA evaluation benchmark that includes 5 K extractive QA instances (12 K in English) in seven languages (English, Hindi, Vietnamese, German, Arabic, Spanish, and Simplified Chinese). Like SQuAD, MLQA is also based on Wikipedia articles, and the questions have been translated by professional translators. The answers are taken directly from the various languages of the corresponding Wikipedia article to obtain parallel sentences. The details of the MLQA dataset are given in Tables 1 and 2.

Implementation Details: Our proposed model uses the XLM-RoBERTa [4] as the backbone model. It is a multilingual model trained on 100 languages and tokenized by SentencePiece [11]. It comprises of 24 layers, with 1,024 hidden states per layer. The dimensionality of the feed-forward layer is 4,096. It uses 16 attention heads and vocabularies of size 250 k; There are 550 million parameters in total for XLM-RoBERTa. We follow a similar setup for our model. We train on the SQuAD v1.1 [18] dataset and evaluate using the MLQA dataset in a zero-shot cross-lingual setting. The development data is in English-MLQA-en; test data is available in several target languages. The lambda hyperparameters ($\lambda_{SD} = 0.01$, $\lambda_{LN} = 1$, and $\lambda_{VD} = 0.1$) were selected based on grid search using validation F_1-scores on a subset of the MLQA development dataset. Specifically, λ_{SD} was explored over [0.001, 0.01, 0.05, 0.1], λ_{LN} over [0.1, 0.5,1, 0.05], and λ_{VD} over [0.01, 0.1, 0.2, 0.5], with optimal settings determined by highest validation performance. We implemented our model using the PyTorch framework [17] within the Google Colab Pro environment.

Table 1. Number of Wikipedia articles with a context in MLQA.

	en	de	es	ar	zh	vi	hi
Number of Articles	5530	2806	2762	2627	2673	2682	2255
Number of Contexts	10894	4509	5215	5085	4989	5246	4524

Table 2. Total number of parallel instances (all parallel with English) between target language pairs. Here, the languages are Hindi (hi), Simplified Chinese (zh), Vietnamese (vi), Arabic (ar), German (de), and Spanish (es).

	de	es	ar	zh	vi	hi
de	5029					
Es	1972	5753				
ar	1856	2139	5852			
zh	1811	2108	2100	5641		
vi	1857	2207	2210	2127	6006	
hi	1593	1910	2017	2124	2124	5425

5 Results and Analysis

F_1-score is a standard metric that is used for QA Systems. Table 3 shows the results of the different existing models along with the proposed model. XLM-R+ outperforms the existing methodologies. The Fig. 3 shows the heatmap, including scores of our proposed model and the SOTA (G-XLT [14]).

5.1 Performance Analysis

The F_1-scores of the proposed XLM-R+ model on the MLQA dataset (Fig. 3) reveal consistent improvements over SOTA baselines across multiple language pairs, underscoring the impact of the applied regularization techniques. For instance, in the English-Spanish (en-es) setting, XLM-R+ achieved an F_1-score of 84.42% , outperforming the

SOTA score of 74.90% - a significant gain of 9.5% . Similarly, English-German (en-de) reached 82% compared to 65% from prior models. Although improvements in pairs such as English-Hindi (en-hi) were more modest, the results still suggest strong generalization and highlight areas for future enhancement. These gains are largely attributed to the integration of stochastic depth, layer normalization, and variational dropout, which collectively reduce overfitting and improve training stability.

Table 3. Comparison of F_1-scores of various models on MLQA dataset for the cross-lingual task

Model	F_1-score						
	en	es	de	ar	hi	vi	zh
BERT-Large [7]	80.2	-	-	-	-	-	-
Multilingual-BERT [7]	77.7	64.3	57.9	45.7	43.8	57.1	57.5
XLM [18]	74.9	68.0	62.2	54.8	48.8	61.4	61.1
XLM- R_{Base} [5]	77.1	67.4	60.9	54.9	59.4	64.5	61.8
XLM-R [5]	80.6	74.1	68.5	63.1	69.2	71.3	68.0
XLM-R+	**84.42**	**75.72**	**71.08**	**65.23**	**71.37**	**71.4**	**69.70**

Here '-' indicates that the experimental results were not reported in the original papers. Best results indicated in **bold**.

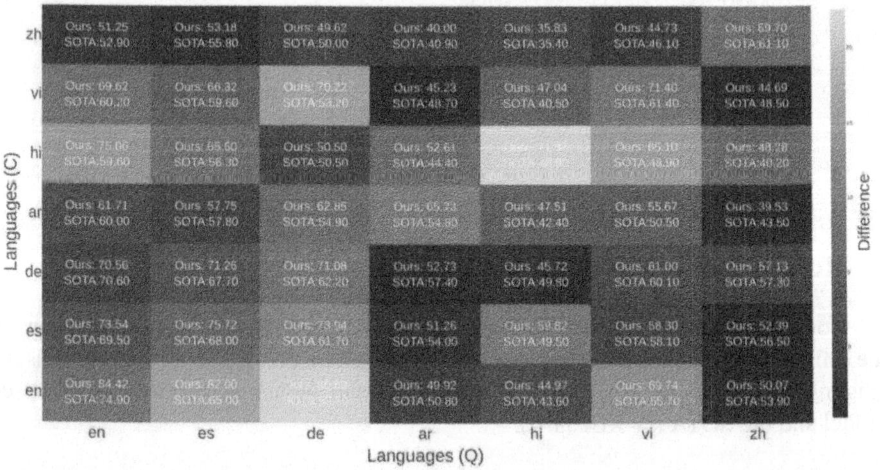

Fig. 3. F_1-scores comparison of existing XLM-R and proposed XLM-R+ model for MLQA.

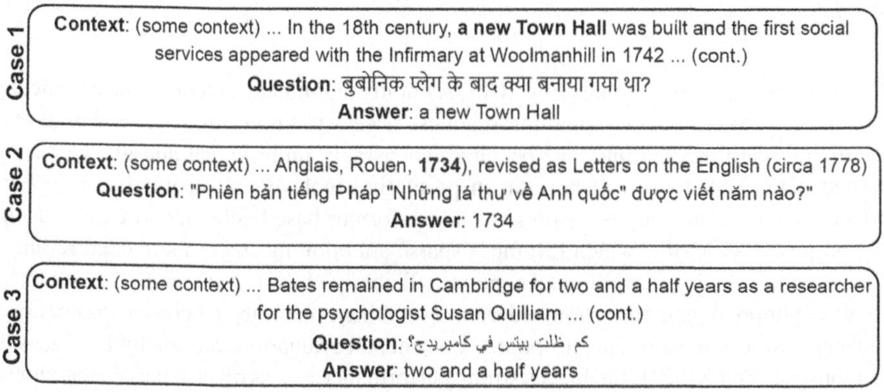

Fig. 4. Example cases for English being Context and the Questions are from different languages.

5.2 Impact of Learning to Cross-Lingual Question Answering

Our approach addresses this by leveraging high-resource languages to support QA in low-resource languages, effectively democratizing information access. Users can ask questions in their native language and retrieve relevant content composed in another. It is a vital capability for real-world domains such as education, healthcare, legal services, and public communication, where language diversity is critical. To illustrate this, Fig. 4 presents qualitative examples where the *Context* in English, *Question* in a different language (e.g., Hindi, Vietnamese, Arabic), and *Answer* in English. The notation (e.g., *en-hi*) indicates a context in English and a question in Hindi.

5.3 Applications of CLQA for Inclusive and Personalized Learning

- *Multilingual Accessibility*: Learners ask in their language and get answers from different-language content using CLQA.
- *Personalized Virtual Tutors*: AI tutors respond in real time across languages and formats, including text and video.
- *Global Collaboration*: CLQA allows multilingual learners to access and query shared resources in global education programs.
- *Access in Low-Resource Settings*: Learners from underrepresented regions can access rich content using cross-lingual model support.
- *Assessment and Feedback*: Automated multilingual assessments and feedback improve the understanding of the learner and personalized educational support
- *Cross-Language Learning*: Students enhance language skills by comparing content and answers in multiple languages via CLQA.
- *Support for Teachers*: In multilingual classrooms, teachers deliver and clarify content using the native languages of students efficiently.

6 Conclusion

Cross-lingual Question Answering (CLQA) holds significant potential for enhancing educational experiences by enabling seamless access to knowledge across languages. As digital learning environments become increasingly multilingual and globally connected, CLQA systems will be vital in promoting inclusive and equitable access to educational content. This work presents a transformer-based approach to CLQA using the proposed XLM-R+, which leverages sparse attention mechanisms to capture long-range dependencies in multilingual contexts efficiently. We integrate regularisation techniques to improve generalization and training stability, including stochastic depth, layer normalization, and variational dropout. Experimental evaluations on benchmark datasets demonstrate that XLM-R+ achieves strong performance across diverse languages, showing particular gains in low-resource settings. We aim to extend this work by combining XLM-R+ with symbolic reasoning methods to support multimodal QA.

References

1. Artetxe, M., Ruder, S., Yogatama, D.: On the cross-lingual transferability of monolingual representations. In: Proc. of the 58th Annual Meeting of the ACL, pp. 4623–4637. ACL (2020)
2. Asai, A., Eriguchi, A., Hashimoto, K., Tsuruoka, Y.: Multilingual extractive reading comprehension by runtime machine translation. CoRR **abs/1809.03275** (2018)
3. Child, R., Gray, S., Radford, A., Sutskever, I.: Generating long sequences with sparse transformers. CoRR **abs/1904.10509** (2019)
4. Conneau, A., Khandelwal, K., Goyal, N., et al.: Unsupervised cross-lingual representation learning at scale. In: Jurafsky, D., Chai, J., Schluter, N., Tetreault, J.R. (eds.) Proc. of the 58th Annual Meeting of the ACL, July 5–10, pp. 8440–8451 (2020)
5. Devlin, J., Chang, M.W., Lee, K., Toutanova, K.: BERT: Pre-training of Deep Bidirectional Transformers for Language Understanding. In: Proc. of the 2019 Conf. of the North American Chapter of the ACL: Human Language Technologies, pp. 4171–4186. ACL, Minnesota (2019)
6. Gupta, D., Kumari, S., Ekbal, A., Bhattacharyya, P.: MMQA: A Multi-domain Multi-lingual Question-Answering Framework for English and Hindi. In: LREC (2018)
7. Hardalov, M., Koychev, I., Nakov, P.: Beyond English-only reading comprehension: Experiments in zero-shot multilingual transfer for Bulgarian. In: Mitkov, R., Angelova, G. (eds.) Proceedings of the International Conference on Recent Advances in Natural Language Processing, pp. 447–459. INCOMA Ltd., Varna, Bulgaria (2019)
8. Hermann, K.M., Kociský, T., Grefenstette, E., Espeholt, L., et al.: Teaching machines to read and comprehend. In: Advances in Neural Information Processing Systems 28: Annual Conf. on Neural Information Processing Systems, December 7–12, pp. 1693–1701. Montreal, Canada (2015)
9. Hu, J., Ruder, S., Siddhant, A., Neubig, G., et al.: XTREME: A massively multilingual multi-task benchmark for evaluating cross-lingual generalisation. In: Proc. of the 37th Int. Conf. on Machine Learning, ICML 2020. Proc. of Machine Learning Research, vol. 119, pp. 4411–4421 (2020)
10. Joshi, M., Choi, E., Weld, D., et al.: TriviaQA: A Large Scale Distantly Supervised Challenge Dataset for Reading Comprehension. In: Proc. of the 55th Annual Meeting of the ACL, pp. 1601–1611. Canada (2017)

11. Kudo, T., Richardson, J.: Sentencepiece: a simple and language independent subword tokenizer and detokenizer for neural text processing. In: Proc. of the 2018 Conf. on Empirical Methods in Natural Language Processing, EMNLP, Brussels, Belgium, pp. 66–71. ACL (2018)
12. Lee, K., Park, S., Han, H., et al.: Learning with Limited Data for Multilingual Reading Comprehension. In: Proc. of the 2019 Conf. onEmpirical Methods in NLP and the 9th Int. Joint Conf. on NLP (EMNLP-IJCNLP), pp. 2833–2843. ACL, Hong Kong (2019)
13. Lee, K., Yoon, K., et al.: Semi-supervised Training Data Generation for Multilingual Question Answering. In: Proc. of the Eleventh Int. Conf. on Language Resources and Evaluation (LREC 2018). European Language Resources Association (ELRA). Miyazaki, Japan (2018)
14. Lewis, P.S.H., Oguz, B., Rinott, R., Riedel, S., Schwenk, H.: MLQA: evaluating cross-lingual extractive question answering. In: Proc. of the 58th Annual Meeting of the ACL, pp. 7315–7330 (2020)
15. Liang, Y., Duan, N., Gong, Y., Wu, N., Guo, F., et al.: XGLUE: A new benchmark datasetfor cross-lingual pre-training, understanding and generation. In: Proc. of the 2020 Conf. on Empirical Methods in Natural Language Processing, EMNLP, pp. 6008–6018 (2020)
16. Liu, J., Lin, Y., Liu, Z., Sun, M.: XQA: A Cross-lingual Open-domain Question Answering Dataset. In: Proc. of ACL 2019 (2019)
17. Paszke, A., et al.: Automatic differentiation in pytorch. In: NIPS 2017 Workshop on Autodiff (2017)
18. Rajpurkar, P., Zhang, J., Lopyrev, K., Liang, P.: Squad: 100, 000+ questions for machine comprehension of text. In: Proc. of the 2016 Conf. on Empirical Methods in Natural Language Processing, EMNLP 2016, Austin, Texas, USA, November 1–4, pp. 2383–2392 (2016)
19. Richardson, M., Burges, C.J.C., Renshaw, E.: Mctest: A challenge dataset for the open-domain machine comprehension of text. In: Proc. of the 2013 Conf. on Empirical Methods in Natural Language Processing, EMNLP 2013, 18–21 October 2013, Seattle, Washington, USA, A meeting of SIGDAT, a Special Interest Group of the ACL, pp. 193–203. ACL (2013)
20. Shah, S.R.B., Chadha, G.S., Schwung, A., Ding, S.X.: A sequence-to-sequence approach for remaining useful lifetime estimation using attention-augmented bidirectional lstm. Intelligent Systems with Applications **10–11**, 200049 (2021)
21. Singh, J., McCann, B., Keskar, N.S., et al.: XLDA: Cross-Lingual Data Augmentation for Natural Language Inference and Question Answering. arXiv:1905.11471 [cs] (2019)
22. Yang, Y., Yih, W., Meek, C.: Wikiqa: A challenge dataset for open-domain question answering. In: Proc. of the 2015 Conf. on Empirical Methods in Natural Language Processing, EMNLP 2015, Lisbon, Portugal, September 17–21, pp. 2013–2018. The ACL (2015)

Drawing for You: Exploring the Impact of Integrating Educational Technology into Picture Book Creation on Students' Understanding of Special Education

Mei-Yun Chang(✉), Chi-Yu Yang, and Chia-Hua Hsiao

Department of Childhood Education and Enterprise Management, Central Taiwan University of Science and Technology, Taichung 406053, Taiwan
{mychang,106817,108463}@ctust.edu.tw

Abstract. This study aims to explore the application of educational technology in creating picture books for special education and analyze its impact on undergraduate students' understanding of special education theories. Fifty post-baccalaureate students participated, using ChatGPT to generate picture book texts and tools like Canva and Bing Image Creator to design illustrations. The latest version of the picture books was used for shared reading activities in preschool, and feedback from children was incorporated to revise the content. The results show that students created picture books covering six types of special needs, such as hearing impairment, autism, and ADHD. Peer reviews indicated that about one-third to half of the group works met evaluation standards, and students generally agreed that creating picture books helped deepen their understanding of special education theories. While ChatGPT assisted with text generation, multiple revisions were needed to tailor content to children's needs, highlighting the crucial role of professionals in adapting language and shaping scenarios. Children's feedback helped students refine their picture books, aligning them better with developmental characteristics and enhancing educational effectiveness. Through this process, students learned about emerging AI technologies and digital tools, boosting their confidence and sense of achievement in innovative teaching and creation.

Keywords: Educational Technology · Picture Book Creation · ChatGPT

1 Introduction

Developing students' transferable competencies, enabling them to flexibly apply acquired knowledge and skills to meet the demands of the 21st century, has become a critical issue in the field of education. As early as 2002, the Partnership for 21st Century Skills (P21) advocated for educational reform and, in its 2008 international conference, identified three core competencies essential for future talents: learning and innovation skills, information, media, and technology skills, and life and career skills [1]. This highlights the pivotal role of digital literacy in preparing future professionals.

W.-S. Wang et al. (Eds.): ICITL 2025, LNCS 15913, pp. 38–47, 2026.
https://doi.org/10.1007/978-3-031-98185-2_5

The rapid advancement of generative AI technology at the end of 2022 has had a profound impact across various fields, particularly in medicine, engineering, and business. In the realm of education, generative AI has reshaped digital learning trends by assisting educators in designing more appropriate instructional content and offering learners personalized learning solutions that accommodate diverse temporal and disciplinary needs for in-depth learning.

In the field of early childhood education, the application of AI has also made significant strides. From instructional setting design to teacher-parent communication, AI-assisted technologies have enhanced educators' creativity in selecting and designing instructional content. One notable example is the "text-to-image" function of generative AI, which enables educators to create images that align with children's needs and comprehension levels. This technology facilitates discussion and sharing activities in the classroom, using images to enhance young children's cognitive development and imagination. Picture books serve as essential instructional tools in early childhood education, characterized by concise text, vivid illustrations, and narratives closely related to daily life. These books are well-suited for parent-child reading and carry profound educational implications. Research indicates that picture books rich in imaginative elements are particularly effective in stimulating children's learning interests [2]. The researcher, with a long-standing focus on special education, has observed that students engaged in collaborative creation of picture books on special education topics experience a sense of accomplishment and fulfillment, even when facing challenges such as difficulties in illustrating their envisioned images. With the widespread adoption of AI-generated content and educational technology tools, this study explores the feasibility of integrating educational technology into the creation of picture books on special education topics. The objective is to enable students to apply their theoretical knowledge of special education by generating and crafting narratives using ChatGPT, designing illustrations with tools such as Canva and Bing Image Creator, and subsequently implementing their picture books in preschool teaching. Based on children's feedback, students refine and revise their work to enhance its effectiveness.

Given this background, this study aims to examine the factors influencing students' decisions when selecting the special needs category for their picture book protagonists, the challenges encountered during the creative process, and the strategies employed to address these challenges. Additionally, by analyzing picture book creation checklists and learning outcome questionnaires completed at the end of the semester, this study assesses the impact of picture book creation on students' comprehension of special education theories.

2 Literature Review

2.1 Application of Educational Technology

Since the beginning of the 21st century, the rapid development of Artificial Intelligence (AI) and mobile network technologies has driven a new wave of digital learning, with various innovative applications becoming increasingly popular among students. In educational settings, the integration of technological tools has fostered a student-centered learning environment, enabling learners to express their views, share knowledge, and interact with others. Compared to traditional classrooms, this model offers greater flexibility in terms of relationships, time, and space [3]. The integration of information technology into teaching has demonstrated a moderately positive effect on students' learning attitudes and has shown significantly better outcomes than traditional teaching approaches [4].

ChatGPT, developed by OpenAI, is an advanced language model based on the Generative Pretrained Transformer (GPT) architecture. It is capable of generating natural language text, answering questions, offering suggestions, and engaging in dialogue. ChatGPT acts as an intelligent assistant in personalized learning, providing appropriate support and real-time feedback based on students' learning styles, interests, and abilities. This facilitates task completion and problem-solving [5, 6]. Furthermore, Canva, a multifunctional tool for educational material creation, allows students to easily produce text-based content and presentations, thereby lowering the learning threshold for AI technology. Students are not only users of AI but also have the opportunity to become content creators in collaboration with AI [7].

In summary, the application of AI has advanced the development of digital learning by offering students more opportunities for expression and sharing. It has also had a significantly positive impact on their learning attitudes. Consequently, future educators and childcare professionals must be equipped with the ability to utilize information technology in order to establish student-centered learning environments and promote autonomous learning.

2.2 Picture Book Creation

Former Minister of Education, Ovid Tzeng, once stated, "Reading helps children internalize the experiences of others into their own knowledge, which in turn enables them to absorb more information, elevating their perspective and comprehension as if ascending a spiral staircase" [8]. A high-quality picture book should possess the following characteristics: it should be interesting, original, and developmentally appropriate for children. The content should reflect diverse aspects of human nature (such as good and evil, strength and weakness), allow children to comprehend the themes independently, and avoid excessive moralizing. Characterization should not be overly idealized or exaggerated; protagonists should demonstrate problem-solving abilities and exhibit traits that children can emulate. Authors and illustrators should avoid conveying discriminatory messages or misinformation when developing characters [9]. In picture books, text and illustrations are equally important. At a minimum, they should include three key elements: the meaning conveyed by the text, the meaning expressed through the illustrations, and the combined interpretation of both. A fourth critical element is the personal connection formed between the child and the picture book. Picture books may be fictional or nonfictional, and illustrations can take the form of photographs, drawings, or collages [10].

Research has shown that guiding students to create picture books on the theme of adult life as part of project-based learning results in meaningful reflections. Students reported that illustrations sometimes conveyed more emotional power than text, deeply affecting readers and offering great insight [11]. Action research has also been used to incorporate Amis tribal culture into indigenous legends, resulting in a collaboratively created picture book titled Asiluai [12]. Weekend program students found that creating e-picture books (e-Picture-Book Creating, e-PBC) enhanced their knowledge of picture books, critical thinking, and multimedia literacy [13]. In addition, picture book reading supports the development of children's social skills, including empathy, critical thinking, communication, collaboration, and inclusiveness [14].

In conclusion, the use of ChatGPT to support picture book creation, coupled with Canva as a learning aid, enables students to personalize their use of educational technology. Picture book creation should emphasize meaningful and valuable content while ensuring well-developed characters, thereby enhancing the educational and psychological value of picture books.

3 Research Methodology and Design

3.1 Research Participants and Implementation Process

This study involved 50 post-baccalaureate students enrolled in a special education course, utilizing a survey-based approach to collect rubric scores on picture book creation, learning outcome questionnaires, and reflective records. The research process began with an introduction to special education, covering the characteristics, needs, and educational strategies for children with special needs, along with examples of student-created and commercial picture books. Students then learned to use educational technology tools like ChatGPT, Canva, and Bing Image Creator for text generation and image design. They designed story protagonists based on different disabilities, developed plots, and created content using these tools. The completed picture books were shared with preschool children, and revisions were made based on their feedback. Finally, a learning outcomes questionnaire assessed the impact of picture book creation on students' understanding of special education theories.

3.2 Research Instruments

The research instruments included learning portfolio data, a picture book creation rubric, and a questionnaire on the effectiveness of picture book creation in enhancing students' understanding of special education theories, as described below:

(1) Learning Portfolio Data

This comprised both group and individual reflective records, documenting students' decision-making in selecting disability categories, developing picture books, and revising content following shared reading activities. These records captured students' learning processes and revision strategies.

(2) Picture Book Creation Rubric

The rubric assessed five dimensions: (A) Description of the protagonist's special needs characteristics; (B) Content depicting interactions with the protagonist; (C) The degree of correspondence between text and images; (D) The extent to which the book captures young children's attention; and (E) Aesthetic quality of the illustrations. Each dimension was rated on a 4-point scale, with higher scores indicating better performance. The reliability of the scale (Cronbach's α) was .844.

(3) Questionnaire on the Effectiveness of Picture Book Creation in Enhancing Students' Understanding of Special Education Theories

This end-of-semester questionnaire consisted of 17 items rated on a 4-point Likert scale, ranging from "Strongly Agree" (4 point) to "Strongly Disagree" (1 points). It measured students' perceived learning benefits, with a reliability coefficient (Cronbach's α) of .895.

For data analysis, quantitative analysis was conducted using percentage-based representations of agreement levels in the picture book creation checklist and the learning outcomes questionnaire. Qualitative analysis involved examining students' reflective records. Items 1 to 6 represented group reflections, with each group submitting one record, coded with identifiers (e.g., G03 for Group 3). Item 7 captured individual reflections, coded sequentially based on submission order (e.g., N02 for the second student's reflection in the class).

4 Results and Discussion

4.1 Analysis of Learning Portfolio Data and Findings

(1) Selection of Picture Book Protagonists Based on Prior Experiences

This study collected a total of ten picture books created by students. The protagonists represented six types of special needs: hearing impairment (2 books), autism spectrum disorder (2 books), attention deficit hyperactivity disorder (ADHD) (3 books), Tourette syndrome (1 book), and selective mutism (1 book). The selection of special needs categories for the protagonists was based either on the personal experiences of students with their children or on their encounters with young children in professional settings.

One of our group members has a child diagnosed with ADHD, which has given us a deeper understanding and awareness of the needs and challenges faced by this group (G02).

This type of special need is commonly observed in preschool environments and is suitable for guidance and education through picture books (G01).

While discussing our experiences with autistic children in our professional settings, we discovered similarities in our teaching encounters, leading us to choose autism as the theme for our picture book (G07).

(2) Utilizing ChatGPT to Assist with Story Development

Most students expressed a willingness to use ChatGPT for story ideation, but the final content was determined through multiple rounds of group discussion.

We extended the story based on real-life observations of a child in the classroom, then collectively developed a core storyline. ChatGPT was used to generate text (G01).

We used ChatGPT to generate the story text, but much of the AI-generated content did not align with our needs. Ultimately, we rewrote over 80% of the story (G08).

Our group collaboratively developed the story, with each member contributing sequentially to complete the special education picture book text (G07).

By generating multiple versions of the text with ChatGPT, we discussed and selected the most appropriate content, making necessary refinements (G03, G05).

(3) Feedback from Young Children Contributed to Refining the Picture Books
The students noted that while young children showed great interest in the picture book content, certain textual descriptions surpassed their lived experiences, resulting in comprehension challenges. Consequently, the content was revised in response to the children's reactions. This is consistent with findings from previous studies, which emphasize that picture books should possess qualities of interest, originality, and developmental appropriateness for young children [9].

Preschool children were curious about the protagonist's hearing aid, prompting us to simplify the story language and enlarge the hearing aid illustration to highlight the protagonist's unique feature (G03).

Although the text was simple, the characteristics of the special needs child were not distinct enough. As a result, we added three additional illustrations and more descriptive text to clarify the special traits, making it easier for children to understand (G06).

The vibrant colors of the illustrations attracted children's attention, but some struggled to understand the function of hearing aids. To address this, we added a more straightforward explanation and interactive teaching components to enhance their understanding (G04).

4.2 Peer Evaluation of Picture Book Creations

Students conducted peer evaluations of each group's picture books, as detailed in Table 1. Among the ten books, Group 8 received the highest ratings, followed by Group 3.

Table 1. Peer Evaluation Results of Picture Book Creation.

Rubric (4 points)	Group3 (%)	Group4 (%)	Group5 (%)	Group7 (%)	Group8 (%)
Description of protagonist's special needs	61	77.3	-	-	71.8
Details of interaction with protagonist	-	77.3	63.4	-	66.7
Coherence between text and images	71.8	-	63.4	60.5	76.9
Ability to maintain children's attention	64.1	72.7	-	60.5	71.8
Aesthetic quality of images	66.7	-	61.0	60.5	69.2

4.3 Learning Outcomes of Picture Book Creation on Students' Understanding of Special Education Theories

(1) Picture Book Creation Enhanced Understanding of Special Education Theories
Results from the questionnaire (N = 43) indicated that students scored above 2.5 on all items, with average scores ranging from 2.51 to 3.91 and standard deviations between 0.29 and 0.96. The top three highest-rated items were: "Through this picture book creation process, I gained a deeper understanding of the physical

and psychological characteristics of children with special needs" (M = 3.91; SD = 0.29); "Through this picture book creation process, I better understood the reasons behind the behaviors of children with special needs" (M = 3.91; SD = 0.29); and "The special education picture books introduced by the instructor in class helped me better understand the physical and psychological characteristics of children with special needs" (M = 3.90; SD = 0.29). The lowest-rated items were: "I find it easy to use ChatGPT to generate picture book stories related to children with special needs" (M = 2.72; SD = 0.82) and "I find it easy to use ChatGPT, Canva, or other educational technology tools to generate picture book illustrations related to children with special needs" (M = 2.51; SD = 0.96). Students generally perceived the use of educational technology tools for special education picture book creation as a valuable skill in modern society (M = 3.81; SD = 0.39), aligning with Van Laar et al.'s (2017) framework on the key competencies required for future professionals [1].

(2) The Role of Educational Technology helps Enhance Students' Cognition, Attitudes, and Skills

The students expressed that learning new AI technologies was a valuable experience. After the picture books were completed, the children listened attentively, and the activity had a counseling effect, which aligns with the findings of previous studies [2, 11, 13].

"When I first heard that we would use AI-generated images to create picture books, I thought it was so cool! Without this course, I would never have explored this field in my lifetime. After completing the picture book, I tried telling the story to younger children who arrived home late. Seeing their focused expressions made me realize that interacting with children is not as difficult as I once thought" (N002).

"Completing the picture book gave me a strong sense of accomplishment. I am grateful that neither my teammates nor I gave up easily. When I told the story, the children not only listened attentively but also remembered the content afterward, which moved me deeply" (N010).

"This was an entirely new experience for me and an excellent learning opportunity. It enhanced my professional knowledge of AI-generated imagery and reminded me not to be confined to traditional teaching methods but to embrace innovation when necessary" (N005).

(3) The Role of Human Judgment in Overcoming Challenges in Educational Technology

While AI provided valuable support for content generation, human intervention was necessary to refine and adapt outputs to ensure educational effectiveness. The primary challenges encountered by students included the lack of child-friendly language in AI-generated text, the pursuit of higher-quality images, and the need for consistency in visual elements. The following sections outline the approaches taken to address these challenges.

(A) Adapting AI-Generated Text for Child-Friendliness

Students observed that AI-generated text tended to be overly complex and lacked child-friendly phrasing, making it difficult for young children to comprehend and engage with the content. Strategies to address this included refining AI prompts and manually adjusting the text.

AI struggles to accurately depict real-life special needs situations in a way that is understandable to young children. Through team discussions, we refined the ChatGPT prompts, incorporating real-world scenarios while ensuring that the language remained simple and relatable for children (G01).

Due to our limited professional knowledge, we initially relied on work experiences, which resulted in inaccuracies in depicting specific disabilities. To address this, we gathered medical and educational re-sources on different disabilities and integrated them into the story, making the theme more precise (G07).

ChatGPT-generated text contained many complex, adult-oriented terms. To address this, two team members thoroughly reviewed and re-vised the content to ensure that the vocabulary was accessible to young children (G06).

(B) Achieving Higher-Quality Visuals

Students utilized multiple software tools, including Canva, ChatGPT, PicLumen, MidJourney, DALL-E, Leonardo AI, Bing Image, and traditional hand-drawing tech-niques, demonstrating strong motivation for self-learning.

Our team used PicLumen and Canva to generate illustrations for special needs picture books (G03).

After generating the text, we experimented with different AI tools, such as ChatGPT and Bing Image, and selected the most suitable images for each section of the book (G05).

We combined hand-drawn illustrations with reference images from the internet and used Keynote to assemble the final visuals (G07).

Our team used Leonardo AI as the primary tool for generating illustrations (G08).

(C) Ensuring Visual Consistency in Characters and Scenes

Students encountered difficulties in maintaining visual consistency across images. To address this, they experimented with different AI tools and refined prompts for better continuity.

Initially, we used ChatGPT for image generation, but the illustrations of the main character lacked consistency. Later, we discovered Leonardo AI, which offered better results. The key to overcoming these challenges was continuously refining prompts and generating multiple versions until we achieved a coherent visual style (G08).

Using ChatGPT-generated storyboard scripts often failed to produce desired images. We experimented with Canva, Bing AI, and other tools but faced issues with character continuity and image generation limits. Eventually, we found that PicLumen met our needs, though it required English-language prompts. We then used Canva to add elements like hearing aids to the images (G03).

Initially, we used ChatGPT to generate images, but inconsistencies in style and character depiction emerged. Later, we switched to Canva's AI Dream Studio, which allowed us to generate images in a selected style and refine them with reference images. However, minor inconsistencies remained, requiring precise prompt adjustments (G09).

5 Conclusions and Recommendations

5.1 Conclusions

This study explored the use of educational technology in creating picture books on special needs topics, highlighting its role in enhancing students' learning and creativity. By integrating personal and professional experiences, students developed diverse and practical themes while deepening their understanding of special education theories through iterative refinement of text and images. Although AI tools like ChatGPT assisted in text generation, human expertise was essential in adapting content for young children. Feedback from children further improved language use and visual storytelling, strengthening the educational impact. Overall, this process fostered students' technical proficiency, creative confidence, and innovative teaching approaches, demonstrating the value of educational technology in teacher training.

5.2 Recommendations

To enhance the effectiveness of picture book creation in special education, future curricula should integrate AI literacy training to improve text and image development. Collaboration with experts in psychology and special education can elevate the professional quality of content, while observing children's responses can help refine language and storytelling for better engagement. Providing broader access to educational technology resources will further support students' creative processes. Building on the above insights, it is hoped that future efforts will further enhance the application of picture book creation in special education, enabling students to deepen their understanding of children with special needs through hands-on practice, while also providing young learners with more diverse educational resources. This study responds to key 21st-century competencies, particularly digital literacy and innovation skills, and affirms the potential of generative AI and educational technology in practical teaching and teacher education. It lays a foundation for future interdisciplinary applications in education.

Acknowledgments. This study was supported by the Pilot Teaching Practice Program of Central Taiwan University of Science and Technology, Taiwan.

References

1. Van Laar, E., et al.: The relation between 21st-century skills and digital skills: A systematic literature review. Computers in Human Behavior **72**, 577–588 (2017)
2. Mao, C., Sharudin, S.A., Lu, H., Mo, Y.: A study on the use of children's picture books in community education: An analysis based on typical cases. Journal of Education, Humanities, and Social Research **2**(1), 1–16 (2025)
3. Lin, Y., Chang, S., Chan, C.: Prospect for introducing emerging technologies to school traffic education. Urban Transportation **37**(2), 81–108 (2022)
4. Liang, Y., Chen, F.: The meta-analysis of students' attitude toward the incorporation of information technology into teaching. Secondary Education **66**(2), 100–125 (2015)

5. Baidoo-Anu, D., Ansah, L.O.: Education in the era of generative artificial intelligence (AI): Understanding the potential benefits of ChatGPT in promoting teaching and learning (2023). https://ssrn.com/abstract=4337484 or https://doi.org/10.2139/ssrn.4337484
6. Su, J.H., Yang, W.P.: Unlocking the power of ChatGPT: A framework for applying generative AI in education. Available at SAGE Journals. (2023). https://doi.org/10.1177/20965311231168423
7. Hsu, T.P., Wang, C.C.: Feasible strategies and teaching examples of AI integration in education. The Education Bimonthly **644**, 29–34 (2024)
8. Hsu, H.A., Chiu, H.J.: Life education in picture books. Taiwan Educational Review Monthly **2**(12), 122–125 (2013)
9. Uluğ, E., Bayraktar, A.: Determination of the required features of children's picture books. Journal of Education and Future **6**, 25–42 (2014)
10. Seplocha, H., Strasser, J.: Using picture books to support young children's literacy. Child. Educ. **83**(4), 219 (2007)
11. Chang, M.: Life Education Picture Books for Adults. Journal of General Education **8**(2), 27–46 (2014)
12. Hung, W.: Action research on creating a multicultural education picture book take the picture book "Asiroay" created by Feng-Nian elementary school in Taitung County as an example. J. General Educ. Multicult. **10**, 83–102 (2022)
13. Wang, C., Jiang, S., Wu, W.: E-Picture-Book Creating (e-PBC) in the Children's Literature Classroom. J. Nation. Formosa Univ. **32**(2), 81–98 (2024)
14. Sinamo, J., Panjaitan, L.S.W., Butar Butar, M.L.E.F.: Building children's social Skills through picture story books. Talitakum: Jurnal Pendidikan Kristen Anak Usia Dini **3**(1), 14–21 (2024)

AI-Enhanced Augmented Reality for L2 Medical English Learning and Remote Surgical Collaboration

Yingling Chen[1](✉) and Chinlun Lai[2]

[1] General Education Center, National Defense University, Taoyuan City, Taiwan
cil0226@yahoo.com.tw
[2] Asia Eastern University of Science and Technology, Taipei, Taiwan

Abstract. This paper presents a pilot study of implementing a novel system combining Augmented Reality (AR) and Artificial Intelligence (AI) designed for remote collaboration in clinical surgery and L2 medical English learning. The primary objective of this study is to provide real-time, AI-driven recommendations to surgical teams, especially when encountering unexpected challenges during operations. Traditionally, unforeseen complications during surgery leave medical teams with limited options, often resulting in suboptimal outcomes. However, the proposed system addresses this issue by enabling surgeons to receive optimized medical strategies and guidance from an AI assistant, which is trained to analyze situations and propose real-time solutions based on data and past experiences. In addition to improving surgical decision-making, the system incorporates an AI-driven L2 medical English training module, designed to enhance communication among multilingual surgical teams. This module provides real-time language support, terminology explanations, and speech recognition-based performance evaluation, ensuring effective team coordination in international medical environments. Based on prototype tests in simulated surgical environments, the results demonstrated that the AI-assisted collaboration system successfully provided timely and accurate recommendations, significantly reducing response time and improving overall surgical outcomes. Furthermore, the L2 learning module improved participants' proficiency in medical English, enhancing their ability to communicate critical information effectively. These findings highlight the system's potential in addressing sudden surgical challenges while also contributing to language proficiency development, ultimately leading to improved healthcare outcomes in diverse and globalized medical settings.

Keywords: Augmented Reality · Artificial Intelligence · Clinical Assistance Systems · L2 Medical English Learning · Real-Time Decision-Making · Surgical Collaboration

1 Introduction

Remote collaboration technology has revolutionized surgery by enabling expert support in real time, especially in underserved areas. Advances in Augmented Reality (AR) and Artificial Intelligence (AI) further enhance this capability. AR provides 3D models, live

W.-S. Wang et al. (Eds.): ICITL 2025, LNCS 15913, pp. 48–57, 2026.
https://doi.org/10.1007/978-3-031-98185-2_6

data, and real-time anatomical overlays to improve surgical accuracy, while AI supports decision-making through predictive analytics and treatment optimization. Together, AR and AI enhance precision, visualization, and clinical outcomes in complex procedures. Effective communication is essential in remote, multilingual surgical teams, where language barriers can jeopardize patient safety. This study proposes an AI-enhanced AR system that integrates L2 medical English learning with real-time translation, terminology support, and AI-driven speech evaluation to improve communication among non-native English-speaking professionals. By incorporating L2 learning modules [1, 2], the system not only improves technical surgical guidance but also fosters effective interdisciplinary communication, ensuring that surgical teams can convey critical information accurately and efficiently. Thus, exploring recent research and studies on the potential of AR, AI, and L2 medical English learning [3] in the context of remote surgical collaboration lays the foundation for the proposed system in this paper. By integrating real-time decision support, this approach aims to improve both surgical outcomes and international medical collaboration, ultimately contributing to better healthcare delivery worldwide.

Augmented Reality has been a key focus of research in the field of surgery, particularly for its ability to enhance visualization and precision. Early studies on AR systems in surgery demonstrated their effectiveness in providing surgeons with real-time 3D anatomical models, which improve the accuracy of minimally invasive surgeries. For instance, a series of systematic study reviews [4–7] demonstrated how AR can project pre-operative data such as CT or MRI scans directly onto the patient's body during surgery, allowing for better alignment and precise interventions. That is, AR-based navigation systems enhance surgical accuracy by providing real-time, detailed views of patient anatomy—crucial in precision fields like neurosurgery and orthopaedics. These systems also enable remote experts to share immersive views for better collaboration. However, most lack integrated real-time decision support, limiting dynamic interaction during critical moments.

AI has become increasingly important in healthcare, especially for decision support. In surgery, machine learning and deep learning algorithms analyse large datasets to predict complications, recommend interventions, and offer real-time guidance based on past cases. Recent researches [8–11] explored the application of AI in medical image analysis, where AI models were trained to detect abnormalities such as cancerous tumours with accuracy comparable to human experts. AI-powered systems in surgery assist decision-making by analysing patient data in real time, recommending optimal approaches based on medical history and procedure complexity. Research shows AI improves surgical outcomes, reduces errors, and supports the move toward autonomous surgery. Despite advancements, remote surgical collaboration still faces challenges like communication latency, limited real-time decision-sharing, and the lack of hands-on guidance. Communication lag remains a critical issue, especially in high-stakes procedures requiring immediate intervention. While AR improves visualization, it lacks built-in decision support, placing all critical decisions on surgeons, which can be risky in unexpected situations. Meanwhile, AI tools offer insights but are often standalone and not yet fully integrated with AR for real-time remote collaboration. To address current challenges, a unified system is needed that seamlessly integrates AR's real-time visualization with

AI's decision-making support. For remote surgical teams, especially those spread across regions, minimizing language barriers is also essential for effective collaboration. While AR and AI each enhance surgical performance, there is a clear research gap in combining them for real-time, remote surgical collaboration—AR lacks decision support, and AI is rarely embedded within AR platforms. Thus, the integration of AR and AI for remote collaboration represents an untapped area of research with significant potential. However, there is quite few related studies exists. Only one similar result can be found in [12] where emphasizing the integration of artificial intelligence (AI) and augmented reality (AR) in robotic surgery, particularly within the context of surgical education.

This research aims to address this gap by developing a system that enhances remote collaboration in surgery through the integration of AI and AR, called as **AIR** system. By integrating the interactive features of augmented reality (AR) with the analytical power of artificial intelligence (AI), the proposed system delivers real-time, context-aware assistance to surgeons during intricate medical procedures. Simultaneously, the system incorporates advanced language learning functionalities, enabling medical professionals to improve their communication skills in real-time. By providing interactive, language-enhanced guidance tailored to surgical contexts, the system fosters both procedural efficiency and multilingual proficiency, ultimately contributing to a higher standard of medical care and the possibility of global collaboration.

2 The Research Methodology

2.1 System Design and Architecture

The proposed system for remote surgical collaboration integrates Augmented Reality (AR) with Artificial Intelligence (AI) to assist clinical teams during complex surgeries. This system is built using the Unity3D platform for AR functionalities and Microsoft HoloLens II as the hardware interface for immersive interaction. AI is integrated using Google's Gemini engine, which acts as an intelligent assistant to retrieve data from large databases, analyze real-time situations, and provide optimized solutions. Unity3D is a widely used platform for developing AR and VR applications due to its flexibility, scalability, and robust set of development tools. In our system, Unity3D serves as the core engine that drives AR functionalities, enabling real-time 3D rendering of medical images, anatomical models, and live data overlays. These visual elements provide surgeons with enhanced spatial awareness during surgery. Unity3D allows for the rendering of complex anatomical models derived from medical imaging data (CT, MRI) that can be superimposed on the patient's body through AR devices. Surgeons can manipulate these models using gestures, zooming in for details, or rotating to examine structures from different angles. Another key feature of the Unity3D platform is its ability to integrate live data streams, such as vital signs or intraoperative sensor data, directly into the AR environment. These overlays offer real-time insights into the patient's condition, enhancing decision-making. Finally, most AR devices support advanced gesture-based interactions, which are critical for surgeons who need hands-free control of the AR interface during surgery, thus the surgeons can manipulate 3D models, access medical records, or consult with remote experts without interrupting the procedure.

To choose the suitable AR device, the Microsoft HoloLens II, which maybe proved as the best display platform in collaborative surgery process [13–15], is an advanced mixed-reality headset that provides a highly immersive experience for users, making it the ideal hardware choice for this system. Its combination of high-resolution displays, spatial mapping, and advanced gesture recognition enables surgeons to interact with digital content seamlessly during operations. By using the HoloLens II display platform, a real-time collaboration allowing remote experts to interact in the same AR environment as the operating team, can be easily implemented. This feature enables remote specialists to annotate the surgeon's view or provide verbal guidance while observing the procedure through their own HoloLens device or other connected systems.

Thus, via using the HoloLens II platform, we have not only achieved real-time synchronized connections for multiple users in different locations, enabling interaction with audio, video, and 3D objects, but we have also integrated an invisible AI intelligent assistant to complement the expertise of remote specialists. At the same time, the AI assistant is designed to serve as a support system during emergencies, providing crucial assistance when immediate expert intervention may be limited. That is, an AI assistant is integrated into the system using Google's Gemini engine, a large language model capable of understanding complex medical queries and providing real-time recommendations. The AI assistant remains invisible until we call upon it for assistance, seamlessly stepping in when needed, and offering real-time support to the surgical team by retrieving relevant data, analyzing situations, and suggesting optimal solutions. Once the AI assistant is integrated, collaborating experts can simply call upon the assistant with the voice command "Hey, Doctor" to perform any of the following functions: 1. Data Retrieval and Analysis, 2. Real-time Decision Support, 3. Optimized Solutions and Strategy Recommendations, and 4. Natural Language Processing for Collaboration.

After integrating AR and AI functions into the proposed surgical assistant system, several advantages can be obtained. First, the AR system ensures that surgeons have a clear, augmented view of the patient's anatomy, reducing the risk of errors during surgery, while AI enhances this by providing real-time decision support based on a vast repository of medical knowledge. Second, the ability to bring remote specialists into the operating room via AR makes it easier for surgical teams to access expert advice during critical moments, leading to better outcomes, particularly in complex cases where local expertise may be limited. Third, the AI-powered real-time analysis capabilities, such as those implemented in Gemini AI, allow the system to adapt dynamically to unexpected situations, offering optimized suggestions that help surgeons respond more effectively to challenges during surgery. In addition to these technical advancements, the system incorporates an L2 medical English learning module, ensuring that multilingual surgical teams can communicate effectively in high-pressure situations. This module provides real-time language support, medical terminology explanations, speech recognition-based assessments, and AI-driven feedback on pronunciation and fluency. By improving medical English proficiency, the system enhances collaboration in multinational surgical environments, reducing misunderstandings and ensuring precise communication of critical instructions.

Finally, by automating data retrieval, decision support, and language assistance, the system reduces cognitive load, allowing surgical teams to focus on the task at hand

and improving both surgical efficiency and communication accuracy. This integration of AR, AI, and L2 learning not only advances surgical outcomes but also strengthens international medical collaboration, ultimately contributing to higher standards of global healthcare.

2.2 System Efficacy Validation Method

After completing the prototype of our Augmented Reality (AR) and Artificial Intelligence (AI)-assisted remote collaboration system, a qualitative assessment was conducted, similar to research [16], to validate its performance and identify areas for further improvement. Given that this study primarily focuses on the feasibility of developing a surgical assistance system, we were constrained by the inability to test the system in actual clinical surgeries due to limitations such as restricted access to hospital environments and the sensitivity of clinical settings. As a result, our testing was limited in scale and setting, involving only three clinical surgeons from different specialties who operated the system in a simulated surgery environment in the lab. In addition to evaluating surgical performance and system usability, we also explored the integration of an L2 medical English learning module. This feature is particularly relevant for non-native English-speaking surgeons, as it provides real-time language support, terminology explanations, and AI-driven speech evaluation. By incorporating language learning into the system assessment, we aim to determine its potential to improve communicating in multilingual surgical environments. Additionally, we submitted the prototype to an international innovation competition to gather feedback from expert judges, further enhancing our understanding of the system's strengths and areas that require refinement, including its role in medical English training for global surgical teams.

3 Experimental Results and Discussions

3.1 The Implementation of the System

The proposed assistance system is designed and simulated on the Unity3D 2021 platform. The hardware architecture includes high-end laptops (equipped with Intel Core i9 CPU, 16 GB DDR RAM, and NVIDIA RTX3070). The system prototype is exported to standalone AR headset (HoloLens II) for end players. Some examples used to demonstrate the system implementation are shown in Figs. 1, 2, 3, 4 and 5. The prototype was tested in a controlled environment that simulated emergency scenarios typically encountered during surgical procedures. Each participating surgeon, connected remotely, could communicate and interact with both the system and one another. The main functions tested included:

- An AR interface using Microsoft HoloLens II, allowing for the visualization of the surgical site and surrounding data. The interface supported voice communication, annotation, and interaction with 3D objects.

- An AI assistant, capable of retrieving relevant medical data and providing optimized procedural advice based on historical case data, including images, documents, or audio-visual materials. Additionally, the AI can support L2 medical English learning by offering real-time language assistance, such as medical terminology explanations and pronunciation guidance, helping non-native English-speaking surgeons improve their communication skills during surgery.
- Real-time collaboration features, enabling remote participants to view, offering suggestions, and annotate the ongoing surgical process. To further enhance collaboration in multilingual surgical teams, the system integrates AI-driven English learning support, ensuring clear and precise communication through automated translations, terminology assistance, and real-time speech evaluation. This feature helps bridge language gaps, facilitating more effective teamwork and reducing the risk of miscommunication in high-stakes surgical environments.

3.2 The In-Depth Interviews

During the pilot tests, three surgeons performed simulated operations that included unexpected surgical challenges designed to evaluate the system's impact on performance, decision-making, communication, and language support. Following the simulations, in-depth interviews and observational analyses were conducted to assess system usability and gather empirical feedback. While the sample size was limited, triangulated data from user actions, interview responses, and language module performance logs revealed several concrete outcomes linked to the system's features. The findings below highlight key strengths of the system, supported by specific evaluation results.

- Precision of Visual Aids: All three surgeons emphasized that the AR interface's 3D anatomical overlays and real-time data significantly improved their spatial orientation. Observational data showed that during minimally invasive procedures, surgeons using the system completed navigation tasks more quickly, with fewer directional errors than during baseline trials without AR support. Specifically, the improvement in target identification speed was noted across participants.
- Quick Retrieval of Real-Time Data: The AI assistant's ability to access relevant historical data and case recommendations in real time proved crucial in time-sensitive scenarios. Three surgeons reported greater confidence in decision-making, which was reflected in reduced hesitation during simulated complications. Furthermore, the L2 medical English learning module supported non-native English-speaking surgeons by offering real-time translation and terminology assistance. The integrated speech recognition feedback led to observable improvements in pronunciation and terminology accuracy during post-task assessments. Two of the three surgeons showed measurable improvement in correctly using specialized terms in the post-simulation debriefing, aligning with the system's language learning objectives.
- Convenience of Remote Collaboration: The real-time remote collaboration feature was used during two of the simulated procedures. Both remote and on-site surgeons reported that the synchronized AR view facilitated accurate and timely communication. Review of system interaction logs revealed that collaborative tasks conducted with remote input involved fewer clarification prompts than tasks performed without

remote assistance, suggesting improved communication flow and decision-making efficiency.

- Fluidity of Surgical Workflow: Surgeons noted that system prompts and AI/AR support were well-integrated into the workflow and did not require manual input that could interrupt procedures. According to qualitative feedback observation, all participants were able to remain focused without frequently shifting attention away from the surgical area. Although formal cognitive load testing was not conducted, participants subjectively rated their cognitive burden as lower during AR-assisted tasks compared to earlier trials.
- Intuitive System Operation: The three surgeons generally found the system interface intuitive, with gesture and voice controls enabling hands-free interaction. Despite recommending refinements to the UI layout, they successfully completed over 85% of interactions without external assistance. The embedded L2 English support was specifically noted as helpful for on-the-fly clarification of complex terminology, and one surgeon reported incorporating newly learned terms into real-time verbal communication during the simulation. Speech recognition logs confirmed improvements in command pronunciation and context-appropriate usage.

3.3 Suggestions for Improvements

Overall, the surgeons unanimously agreed that the system holds significant potential for future surgeries, offering powerful technical support to enhance precision, efficiency, and collaboration in the operating room. On the other hands, improvement suggestions are also provided as follows:

- Enhanced Real-Time Data Retrieval: While the AI assistant's ability to access relevant case histories and propose optimized strategies was praised, the surgeons suggested that the system could be further improved by integrating more dynamic data sources, such as real-time vital signs and intraoperative imaging. This would enable more precise and contextually relevant advice during surgery.
- Improved User Interface: The AR interface was generally well-received, but some surgeons reported difficulties in navigating the holographic menus, particularly during high-stress moments. They recommended streamlining the user interface to minimize distractions, possibly through gesture controls that do not require hand movements away from the surgical field.
- Context-Aware AI Responses: Surgeons highlighted that while the AI assistant provided accurate recommendations, it occasionally lacked context sensitivity regarding the current stage of the surgery. They suggested integrating a contextual awareness module that could recognize the progress of the procedure and tailor suggestions more precisely to the moment's needs. Additionally, they emphasized the importance of real-time L2 medical English support, where the system could adjust language complexity based on the user's proficiency level and provide context-aware translations, terminology clarifications, and pronunciation feedback. This would ensure that non-native English-speaking surgeons fully understand and effectively communicate critical information at each surgical stage, enhancing both decision-making accuracy and international collaboration.

- Remote Collaboration Synchronization: While the system allowed for real-time input from remote collaborators, there were occasional lags in the display of annotations and comments. Surgeons recommended improving the synchronization of these inputs to ensure that remote experts can offer immediate guidance without delay, especially during critical moments.
- Customization of AI Recommendations: Finally, the surgeons suggested that the system allow for more customization in terms of the AI assistant's recommendations. Specifically, they proposed that individual surgeons be able to input personal preferences or commonly used techniques, which the AI could be taken into account when generating advice.

3.4 Summary of Experimental Results and Discussions

Despite the limitations and suggestions for improvement, all three surgeons agreed that the system holds significant potential to enhance collaborative surgery, especially in emergency cases where immediate expert advice may be required. The ability to have AI-driven assistance that analyzes vast amounts of data to provide real-time support was seen as a major advancement in improving both decision-making and surgical outcomes. Additionally, the system's AI-driven feedback mechanism offers real-time language support, helping surgeons enhance their English proficiency while making critical decisions, thereby reducing miscommunication in high-pressure situations.

Moreover, they acknowledged the system's capacity to enhance training for junior surgeons, allowing them to experience advanced decision-making processes under the guidance of experienced remote colleagues. Additionally, the integration of an L2 medical English learning module further supports training by improving communication skills in multilingual surgical environments. Through real-time language support, medical terminology explanations, and AI-driven speech evaluation, junior surgeons can enhance their proficiency in medical English, ensuring more effective collaboration and precise communication in international surgical teams. The feedback provided by the surgeons highlights a number of important factors to consider for future iterations of the system. The need for enhanced context-awareness, more streamlined user interfaces, and improved real-time data integration are all areas that can be addressed through further development and refinement. Additionally, the inclusion of customizable AI responses would allow for greater flexibility in matching the system to unique preferences and procedures of different surgeons. Expanding the system's language-learning capabilities, such as integrating adaptive English interactions training would further support surgeons in mastering both medical procedures and effective communication, ensuring greater efficiency and safety in multilingual surgical settings.

The AIR system designed for L2 Medical English learning and remote surgical collaboration is currently in its testing and validation stage and also working on widely deployed. While our sample size was limited, the insights gained from this qualitative analysis offer a clear pathway for improving the system before wider deployment. The overall positive reception of the system's potential suggests that, with further refinement, this AR and AI-assisted remote collaboration tool could become an integral part of modern surgical practice, especially in situations requiring urgent expert input from remote locations.

Fig. 1. Demo scene 1: The collaborative AIR system Overview.

Fig. 2. Demo scene 2: Interaction of surgical operation between surgeons.

Fig. 3. Fig. 3. Demo scene 3: Surgeons can simply call the AI assistant with voice com-mand "Hey, Doctor" to perform the designed functions for help.

Fig. 4. Demo scene 4: The AI assistants can provide surgical decision-making suggestions, offer similar past case examples, include AV materials.

Fig. 5. Demo scene 5: If needed, the AI assistant will proactively invite and connect other experts to join in the operations.

4 Conclusions

This paper presents a pilot study aimed at designing and implementing a remote surgical collaboration system that integrates Augmented Reality (AR) with Artificial Intelligence (AI) assistance. To overcome the limitations of current AR surgical collaboration systems, our prototype is intended to provide real-time AI-driven solutions in response to emergency situations, thereby enhancing clinical decision-making efficiency and improving the quality of medical care. Our goal is to strengthen collaboration, precision, and communication during surgical procedures through this system, ultimately elevating the overall standard of healthcare services.

From the preliminary qualitative assessments, it is observed that the proposed system is not only feasible but also functionally robust, effectively supporting clinical surgeons by offering real-time assistance during operations. Surgeons who participated in the tests acknowledged the system's practical value, particularly its ability to respond to unexpected challenges during surgery. The AI's timely recommendations and responses were highlighted as key features contributing to improved surgical accuracy and efficiency. Additionally, the integration of an L2 medical English learning module was recognized as a valuable component, helping multilingual surgical teams enhance communication skills. The system provides real-time translations, medical terminology explanations, and speech recognition-based feedback, ensuring clear and precise communication during high-pressure surgical situations.

Future work will focus on refining and optimizing the system based on feedback from the initial testing phase. More comprehensive qualitative and quantitative evaluations will be conducted to further validate the system's practicality, reliability, and effectiveness in L2 learning support. These practices will encompass a broader range of clinical scenarios and involve surgeons from various specialties and linguistic backgrounds to ensure the system operates consistently under diverse surgical and multilingual conditions. Ultimately, we aim to progress toward clinical trials, positioning this system as a foundation for future medical product applications and advancing surgical collaboration technologies while also contributing to medical English proficiency in global healthcare settings.

References

1. Using AI to translate speech for a primarily oral language, https://about.fb.com/news/2022/10/hokkien-ai-speech-translation. Last accessed 3 February 2025
2. The impact of artificial intelligence on Language Translation: A Review, IEEE Journals & Magazine Homepage, https://ieeexplore.ieee.org/document/10438431. Last accessed 3 February 2025
3. Chen, Y.: Augmented Reality as a Reinforcement to Facilitate ESP Learning for Nursing Students. Communications in Computer and Information Science. **CCIS1131**, 131–141 (2020)
4. Vávra, P., et al.: Recent development of augmented reality in surgery: a review. J. Healthc. Eng. **1**, 4574172 (2017)
5. Yoon, J.W., et al.: Augmented reality for the surgeon: systematic review. The International Journal of Medical Robotics and Computer Assisted Surgery **14**(4), 1914 (2018)
6. Lungu, A.J., et al.: A review on the applications of virtual reality, augmented reality and mixed reality in surgical simulation: an extension to different kinds of surgery. Expert Review of Medical Devices **18**(1), 47–62 (2021)
7. Barcali, E., et al.: Augmented reality in surgery: a scoping review. Applied Sciences **12**(14), 68–90 (2022)
8. Hashimoto, D.A., Rosman, G., Rus, D., Meireles, O.R.: Artificial intelligence in surgery: promises and perils. Annals of Surgery **268**(1), 70–76 (2018)
9. Guni, A., et al.: Artificial intelligence in surgery: the future is now. European Surgical Research **65**(1), 22–39 (2024)
10. Gumbs, A.A., et al.: Artificial intelligence surgery: How do we get to autonomous actions in surgery?. Sensors **21**(6), 5526 (2021)
11. Wagner, M., et al.: Artificial intelligence for decision support in surgical oncology-a systematic review. Artificial Intelligence Surgery **2**(3), 159–172 (2022)
12. Long, Y., et al.: Integrating artificial intelligence and augmented reality in robotic surgery: An initial dvRK study using a surgical education scenario. In: 2022 International Symposium on Medical Robotics Proceedings, pp. 1–8. Atlanta (2022)
13. Park, S., Bokijonov, S., Choi, Y.: Review of microsoft hololens applications over the past five years. Applied Sciences **11**(16), 7259 (2021)
14. Palumbo, A.: Microsoft HoloLens 2 in medical and healthcare context: state of the art and future prospects. Sensors **22**(20), 7709 (2022)
15. Gsaxner, C., et al.: The HoloLens in medicine: a systematic review and taxonomy. Medical Image Analysis **85**, 102757 (2023)
16. Zhao, B., et al.: Making the jump: a qualitative analysis on the transition from bedside assistant to console surgeon in robotic surgery training. J. Surg. Educ. **77**(2), 461–471 (2020)

AI-Driven Constructivist Framework in Child Welfare and Social Work Education

Synnøve Thomassen Andersen(✉)

UiT, The Arctic University of Norway, Follumsvei 31, 9510 Alta, Norway
Synnove.T.Andersen@uit.no

Abstract. This article examines how child welfare and social work students at Norwegian universities use AI, analyzing their experiences through social constructivist learning theory. The findings suggest that educational institutions can address related challenges by developing dynamic ethical guidelines, integrating critical thinking and AI ethics training, and encouraging reflective, balanced use of AI. This study offers insights into preparing future professionals to integrate AI into their work while maintaining ethical standards and sound judgement.

Keywords: AI · ChatGPT · Social Constructivist Theory · Child Welfare

1 Introduction

This article examines a group of students' use of artificial intelligence (AI), specifically Chat Generative Pre-Trained Transformer (ChatGPT), within the fields of child welfare and social work at various universities in Norway, and analyzes this usage in relation to constructivist learning theory [1–4].Constructivism is positioned as one of four main theories in pedagogy [5, 6], behaviorism [7], cognitivism [8], and social constructivism [1–4, 8]. The sociocultural learning perspective views learning as a social phenomenon, where knowledge is formed through interaction with other individuals and tools [9]. AI technologies in academia bring new opportunities and challenges, especially for content creation. Universities must address impacts on learning and responsibility by regularly updating ethical guidelines and setting new standards for student work [10]. This study analyzes how a group of students' use of ChatGPT affects their learning processes. The following research question is analyzed: *How does students' use of ChatGPT in child welfare and social work influence their construction of knowledge, viewed through the lens of constructivist learning theory?* This study contributes to the research field by examining how future education programs, researchers, and practitioners within these fields integrate and relate to AI in their academic and professional work.

2 Social Constructivism Learning Theory

Social constructivist learning theory emphasizes that knowledge is built through social interaction and collaboration within cultural contexts [2–4, 11]. Unlike individualistic theories [11, 13], it highlights that learning is mediated, situated, and actively constructed

W.-S. Wang et al. (Eds.): ICITL 2025, LNCS 15913, pp. 58–63, 2026.
https://doi.org/10.1007/978-3-031-98185-2_7

[12]. This perspective is especially relevant in child welfare and social work, where users' perceptions are socially shaped [11]. Integrating AI challenges traditional learning models, making critical reflection on its role essential and reinforcing the importance of social context in knowledge construction [14, 15]. The theory is characterized by several key features:

Knowledge as social interaction: The theory posits that knowledge and learning occur through social interaction and collaboration, not primarily through individual cognitive processing [2]. Dialogue and discussion are central elements, and knowledge is developed collectively. ***Contextual learning***: Learning is context-dependent, meaning knowledge and skills develop in specific situations and environments [2–4] ***Active learning process***: Students are active participants in the learning process, constructing their own understanding through experiences and reflection [2–4]. ***Collaboration:*** The theory emphasizes agreement between individuals rather than absolute truth, acknowledging that all knowledge is subjective [2–4]. ***Central role of language:*** Language is a crucial tool for developing and sharing knowledge, viewed as a cultural phenomenon fundamental to the learning process [2]. ***Teacher's role as facilitator***: In educational settings, the teacher is seen as a facilitator and guide for learning and activity among students, rather than a transmitter of finished knowledge [14–18]. ***Building on existing knowledge***: New knowledge is constructed on existing understanding, with reality perception continuously shaped through experiences, situations, and communication with others [2–4]. Social constructivism offers a distinct approach to learning and knowledge development, emphasizing the social and cultural aspects of human understanding and meaning making. It views learning as a dynamic and continuous process occurring in interaction with the environment and other individuals. Students are encouraged to engage in problem-solving and critical thinking, promoting deeper learning and understanding [2–4, 17, 18].

3 Methodology

The study uses a hermeneutic qualitative approach to explore human experiences in pedagogy and social work [19]. Qualitative methods like informal interviews are ideal for deeply exploring complex social phenomena [20, 21]. This exploratory study utilized data from two informal, semi-structured interviews (45 min each) conducted between November 2024 and January 2025 with nine participants (two men, seven women) enrolled in child welfare and social work programs at Norwegian universities. Participants spanned academic levels (bachelor's to Ph.D.) and were purposively sampled to reflect diverse experiences with AI. All participants demonstrated foundational digital competence, defined as the ability to use digital tools securely and critically [22]. However, limitations of data collection are the small sample size ($n = 9$), and limited data collection (two interviews) restrict the generalizability of findings. While the informal structure fostered rich dialogue, the absence of formal interview protocols and the homogeneity of participants (all from Norwegian universities) may limit transferability to broader contexts. To enhance methodological transparency, the analysis followed a systematic process. The interviews were transcribed verbatim, with non-verbal cues (e.g., laughter) noted to contextualize responses. Transcripts were analyzed using open coding to identify emergent themes to ensure inter-coder reliability, resolving discrepancies through discussion. Codes were grouped into themes (e.g., AI like Chat GPT as a learning tool, ethical concerns) using NVivo software. Contrasting perspectives (e.g., enthusiasm vs. skepticism) were explicitly flagged to capture nuance. Preliminary findings were shared with participants for member checking, though only three responded due to time constraints.

Informal Interviews focused on students' use of AI and ChatGPT. Students provided informed consent, and anonymized identifiers (NN1–NN9) protect confidentiality. At the start of the meeting, informants were advised that they could conduct the meeting as a conversation, and that if silence ensued, the interviewer would follow up with questions. There was no need for follow-up questions during the interviews, as all informants participated actively, reasoned, and discussed freely in both meetings. All informants were familiar with various ChatGPT models, particularly their universities' proprietary ChatGPT solutions. One informant NN1 reported using ChatGPT only once, resulting in limited knowledge of its use. The informant stated, *"I haven't had time to familiarize myself with this and how to use it, but everyone says it's so simple."* All informants responded to this statement and called for training in the use of ChatGPT, as they all deemed it necessary. Another informant NN2 suggested, *"Can't we organize a separate Teams area for the different student groups, where current information about AI and ChatGPT can be shared? It would be nice if we could collaborate on our own Teams area about this."* All informants responded positively to this suggestion. A new informant NN3 followed up by saying, *"The use of AI and ChatGPT extends into practice, and the question is how we should make good assessments… How we should reflect and evaluate both as students and when we're working? Universities have guidelines, but there are still many gray areas about what is acceptable and what is considered cheating."* Informant NN4 said, *"How should one use ChatGPT well, and not least, how should the field of practice keep up? I think ChatGPT is fine to use because it's difficult for me to meet on campus; I'm a bit alone as a student. I therefore experience being able to use ChatGPT as an okay and good tool to have as a form of digital partner."* A third informant NN8 said, *"I use ChatGPT to improve my writing skills and to get feedback on my own text. It's great to get immediate feedback on what I'm wondering about, how I can express myself more precisely. And I use AI to transcribe my data, but I double-check to make sure they're correct, but I save a lot of time, and maybe ChatGPT makes me more efficient."* Yet another informant NN5 continued, *"It's so easy, I have my mobile phone, and thus I can use ChatGPT if I'm stuck with something… Quite wild really. In many ways, I think learning has become better because I get feedback from ChatGPT while I'm working on an assignment if I'm unsure about things. I often feel I get more ideas while I'm working on an assignment. It's not always as quick to get answers from the supervisor."* A new informant NN7 replied, *"Yes, I'm very satisfied with ChatGPT. I get answers at my own pace and can delve into what I need more time on – in a different way, it becomes more thorough in a way…"* Informant NN2 reasoned aloud, *"Yes, ChatGPT is an assistant, but it lacks ethical ability as it can perform tasks, give you answers you think are good. Ethical assessments in our profession are essential. It's important that employees in the field understand this."* Another informant responded immediately, *"I'm concerned about its use because several reports show that good enough assessments are not being made in* *child welfare."* Yet another informant NN6 commented, *"ChatGPT can be used ethically and constructively, as an addition for one's own reflection and learning in collaboration with ChatGPT, both for students and for employees at work. But if ChatGPT is used as a definitive answer, as a replacement, it's worrying."* All informants reasoned aloud and believed it was very important that students were conscious and critically evaluated what ChatGPT produced. One informant NN8 stated, *"If we who use ChatGPT cannot be constructive and critical, we will lose the ability to distinguish between right and wrong answers»* The informal interviews gave students space to share nuanced insights on AI, yielding candid responses and valuable research perspectives. However, the small, homogenous sample and limited interviews restrict broader validity and depth. Future studies should use more diverse samples, mixed methods, and longitudinal designs to better capture AI's evolving role in education.

4 Analysis and Discussion

Analysis and discussion of findings on students' perceptions and use of AI and ChatGPT, based on key characteristics of social constructivist learning theory. ***Knowledge as Social Construction,*** the theory holds that knowledge is built mainly through social interaction and collaboration, not just individual thinking [16]. Dialogue is central, as shown by students creating a shared Teams area to collectively learn about ChatGPT, demonstrating their preference for learning through discussion and interaction even with new technology [22]. The study's informal structure fostered rich data by encouraging candid responses, such as NN5's admission of using AI for ideation ("*I get more ideas while working*"). Including Ph.D. students further deepened discussions about AI's role in research (e.g., transcription support), illustrating how diverse perspectives contribute to collective knowledge construction. For example, NN3's reflection on ChatGPT's role in practice ("*how we should reflect and evaluate... There are still many gray areas*") highlights the tension between institutional guidelines and real-world ambiguity, a tension best explored through collaborative meaning-making. ***Contextual Learning,*** learning is context-dependent, meaning that knowledge and skills are developed in specific situations and environments. It is crucial to understand how knowledge is applied in practice [16]. The informal interview format allowed students to elaborate freely, generating nuanced insights into AI adoption. This approach aligns social constructivist learning theory, which emphasizes that knowledge is actively constructed through dialogue, interaction, and reflection within a social context. The statement "*The use of AI and ChatGPT extends into practice*" illustrates how students view learning as situated in a specific professional context [3, 4]. They are concerned with how the tool can be applied in practical situations, which is particularly relevant for professional education in child welfare and social work, where theoretical knowledge must be translated into practical actions. This underscores that learning is a process involving constant adaptation and reflection, aligning with the notion that our understanding of reality is dynamic and continuously shaped by experiences and dialogue [23]. ***Active Learning Process,*** several students actively use ChatGPT to improve skills, get feedback, and generate ideas, demonstrating their active engagement in learning-key to social constructivist theory [3, 4, 23]. For example, using ChatGPT via mobile when stuck shows initiative in seeking knowledge. While most praised AI's efficiency, some raised ethical concerns, highlighting contrasting perspectives (NN8 versus NN2). ***Collaboration,*** Social constructivism values collaboration and recognizes knowledge as subjective; group work and shared platforms like Teams enable students to learn from each other's experiences and viewpoints [2–4, 23]. ***Central Role of Language,*** language plays a fundamental role in social constructivist learning theory [16], and its significance in the learning process is evident in students' reflections on ChatGPT. The statement "*how should one use ChatGPT well*" shows that students are aware that AI is a tool for communication and knowledge production. This awareness is particularly relevant given that ChatGPT is based on linguistic analysis [23]. Students also report using ChatGPT to improve writing skills and receive feedback on text, demonstrating the central role of language in the learning process [2–4]. ***Teacher's Role as Facilitator,*** in sociocultural learning theory, the teacher is seen as a facilitator of learning [17]. Students' demand for training in the use of ChatGPT indicates a need for knowledge and guidance in encountering new technologies. This shows that even in a digital age, the human factor and the teacher as a facilitator, rather than a traditional knowledge transmitter, remain central to the learning process [23]. ***Building Knowledge,*** students' use of AI for idea development in assignments reflects social constructivist learning, building new knowledge from existing understanding. However, their experiences also reveal ethical concerns and challenges for critical thinking in professional practice [10], highlighting the need for targeted AI training. This calls for a balanced approach that integrates technological innovation with established pedagogy, especially in fields like child welfare and social work where ethics and human interaction are vital. The study's small, homogenous sample and limited interviews restrict broader validity. While inductive coding captured broad themes, a deductive approach using predefined theoretical frameworks could have further strengthened analytical depth. Future research should include more diverse and international participants, use mixed methods to triangulate findings, and adopt longitudinal designs to better capture AI's evolving educational role. Institutions should develop adaptable ethical guidelines, offer hands-on AI training with critical reflection, and encourage cross-cultural collaboration. Ultimately, child welfare and social work education must prioritize digital literacy and ethics to prepare students for a rapidly changing technological landscape. This would foster a richer, more collaborative knowledge-building process, consistent with social constructivist principles.

5 Concluding Remarks

Integrating AI into higher education brings both opportunities and challenges, especially in child welfare and social work. Social constructivist learning theory helps guide this integration. Educational institutions should: (i) develop adaptable ethical guidelines for AI, (ii) include critical thinking and AI ethics in curricula, (iii) balance technological innovation with traditional, interactive learning, (iv) promote reflective use of AI as a supplement to students' own thinking, and (v) regularly update teaching methods for relevance. With a clear strategy, universities can prepare students to use AI responsibly while upholding strong professional and ethical standards.

References

1. Säljö, R.: Learning, theories of learning, and units of analysis in research. Educ. Psychol. **44**(3), 202–208 (2009). https://doi.org/10.1080/00461520903029030
2. Vygotsky, L.S.: Mind in Society: The Development of Higher Psychological Processes. Harvard University Press. Cambridge, MA (1978)
3. Vygotskij, L.S.: Psykologi och dialektik (L.-C. Hydén, Overs.). Norstedt. Stochokm (1980)
4. Vygotsky, L.S.: Thought and language (Rev. edt., A. Kozulin, Eds.). MIT Press. Cambridge, MA (1986)
5. Imsen, G.: Elevens verden. Innføring i pedagogisk psykologi. Universitetsforlaget, Oslo (2005)
6. Imsen, G.: Hva er pedagogikk. Universitetsforlaget, Oslo (2011)
7. Baum, W.M.: Understanding Behaviorism: Behavior Culture and Evolution. Blackwell, London (2005)
8. Dysthe, O.: Sosiokulturelle teoriperspektiver på kunnskap og læring. In: Dysthe, O. (eds.) Dialog, samspell og læring. Abstrakt forlag as. Oslo (2001)
9. Skaalvik, E.M., Skaalvik, S.: Skolen som læringsarena: selvoppfatning, motivasjon og læring (3. utg.). Universitetsforlaget, Oslo (2018)
10. Forskningsetisk betenkning om kunstig intelligens 1. utg., De nasjonale forskningsetiske komiteene. Oslo (2019)
11. Schaathun Welie, A., Schaathun, H.G.: Mellom klassisk betinging og støttende stillas, Offentleg sektor i endring, Fjordantologien, Oslo (2016)
12. Aadland, E.: Og eg ser på deg: vitenskapsteori i helse- og sosialfag. Universitetsforlaget, Oslo (2011)
13. Piaget, J. Barnets psykiske utvikling (org. Six études de psychologie) introduction by David Elkind, translate, R. Nielsen, 1 etg. Gyldendal. Oslo (1973)
14. Dikilitaş, K., Furenes Klippen, M.I., Keles, S.: A systematic rapid review of empirical research on students' use of ChatGPT in higher education. Nordic J. Systematic Rev. Educ. (2024). https://doi.org/10.23865/njsre.v2.6227
15. Kongsgården, P., Krumsvik, R.J.: Bruk av digitale verktøy i elevers læringsarbeid – med fokus på sammenhengen mellom læring og vurdering for læring. Acta Didactica Norge (2013). https://doi.org/10.5617/adno.1116
16. Lent, P.: T: Hvor kommer sosialkonstruksjonisme fra? Lent, Oslo (2024)
17. Tjora, A., Haugseth, J.F.: Sosialkonstruktivisme. Store norske leksikon. NTNU. Trondheim (2020). https://snl.no/sosialkonstruktivisme
18. O'Flaherty, J., Phillips, C.: The Use of Flipped Classrooms in Higher Education: A Scoping Review. The Internet and Higher education, vol. 25, pp. 85–95. Elsevier, London (2015)
19. Johannessen, A., Christoffersen, L., Tufte, P.A: Introduksjon til samfunnsvitenskapelig metode, vol. 5. Abstrakt forlag, Oslo (2016)
20. Thagaard, T.: Systematikk og innlevelse: En innføring i kvalitative metoder (5.utg.) Fagbokforlaget, Oslo (2018)
21. Creswell, J.W. Poth, C.N.: Qualitative Inquiry and Research Design: Choosing Among Five Approaches, 4th vol. Sage Publications Ltd. (2018). https://doi.org/10.1177/1524839915580941
22. Diku, Direktoratet for internasjonalisering og kvalitetsutvikling i høyere utdanning. Digital tilstand 2018. Perspektiver på digitalisering for læring i høyere utdanning, Diku rapport 6, Oslo (2019)
23. Stai, S.: Vygotskij og kognitiv utvikling. NDLA. https://ndla.no/article/29412. Trondheim (2021)

Teaching AI Textual Interpretation: A Catalyst for Enhanced Literary Skills

Peter Øhrstrøm[1(✉)], David Jakobsen[1], and Simon Pacis[2]

[1] Department of Communication and Psychology, Aalborg University, 9000 Aalborg, Denmark
{poe,davker}@ikp.aau.dk

[2] Pacis Inc., 9530 Støvring, Denmark
simon@pacis.dk

Abstract. This paper presents a pilot study investigating the potential for enhancing literary skills through an innovative pedagogical approach in which students engage in teaching an artificial intelligence (AI) system to interpret literary texts. Drawing on educational research on teaching as a learning strategy, the study examines a specific case involving the interpretation of "The Word", a play by the Danish playwright Kaj Munk. Utilizing dialogues with a chatbot based on a large language model (LLM) and along with the latest translation of Munk's text into English, the study explores the potential and the effectiveness of this method in fostering deeper textual comprehension and critical engagement. The paper discusses both the potential benefits, and the challenges associated with this approach, contributing to the broader discourse on AI-assisted learning in literary studies.

Keywords: Generative AI · learning by teaching · Socratic learning · literary interpretation · Kaj Munk

1 Teaching as a Learning Strategy

Teaching as a learning strategy has garnered considerable attention in educational psychology, with research highlighting its cognitive and social benefits. Keith J. Topping [8] provides a comprehensive analysis of peer learning, emphasizing its effectiveness for both the tutor and the tutee. This body of research strongly supports the notion that teaching enhances learning by fostering deeper understanding, increasing cognitive engagement, and developing transferable skills. More recent studies ([2, 4]) further validate these findings, reinforcing the role of teaching as a powerful learning strategy.

However, while the benefits of this approach are well-documented, it is also important to consider potential limitations and challenges. Obviously, a rather trivial limitation arises in situations where no realistic peer is available for the learner. Given the advancements in large language models (LLMs) and generative AI, it is worth exploring the potential of chatbots to serve as artificial "peers" in this context. This suggests a need for further investigation into the design of learning systems that leverage the act of teaching as a central mechanism—specifically, systems in which learners enhance their

W.-S. Wang et al. (Eds.): ICITL 2025, LNCS 15913, pp. 64–73, 2026.
https://doi.org/10.1007/978-3-031-98185-2_8

understanding by instructing or explaining concepts and perspectives to an AI-based chatbot. Our working hypothesis is that the user can gain valuable new insights into the task of interpreting literary texts and significant competence in the field by undertaking the task of guiding the chatbot through the analyses of the text that may be relevant in formulating a reasonable and interesting interpretation of the text.

While Topping [8] provides strong evidence for teaching as a learning strategy, he also emphasizes the importance of structured implementation. Unstructured peer learning can lead to ineffective interactions. Studies since then continue to stress the need for training peer tutors, designing effective scaffolding, and ensuring quality feedback mechanisms [3].

Topping [8] highlights that structured peer tutoring fosters higher-order thinking skills. Tutors must diagnose misleading explanations. This dynamic engagement mirrors the cognitive processes developed by expert learners, supporting the notion that teaching accelerates intellectual growth. Similar to the insights presented in [5], we suggest viewing the AI-based chatbot as an expert assistant rather than an expert in its own right. This approach reflects Socratic principles, emphasizing that learning occurs through and depends on dialogue.

2 The Case: Literary Interpretation of Kaj Munk's "the Word"

An interesting case of using an AI-based chatbot occurs when a person wants to study literary interpretation online. This may, for instance, be relevant for users of The Digital Kaj Munk Archive at Aalborg University.

Kaj Munk (1898–1944) was a Danish playwright, pastor, and a key cultural figure whose works remain central to the study of faith, art, and national resistance. Known for his outspoken criticism of totalitarianism, which ultimately led to his assassination by the Nazis in 1944, Munk's legacy extends beyond his political activism. His theological and dramatic works probe the depths of human existence, exploring the interplay of doubt, faith, and miracles. Among his most significant contributions to Danish literature is the play "The Word", written in 1925, which has since been immortalized not only on stage but also through Carl Th. Dreyer's celebrated 1955 film adaptation ([1, 6]).

In the following it will be discussed how a user of the archive who is interested in obtaining a better understanding of the literary works of Kaj Munk may proceed. Kaj Munk's most famous play, "The Word", will be used in this pilot study. The aim is to design a procedure for the use of an AI-based chatbot that supports the user in obtaining enhanced skills in literary interpretation. A design of this kind may of course be interesting as a potential learning module implemented as a part of The Digital Kaj Munk Archive [11].

"The Word" is set in the austere landscape of rural West Jutland, Denmark, a region whose starkness reflects the play's spiritual and existential themes. It centers on the Borgen family, where three generations struggle with divergent expressions of faith: the patriarch, Mikkel Borgen, embodies a traditional Lutheran piety; his son Johannes, having suffered a mental breakdown, proclaims himself to be Christ reincarnated; while the youngest son Anders is drawn to the daughter of a lay preacher, a union complicated by theological and familial tensions. The drama escalates when Inger, Young Mikkel's wife, and Mikkel Borgen's pregnant daughter-in-law and the family's moral center, dies during childbirth, only to be miraculously resurrected in the play's climactic scene.

Carl Theodor Dreyer's 1955 adaptation of "The Word" transformed the play into an internationally acclaimed cinematic work. It preserves the essence of Munk's drama while employing a distinct visual and narrative style that amplifies its spiritual resonance [6].

The film was met with critical acclaim, winning the Golden Lion at the Venice Film Festival in 1955. It achieved further recognition when it won the Academy Award for Best Foreign Language Film in 1956, marking the first time a Danish film received this honour. This international recognition cemented Dreyer's reputation and brought Munk's "The Word" to a global audience.

3 The Set-Up of the AI-Based Chatbot

The chatbot used in the pilot study is designed to participate in a dialogue on Kaj Munk's play, "The Word". The chatbot is able to access and refer to the online publication [7] of the latest translation into English of the play, which also includes a preface and a brief introduction to the play. The chatbot uses Meta's Llama 3.3 large language model, a version specifically enhanced for text-only applications. To improve accuracy, we added Retrieval-Augmented Generation (RAG) functionality. For every user prompt, the chatbot retrieves the five most semantically similar results from the Munk 2024 publication and uses these to generate its response. This approach minimizes the risk of the LLM hallucinating and allows users to verify the response's correctness through references to the publication. The chatbot's online interface also displays the RAG results used for each response, further enhancing transparency. This approach depends on a mathematical model that makes it possible to calculate semantical similarity. The model uses a 1024-dimensional vector space.[1] To calculate the semantic similarity of a prompt to the publication, we first split up the publication into distinct semantic chunks using a sentence transformer. Each chunk constitutes roughly one sentence, as determined by the sentence transformer [9]. When a user prompts the chatbot, the same sentence transformer transforms the prompt into a vector space, so that we can compare the prompt to the publication [10].

We calculate the similarity for each of the sentence chunks and the user prompt. This gives us a list of similarity scores, where each entry in the list is the similarity between the user's prompt and the given sentence chunk from the publication. We then sort the resulting list of similarity scores, and append the top five results to the prompt, before passing it on to the LLM. We do not, of course, give the vector space to the LLM, but we give it the original sentence chunk from the publication that was previously transformed into a vector space. Along with the sentence chunk itself we also pass metadata, in the form of the page on which the sentence chunk was found. In this way, the LLM can refer to the specific page in the publication where it got the information that it is referring to.

[1] 1024 dimensions is an arbitrary number, and it was chosen to strike a balance between computational cost and detail.

This setup ensures that the chatbot's responses are grounded in the source material, reducing the risk of hallucinations and enabling users to verify the accuracy of the information provided.

4 Interacting with AI on the Interpretation of "the Word"

In the following interaction we have taken the role as the user who is trying to enhance his literary skills acting as a teacher whereas the chatbot is a student who is being guided by the user in the exploration of Kaj Munk's play. To take care of this guidance in a qualified manner the user needs a strategy to lead the chatbot towards an interpretation of the play. The choice of such a strategy is difficult, and it should be discussed based on professional studies in literature that are beyond the scope of this paper. However, we may imagine that the user is in fact training to become a teacher in literary studies. It is suggested that interactions like the following might be part of the user's training to become a skilled scholar in literary studies and maybe even a qualified teacher in the field. The aim is to develop a learning module as part of the Digital Kaj Munk Archive. It is crucial that this module provides the user with access to qualified advice on literary interpretation of texts, so that he or she can receive high-level assistance in guiding the chatbot towards the outcome that best aligns with the current interpretive aim. The following dialogue represents an early experimental step towards the development of such a module. At this preliminary stage, the primary aim is to explore the practical possibilities for productive dialogue with the available prototype, as well as to identify some of the issues that need to be addressed during the system's development and testing.

There are several possible ways to open a discussion on "The Word". One obvious first approach would be to focus on the characters in the play. The following dialogue with the chatbot is obtained using this approach (December 18, 2024):

> *User*:List the characters in Kaj Munk's play, "The Word".
>
> *AI:* The characters in Kaj Munk's play, "The Word", include Johannes, Pastor Bandbul, and Mikkel Borgen, as well as Ruben Snipper, a tailor who is a member of the inner Mission.
>
> *User*:There are several others. Try again.
>
> *AI*: The characters in Kaj Munk's play, "The Word", include Johannes, Pastor Bandbul, Mikkel Borgen, Ruben Snipper, Maren, Doctor, Young Mikkel, and others.

In the first place the chatbot when asked to list the characters in "The Word" only mentions Johannes, Pastor Bandbul, Mikkel Borgen, and Ruben Snipper. When asked to reconsider three other characters in the play are mentioned. Regarding this simple dialogue, the important observation is that the user must critically evaluate the responses provided by the chatbot. The answers could be insufficient or even misleading. If this is possible, it becomes the user's task during the interaction to ask relevant follow-up questions.

A way from listing the characters to a significant contribution to a broader understanding of the play could be to ask for the most important character in the play (December 18, 2024 continued from the above dialogue):

User:Who is the most important character in the play?

AI: The most important character in the play "The Word" is Johannes.

User:Why is Johannes the most important character in the play?

AI: The most important character in the play "The Word" is Johannes. This is because the entire play revolves around his journey, his faith, and his relationship with God. The other characters in the play, including his father Mikkel Borgen, Pastor Bandbul, and Doctor, are all reacting to Johannes's crisis of faith and his desire to understand God's will. The play's themes of doubt, faith, and the supernatural are all explored through Johannes's experiences and interactions with the other characters.

It seems that the reasons for asserting that Johannes is the most significant character in the play provides a valuable preliminary insight into the essence of "The Word". This line of inquiry could certainly have been further developed. However, as an alternative, we might consider requesting a comprehensive analysis of the play from the chatbot directly, as illustrated in the following example (January 20, 2025):

User: Write a short essay on the aim of Kaj Munk's play, "The Word"

AI: The aim of Kaj Munk's play, "The Word", is to explore the themes of faith, death, and the meaning of life, as evident in the introduction to the play. Munk wrote the play while waiting for the decision of the Danish Royal Theatre's administration concerning the acceptance of his other play, and it was inspired by his own experiences with grief and loss, including the death of his parents and the tragedy of a young neighbor and her newborn baby. The play is a "legend of today" that may be interpreted in various ways, and its meaning was hotly debated at its original production. The play's construction is perhaps the best of all Kaj Munk's plays, with characters that are types he knew firsthand, and he consciously set out to write a play in which country folk were to be taken seriously (7)[2]. The play's aim is also to explore the idea of miracles and the power of faith, as seen in the climax of the play, which was a topic of debate and protest at the original production (7). Overall, the aim of "The Word" is to explore complex themes and ideas, and to challenge the audience to think critically about their own beliefs and values.

User:Which miracles take place in the drama?

AI: The miracles that take place in the drama "The Word" are not explicitly stated, but there are several references to miracles throughout the play. For example, Mikkel Borgen mentions that it's a "positive miracle" when his daughter-in-law's condition improves (52). Additionally, the character of Reuben Snipper refers to the miracle of his own conversion and the conversion of others, such as Anna Maria and Thatcher Kristen (31). Furthermore, Inger mentions that God might perform miracles, and Borgen talks about the Catholics saying miracles happen at Lourdes (14). However, the Doctor is skeptical of miracles and believes that everything can be explained by natural causes (52).

---

[2] The numbers given by the chatbot are references to pages in the published edition of Kaj Munk's play, (Munk 2024).

It is evident that the concept of 'miracles' constitutes a fundamental theme within the text, with various types of miracles being explicitly referenced throughout the play. Consequently, a systematic classification of the different categories of miracles presented in the play would be beneficial for a comprehensive understanding of their significance (January 20, 2025, continued from the dialogue above):

> *User*:These miracles seem to be very different. Please classify them.
>
> *AI*: The miracles mentioned in the play can be classified into two main categories: physical miracles and spiritual miracles. Physical miracles refer to events that defy the laws of nature, such as healing or other supernatural occurrences. For example, Mikkel Borgen mentions that it's a "positive miracle" when his daughter-in-law's condition improves (52). On the other hand, spiritual miracles refer to events that are seen as miraculous in a more metaphorical sense, such as a change of heart or a newfound sense of faith. For instance, Reuben Snipper refers to the miracle of his own conversion and the conversion of others, such as Anna Maria and Thatcher Kristen (42). Additionally, Johannes mentions that he went from miracle to miracle to quicken the omnipotence of love in the eyes of mankind (21). It's also worth noting that the Pastor and the Doctor have different views on miracles, with the Pastor believing that miracles are possible but not something that God would normally do, and the Doctor being skeptical of miracles and believing that everything can be explained by natural causes (52).

The debate regarding the possibility of miracles is central to the play. In this context, the doctor emerges as the most skeptical character, consistently rejecting all supernatural phenomena. In a discussion of the Word, it is particularly pertinent to pay close attention to his stance on the miracles described within the text (January 20, 2025, continued from the dialogue above):

> *User*:Give an example of a miracle that the doctor rejects as impossible.
>
> *AI*: The Doctor rejects the idea of miracles that involve a break in the laws of nature, as he believes that everything can be explained by natural causes (52). For example, when Mikkel Borgen attributes his daughter-in-law's improvement to a "positive miracle", the Doctor responds by saying that he can trace every step of the improvement and that it is all perfectly natural (52). Additionally, the Doctor also rejects the idea of Christ's miracles, saying that even those can be assigned a natural cause by a sufficiently skilled investigator.

It may seem somewhat surprising that the most spectacular miracle described in the play is not mentioned here. Consequently, it is natural for the user to inquire further about this particular miracle (January 20, 2025, continued from the dialogue above):

> *User*:What is the most important miracle that happens in the drama?
>
> *AI*: The most important miracle that happens in the drama "The Word" is the miracle of Inger's recovery from her illness, as mentioned by Mikkel Borgen, who attributes her improvement to a "positive miracle" (52). This miracle is significant because it is a turning point in the play and has a profound impact on the characters,

particularly Mikkel Borgen, who sees it as a sign of God's blessing and intervention in their lives. However, it's worth noting that the Doctor is skeptical of this miracle and attributes Inger's recovery to natural causes, saying that he can "trace every step" of her improvement and that it is "all perfectly natural" (52).

This interpretation constitutes a clear misreading of Kaj Munk's play. Inger's recovery from her illness is not enduring, as she succumbs shortly after what was presumed to be her recovery. Thus, the events that transpire should not be classified as a genuine miracle. This significant misstep underscores a fundamental point. As everybody should know in advance: the chatbot has not grasped the essence of the play (nor is it equipped to do so). Despite the chatbot's remarkable capacity to generate textual content regarding the play, it lacks a substantive understanding of its themes and nuances. It resembles a type of student who can articulate a considerable amount but has not engaged with the material on a deeper level. Consequently, it is imperative for the user, who is responsible for instructing the chatbot, to recognize and correct this notable mistake. Such an intervention appears to be essential for the user's learning process. The dialogue from January 20, 2025 continues in the following way:

User:I disagree. A much greater and more important miracle takes place later in the play. Please reconsider.
AI: The most important miracle that happens in the drama "The Word" is actually the resurrection of Inger, Young Mikkel's wife, as hinted at by Johannes when he says "if you hadn't enough Christian blood in you to count on the triumph of Easter, you might at least have had the courage of prayer and have asked Him whether you might have her back" (62). This miracle is significant because it is a turning point in the play and has a profound impact on the characters, particularly Young Mikkel, who is grieving the loss of his wife. The resurrection of Inger is a testament to the power of faith and prayer, and it challenges the Doctor's skepticism about miracles (52).

User:What is "the triumph of Easter"?

AI: The "triumph of Easter" refers to the resurrection of Jesus Christ, which is a central event in the Christian faith. In the context of the play, Johannes mentions that if one hasn't enough Christian blood in them to count on the triumph of Easter, they might at least have the courage of prayer and ask God whether they might have their loved one back.

In addition to the traditional Christian view on miracles, Kaj Munk's play also offers two intellectual and rather critical and skeptical views, represented by The Doctor and the Pastor. The Doctor's view is rather straightforward:

User:What is the Doctor's view on miracles?

AI: The Doctor's view on miracles is that they do not occur in the natural world, and that every event can be explained by natural causes. He states, "No, my good Pastor, there never in this world has occurred or will occur anything for which a sufficiently skilled, knowledgeable investigator couldn't assign a natural cause" (52). He also mentions that he believes in himself and his scientific knowledge, and that he performs "miracles" through his medical skills, but these are not supernatural events (53). Additionally, when Borgen suggests that the Doctor is a believer in miracles, the Doctor responds by saying that he believes in his own abilities and scientific knowledge, implying that he does not believe in supernatural miracles (53).

The Doctor's view on supernatural miracles is the traditional atheistic view, and the chatbot offers a clear and understandable account of this view. Things become much more complicated when we turn to Kaj Munk's presentation of the view defended by Pastor Bandbul:

User:What is the Pastor's view on miracles?

AI: The Pastor's view on miracles is that the physical possibility of a miracle can never be denied, since the Creator must always be lord of what He created, but a break in the laws of nature would of course mean a disturbance of God's design for this world (52). He also states that God could of course perform miracles, but of course He never does, and for that we are grateful (52). Additionally, the Pastor notes that at the great turning-points in the history of the world, the question of miracles shapes itself rather differently (52). The Pastor's view is that miracles are not something that can be expected to happen in the natural world, but rather something that can be considered in the context of faith and the grand design of God's world.

In Kaj Munk's text it looks as if Pastor Bandbul claims that a supernatural miracle would be an ethical problem. It is somewhat surprising that the occurrence of a miracle could give rise to an ethical problem. How does ethics relate to the question of miracles at all? The chatbot accounts for Bandbul's view on the relation between miracles and ethics in the following manner (January 20, 2025, continued from the dialogue above):

User:Does the Pastor see a relation to ethics here?

AI: The Pastor sees a relation to ethics in the context of miracles, as he mentions that a break in the laws of nature would mean a disturbance of God's design for this world, and that God could perform miracles, but of course, He never does, and for that, we are grateful (52). This suggests that the Pastor believes there is an ethical aspect to the concept of miracles, as it relates to the idea of God's design and the natural order of the world. The Pastor also notes that the question of miracles shapes itself rather differently at the great turning-points in the history of the world (52), implying that ethics may play a role in how we understand and interpret miracles in different contexts.

User: Why is a break in the laws of nature an ethical problem?

AI: A break in the laws of nature is considered an ethical problem because it would mean a disturbance of God's design for this world, and the grand thing with God is precisely that – that we can rely on Him (52). This suggests that the idea of a break in the laws of nature is not just a matter of scientific curiosity, but also has implications for our understanding of the world and our place in it, and therefore raises ethical concerns. The Pastor notes that God could of course perform miracles, but of course, He never does, and for that, we are grateful (52), implying that the idea of a break in the laws of nature is not just a matter of fact, but also has moral and ethical implications.

The point is apparently that although the occurrence of a supernatural miracle does not give rise to any logical of physical problem, such an occurrence will have ethical consequences in the sense that it will destroy Pastor Bandbul's conception of ethics. The reason is that the possibility of supernatural miracles in our era means that we can't have unconditionally trust in the natural laws, but we ought to take the possibility of miracles into account when we decide what to do in a given situation. This will clearly change ethical reasoning significantly.

The kind of reasoning is a bit surprising and certainly rather complex, and many human readers will probably have to struggle with it in order to comprehend it fully. In this light, it is remarkable that the AI-based chatbot somehow manages to account for Bandbul's strange worldview so precisely as shown above.

5 Evaluation and Perspectives

Topping [8] has provided substantial support for teaching as a learning strategy by demonstrating its cognitive, social, and emotional benefits. His findings align with and have been reinforced by later research, confirming that structured peer teaching enhances both comprehension and skill development. However, for this strategy to be effective, careful planning and implementation are necessary.

In this pilot study, we have observed that the user, in the role of the chatbot's teacher, can become aware of a range of minor and major errors in the responses provided by the chatbot through questioning. The hypothesis is that the user can learn significantly by identifying the mistakes made by the chatbot during the dialogue and by prompting the chatbot to correct these errors in the form of improved responses. It is also assumed that the user can derive substantial insights from the surprising and interesting responses that the chatbot occasionally provides. The role of adjudicator regarding the quality of the chatbot's responses is expected to yield insights into the main themes of the play and its many compelling details. Overall, it is posited that by teaching the chatbot to interpret a drama through a dialogue such as the one described, the user will learn a great deal about the interpretation of the literary work. It is hypothesized that the numerous experiences related to teaching as a learning strategy will be highly relevant in the described context.

To test the hypotheses generated by this pilot study, a logical next step would be to develop a learning module that could facilitate dialogues similar to the one outlined above. This learning module should be developed in collaboration with professional literature educators to ensure that it also includes a guide for selecting the questions that the user chooses to pose to the chatbot. Optionally, the selection of questions could be guided by an overarching problem that is to be explored further through dialogue with the chatbot. It will be particularly interesting to test such a learning module in the context of remote teaching, where the introduction of interactive opportunities in the instruction is expected to be especially appealing.

It remains an open question, at this stage, whether the use of a learning module of the described nature in dialogue with an AI based chatbot can enhance the user's literary skills more than what can be obtained through traditional learning. The answer to this question must depend on concrete assessment of the learning outcomes associated with the use of the learning module compared to those obtained through more traditional teaching methods. It will be a significant challenge for future research in light of the findings from this pilot study to design and conduct comparative studies that evaluate the approach taken in the pilot study against more traditional forms of literature learning. A fundamental prerequisite for these studies will be identifying ways to quantify the outcomes of literature learning. Moreover, these studies should encompass diverse student demographics. Within this framework, it is essential to explore whether certain groups of students encounter particular difficulties in developing a critical approach to the chatbot's texts, thereby hindering their ability to effectively engage with the method proposed by the pilot study.

References

1. Bordwell, D.: The Films of Carl-Theodor Dreyer. University of California Press, Berkeley (1981)
2. Duran, D.: Learning-by-teaching: Evidence and implications as a pedagogical mechanism. Innovación Educativa **17**(74), 19–39 (2017)
3. Chi, M.T.H., Siler, S.A., Jeong, H., Yamauchi, T., Hausmann, R.G.: Learning from human tutoring. Cogn. Sci. **25**, 471–533 (2001)
4. Fiorella, L., Mayer, R.E.: Role of expectations and explanations in learning by teaching. Contemp. Educ. Psychol. **39**(2), 75–85 (2014)
5. Jakobsen, D.: Reasoning with generative AI. In: Arai, K. (ed.) Advances in Information and Communication: Proceedings of the 2025 Future of Information and Communication Conference (FICC), vol. 1, pp. 172–178. Springer Nature Switzerland, Cham (2025). https://doi.org/10.1007/978-3-031-84457-7_10
6. Macnab, G.: Carl Th. Dreyer's Ordet: A Visual Hymn. Sight & Sound (2015)
7. Munk, K.: The Word. New edition by Asger Holde. Extended version of R.P. Keigwin's translation from 1953 (2024). https://arkiv.kajmunk.aau.dk/documents/6960
8. Topping, K.J.: Trends in peer learning. Educ. Psychol. **25**(6), 631–645 (2005)
9. Tucudean, G., Bucos, M., Dragulescu, B., Caleanu, C.D.: Natural language processing with transformers: a review. Peer J. Comput. Sci. **10**, e2222 (2024). https://doi.org/10.7717/peerj-cs.2222
10. Vasileiou, A., Eberle, O.: Explaining Text Similarity in Transformer Models. In: Proceedings of the North American Chapter of the Association for Computational Linguistics (2024). https://arxiv.org/abs/2405.06604v1
11. Øhrstrøm, P., Pacis, S., Jakobsen, D.: The Digital Kaj Munk Archive (2024). https://www.kajmunk.aau.dk/

Lesson Plan Designing in the Digital Age: A Multimodal Approach with ChatGPT

Roza Zhussupova[1], Ainura Nurzhanova[1](✉), Zhanargul Beisembayeva[1], Aigul Baibatyrova[1], Rustam Shadiev[2], Zhainash Nurzhanova[1], Gulzhan Gauriyeva[1], Madina Kozhakanova[3], and Bibol Alipbay[1]

[1] L.N. Gumilyov Eurasian National University, Astana 010000, Kazakhstan
nurzhanova.ainura@gmail.com
[2] Zhejiang University, Zhejiang Province, Hangzhou 310058, China
[3] Kazakh National Agrarian Research University, Almaty 050000, Kazakhstan

Abstract. The rapid development of Artificial Intelligence (AI) is reshaping educational practices, particularly in teacher training. This study explores the integration of Digital Multimodal Simulation (DMS) and ChatGPT in enhancing lesson planning skills among Pre-service English Language Teachers (PELTs). Using a mixed-methods approach that combines rubric-based evaluation, classroom observation, and thematic analysis, the study examines the effectiveness of AI-assisted lesson planning and its perceived benefits. Findings reveal that DMS supported by ChatGPT significantly improved PELTs' ability to structure, personalize, and align lesson plans with pedagogical standards. While ChatGPT-generated plans demonstrated strengths in clarity and differentiation, human-designed plans showed deeper engagement and resource use. Additionally, PELTs reported increased confidence, practical skills, and reflection through real-time feedback within the simulation environment. The study contributes to the growing body of research on AI integration in teacher education and highlights the complementary role of human and AI collaboration in pedagogical design.

Keywords: artificial intelligence in education · digital multimodal simulation · ChatGPT in language teaching · lesson planning · pre-service language teacher training · teacher education and technology · AI-assisted instructional design

1 Introduction

The modern classroom demands innovative teaching methods that keep pace with rapid technological advancements and address diverse student needs. The shift to digital learning, accelerated by the recent pandemic, exposed the limitations of traditional chalk-and-board instruction, prompting increased interest in approaches that enhance engagement, flexibility, and critical thinking [1–3]. Multimodal pedagogy addresses these demands by combining various forms of communication—textual, auditory, visual, and spatial—into cohesive learning experiences [4–6]. Meaning in education is increasingly constructed through the interaction of multiple modes [7, 8]. Multimodal texts include written content and videos, infographics, and interactive materials, all of which encourage deeper engagement and diversified learning paths [9, 10].

W.-S. Wang et al. (Eds.): ICITL 2025, LNCS 15913, pp. 74–83, 2026.
https://doi.org/10.1007/978-3-031-98185-2_9

This study explores the potential of DMS integrating with ChatGPT to support PELTs in developing lesson-planning skills. DMS provides immersive, scenario-based training that mirrors real classroom situations. This integration also addresses learners' varying levels of digital literacy and promotes inclusive, flexible learning environments [11]. Accordingly, this research investigates the effectiveness of using DMS supported by ChatGPT to improve lesson-planning competencies and reflective practices among PELTs. It is guided by the following research questions:

1. How does the integration of ChatGPT into Digital Multimodal Simulation influence the lesson-planning competencies of pre-service English language teachers?
2. What are the perceived benefits and challenges of integrating ChatGPT into the practicum preparation process among PELTs?

By addressing these questions, this study contributes to the evolving discourse on AI integration in education and offers practical insights for enhancing teacher education programs through scalable, multimodal, and AI-supported models.

2 Literature Review

2.1 Multimodality in English as a Foreign Language Teaching (EFLT)

Multimodal approaches in English as a Foreign Language Teaching (EFLT) integrate textual, auditory, visual, and interactive elements to enhance learner engagement and comprehension [12, 13]. Unlike traditional methods, these approaches support diverse meaning-making pathways, aligning with students' cognitive and perceptual processes. While research such as Magnusson and Godhe has highlighted the benefits of multimodality, much of it focuses on first language education, leaving gaps in its application to EFL learners across diverse cultural contexts [10]. Moreover, issues such as cultural inclusivity and linguistic diversity remain underexplored within multimodal frameworks.

2.2 Digital Multimodal Simulation and AI Tools in Education

DMS builds multimodal pedagogy by providing immersive, scenario-based learning that promotes critical thinking and practical teaching skills. Serbinovskaya emphasizes the importance of prebriefing, debriefing, and role-play tasks in enhancing learner agency within simulations [11]. When integrated with AI tools such as ChatGPT, DMS gains the ability to offer real-time feedback, generate lesson content, and support differentiated instruction [14]. Despite these benefits, studies like Al-khresheh raise concerns about ChatGPT's limited cultural sensitivity and inability to tailor outputs to local peda-gogical norms [15]. Rahimi et al. further note a lack of empirical evidence demonstrating ChatGPT's effectiveness in aligning with curricular goals or improving long-term teaching outcomes [16].

2.3 Ethical Considerations and Practical Constraints

While ChatGPT has demonstrated advantages such as multilingual support and structured output generation, ethical concerns regarding originality, data privacy, and academic integrity remain critical [17]. ChatGPT 4.0, chosen for this study, offers improved contextual understanding, yet may still produce overly generalized responses or lack nuanced alignment with national education standards.

3 Methodology

3.1 Participants and Course Context

This study involved 150 fourth-year pre-service English language teachers (PELTs), aged 20–21, primarily Kazakh and Russian speakers, with English as their second or third language. All participants were enrolled in the 15-week course "Practicum in English Language Classrooms" (January–May 2024), designed to enhance teaching proficiency through the integration of digital tools. The course was facilitated by seven instructors, who introduced students to national teaching standards, policies, and ethical practices.

Participants were pre-assigned to academic groups based on the university's enrollment procedures and randomly distributed among instructors to maintain objectivity and avoid selection bias. Participation in the study was voluntary, and students were informed about the research goals and procedures. Efforts were made to ensure anonymity and reduce bias, including clear communication of voluntary involvement and equal inclusion opportunities for all eligible students.

All 150 PELTs took part in the Digital Multimodal Simulation (DMS) intervention and submitted both manually created and ChatGPT-assisted lesson plans, along with written reflections. For comparative analysis, a subset of 50 students (7–8 from each group) voluntarily completed a Google Forms survey during the analysis phase. These data were used for both quantitative and qualitative evaluation of the impact of DMS on lesson planning skills.

3.2 Instructional Design and Implementation of DMS

The 15-week instructional process followed a structured DMS framework, implemented over five key stages (Appendix – Table A1) [11]: 1. **Scenario Development.** Students visited schools to explore lesson components, classroom management, and normative documents. 2. **Scripted Lesson Planning.** Students developed lesson plans aligned with Kazakhstan's national curriculum (KZ Law #130), incorporating differentiation, age-appropriate language skills, and thematic content. 3. **AI-Assisted Planning and Comparison.** Participants created one lesson plan manually and another using ChatGPT (version 4.0), then analyzed both using a standardized evaluation rubric (see Appendix). 4. **Prebriefing and Debriefing with ChatGPT.** Learners used AI-generated feedback to identify strengths and areas for improvement. 5. **Self-Reflection.** Students revised their plans based on ChatGPT's input and submitted critical reflections on the university's Moodle platform.

3.3 Skills Developed Through DMS

Through participation in DMS, students developed a range of instructional and digital competencies, including interpreting curriculum requirements, aligning lesson objectives and activities with national standards, and customizing plans to meet diverse learner needs. They also learned to use rubrics and AI-generated feedback for critical analysis and refinement of lesson plans.

3.4 Data Collection and Analysis

A mixed-methods approach was adopted. **Quantitative Data:** Each participant submitted two lesson plans, one manual and one AI-generated. Fifty students completed a comparison analysis via Google Forms, and all students submitted final reflections on Moodle. **Qualitative Data:** Weekly interviews with PELTs were conducted by 7 Instructors in small groups for about 2 h every week. The interview guides consisted of Question items structured to capture the DMS implementation's objectives, avoid its challenges, and check its efficiency. A recorder was used to record and transcribe the proceedings afterward. The interviews lasted for 15 weeks.

3.5 Thematic Analysis

Interview data were analyzed using Braun and Clarke's thematic analysis framework [19]. Three expert coders independently reviewed transcripts, generated codes using a shared codebook, and identified recurring themes. After discussion and consensus, themes were finalized and validated with participants to ensure authenticity.

3.6 Observation and Evaluation

Instructors monitored students' engagement with DMS, the effectiveness of ChatGPT feedback, and how lesson plans evolved. Observations were recorded using structured checklists, written reports, and Moodle logs. The evaluation was guided by the Lesson Plans Evaluation Rubric, which assessed 11 components such as clarity of objectives, use of technology, inclusivity, and assessment methods across four performance levels: Needs Improvement, Meets Expectations, Exceeds Expectations, and Exemplary. The rubric, adapted from Ozogul et al. [18], underwent expert validation in-volving three senior ELT specialists. Inter-rater reliability among the seven raters was assessed using the Intraclass Correlation Coefficient (ICC), yielding a high reliability score of ICC = 0.89, indicating strong agreement.

4 Findings

4.1 Quantitative Analysis

See Table 1.

The analysis of lesson plans revealed that most students performed well in aligning their plans with national standards (84%) and in stating clear learning objectives (71.4%). Content objectives were another strong area. However, creativity in activities and use of resources remained limited, with only 17.9% rated exemplary. Differentiation and technology integration showed moderate success, while cultural sensitivity was the weakest area, with 32.1% needing improvement. Scaffolding and assessment

Table 1. Lesson plan created by a teacher.

#	Component of LP	The criteria for lesson plans			
		Needs Improvement	Meets expectations	Exceeds expectations	Exemplary
1	Clarity of learning objectives	17.9%	46.4%	10.7%	25%
2	Clarity of Content Objectives	3.5%	39.3%	14.3%	42.9%
3	Variety of activities/resources/materials	28.6%	25%	28.6%	17.9%
4	Differentiation and personalization	17.9%	32.1%	25%	25%
5	Alignment with a standard	3.5%	42.9%	10.7%	42.9%
6	Engagement/Interaction/Collaborative learning	14.3%	39.3%	25%	21.4%
7	Integration of Technology	21.4%	25%	25%	28.6%
8	Cultural sensitivity and Inclusivity	32.1%	25%	25%	17.9%
9	Assessment Methods and Strategies	10.7%	50%	17.9%	21.4%
10	Scaffolding	17.9%	32.1%	32.1%	17.9%
11	Clear Instructions/Time management	3.5%	53.6%	21.4%	21.4%

Table 2. Lesson plan created by ChatGPT.

#	Component of LP	The criteria for lesson plans			
		Needs Improvement	Meets expectations	Exceeds expectations	Exemplary
1	Clarity of learning objectives	25%	53.6%	10.7%	10.7%
2	Clarity of Content Objectives	25%	32.1%	25%	17.9%
3	Variety of activities/resources/materials	17.9%	42.9%	21.4%	17.9%
4	Differentiation and personalization	28.6%	17.9%	25%	28.6%
5	Alignment with a standard	28.6%	46.4%	10.7%	14.3%
6	Engagement/Interaction/Collaborative learning	17.9%	28.6%	35.7%	17.9%
7	Integration of Technology	14.3%	32.1%	28.6%	14.3%
8	Cultural sensitivity and Inclusivity	39.3%	21.4%	14.3%	25%
9	Assessment Methods and Strategies	14.3%	35.7%	28.6%	21.4%
10	Scaffolding	7.1%	39.3%	35.7%	17.9%
11	Clear Instructions/Time management	3.5%	42.9%	25%	28.6%

also required development, though time management and instructions were generally effective (Table 2).

ChatGPT-generated lesson plans showed overall satisfactory performance, especially in clarity of instructions and time management. Learning objectives and assessment methods were generally adequate, but often lacked depth. Differentiation and alignment with standards varied, with around 28.6% needing improvement. Cultural sensitivity was the weakest area, with 39.3% of plans falling short, highlighting a need for more inclusivity. While AI-supported plans offered structure and consistency, improvements are needed in personalization and cultural adaptation to match pedagogical quality standards.

Figure 1 compares manual and AI-generated lesson plans using a rubric across four rating levels: Needs Improvement, Meets Expectations, Exceeds Expectations, and Exemplary.

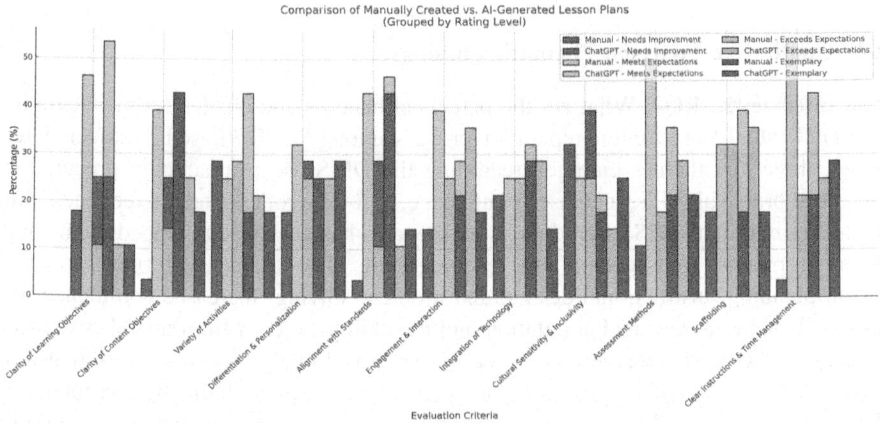

Fig. 1. Comparison of manually created vs. AI-generated lesson plans across 11 evaluation criteria.

Figure 1 compares lesson plans created manually by PELTs and those generated with ChatGPT across key pedagogical criteria. Manual plans scored higher in structure and engagement, while AI-generated plans performed better in differentiation and time management. However, AI plans showed weaknesses in cultural inclusivity and engagement.

While AI-generated plans provide efficiency and structure, they show clear gaps in key areas. Figure 2 highlights aspects needing refinement, underscoring the value of human input.

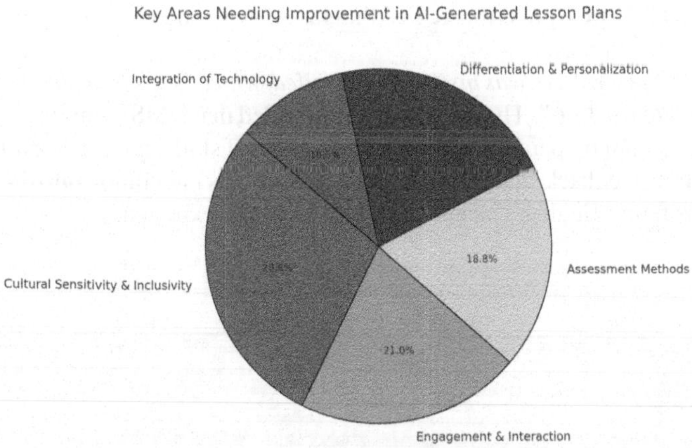

Fig. 2. Key areas needing improvement in AI-generated lesson plans.

Figure 2 highlights key weaknesses in AI-generated lesson plans, with cultural sensitivity, engagement, differentiation, and assessment as top areas needing improvement. These results emphasize the ongoing need for human input to ensure pedagogical quality and cultural relevance.

4.2 Qualitative Analysis: Thematic Findings

The Interviews. RQ2: What are the perceived benefits and challenges of integrating ChatGPT into the practicum preparation process among PELTs? Based on student interviews, three key themes emerged regarding the DMS use in practicum preparation: enhanced practical skills, increased confidence, real-time reflection, and feedback. Students reported that DMS offered realistic, scenario-based tasks that helped them apply theory to practice and develop core teaching skills. The interactive format supported lesson planning, instructional design, and problem-solving. Increased confidence was another benefit, as repeated simulation and the ability to learn from mistakes reduced anxiety and boosted preparedness for real classrooms. Finally, students valued real-time feedback from ChatGPT allowed them to revise lesson plans immediately, reflect on their performance, and improve teaching strategies. These insights underscore DMS's role as an effective, reflective, and formative tool in pre-service teacher education.

Theme 1: Enhanced Practical Skills. Students reported that DMS facilitated hands-on experience and problem-solving.

PELT 1: *"Using the simulation felt just like being in a real practicum setting. It helped me practice skills that I was nervous about"*. PELT 6: *"Being able to practice stage by stage was helpful, promoting continuous learning"*.

Theme 2: Increased Confidence. Repetitive practice within the simulation environment boosted confidence.

PELT 2: *"I felt much more confident walking into my practicum because I had already experienced similar scenarios through the simulation"*. PELT 4: *"The simulation was interactive and fun"*. PELT 5: *"DMS kept me motivated to keep practicing"*.

Theme 3: Real-Time Reflection & Feedback. AI-generated feedback enabled immediate lesson adjustments.

PELT 3: *"The feedback was instant and detailed, which helped me understand exactly what I needed to work on"*. Thematic analysis revealed that DMS significantly supported students' practicum preparation by enhancing practical skills, building confidence, providing real-time feedback, and increasing engagement. Its integration into the curriculum better equips future English teachers for real classroom experiences.

5 Discussion and Conclusion

The comparison and analysis of the reports revealed key strengths and weaknesses in both manually composed and ChatGPT-generated lesson plans, highlighting their effectiveness and areas for improvement across structure, language skills, resources, engagement, assessment, and differentiation. While foundational work by Kress et al. emphasized multimodality as the integration of textual/visual/auditory, and spatial modes through pre-designed materials, our study extends this framework by showing how AI-powered DMS transforms meaning-making into a dynamic, interactive process [8]. Rather than interpreting static resources, learners in AI-driven environments co-construct content, receive real-time feedback, and adapt communication strategies on the fly. Building on Kress's theory, we demonstrate that integrating ChatGPT expands teach-ers' semiotic repertoires, supporting dynamic interplay between digital, visual, and linguistic modes. These AI-generated plans enhance multimodal literacy by modeling strategies often overlooked in traditional instruction. While multimodality is often praised for promoting engagement, our findings also reveal limitations, particularly AI's struggles with cultural nuance and curriculum alignment [15, 16]. Ultimately, our study both supports and extends multimodal theory, showing how AI integration repositions pre-service teachers as active content creators. It also surfaces new ethical, cultural, and pedagogical tensions that arise when machine-mediated learning becomes the norm. Across multiple reports, personally composed lesson plans demonstrated clear advantages over those generated by ChatGPT in several key areas. Manually created plans showed stronger structural organization, providing clear progression and comprehensive coverage of learning objectives, which facilitated student understanding. They also incorporated a wider range of language development activities, promoting critical thinking, communication, writing, and analytical skills. In contrast, ChatGPT plans often focus narrowly on specific skills like speaking, lacking the depth needed for broader learning outcomes. Resource use was another distinguishing factor—manual plans included diverse and meaningful materials such as books, multimedia, and ICT tools, whereas AI-generated plans frequently relied on generic content. Engagement and interaction were also more prominent in human-authored plans, which included collaborative and participatory tasks, unlike ChatGPT plans that emphasized individual work. Finally, assessment/feedback mechanisms were more developed in the manually written plans, offering varied methods and clear evaluation strategies, while AI-generated versions often lacked sufficient detail for meaningful learner progress tracking.

While both teachers composed and ChatGPT-lesson plans met learning objectives, human-created plans showed stronger structure, richer skill development, and more effective use of resources and assessment. Despite concerns that AI might reduce critical thinking, our findings suggest ChatGPT served as a complementary tool, enhancing teacher confidence and innovation, particularly in Kazakhstan's traditionally structured educational environment. AI-generated plans, though less comprehensive, offered creative starting points that, when combined with human input, helped produce more engaging and adaptable lessons.

Disclosure of Interests. The authors declare that there are no conflicts of interest related to the content of this article.

Appendix

Table A1. Multimodal simulation procedure.

Week	Stages	Aim	Key Activities	Skills Developed
1–2	1 Scenario	Understand school norms and curriculum standards	Study school documents; learn lesson components; manage time; integrate standards into lesson plans	Curriculum Integration
3–4	2 Roles/Scripts	Learn to create lesson plans	Develop plans using school calendar and KZ Law #130 template	Critical Lesson Planning
5–7	2 Roles/Scripts	Use ChatGPT in lesson planning	Create lesson plans using ChatGPT based on official templates and thematic plans	AI-enhanced Planning & Evaluation
8–10	3 Case	Compare planning approaches	Evaluate self-made vs. ChatGPT plans using Ozogul et al. criteria [18]; write comparative feedback	Comparative Analysis
10–12	4 Prebriefing and Debriefing questions	Critical analysis via ChatGPT	Use ChatGPT to analyze strengths/weaknesses of both plans; assess source credibility and content quality	Critical Thinking & Evaluation
13–15	5 Self-reflection	Improve lesson planning	Refine personal lesson plans using ChatGPT feedback; reflect on best practices	Reflective Practice & Synthesis

References

1. Shadiev, R., Feng, Y., Zhussupova, R., Huang, Y.: Intercultural competence development through a tele-collaborative project supported by speech-enabled corrective feedback technology. J. Comput. Assist. Learn. **40**(2), 697–714 (2023). https://doi.org/10.1111/jcal.12906

2. Auxier, B., Anderson, M.: Parenting children in the age of screens (2020). https://www.pewresearch.org/internet/2020/07/28/parenting-children-in-the-age-of-screens/. Last accessed 21 Feb 2025
3. Yan, C., Wang, L.: Experienced EFL teachers switching to online teaching: a case study from China. System **105**, 102717 (2022). https://doi.org/10.1016/j.system.2021.102717
4. Blinova, O.A.: Magazine cover as multimodal text. Nauchnyy dialog (2019). https://doi.org/10.24224/2227-1295-2019-5-9-24
5. Bezemer, J., Kress, G.: Multimodality, Learning and Communication: A social semiotic frame, 1st edn. Routledge, London and New York (2016)
6. Ezeh, C.: Multimodal spaces for digital translanguaging: Using "StoryJumper" to engage Bi/Multilinguals in interactive storytelling. Teach. English Technol. **20**(2), 118–130 (2020). http://files.eric.ed.gov/fulltext/EJ1253183.pdf
7. Cowan, K., Kress, G.: Documenting and transferring meaning in the multimodal world: reconsidering "transcription!" In: Serafini, F., Gee, E. (eds.) Remixing Multiliteracies: Theory and Practice from New London to New Times, pp. 50–61. Teachers College Press, New York (2017)
8. Kress, G.R., Leeuwen, T.V.: Multimodal Discourse: The Modes and Media of Contemporary Communications. Edward Arnold, London (2001)
9. Kress, G.: Multimodal discourse analysis. In: Gee, J.P., Handford, M. (eds.) The Routledge handbook of discourse analysis, pp. 35–50. Taylor & Francis Group, Oxfordshire (2012)
10. Magnusson, P., Godhe, A.-L.: Multimodality in Language education – Implications for teaching. Designs Learn. **11**(1), 127–137 (2019). https://doi.org/10.16993/dfl.127
11. Serbinovskaya, A.: Digital Multimodal Simulation for Speaking Communication (2023). https://tcnewsletter.s3.amazonaws.com/newsmanager.commpartners.com/tesolc_mobi/issues/2023-07-01/4.html. Last accessed 23 Feb 2025
12. Danielsson, K., Selander, S.: Reading Multimodal Texts for Learning – a model for cultivating multimodal literacy. Designs Learn. **8**(1), 25–36 (2016). https://doi.org/10.16993/dfl.72
13. Åkerfeldt, A., Åberg, E.S.: Designs for learning: a research approach. Int. J. Educ. Methodol. **7**(4), 547–555 (2021). https://doi.org/10.12973/ijem.7.4.547
14. Zhang, R., Zou, D., Cheng, G.: A review of chatbot-assisted learning: Pedagogical approaches, implementations, factors leading to effectiveness, theories, and future directions. Interact. Learn. Environ. 1–29 (2023)
15. Al-khresheh, M.H.: Bringing technology and pedagogy from a global lens: Teachers' perspectives on integrating ChatGPT in English language teaching. Comput. Educ: Artificial Intelligence **6**, 100218 (2024)
16. Rahimi, A.R., Sevilla-Pavón, A.: The role of ChatGPT readiness in shaping language teachers' language teaching innovation and meeting accountability: a bisymmetric approach. Comput. Educ. Artific. Intell. **7**, 100258 (2024). https://doi.org/10.1016/j.caeai.2024.100258
17. Crawford, J., Cowling, M., Allen, K.-A.: Leadership is needed for ethical ChatGPT: Character, assessment, and learning using artificial intelligence (AI). J. Univ. Teach. Learn. Pract. (2023). https://doi.org/10.53761/1.20.3.02
18. Ozogul, G., Olina, Z., Sullivan, H.: Teacher, self and peer evaluation of lesson plans written by preservice teachers. Education Tech. Research Dev. **56**(2), 181–201 (2006). https://doi.org/10.1007/s11423-006-9012-7
19. Braun, V., Clarke, V.: Using thematic analysis in psychology. Qual. Res. Psychol. **3**(2), 77–101 (2006). https://doi.org/10.1191/1478088706qp063oa

GenAI Chatbot Tutors as Agents of Inclusive Education: A Review Guided by Ethics of Care and Critical Pedagogy

Corna Olivier(✉) and Lizette Weilbach

University of Pretoria, Pretoria, South Africa
corna.olivier@gmail.com

Abstract. Generative Artificial Intelligence (GenAI) chatbots in education presents both opportunities and ethical challenges. While these tools can enhance inclusivity through personalized learning and assistive support, they also raise concerns. Without ethical oversight, GenAI risks reinforcing the very inequalities it seeks to address. This study conducted a Systematic Literature Review (SLR) of 43 peer-reviewed papers, guided by PRISMA methodology. Thematic analysis identified five key challenges in GenAI-supported education. These were interpreted using the Ethics of Care and Critical Pedagogy frameworks, which provided a lens to assess AI's impact on student well-being, relational ethics, and educational equity. Findings show that GenAI chatbots often reproduce systemic bias, offer limited transparency, compromise data protection, and pose threats to academic integrity and the educator's role. To address these issues, the study recommends bias-aware design, explainable AI models, AI-integrated curricula, robust data governance, and hybrid learning models that preserve human interaction.

Keywords: GenAI chatbots · Ethical challenges · Inclusive education · Ethics of Care Framework · Paulo Freire's Critical Care Pedagogy

1 Introduction

Generative AI (GenAI) chatbot tutors present significant opportunities for enhancing and supporting inclusivity in education by providing personalized learning experiences, supporting marginalized students, and bridging gaps in digital education [1, 2]. However, despite their transformative potential, the deployment of GenAI chatbots raises critical ethical concerns such as algorithmic bias and power imbalances, that must be addressed to ensure their responsible development and implementation [3, 4].

This paper aims to critically examine the ethical concerns associated with GenAI chatbots in education through a Systematic Literature Review (SLR). To understand and map these ethical concerns, the paper applies two theoretical frameworks: the Ethics of Care and Critical Pedagogy. The Ethics of Care framework emphasizes relational ethics, empathy, and student well-being, ensuring that AI-driven tutors support diverse learners rather than standardizing educational experiences [5, 6]. Critical Pedagogy, drawing from

W.-S. Wang et al. (Eds.): ICITL 2025, LNCS 15913, pp. 84–93, 2026.
https://doi.org/10.1007/978-3-031-98185-2_10

Paulo Freire's work, provides a cautionary perspective, highlighting how AI technologies can reinforce power imbalances, limit student agency, and perpetuate educational inequities if not carefully designed and implemented [7, 8]. By applying these frameworks, this study not only identifies existing challenges but also develops recommendations for overcoming them. The study contributes to the broader discourse on responsible AI development, advocating for ethical guidelines and governance frameworks to ensure that GenAI chatbots in education enhance rather than undermine inclusivity, fairness, and student empowerment.

2 Literature Review

The integration of AI into inclusive education presents important opportunities to enhance accessibility and deliver personalized support for students with diverse needs. AI-powered assistive technologies—such as screen readers, speech recognition, and predictive text—have been especially effective in supporting students with cognitive and physical disabilities by reducing barriers to communication and learning [6] AI also enables early identification of at-risk students through predictive analytics, helping educators intervene before challenges escalate [7]. For neurodivergent learners, AI-driven personalization supports tailored instruction, aligning with students' individual learning styles, fostering inclusive learning [8]. AI also plays a key role in bridging linguistic and cultural divides, although the dominance of English-language datasets limits the inclusivity of current models [9]. Despite these benefits, the implementation of AI in education requires caution. Without ethical design and governance, these tools risk reinforcing existing inequalities.

2.1 GenAI Use in Inclusive Education Through a Theoretical Lens

The Ethics of Care Framework. The ethically grounded approach of the Ethics of Care framework offers a valuable guide to ensure that GenAI tutors promote inclusivity by emphasizing empathy, relationships, and contextual sensitivity in decision-making processes [10]. In educational settings, this means centring AI design on students' holistic development—supporting not just academic outcomes, but also their emotional and social needs [11]. Despite its strong moral foundation, integrating the Ethics of Care into AI development presents several challenges. One of the primary obstacles is the commercialization of AI technologies. Many AI systems are developed by private companies whose primary objective is profitability rather than student well-being [12]. As a result, transparency is often lacking, and there is little opportunity for marginalized communities to influence AI design. Algorithmic bias remains another major challenge in aligning AI with the Ethics of Care. If training datasets fail to include diverse student experiences, AI models risk perpetuating educational inequalities rather than addressing them [13].

Paulo Freire's Critical Pedagogy. While the Ethics of Care ensures relational ethics and student-centred AI development, Critical Pedagogy serves as a necessary counterbalance by questioning power dynamics embedded in AI-driven learning. Paulo Freire's Critical Pedagogy challenges the ways in which AI technologies can replicate existing power imbalances and restrict students' ability to think critically and independently [14]. Freire's concept of the "banking model" of education, in which students passively receive knowledge rather than engaging in dialogue and critical reflection, mirrors the risks posed by AI-driven education [15]. GenAI systems, if not carefully designed, can promote standardized, one-size-fits-all learning models that fail to consider the unique perspectives and needs of individual students while undermining critical thinking, disempowering vulnerable students. Taken together, Ethics of Care and Critical Pedagogy highlight both the opportunities and challenges presented by GenAI in inclusive education.

3 Methodology

To critically examine the ethical and pedagogical implications of GenAI chatbots in inclusive education, a SLR was conducted in accordance with the Preferred Reporting Items for Systematic Reviews and Meta-Analyses (PRISMA) guidelines [16]. The literature search was performed using Google Scholar, Scopus, and Web of Science, combining Boolean search techniques with keywords such as "GenAI chatbots in education" AND "bias", "transparency", "privacy", and "ethics". The inclusion criteria specified peer-reviewed journal articles or conference proceedings published between 2015 and 2025, with particular emphasis on recent research (2023–2025). Eligible studies were required to explicitly address GenAI chatbot applications in educational contexts and examine ethical or pedagogical implications. Only English-language studies with full-text access were included, while studies focused solely on technical AI advancements, non-educational applications, or non-peer-reviewed materials were excluded. A total of 43 papers met the inclusion criteria and were included in the final analysis. Rayyan software was used to streamline the selection process, facilitating duplicate removal, title and abstract screening, and full-text eligibility assessment. Thematic analysis followed Clarke and Braun's six-phase approach [17], which involved coding and categorizing recurring concerns. Rayyan assisted in organizing the data, ensuring analytical consistency.

4 Findings and Discussion

The thematic analysis identified five critical ethical and pedagogical concerns related to the integration of GenAI chatbot tutors in education, namely algorithmic bias and fairness, transparency and explainability issues, academic integrity and plagiarism risks, privacy and data protection concerns, and the replacement of human educators with AI. Each of these themes presents unique challenges that must be addressed to ensure that AI-driven education remains inclusive, ethical, and equitable.

4.1 Unique Challenges Identified

Algorithmic Bias and Fairness. Algorithmic bias remains one of the most pressing ethical issues in AI-driven education. GenAI chatbots are often trained on datasets that reflect existing societal inequalities, leading to biased outputs that disproportionately affect marginalized student populations. AI models frequently reinforce Western-centric narratives, overlooking linguistic and cultural diversity [18]. This bias manifests in educational assessments, where non-native English speakers' submissions are incorrectly flagged as AI-generated, resulting in unfair academic penalties [3]. Similarly, gender and racial biases embedded in chatbot responses limit access to equitable learning experiences [19, 20].

AI-powered tutoring systems also struggle to accommodate neurodivergent learners, failing to adjust to varying cognitive needs and learning styles [6]. The risks extend to socioeconomic disparities, where students from affluent backgrounds benefit from AI-driven personalized learning, while those with limited digital literacy skills receive lower-quality feedback [21]. Bias is also observed in multilingual settings, where AI tutors favour dominant languages over indigenous and regional dialects, further marginalizing non-English-speaking students [22].

Transparency and Explainability Issues. The opaque nature of AI decision-making processes continues to raise concerns about transparency and accountability in AI-enhanced education. Many GenAI chatbots operate as black-box models, making it difficult for students and educators to understand how responses are generated [23], failing to provide sufficient explanations for their outputs [24]. Students often place unwarranted trust in chatbot responses, assuming them to be authoritative despite lacking verifiability [25]. Transparency is particularly critical in AI-powered assessment tools, where automated grading systems have been found to lack justification mechanisms, making it difficult for students to appeal decisions [26]. Blockchain-based verification systems have been proposed as a means to enhance explainability, allowing students and educators to trace and authenticate AI-generated responses [1]. However, despite these advances, most institutions lack clear regulatory frameworks for AI transparency, leading to inconsistencies in how AI is integrated into academic settings [27, 28].

Academic Integrity and Plagiarism Risks. The use of GenAI chatbots in academic writing and assessment has introduced complex challenges regarding plagiarism and student originality. AI-generated text closely mimics human writing, blurring the distinction between student-authored work and chatbot-assisted output [29]. Existing plagiarism detection tools struggle to differentiate between AI-generated and human-written content, frequently flagging legitimate student work as AI-produced and vice versa [4, 30]. The accessibility of GenAI tools has led to concerns about students using chatbots to bypass critical thinking and effort, in academic tasks [24, 31]. While AI-assisted learning has potential benefits, the reliance on GenAI for assignment completion undermines independent research, and cognitive skill development [21, 32].

Privacy and Data Protection Concerns. The widespread use of GenAI chatbots in education has raised serious privacy concerns regarding student data collection, storage, and surveillance. AI-powered learning platforms collect vast amounts of student data, often without clear policies on data retention or user consent [33, 34]. Student interactions with chatbots generate metadata that can be exploited for commercial purposes or inadvertently expose learners to cybersecurity risks [35, 36]. The lack of privacy safeguards disproportionately affects marginalized students, who may be subject to greater surveillance and profiling through AI analytics [37]. Institutions are increasingly called upon to implement privacy-by-design principles, ensuring that AI systems adhere to strict data protection standards while granting students greater control over their personal information [38].

AI Replacing Human Educators. The increasing reliance on AI chatbots in education has raised concerns about the diminishing role of human educators and its impact on student-teacher relationships. While AI tutors enhance accessibility and personalized learning, their overuse may weaken essential aspects of human-centred education, such as mentorship, critical discourse, and emotional intelligence [39, 40]. Students who depend heavily on AI tutors develop weaker problem-solving skills, as chatbots provide instant solutions without fostering deeper engagement [25, 32]. Additionally, institutions facing financial constraints may prioritize AI-based instruction over human-led teaching, reducing opportunities for interpersonal interaction [41, 42]. A hybrid learning model in which AI complements human educators rather than replaces them, would ensure that relational pedagogy remains central to education [43, 44]. To safeguard pedagogical integrity, AI-assisted learning environments must be designed with human-in-the-loop approaches, where educators retain oversight of AI-generated content while fostering student engagement and critical inquiry [27, 45]. The future of AI in education must balance automation with human relational ethics, ensuring that GenAI remains a tool for empowerment rather than a substitute for meaningful teaching and mentorship.

5 Applying the Ethics of Care and Critical Pedagogy Lens

The ethical and pedagogical concerns identified in Sect. 4 can be better understood through the Ethics of Care and Critical Pedagogy frameworks. Ethics of Care highlights the need for AI to prioritize student well-being, relational ethics, and inclusivity, ensuring AI-driven education supports diverse learners equitably [10]. Critical Pedagogy offers a structural critique of power dynamics, questioning whether AI chatbots reinforce or challenge systemic educational inequalities [14].

5.1 Ethical and Pedagogically Sound GenAI Chatbot Integration.

As the emphasis of care ethics enrich the dialogical and liberatory goals of critical pedagogy [10], while the critical lens of Freirean thought inform a more socially aware and justice orientated application of care ethics [5], interweaving these frameworks provides an effective guide to ethical AI design, and inform the recommendations for responsible GenAI integration in this study.

Ethics of Care: Prioritizing Inclusion and Well-Being: AI chatbots often fail to equitably support marginalized students, reinforcing linguistic, cultural, and neurodivergent biases [6, 18, 19]. Addressing these disparities requires fairness audits, inclusive dataset representation, and adaptable AI models [3, 21]. Transparency is also critical. Students often trust opaque AI-generated responses without understanding their basis, leading to misinformation and misplaced reliance [23, 28]. To align with Ethics of Care, AI systems should implement explainable AI (XAI) models that provide clear justifications for decisions [27]. Privacy concerns further highlight the importance of ethical AI governance.

AI tools collect student data without clear consent policies, disproportionately impacting vulnerable learners [33, 36]. Institutions must enforce strict data protection measures, ensuring privacy-by-design principles and student control over personal information [20, 46].

Critical Pedagogy: Addressing Power and Educational Inequities. Over-reliance on chatbots risks reducing education to AI-driven content consumption, sidelining dialogical learning [5, 31]. Moreover, AI disproportionately benefits students with strong digital literacy, while low-income students receive lower-quality interactions, widening educational inequities [37, 47]. AI should be a tool for empowerment, not a barrier reinforcing socioeconomic divides [21, 22]. The risk of AI replacing human educators further contradicts Critical Pedagogy's emphasis on relational and participatory learning [39, 44]. AI should complement—not replace—teachers, preserving human oversight in AI-assisted learning [42, 43].

6 Recommendations

6.1 Aligning Ethical Care and Critical Pedagogy in GenAI Integration

The Ethics of Care and Critical Pedagogy frameworks together emphasize the need for AI systems to be transparent, inclusive, and participatory. AI must prioritize fairness-aware algorithms, student-centred privacy protections, and human-AI collaboration rather than passive, one-directional learning models [23, 36]. Building on the findings and theoretical analysis, this section outlines key recommendations for ensuring ethical and pedagogically responsible GenAI chatbot integration in inclusive education.

Addressing Algorithmic Bias and Fairness. To mitigate bias and ensure inclusivity, AI developers must implement fairness-aware algorithms, expand dataset diversity, and conduct regular bias audits [18, 19, 21]. Institutions should require bias testing before deployment, ensuring AI systems adapt to multilingual, neurodivergent, and socioeconomically diverse learners [3, 6]. Additionally, educators and students should have agency in refining AI outputs, enabling customization to reflect linguistic, cultural, and individual learning needs [20, 22]. Ensuring transparency in AI training data will also reduce hidden biases and improve trust in chatbot interactions [27].

Enhancing Transparency and Explainability. To address AI's black box nature, institutions must adopt explainable AI (XAI) models that justify AI-generated responses in real-time [23]. User-friendly dashboards should allow educators and students to trace AI-generated content back to its sources, fostering critical engagement rather than passive trust [28]. Moreover, regulatory frameworks should enforce standardized AI explainability protocols to ensure that all AI-driven educational tools provide interpretable decision-making processes [27, 42], mitigating the risk of students risk blindly accepting AI-generated content without deeper inquiry [48].

Safeguarding Academic Integrity. To prevent plagiarism and over-reliance on AI, institutions should integrate AI literacy into curricula, equipping students with ethical guidelines on AI-assisted learning [29, 47]. Rather than banning AI use, assessment models should evolve to evaluate students' ability to critically engage with AI-generated content [21, 32]. Educators should design assessments that require student reflection, analysis, and synthesis, reducing mechanical AI use [49]. AI detection tools should be paired with pedagogical strategies rather than punitive measures to promote responsible AI integration [30].

Strengthening Privacy and Data Protection. To protect student data, AI systems should adopt privacy-by-design principles, ensuring students control how their data is collected, stored, and used [33, 36]. Institutions must implement clear data retention policies and provide opt-in consent models for AI-driven interactions [20, 46]. Regulatory bodies should establish ethical guidelines for AI surveillance and tracking, preventing AI-powered analytics from disproportionately affecting marginalized students [37, 44]. Encryption-based protections and time-limited data storage mechanisms should be mandated to prevent unregulated AI data exploitation [27, 38].

Preserving the Role of Human Educators. AI chatbots should complement, not replace, human educators. Institutions must prioritize hybrid learning models where AI enhances instruction without diminishing student-teacher relationships [39, 40]. AI tools should facilitate collaborative, student-centred learning rather than passive knowledge consumption, preserving critical thinking, mentorship, and relational learning [41, 43]. To ensure human oversight, educators must be actively involved in AI-assisted pedagogy, setting parameters for AI-generated interactions [25, 42].

7 Conclusion

The integration of GenAI chatbots into education offers significant opportunities for personalized and accessible learning, but it also raises pressing ethical concerns. This study identified key challenges—algorithmic bias, lack of transparency, academic integrity risks, data privacy issues, and the diminishing role of human educators—through a systematic literature review and analysed them using the Ethics of Care and Critical Pedagogy frameworks. Findings show that GenAI systems often reinforce existing inequalities, lack explainability, and risk undermining critical thinking and human relationships in education. Addressing these challenges requires targeted interventions, including bias audits, explainable AI models, AI literacy initiatives, robust data protection, and maintaining the essential role of educators.

The study's recommendations emphasize ethical design and inclusive implementation, aligning with both care ethics and critical pedagogy. Ultimately, the responsible use of GenAI in education depends on collaboration among developers, educators, policymakers, and students to ensure these tools support empowerment, not exclusion. As AI continues to shape learning environments, ethical vigilance and inclusive innovation will be key to ensuring equity and integrity in education.

References

1. Al-Tamimi, A.-K., Moore, R., Javed, Y., Babu, S., Freeman, E.: Chatbots in education: Addressing student needs and transforming learning in the post-COVID-19 era. Building Resiliency in Higher Education: Globalization, Digital Skills, and Student Wellness, pp. 99–127. IGI Global (2024)
2. Panda, A.: Achieving Inclusive Education: Strategies, Barriers, and Solutions (2024)
3. Perkins, M., Roe, J., Vu, B.H., Postma, D., Hickerson, D., McGaughran, J., Khuat, H.Q.: GenAI detection tools, adversarial techniques and implications for inclusivity in higher education. arXiv preprint arXiv:2403.19148 (2024)
4. Popenici, S.A., Kerr, S.: Exploring the impact of artificial intelligence on teaching and learning in higher education. Res. Pract. Technol. Enhanc. Learn. **12**, 22 (2017)
5. Nugraha, A.E., Wibowo, D., Hendrawan, B.: Paulo Freire's critical pedagogy analysis of educational transformation. MSJ: Majority Sci. J. **2**(2), 220–228 (2024). https://doi.org/10.61942/msj.v2i2.157
6. Nacheva, R., Czaplewski, M.: Artificial Intelligence In Helping People With Disabilities: Opportunities and Challenges. HR and Technologies 102–124 (2024)
7. Latif, G., Alghazo, R., Pilotti, M.A., Brahim, G.B.: Identifying" at-risk" students: an AI-based prediction approach. Int. J. Comput. Digit. Syst. (2021)
8. Barua, P.D., et al.: Artificial intelligence enabled personalised assistive tools to enhance education of children with neurodevelopmental disorders—a review. Int. J. Environ. Res. Public Health **19**, 1192 (2022)
9. Pinhanez, C., et al.: Harnessing the Power of Artificial Intelligence to Vitalize Endangered Indigenous Languages: Technologies and Experiences. arXiv preprint arXiv:2407.12620 (2024)
10. MacGill, B.: A paradigm shift in education: pedagogy, standpoint and ethics of care. Int. J. Pedagogies Learn. **11**, 238–247 (2016)
11. Yew, G.C.K.: Trust in and ethical design of carebots: the case for ethics of care. Int. J. Soc. Robot. **13**, 629–645 (2021)
12. Lu, S.: Algorithmic opacity, private accountability, and corporate social disclosure in the age of artificial intelligence. Vand. J. Ent. Tech. L. **23**, 99 (2020)
13. Baker, R.S., Hawn, A.: Algorithmic bias in education. Int. J. Artific. Intell. Educ. 1–41 (2022)
14. Ayoub Mahmoudi, D., Khoshnood, A., Babaei, A.: Paulo Freire's critical pedagogy and its implications in curriculum planning. J. Educ. Pract. **5**, 86–91 (2014)
15. Govender, N.: Alienation, reification and the banking model of education: Paulo Freire's critical theory of education. Acta Academica **52**, 204–222 (2020)
16. Vrabel, M.: Preferred reporting items for systematic reviews and meta-analyses. Number 5/September 2015 42, 552–554 (2015)
17. Clarke, V., Braun, V.: Thematic analysis. J. Posit. Psychol. **12**, 297–298 (2017)
18. Mirowsky, J.E.: Assessing biases in the names generated by generative artificial intelligence chatbots. J. Chem. Educ. **101**, 5142–5146 (2024)
19. Mohamed, M.S.P.: Exploring ethical dimensions of AI-enhanced language education: a literature perspective. Technol. Lang. Teach. Learn. **6**, 1813 (2024)
20. Khazanchi, R., Khazanchi, P.: Generative AI to improve special education teacher preparation for inclusive classrooms. Exploring new horizons: Generat. Artific. Intell. Teacher Educ. **159** (2024)
21. Lai, J.W.: Adapting self-regulated learning in an age of generative artificial intelligence chatbots. Future Internet **16**, 218 (2024)
22. Zou, Z.: Exploring the impact of using Chatbots on teacher-student relationships in today's higher education. J. Educ. Humanit. Soc. Sci. **45**, 33–39 (2024). https://doi.org/10.54097/0pev3z68

23. Feng, C., Botha, E., Pitt, L.: From HAL to GenAI: Optimize chatbot impacts with CARE. Business Horizons (2024)
24. Wood, D., Moss, S.H.: Evaluating the impact of students' generative AI use in educational contexts. J. Res. Innov. Teach. Learn. **17**, 152–167 (2024)
25. Huang, Y., et al.: A general multi-method approach to data-driven redesign of tutoring systems. In: LAK21: 11th International Learning Analytics and Knowledge Conference, pp. 161–172 (2021)
26. Lan, G., Feng, X., Du, S., Song, F., Xiao, Q.: Integrating ethical knowledge in generative AI education: constructing the GenAI-TPACK framework for university teachers' professional development. Educ. Inform. Technol. 1–24 (2025)
27. Francis, N.J., Jones, S., Smith, D.P.: Generative AI in higher education: balancing innovation and integrity. Br. J. Biomed. Sci. **81**, 14048 (2025)
28. Bozkurt, A., Sharma, R.C.: Trust, credibility and transparency in human-AI interaction: why we need explainable and trustworthy AI and why we need it now. Asian J. Dist. Educ. **19** (2024)
29. Rasul, T., et al.: Enhancing academic integrity among students in GenAI Era: a holistic framework. Int. J. Manage. Educ. **22**, 101041 (2024)
30. Chocarro, R., Cortiñas, M., Marcos-Matás, G.: Teachers' attitudes towards chatbots in education: a technology acceptance model approach considering the effect of social language, bot proactiveness, and users' characteristics. Educ. Stud. **49**, 295–313 (2021)
31. Zadorozhnyy, A., Lai, W.Y.W.: ChatGPT and L2 written communication: a game-changer or just another tool? Languages **9**(1), 5 (2023). https://doi.org/10.3390/languages9010005
32. Lee, S.S., Moore, R.: Harnessing generative AI (GenAI) for automated feedback in higher education: a systematic review. Online Learn. (2024)
33. Venkat, S.: Ethics of generative AI use in higher education: a focus group study (2024)
34. Olohunfunmi, I.A., Khairuddin, A.Z.: Exploring ethical dilemmas of AI generative tools among higher education students: a systematic review. In: International Conference on Innovation & Entrepreneurship in Computing, Engineering & Science Education (InvENT 2024), pp. 255–275. Atlantis Press (Year)
35. Yan, L., et al.: Practical and ethical challenges of large language models in education: a systematic scoping review. Br. J. Edu. Technol. **55**, 90–112 (2024)
36. Holmes, W., Zhgenti, S.: Exploring the ethics of generative AI, education, and democracy. J. Artific. Intell. Sustain. Dev. **1**, 1–9 (2024)
37. Luckyardi, S., Karin, J., Rosmaladewi, R., Hufad, A., Haristiani, N.: Chatbots as digital language tutors: revolutionizing education through AI. Indonesian J. Sci. Technol. (2024)
38. Kangwa, D., Msafiri, M.M., Fute, A.: Balancing innovation and ethics: promote academic integrity through support and effective use of GenAI tools in higher education. AI and Ethics 1–4 (2025)
39. Nguyen, H., Nguyen, V., Ludovise, S., Santagata, R.: Value-sensitive design of chatbots in environmental education: Supporting identity, connectedness, well-being and sustainability. British J. Educ. Technol. (2025)
40. Zawacki-Richter, O., Marín, V.I., Bond, M., Gouverneur, F.: Systematic review of research on artificial intelligence applications in higher education–where are the educators? Int. J. Educ. Technol. High. Educ. **16**, 1–27 (2019)
41. Bozkurt, A.: Unleashing the potential of generative AI, conversational agents and chatbots in educational praxis: A systematic review and bibliometric analysis of GenAI in education. vol. 15, pp. 261–270. International Council for Open and Distance Education Oslo, Norway (2023)
42. Hoernig, S., Ilharco, A., Pereira, P.T., Pereira, R.: Generative AI and Higher education: Challenges and opportunities. Institute of Public Policy (2024)

43. Hanip, A., Sarower, A.H., Bhuiyan, T.: The transformative role of generative AI in education: challenges and opportunities for enhancing student learning and assessment through mass integration. Int. J. Adv. Res. Eng. Technol. **15**, 161–175 (2024)
44. Holmes, W., et al.: Ethics of AI in education: towards a community-wide framework. Int. J. Artific. Intell. Educ. 1–23 (2022)
45. Chakraborty, S.: Generative AI in Modern Education Society. arXiv preprint arXiv:2412.08666 (2024)
46. Cordero, J., Torres-Zambrano, J., Cordero-Castillo, A.: Integration of generative artificial intelligence in higher education: best practices. Educ. Sci. **15**(1), 32 (2024). https://doi.org/10.3390/educsci15010032
47. González-González, C., Muñoz-Cruz, V., Toledo, P., Nacimiento-García, E.: Personalized Gamification for Learning: A Reactive Chatbot Architecture Proposal. Sensors (Basel, Switzerland) **23** (2023)
48. Nguyen, K.V.: The use of generative AI tools in higher education: ethical and pedagogical principles. J. Acad. Ethics (2025). https://doi.org/10.1007/s10805-025-09607-1
49. Cislowska, A., Peña-Acuña, B.: Integration of chatbots in additional language education: a systematic review. Europ. J. Educ. Res. **13**(4), 1607–1625 (2024). https://doi.org/10.12973/eu-jer.13.4.1607

Postgraduate Students' Perspective of Generative Artificial Intelligence for Learning

Komla Pillay(✉)

Department of Business Management, University of Johannesburg, Johannesburg, South Africa
komlap@uj.ac.za

Abstract. The paper presents a study that used the Unified Theory of Acceptance and Use of Technology (UTAUT) model to determine the postgraduate students' perception of AI in education. The six dimensions of performance expectancy, effort expectancy, social influence, facilitating conditions, attitude and anxiety were analysed. The interpretative study employed a mixed method approach. The questionnaire research instrument consisted of both quantitative and qualitative questions. With a sample of thirty postgraduate students, the study reveals that postgraduate students have a positive perception of using AI in education. Four of the six dimensions reflect a positive perception with two dimensions social influence and anxiety not being entirely positive. This study can assist in identifying strategies to help postgraduate students overcome their anxiety. Higher education institutions may consider the findings when formulating strategies for the incorporation of generative artificial intelligence into postgraduate teaching, research and assessment.

Keywords: Artificial intelligence in education · postgraduate students' perception of AI · Unified Theory of Acceptance and Use of Technology model

1 Introduction and Background

The rapid growth of Artificial Intelligence (AI) technology has prompted development and change in the processes and functioning within higher education. Academics and students have differing and mixed perceptions of the use of artificial intelligence in higher education. This research aims to determine what are the true perceptions of students toward artificial intelligence. The research question that this research aims to answer is "What is postgraduate students' perception of the role of AI in education?". The sub research question is "Do postgraduate students' accept the change that AI brings to Higher Education?". The study uses the Unified Theory of Acceptance and Use of Technology (UTAUT) model. This model examines the acceptance of technology. It considers factors such as performance expectancy, effort expectancy, social influence, and facilitating conditions to explain user intentions to use an information system and subsequent usage behaviour.

The Research Objectives of this study was to determine postgraduate students' perception of the role of AI in education and to determine if postgraduate students accept

W.-S. Wang et al. (Eds.): ICITL 2025, LNCS 15913, pp. 94–103, 2026.
https://doi.org/10.1007/978-3-031-98185-2_11

the change that AI brings to Higher Education. Students are familiar with many social AI platforms but lack full understanding of the educational AI abilities. AI supports learning and teaching and is only as effective as the student's willingness to use and challenge the different features [1].

There is still scope for students to learn how to interpret AI data and to foster critical thinking [2]. One study on students' perceptions of AI outline that better educational outcomes are achieved when AI based learning was co-created with the lecturers [3]. Other studies delved into the different student cohorts' perceptions of AI and what factors contributed to improved AI literacy [4].

There is still a gap in existing literature regarding how postgraduate students perceive AI. While the current literature provides insights into some important aspects of AI in higher education, many research gaps still exist. Literature is lacking in providing a comprehensive AI perspective in promoting superior postgraduate student outcomes.

This study seeks to fill in the gaps of AI in education by providing the perception of AI in postgraduate education to support the integration of AI into education and to promote positive AI learning experiences for postgraduate students.

The remaining sections of the paper are structured as follows: In Sect. 2, the relevant literature is discussed. This includes an overview of artificial intelligence in education and the Unified Theory of Acceptance and Use of Technology model. The research method is presented in Sect. 3. Detailed discussions on the perceptions of artificial education of postgraduate students are presented in Sect. 4. Section 5 concludes the paper.

2 Literature Review

2.1 Artificial Intelligence in Education

Artificial intelligence has a presence in the everyday lives of people, from reserving tickets to arranging appointments. The role that AI plays in education is transformative. AI technologies can accommodate different learning styles, identify individual student requirements or preferences and provide personalized educational mediations [1].

AI has transformed the educational environment by enabling personalized learning, automating educational administrative tasks and improving the overall impact on education [5].

AI in education are the different technologies that enable computers to perform human intelligent assignments like speech recognition, smart decision making, and problem solving. Generative AI is used by both students and lecturers to do assignments and other educational tasks [6]. Educational AI technologies improve teaching and learning, by facilitating personalised learning. AI is used to better manage the pace and structure of the content, and assessments, thereby better catering to student's needs [3, 7]. AI assists lecturers by automating their routine administrative tasks and marking, thereby enabling them to focus more on student engagement and critical thinking [8]. AI in education support the scaling of education to accommodate the worldwide growth in the student population [9]. The result is more students having access to AI assisted education, despite their location [9]. The students would have to have access to the correct technology to access this AI assisted education.

ChatGPT is a popular generative AI application. There has been research done on ChatGPT which highlights insights into usage, capabilities, regulatory and ethical concerns, user satisfaction and attitudes, academic issues and outcomes, skills development, labor market dynamics and skills mismatches, and emotional responses. Students use ChatGPT due to it being easy to use, they find it useful, enjoy the tool, and the tool has a social presence [10]. The use of ChatGPT aids in preparing assessments, translating documents, programming support, and improved scientific writing. ChatGPT fosters interactive problem-solving aimed at helping students break down complex problems. There is real-time feedback on grammar in multiple languages. ChatGPT also assists in synthesizing research ideas and arguments. ChatGPT debugs programming code. All these characteristics confirm the usefulness of ChatGPT in creating personalized learning spaces [11].

The capabilities of ChatGPT is broad and multipurpose. The higher education learning experience is enhanced as the tool communicates in natural language and in people's native language. ChatGPT supports critical thinking supporting blended learning while playing the roles of a peer and an examiner [12]. Universities are grappling with the challenges and opportunities posed by generative AI. The major areas of concern are policy formation, data privacy, and an over dependence on AI-generated content. Universities have implemented diverse approaches from outlining guidelines on how to use generative AI in assessments and some have issued a ban for all credit bearing submissions. Leading universities like Harvard and Cambridge have ongoing policies that are subject to continuous updates based on latest innovations. Universities are communicating to students what is acceptable use of generative AI and what constitutes academic misconduct. AI can blur the line between helping and complete authorship. Definition of plagiarism must be revisited. Concerns around students losing their critical thinking skills are being addressed by helping educators integrate AI ethically into teaching, while students are being taught how to critically evaluate and responsibly use AI tools.

Many higher education institutions have difficulty integrating AI so they have resorted to banning AI tools like ChatGPT for compiling research reports. There is the added privacy dimension of inputting collected data into the tool, this raises ethical concerns about who can access the input data. Most times, participants are assured that their privacy will always be maintained, using AI generative tools [13]. AI can reduce academic work, making academic tasks easier, but it may impact academic integrity [14].

2.2 Theoretical Framework

This study used the Unified Theory of Acceptance and Use of Technology (UTAUT) model to determine postgraduate students' acceptance of AI for their studies. The theoretical UTAUT model purports that the use of technology is determined by behavioural intention. The "perceived probability" of accepting new technology is dependent on the effect of four key constructs, namely performance expectancy, effort expectancy, social influence, and facilitating conditions. [15]. Each variable is explained below.

Performance expectancy is "the degree to which an individual believes that using the system will help him or her to attain gains in job performance" [15]. It is a solid predictor of the intention to use [16]. Effort expectancy is "the degree of ease associated with the use of the system" [15]. Social Influence is "the degree to which an individual perceives that important others believe he or she should use the new system" [15]. Social influence can be compared to subjective norms and social factors. Facilitating conditions is "the degree to which an individual believes that an organisation's and technical infrastructure exists to support the use of the system" [15].

The UTAUT model refers to anxiety as being in a negative emotional state when using new technology. The parameter was added to the UTAUT model to better understand the emotions involved when adopting new technology. This parameter is seen to negatively affect the behavioural intention to use technology. This parameter can also affect the individual's decision to adopt a particular technology. If anxiety is experienced, this may result in the technology not being adopted [15].

3 Method

The study employed a mixed method approach. The research instrument which is the questionnaire had both quantitative and qualitative questions. This approach supports the interpretative research paradigm.

This study took place in the South African higher education space among postgraduate students. Due to the research nature of postgraduate assessments, the postgraduate student sample is most relevant as AI tools are used for these types of assessments. The target sample was 20 and the sample could include current postgraduate students or already graduated postgraduate students. The final respondent number was 30. The sample was targeted using higher education networks on the WhatsApp private messaging platform. A link to the questionnaire was posted on several postgraduate student WhatsApp groups. Students were also encouraged to distribute the link via their private chats and personal networks.

The mixed methods questionnaire was designed according to the UTAUT model. The quantitative questions were designed to use the five-point Likert scale ranging from strongly agree to strongly disagree. The qualitative questions were open-ended questions. The questions according to each dimension of the model using the Likert scale (Strongly Agree; Agree; Neutral; Disagree; Strongly Disagree) were as follows:

Performance Expectancy

PE 1.1 AI technology is useful for teaching/learning.

PE 1.2 Using AI increases my productivity.

1.3 Describe how AI increases your productivity.

Effort Expectancy
EE 2.1 I understand how to use AI.
EE 2.2 It is easy for me to become skillful using AI.
2.3 Discuss what makes it easy/difficult for you to use AI.

Social Influence
SI 3.1 People who influence my behaviour think that I should use AI.
SI 3.2 I feel pressurized to use AI.

Facilitating Conditions
FC 4.1 I have the resources necessary to use AI.
FC 4.2 I have the knowledge necessary to use AI.
FC 4.3 AI is not compatible with the other systems I use.
4.4 What resources do you think you need to better use AI.

Attitude Toward Using Technology
ATT 5.1 Using AI is a good idea.
ATT 5.2 AI makes lecturer/student engagement more interesting.
5.3 What features of AI make engaging with students or lecturers interesting?

Anxiety
ANX 6.1 I feel apprehensive about using AI.
ANX 6.2 AI intimidates me.
ANX 6.3 I hesitate to use AI for fear of making mistakes I cannot correct.
5.4 Discuss, what about AI intimidates you. (if anything)

Behavioural Intention to Use The System
7.1 I intend to use AI in the next _____ months. (fill in the blank space)
7.2 Outline your future plan to incorporate AI into your life. (if you have any)

Data analysis included describing, organising, and compiling both the quantitative and qualitative data. The study used descriptive statistics and thematic analysis. The study contributes to academia by demonstrating postgraduate students' perceptions of using generative AI in their academic studies. Having this information will provide the foundation for future planning for postgraduate studies.

Ethical clearance was obtained from the Department of Business Management Ethics Committee at the University of Johannesburg. Consent to participate in the study was obtained from all respondents.

4 Results and Discussion

Figure 1 shows the responses to the quantitative Likert scale questions.

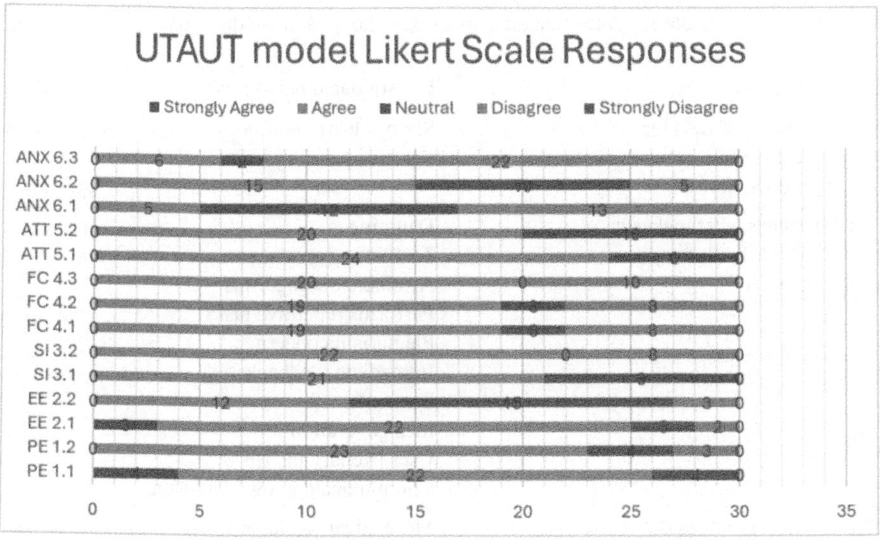

Fig. 1. Responses to the quantitative Likert scale questions

Qualitative Responses

Table 1 outlines the consolidated responses to the qualitative questions.

Performance Expectancy

There was a positive response for both scale questions highlighting the usefulness of AI for learning and increasing productivity. The students outlined that shorter learning time and creative learning as the reasons for increase in their productivity.

Effort Expectancy

Most respondents indicated that they understand how to use AI. More students were neutral about their ability to become skilful using AI. Students highlighted the factors that make it easy for them to use AI as: available on fingertips, performs repetitive tasks, immediate feedback, idea generation, user friendly interface and communicate in own language.

Respondents highlighted the factors that make it difficult for them to use: AI is daunting, too many new features, plagiarism concern and Untrustworthy potential misinformation, untested response accuracy, data quality issues, and ethical considerations.

Social Influence

Sixty percent of students are influenced by peers and forty percent of respondents are neutral about/are not influenced. Seventy three percent of respondents feel pressurized to use AI – this was the first "dimension" that received a negative response.

Table 1. Consolidated responses to the qualitative questions

No	Questions	Consolidated responses
1.3	Describe how AI in creases your productivity	Shorter learning time Creative learning
2.3	Discuss what makes it easy/difficult for you to use AI	Daunting Too many new features Available on fingertips Performs repetitive tasks Plagiarism concern Immediate feedback Un/trustworthy Idea generation User friendly interface Communicate in own language
4.4	What resources do You think you need to better use AI	More advanced laptop Later version of phone with larger memory Consistent data connection
5.3	What features of AI make engaging with students or lecturers in teresting?	Mark analytics Immediate feedback Track progress
6.4	Discuss, what about AI intimidates you. (if an ything)	It knows more than me What exactly is happening be hind the app Can do my job Who can see what query I typed
7.1	I intend to use AI in the next _____ months. (fill in the blank space)	All responses were not applica ble or blank
7.2	Outline your future plan to incurporate AI into your life. (if you have any)	If my job allows me, I want to do my work using AI Try to learn how to better request information from AI applications Learn how to request anonymously from AI applications Get better AI apps Get better AI devices

Facilitating Conditions

More than sixty percent of respondents have the necessary skills and resources to use AI or compatible systems. Approximately thirty percent of respondents do not have the necessary skills and knowledge, or their systems are not compatible with AI. Respondents require these resources to better use AI: more advanced laptop, later version of phone with larger memory, and consistent data connection.

Attitude Toward Using Technology

Up to eighty percent of respondents agree that using AI is a good idea and it makes student/lecturer engagement more interesting.

The features that make AI more interesting for students are mark analytics, immediate feedback and being able to track progress.

Anxiety

More than eighty percent of respondents are either neutral or feel apprehensive about using AI. More than eighty percent of respondents are either neutral or feel intimidated by AI. More than seventy percent of respondents do not hesitate to use AI for fear of making mistakes. Respondents outlined what intimidates them about AI: AI knows more than me, don't know what exactly is happening behind the application, AI can do my job, and who can see what query was typed.

Behavioural Intention to Use the System

All respondents indicated not applicable to the question asking them when they intend using AI, due to them already using AI. Respondents indicated the following as what they plan to incorporate AI into their lives: "if my job allows me, I want to do my work using AI"; "Try to learn how to better request information from AI applications"; "Learn how to request anonymously from AI applications"; "Get better AI apps"; "Get better AI devices."

The respondents demonstrate their behavioural intention to use the system by planning various tasks to incorporate AI into their lives.

Figure 2 illustrates the six dimensions influencing the postgraduate student's acceptance of AI. Four of the six dimensions reflect a positive perception. One question in the social influence domain reflects a mostly positive perception with the second question

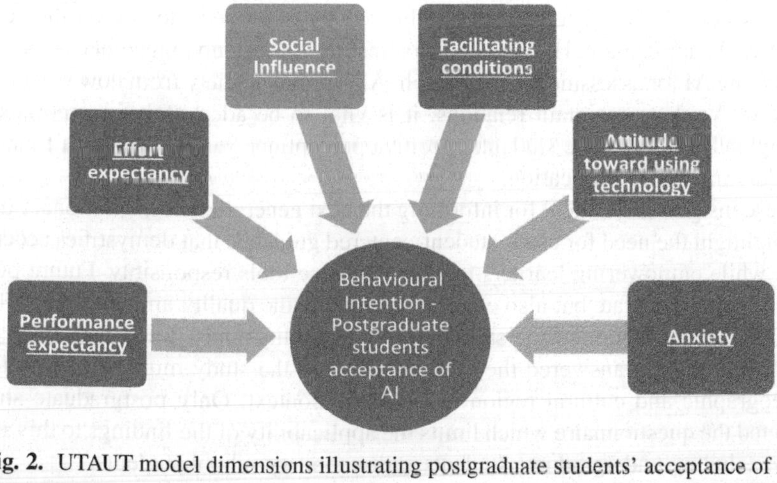

Fig. 2. UTAUT model dimensions illustrating postgraduate students' acceptance of AI

about feeling pressurized representing a negative perception. The anxiety dimension had two of the three Likert scale questions with a negative response. This is the dimension where work needs to be done to help postgraduate students overcome their anxiety.

The model illustrates that postgraduate students are likely to use AI for their postgraduate studies. The students would have to be trained about the regulations and ethics around the use of AI for postgraduate research purposes. If the postgraduate students expected performance and ease of use is met, then AI would become an integral part of their learning journey. Academia's use of AI generative tools has created debate around regulations and ethics. Most higher education institutions do not have policies that govern the if lack rules. The respondents demonstrated that AI could improve ease and comfort of learning, while also expressing concern over academic integrity.

Respondents have a positive attitude with AI in higher education. Generative AI enhances and speeds up research tasks, contributing to the satisfaction. Adopting new AI technologies in higher education elicits both positive and negative emotions in students. This speaks to the anxiety dimension. The respondents also indicated that they use AI to ease the academic burden. Educators need to be aware of the possible over reliance of AI and create assessments such that there is no dependency created. The positive perception of AI in postgraduate student learning will create an enabling environment to accommodate new assessment types and better research approaches.

5 Conclusion

This paper answered the research question of what the perceptions of artificial intelligence among postgraduate students are. To ensure the effective use of generative AI, students must embrace emerging technologies while being responsible and not becoming overly reliant. Some of the fears expressed by respondents were the fear of academic misconduct allegations. To overcome this, there should be proper guidance on what constitutes AI misuse from the institution's perspective. The academic institution must promote academic integrity and ethical use of AI in academia.

The respondents had a mostly positive response to generative AI but expressed some anxiety which can be systematically addressed by improved literacy on the selected generative AI application. Higher education institutions can no longer take the stance of not allowing AI for assessments or research. AI is part of society from how we socialize, to how we work or maintain relations, it is vital to be adequately incorporated into teaching and learning. The students' positive perceptions can be used as a foundation for integrating AI into education.

These insights are critical for informing the next generation of institutional policies. They highlight the need for clear, student-centered guidance that demystifies acceptable AI use while empowering learners to leverage these tools responsibly. Future policies should not only regulate but also educate and enable the quality and integrity of higher education. The limitation of the study is generalizability. Only thirty participants from one African country answered the questionnaire, so the study must be interpreted for that geographic and cultural region and cultural context. Only postgraduate students completed the questionnaire which limits the applicability of the findings to this student group, excluding undergraduate students and secondary school students.

References

1. Marrone, R., Zamecnik, A., Joksimovic, S., Johnson, J., Laat, M.: Understanding student perceptions of artificial intelligence as a teammate. Tech. Know. Learn. (2024). https://doi.org/10.1007/s10758-024-09780-z
2. Walter, Y.: Embracing the future of Artifcial Intelligence in the classroom: the relevance of AI literacy, prompt engineering, and critical thinking in modern education. Int. J. Educ. Technol. High. Educ. **21**(1), 15 (2024)
3. Chiu, T.K.: A holistic approach to the design of artifcial intelligence (AI) education for K-12 schools. TechTrends **65**(5), 796–807 (2021)
4. Dai, Y., Chai, C.-S., Lin, P.-Y., Jong, M.S.-Y., Guo, Y., Qin, J.: Promoting students' well-being by developing their readiness for the artificial intelligence age. Sustainability **12**(16), 6597 (2020)
5. Zawacki-Richter, O., Marín, V.I., Bond, M., Gouverneur, F.: Systematic review of research on artificial intelligence applications in higher education – where are the educators? Int. J. Educ. Technol. High. Educ. (2019). https://doi.org/10.1186/s41239-019-0171-0
6. Baidoo-anu, D., Owusu Ansah, L.: Education in the era of generative artificial intelligence (AI): understanding the potential benefits of ChatGPT in promoting teaching and learning. J. AI **7**(1), 52–62 (2023). https://doi.org/10.61969/jai.1337500
7. Dilmurod, R., Fazliddin, A.: Prospects for the introduction of artifcial intelligence technologies in higher education. ACADEMICIA: An Int. Multidisc. Res. J. **11**(2), 929–934 (2021)
8. Seo, K., Tang, J., Roll, I., Fels, S., Yoon, D.: The impact of artifcial intelligence on learner–instructor interaction in online learning. Int. J. Educ. Technol. High. Educ. **18**, 1–23 (2021)
9. Alam, A.: Possibilities and apprehensions in the landscape of artifcial intelligence in education. In: 2021 International Conference on Computational Intelligence and Computing Applications (ICCICA), pp. 1–8. IEEE (2021)
10. Tiwari, C.K., Bhat, M.A., Khan, S.T., Subramaniam, R., Khan, M.A.: What drives students toward ChatGPT? An investigation of the factors influencing adoption and usage of ChatGPT. Interact. Technol. Smart Educ. **21**(3), 333–355 (2023). https://doi.org/10.1108/ITSE-04-2023-0061
11. Kamalov, F., Calonge, D.S., Gurrib, I.: New era of artificial intelligence in education: towards a sustainable multifaceted revolution. Sustainability **15**(16), 12451 (2023). https://doi.org/10.3390/su151612451
12. Gill, S.S., Xu, M., Patros, P., Wu, H., Kaur, R., Kaur, K.: Transformative effects of ChatGPT on modern education: emerging era of AI Chatbots. Internet Things Cyber-phys. Syst. **4**, 19–23 (2024). https://doi.org/10.1016/j.iotcps.2023.06.002
13. Vij, O., Calver, H., Myall, N., Dey, M., Kouranloo, K.: Evaluating the competency of ChatGPT in MRCP Part 1 and a systematic literature review of its capabilities in postgraduate medical assessments. PLOS ONE **19**(7), e0307372 (2024). https://doi.org/10.1371/journal.pone.0307372
14. Kar, S.K., Bansal, T., Modi, S., Singh, A.: How sensitive are the free AI-detector tools in detecting AI-generated texts? A comparison of popular AI-detector tools. Indian J. Psychol. Med. **47**(3), 275–278 (2024). https://doi.org/10.1177/02537176241247934
15. Venkatesh, V., Morris, M.G., Davis, G.B., Davis, F.D.: User acceptance of information technology: toward a unified view. MIS Q. **27**(3), 425 (2003). https://doi.org/10.2307/30036540
16. Venkatesh, V., Zhang, X.: Unified theory of acceptance and use of technology: U.S. vs. China. J. Global Inform. Technol. Manage. **13**(1), 5–27 (2010)

The Impact of AI-Generated and Non-AI-Generated Images on Learning Outcomes and Attitudes: A Case Study of Visual Narrative in Elementary School English Curriculum

Yung-Shen Huang, Chin-Feng Lai, and Shih-Yeh Chen(✉)

Department of Engineering Science, National Cheng Kung University,
Tainan, Taiwan, R.O.C.
sychen-ncku@gs.ncku.edu.tw

Abstract. This study aims to investigate the impact of Generative Artificial Intelligence (GAI) images and non-GAI images applied in visual narrative-based instructional materials on elementary school students' learning outcomes and learning attitudes. A quasi-experimental design was employed, involving 60 s-grade students from an elementary school in Kaohsiung, Taiwan. The students were randomly assigned to either an experimental group, which used GAI-generated images, or a control group, which used traditionally hand-drawn images for English vocabulary instruction. Both groups were taught by the same teacher using identical content and instructional procedures to eliminate possible confounders. After the lessons, a learning outcomes post-test and a learning attitude questionnaire were administered. The results did not show significant differences in learning outcomes between the two groups. However, the experimental group demonstrated a slightly more favorable trend in several questionnaire items related to learning attitude, suggesting that GAI-generated images may have the potential to enhance student engagement and motivation. In general, GAI technology can reduce the time and cost required for the development of teaching material without negatively affecting learning performance, promote diverse instructional resources, and contribute to the vision of sustainable education.

Keywords: Visual Narrative · Generative Artificial Intelligence · Learning Outcomes · Learning Attitudes

1 Introduction

Visual narrative refers to the use of visual media, such as images, illustrations, murals, or picture books, to convey information and tell stories [1]. It is characterized by its intuitive and cross-cultural nature, allowing people from different linguistic and cultural backgrounds to achieve shared understanding and emotional resonance without relying heavily on textual explanations. In the field of education, integrating visual narratives into

W.-S. Wang et al. (Eds.): ICITL 2025, LNCS 15913, pp. 104–110, 2026.
https://doi.org/10.1007/978-3-031-98185-2_12

digital learning materials has been shown to effectively transform abstract textual content into concrete representations, thereby enhancing students' comprehension, engagement, and motivation in learning [2–6].

With the rise of generative artificial intelligence (GAI), the creation of visual narrative materials has gradually shifted from traditional hand-drawn methods to AI-generated imagery, making the production process more efficient and accessible [7–10]. Multiple studies have utilized GAI, such as latent diffusion models, to generate coherent sequences of story images, showcasing the potential of such technologies in educational material development [11–13]. However, there remains a lack of empirical evidence in educational practice to determine whether GAI-generated images differ significantly from non-GAI images in terms of their impact on students' learning outcomes and attitudes. More research is needed to clarify this issue [14].

Therefore, this study aims to investigate the differences in learning outcomes and attitudes between students exposed to GAI-generated and non-GAI generated visual narrative materials. Specifically, the study applies GAI techniques to convert English vocabulary into visually engaging illustrations and adopts a quasi-experimental design to compare students' performance and attitudes between the two groups. The findings are expected to validate the educational value of GAI-generated visuals and provide practical insights for the future design and development of visual narrative-based teaching materials.

2 Research Method

This study aims to examine the impact of GAI-generated images used in visual narrative materials on students' learning outcomes and attitudes. A quasi-experimental design was adopted, involving 60 s-grade students from an elementary school in Kaohsiung, Taiwan. Participants were randomly assigned to an experimental group or a control group, with 30 students in each group. The experimental group received instructional materials incorporating GAI-generated images, while the control group used materials with non-GAI-generated images. To ensure group equivalence in English proficiency, a prior knowledge pretest was administered before the intervention. After completing the lessons, students were assessed through a post-test measuring learning outcomes and a questionnaire evaluating learning attitudes to determine whether the type of instructional material influenced student outcomes. The experimental procedure is illustrated in Fig. 1.

During the instructional process, both groups of students were taught by the same teacher using identical curriculum content and instructional strategies, with the only difference being the method by which the instructional images were generated. This consistency was maintained to minimize the influence of extraneous variables. The teacher adopted a visual narrative approach, using images to reinforce students' understanding and memory of vocabulary, as illustrated in Fig. 2. After the course, a post-test and a learning attitude questionnaire were administered to both groups. The post-test aimed to assess the students' comprehension of the language content and their ability to apply the visual narrative-based learning approach. The learning attitude questionnaire, adapted from Alderbashi, consisted of 17 items designed to evaluate students' attitudes toward digital storytelling in the classroom [15]. It used a five-point Likert scale ranging from "*strongly disagree*" (1) to "*strongly agree*" (5), quantifying the agreement of the students with various attitude indicators. All data were collected to record in numerical form and analyzed using independent samples t-tests to compare the mean scores between the two groups. The analysis aimed to determine whether the image generation method had a statistically significant effect on the learning outcomes and attitudes of students, thus providing information on the educational potential and limitations of applying GAI technology in the classroom.

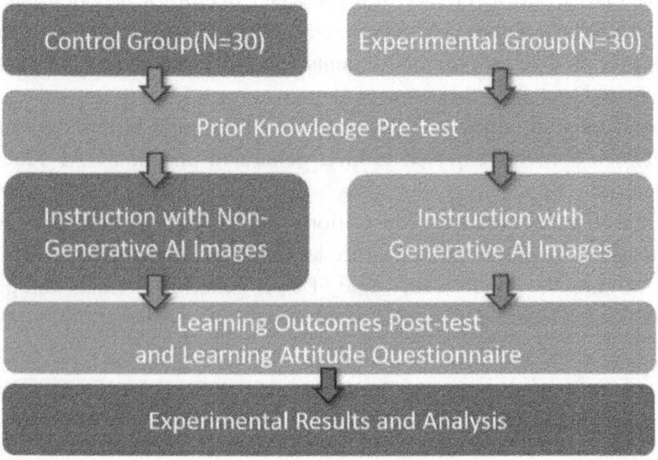

Fig. 1. Research experiment flow chart.

Fig. 2. Teacher using visual narrative strategy in English instruction.

3 Results

3.1 Prior Knowledge Pre-Test

According to the analysis results presented in Table 1, the average pre-test score of prior knowledge for the control group was 74.13 with a standard deviation of 13.441, while the experimental group scored an average of 71.73 with a standard deviation of 15.963. The independent sample t-test yielded a *t*-value of 0.630 and a *p*-value of 0.531, indicating that there was no significant difference between the two groups in terms of prior knowledge. This suggests that the baseline abilities of the two groups were homogeneous, providing a reasonable basis for subsequent comparisons of the impact of GAI-based instructional materials on learning outcomes.

Table 1. Prior knowledge pre-test scores.

	Control group		Experimental group		*t*	*p*
Pre-test	*M*	*SD*	*M*	*SD*	.630	.531
	74.13	13.441	71.73	15.963		

$p > .05$.

3.2 Learning Outcomes Post-Test

As shown in Table 2, the average score in the learning outcomes post-test for the control group was 81.87 with a standard deviation of 11.779, while the experimental group scored an average of 77.20 with a standard deviation of 13.449. The independent sample t-test yielded a *t*-value of 1.427 and a *p*-value of 0.159, indicating that there was no statistically significant difference in learning outcomes between students who received instruction with GAI-generated images and those who used traditional materials. However, this result does not suggest that GAI technology lacks educational value. In contrast, GAI has the potential to significantly reduce the cost and time associated with the production of instructional materials, allowing teachers to create diverse and engaging content more efficiently, contributing to the goals of sustainable education.

Table 2. Learning outcomes post-test scores.

	Control group		Experimental group		*t*	*P*
Post-test	*M*	*SD*	*M*	*SD*	1.427	.159
	81.87	11.779	77.20	13.449		

$p > .05$.

3.3 Learning Attitude Questionnaire

According to the results in Table 3, the differences in mean scores between the control and experimental groups across the 17 items of the learning attitude questionnaire were relatively small, ranging from 0.03 to 0.33. All *p*-values were greater than 0.05, indicating that there were no statistically significant differences in learning attitudes between students who used GAI-generated images and those who used traditionally produced materials. This suggests a high degree of consistency in how both groups perceived and responded to the instructional materials. The findings imply that the method of image generation may not be sufficient to influence learning attitudes in the short term, which are generally considered stable psychological constructs.

Table 3. Learning attitude analysis table.

	Mean		*SD*		*t*	*p*
	CG	EG	CG	EG		
1	4.07	4.23	0.691	0.679	−.942	.350
2	4.40	4.50	0.498	0.572	−.722	.473
3	4.70	4.77	0.702	0.430	−443	.659
4	4.80	4.87	0.407	0.346	−.684	.497
5	4.90	4.87	0.305	0.342	−.396	.694
6	3.60	3.77	0.621	0.626	−1.035	.305
7	4.47	4.50	0.629	0.572	−.215	.831
8	4.53	4.37	0.507	0.615	1.145	.257
9	1.87	1.80	0.507	0.407	.561	.577
10	4.40	4.60	0.498	0.498	−1.555	.125
11	4.07	4.23	0.828	0.679	−.853	.397
12	4.17	4.47	0.648	0.629	−1.820	.074
13	4.17	4.20	0.747	0.664	−183	.856
14	3.20	3.53	0.847	0.900	−1.478	.145
15	4.27	4.33	0.640	0.479	−.457	.650
16	3.37	3.60	0.809	0.621	−1.253	.215
17	4.73	4.77	0.450	0.430	−2.93	.770

$p > .05$.

However, although the overall results were not statistically significant, several items showed slightly higher mean scores in the experimental group. This may imply that GAI-based materials have the potential to enhance students' creativity and motivation. This trend aligns with the appealing and interactive nature of GAI-generated content, though the current data set was not large enough to produce statistically significant results. Future studies could further explore this phenomenon by increasing the sample size or extending the intervention period.

Since learning attitude is a multidimensional construct, its changes may require long-term observation to become statistically evident. Therefore, the short-term nature of this study may have limited the full impact of GAI-generated visuals on students' interest and engagement. It is recommended that future research incorporate qualitative methods, such as interviews or classroom observations, to gain deeper insights into students' perceptions of the materials and.

4 Conclusions

This study examined the effects of instructional materials created with GAI generated images and non-GAI-generated images on students' learning outcomes and learning attitudes. The results indicated that the two types of image-based materials did not lead to significant differences in learning outcomes and learning attitudes, and neither had a negative impact on students. In particular, in several items of the learning attitude questionnaire, students using GAI-based materials scored consistently higher than those using traditional materials, and some items were close to statistical significance. These findings suggest that GAI-generated materials may offer potential advantages in improving student' learning attitudes. GAI has the potential to become a valuable tool for improving instructional quality and enriching the student learning experience, offering new possibilities for the future transformation of educational practices.

Acknowledgments. This study was supported by the National Science and Technology Council, Taiwan, under grant NSTC113-2410-H-006-130-MY2.

Disclosure of Interests. The authors declare that they have no competing financial interests or personal relationships that might have influenced their work.

References

1. Antony, V.N., Huang, C.M.: Id. 8: co-creating visual stories with generative ai. ACM Transactions on Interactive Intelligent Systems **14**(3), 1–29 (2024)
2. Beck, T., Giese, S., Khoo, T.K.: Visual art and medical narratives as universal connectors in health communication: an exploratory study. Journal of Health Communication 1–8 (2025)
3. Calvert, J., Hume, M.: Immersing learners in stories: a systematic literature review of educational narratives in virtual reality. Australas. J. Educ. Technol. **38**(5), 45–61 (2022)
4. Cohn, N.: Your brain on comics: a cognitive model of visual narrative comprehension. Top. Cogn. Sci. **12**(1), 352–386 (2020)
5. Huynh, E., Nyhout, A., Ganea, P., Chevalier, F.: Designing narrative focused role-playing games for visualization literacy in young children. IEEE Trans. Visual Comput. Graphics **27**(2), 924–934 (2020)
6. Jarrah, H., et al.: The impact of storytelling and narrative variables on skill acquisition in gamified learning. Int. J. Data and Netw. Sci. **8**(2), 1161–1168 (2024)

7. Arif, S., et al.: The art of storytelling: Multi-agent generative ai for dynamic multimodal narratives (2024). arXiv preprint arXiv:2409.11261
8. Dhagare, M.R.P.: Generative ai and education: a symbiotic relationship. Int. J. Res. Appl. Sci. Eng. Technol. **12**(11), 1042–1045 (2024)
9. Liu, Y., Awang, H., Mansor, N.S.: To explore sora's potential influence on future education. Educational Research (IJMCER) **6**(5), 98–105 (2024)
10. Pellas, N.: The impact of ai-generated instructional videos on problem based learning in science teacher education. Education Sciences **15**(1), 102 (2025)
11. Maharana, A., Bansal, M.: Integrating visuospatial, linguistic and commonsense structure into story visualization (2021). arXiv preprint arXiv:2110.10834
12. Mittal, U., Sai, S., Chamola, V.: A comprehensive review on generative ai for education. Ieee Access **12**, 142733–142759 (2024). https://doi.org/10.1109/ACCESS.2024.3468368
13. Zhu, Z., Tang, J.: Cogcartoon: towards practical story visualization. Int. J. Comp. Vision 1–26 (2024)
14. Han, A., Cai, Z.: Design implications of generative ai systems for visual storytelling for young learners. In: Proceedings of the 22nd Annual ACM Interaction Design and Children Conference, pp. 470–474 (2023)
15. Alderbashi, K.: Attitudes of primary school students in uae towards using digital story-telling as a learning method in classroom. Res. Humanit. Soc. Sci. **11**(10), 20–28 (2021)

From Technology Acceptance to Teaching Practice: Exploring Pre-service Teachers' User Typologies and Training Needs in ChatGPT Adoption

Pei-Hua Chen[1], Lisbet Rønningsbakk[2], and Yueh-Min Huang[1](✉)

[1] Department of Engineering Science, National Cheng Kung University, Tainan City, Taiwan
huang@mail.ncku.edu.tw

[2] Department of Education, UiT The Arctic University of Norway, Tromsø, Norway
lisbet.ronningsbakk@uit.no

Abstract. This pilot study explores pre-service teachers' acceptance, usage patterns, and training needs regarding ChatGPT in teaching. Integrating constructs from TAM and UTAUT, a survey with 47 university students identified four user typologies to inform differentiated training strategies. Results show that 97.87% had used generative AI tools, with 57.45% applying ChatGPT to teaching tasks. K-means cluster analysis identified Innovators (20%), Pragmatists (42%), Cautious Evaluators (28%), and Resistors (10%), each differing in perceived usefulness, ease of use, and adoption intention. STEM-background participants were more likely to be Innovators or Pragmatists, while non-STEM participants tended to be Cautious Evaluators. The study proposes training strategies tailored to each user type, laying a foundation for future AI-integrated teacher education programs.

Keywords: ChatGPT · Generative AI in Education · Pre-service Teachers · TAM · Teacher Training Strategies · UTAUT

1 Introduction

Generative AI technologies—particularly large language models such as ChatGPT—are rapidly gaining traction in the field of education. Across various levels of schooling, educators and institutions are increasingly exploring how these tools can enhance instructional design, support teaching tasks, and personalize student learning [1]. As ChatGPT becomes more prevalent, teacher education programs are under growing pressure to prepare pre-service teachers with the competencies needed to integrate AI meaningfully into their future classrooms. Although many pre-service teachers express a cautiously optimistic view toward ChatGPT, existing research suggests that uncertainty remains regarding how to apply such tools effectively within pedagogical practice [2].

Current studies have approached teachers' adoption of ChatGPT mainly from two theoretical perspectives: the Technology Acceptance Model (TAM), which emphasizes perceived usefulness and ease of use, and the Unified Theory of Acceptance and Use of

W.-S. Wang et al. (Eds.): ICITL 2025, LNCS 15913, pp. 111–120, 2026.
https://doi.org/10.1007/978-3-031-98185-2_13

Technology (UTAUT), which highlights external factors such as performance expectancy and social influence [3]. While these frameworks have identified key influencing factors, several research gaps remain: insufficient focus on pre-service teachers as a distinct group; the tendency to treat them as a homogeneous population; and limitations in using single-theory approaches to fully explain the complex decision-making process involved in adopting new technologies.

This pilot study adopts a mixed-methods approach that integrates key constructs from TAM and UTAUT, while also introducing a user typology perspective to explore pre-service teachers' views and acceptance of ChatGPT in educational contexts. The aim is to preliminarily identify the characteristics, needs, and challenges of different user types, and to propose differentiated training strategies, thereby laying the groundwork for future large-scale studies. Specifically, this study addresses the following three research questions:

1. What are the potential key factors influencing pre-service teachers' adoption of ChatGPT?
2. How can pre-service teachers be preliminarily categorized based on their usage patterns?
3. What differentiated training strategies may be appropriate for different user types?

2 Related Work

2.1 Applications of ChatGPT in Education

Generative AI—particularly large language models like ChatGPT—is playing an increasingly prominent role in education. Teachers can use ChatGPT to design course syllabi, generate instructional materials, and develop assessment tools, thereby improving lesson preparation efficiency and reducing administrative workload. In classroom settings, ChatGPT can provide real-time answers to student questions, generate discussion scenarios, and simulate instructional contexts, enhancing teacher-student interaction [4]. For students, ChatGPT offers conceptual explanations, personalized practice, and writing feedback, which strengthens learning support. In assessment, it can generate quiz items and offer instant feedback, thus improving learning outcomes [5].

As applications expand, ChatGPT's impact on the teacher's role has attracted attention. While educational technologies have long been shifting the educator's role from knowledge transmitters to learning designers and facilitators, generative AI is accelerating this transformation. AI extends this evolution by demanding stronger self-regulated learning skills from students and requiring teachers to become AI collaborators and critical thinking facilitators. Although previous technologies have expanded human capabilities in educational contexts, AI's unprecedented power intensifies the need for teacher role redefinition and enhanced competencies in technology evaluation and ethical reflection. However, several challenges persist in implementation. [6] pointed out that most teacher education programs have not yet systematically incorporated AI literacy, leading to uncertainty among pre-service teachers about meaningfully applying generative AI while preserving core educational values. Their findings revealed that many pre-service teachers have only a superficial understanding of ChatGPT, with limited hands-on experience, and highly polarized attitudes—highlighting the urgent need to address diverse patterns of technology adoption among future educators.

2.2 Theoretical Models for Pre-service Teachers' Adoption of Educational Technology

Research on pre-service teachers' acceptance of educational technology has primarily drawn on two key theoretical frameworks: the Technology Acceptance Model (TAM) and the Unified Theory of Acceptance and Use of Technology (UTAUT). TAM, introduced by [7], identifies perceived usefulness and perceived ease of use as the main factors influencing technology adoption. UTAUT, proposed by [8], expands this model by incorporating performance expectancy, effort expectancy, social influence, and facilitating conditions. Recent studies have applied these frameworks to examine teachers' use of generative AI tools such as ChatGPT. Existing research has shown that, beyond perceived usefulness, factors such as perceived risk, performance expectancy, and social influence also play important roles in shaping teachers' acceptance of ChatGPT [9].

Despite growing interest in ChatGPT integration, current research on pre-service teachers' adoption of generative AI still faces several key limitations. First, most studies rely on a single theoretical framework to explain complex adoption behavior, without proposing an integrated explanatory model. Second, there is a lack of research specifically focused on pre-service teachers, even though their professional identity may shape how they perceive and engage with AI tools. Third, existing AI training programs tend to treat pre-service teachers as a uniform group, overlooking differences in technology readiness and learning needs. While some scholars have emphasized the need for user typologies to guide differentiated training strategies, empirical studies in this area remain scarce [10].

3 Methodology

3.1 Research Design

This pilot study employed a quantitative survey approach to explore pre-service teachers' acceptance and adoption behaviors related to ChatGPT. The questionnaire integrated core constructs from TAM and UTAUT, collecting data on students' perceptions, acceptance levels, and willingness to use ChatGPT through both quantitative items and open-ended questions. As a pilot study, the primary goal was to capture early trends and lay a foundation for future large-scale research.

The study employed exploratory data analysis techniques including descriptive statistics, correlation analyses to examine relationships among perceived usefulness, perceived ease of use, and adoption intention, and K-means cluster analysis to identify potential user types. Responses to open-ended questions enriched the quantitative findings with additional insights into the characteristics of each user type.

3.2 Participants

The participants of this pilot study were university students, primarily from undergraduate and graduate teacher education programs. Participants were recruited through convenience sampling using departmental email lists and voluntary sign-ups during course sessions. A total of 47 valid responses were collected through the questionnaire. The participants' demographic information is summarized in Table 1. In terms of gender distribution, 11 participants (23.4%) identified as male, while 36 participants (76.6%) identified as female. Regarding academic background, 21 participants (44.7%) were from STEM fields (science, technology, engineering, and mathematics), while 26 participants (55.3%) were from non-STEM disciplines.

Table 1. Demographic Information

Characteristic	*n*	%
Male	11	23.4%
Female	36	76.6%
Major		
STEM	21	44.7%
Non-STEM	26	55.3%
Have you ever used generative AI technologies like ChatGPT?		
Never	1	2.13%
Rarely	8	17.02%
Sometimes	8	17.02%
Often	21	44.68%
Always	9	19.15%
Have you used ChatGPT for teaching-related tasks?		
Yes	27	57.45%
No	20	42.55%

Regarding experience with generative AI tools such as ChatGPT, the vast majority of respondents (97.87%) reported having used such tools, with only one individual (2.13%) indicating no prior use. The frequency of use was distributed as follows: "often" (44.68%), "always" (19.15%), "sometimes" (17.02%), and "rarely" (17.02%).

A total of 57.45% of participants reported having applied ChatGPT to teaching-related tasks, while 42.55% had not yet done so.

3.3 Research Instrument

This study adopted a revised quantitative questionnaire based on the original Technology Acceptance Model (TAM) scale developed by [7] and the Unified Theory of

Acceptance and Use of Technology (UTAUT) scale proposed by [8]. The instrument was further adapted following Islamoglu, Kabakci Yurdakul and Ursavas [9], who developed a mobile learning acceptance scale for pre-service teachers, which informed the refinement of technology acceptance constructs used in this study.

The questionnaire consisted of three main sections. The first section gathered demographic information, including gender, academic year, field of study, and prior experience with ChatGPT. The second section measured the core constructs of TAM and UTAUT, such as perceived usefulness/performance expectancy (e.g., "I believe ChatGPT can help improve my teaching efficiency"), perceived ease of use/effort expectancy (e.g., "I find ChatGPT's interface user-friendly and easy to navigate"), and overall acceptance (e.g., "If given the opportunity, I would continue to use ChatGPT"). All items were rated using a 5-point Likert scale ranging from 1 ("strongly disagree") to 5 ("strongly agree"). The third section assessed the use of ChatGPT in specific teaching scenarios as well as ethical concerns. Items in this section included instructional use cases (e.g., syllabus generation, providing feedback) and potential concerns (e.g., overreliance, impact on critical thinking abilities).

The reliability of the scale was confirmed through internal consistency testing, with Cronbach's alpha coefficients for each subscale ranging from 0.78 to 0.85, indicating acceptable reliability. By utilizing and adapting established scales, the study enhanced the validity of the instrument and ensured comparability with prior research findings.

3.4 Data Analysis

The quantitative data analysis in this study employed basic statistical techniques, with an emphasis on exploratory rather than confirmatory hypothesis testing. First, descriptive statistics were used to present the distribution of each variable. Second, simple correlation analyses were conducted to preliminarily examine the relationships among key variables, with particular attention given to the core constructs of TAM—perceived usefulness, perceived ease of use—and their associations with behavioral intention.

To identify potential user types, this study utilized K-means cluster analysis. Cluster solutions ranging from 2 to 5 were tested, and the most appropriate classification was selected based on the interpretability of cluster characteristics. Given the limited sample size, the clustering results were considered exploratory and served primarily to generate initial hypotheses about possible user typologies. In addition, the study examined differences in key variables based on participants' academic background (e.g., STEM vs. non-STEM), in order to gain a preliminary understanding of how background factors might influence acceptance of AI. Responses to open-ended questions were analyzed using simple content analysis, which served to supplement and contextualize the findings from the cluster analysis. As a pilot study, the interpretation of results focused more on practical significance and conceptual insight rather than on statistical significance.

4 Results

To acknowledge the limitations of this pilot study, it is important to note that with a sample size of 47 participants, the statistical methods employed can only suggest preliminary findings rather than establish definitive conclusions. Results should be interpreted with appropriate caution, as patterns identified through cluster analysis and correlations are exploratory in nature. Nevertheless, this pilot study serves a valuable purpose in providing important background for developing more specific hypotheses and research questions for future large-scale studies. The preliminary typologies and factors identified here offer a foundation upon which more robust investigations can build, ultimately contributing to a more comprehensive understanding of pre-service teachers' adoption of AI technologies in educational contexts.

4.1 Current Use of ChatGPT Among Students

The questionnaire results indicated that the vast majority of respondents (97.87%) had used generative AI tools, with only one participant having no prior experience. In terms of usage frequency, 9 participants (19.15%) reported "always" using ChatGPT, 21 (44.68%) "often," 8 (17.02%) "sometimes," and 8 (17.02%) "rarely." These findings suggest that generative AI tools are already widespread among students, though the intensity of use varies.

With regard to teaching-related applications, 27 participants (57.45%) had used ChatGPT for instructional purposes, while 20 (42.55%) had not. Among those who had used ChatGPT in teaching contexts, the most frequently reported tasks included content summarization (64%), syllabus generation (56%), and instructional content creation (51%), followed by test item generation (49%) and feedback provision (27%).

4.2 Key Factors Influencing Pre-service Teachers' Adoption of ChatGPT

Preliminary quantitative analysis revealed that multiple factors influence pre-service teachers' adoption of ChatGPT. Descriptive statistics for each construct are presented in Table 2. Regarding the TAM construct of perceived usefulness (aligned with UTAUT's performance expectancy), the item "I believe ChatGPT can improve my teaching efficiency/effectiveness" (PU2) had a mean score of 4.32 ($SD = 0.726$), while "I believe ChatGPT is useful in teaching" (PU3) had a mean of 4.17 ($SD = 0.816$), indicating a generally positive perception of ChatGPT's instructional value.

In terms of perceived ease of use (aligned with UTAUT's effort expectancy), "I find ChatGPT's interface user-friendly and easy to operate" (PEU1) had the highest mean score of 4.34 ($SD = 0.731$), and "I can easily learn how to use ChatGPT for teaching activities" (PEU2) scored 4.23 ($SD = 0.758$), suggesting that most respondents found the tool intuitive. However, the item "I rarely encounter technical problems when using ChatGPT" (PEU3) had a lower average score of 3.00 ($SD = 0.692$), indicating concerns about technical reliability.

Regarding behavioral intention, "If given the opportunity, I would continue using ChatGPT" (BI1) received the highest score ($M = 4.43$, $SD = 0.715$), but items reflecting deeper integration—such as "I plan to incorporate ChatGPT more into my future teaching" (BI2, $M = 3.45$, $SD = 1.23$), "Even without external requirements, I would proactively use ChatGPT for lesson planning or instructional design" (BI3, $M = 3.68$, $SD = 1.04$), and "I am willing to invest time and effort to learn how to use ChatGPT more effectively for teaching" (BI4, $M = 3.47$, $SD = 1.16$)—showed lower means and greater variability, suggesting notable individual differences in long-term adoption intention.

Correlation analysis revealed that perceived usefulness was strongly correlated with behavioral intention ($r = 0.68$, $p < 0.01$), supporting the TAM framework's prediction that utility perceptions significantly influence adoption decisions. Perceived ease of use was moderately correlated with behavioral intention ($r = 0.51$, $p < 0.01$), indicating that usability also matters, though to a lesser extent than perceived value.

Additionally, concerns about the ethical implications of ChatGPT were notable. Respondents expressed worries about overreliance (78%), loss of independent thinking (62%), diminished creativity (42%), and reduced critical thinking (42%). These concerns go beyond the scope of traditional TAM constructs, suggesting that, in educational contexts, adoption decisions are influenced not only by practical utility but also by broader educational values.

Table 2. Descriptive Statistics of Acceptance Dimensions for ChatGPT in Teaching Contexts

Dimension	Item Code	Statement	*Mean*	*SD*
Attitude	AT1	I am satisfied with the functions and features of ChatGPT	4.00	0.780
	AT2	Before using ChatGPT, I had a positive expectation of it	4.09	0.855
	AT3	I am satisfied with my overall experience using ChatGPT	4.04	0.779
Perceived Usefulness	PU1	I believe ChatGPT can help me solve instructional problems	4.13	0.875
	PU2	I believe ChatGPT can improve my teaching efficiency/effectiveness	4.32	0.726
	PU3	I believe ChatGPT is useful in teaching	4.17	0.816
	PU4	Using ChatGPT enhances my instructional effectiveness/efficiency	4.04	0.932
Perceived Ease of Use	PEU1	I find ChatGPT's interface user-friendly and easy to operate	4.34	0.731
	PEU2	I can easily learn how to use ChatGPT for teaching activities	4.23	0.758
	PEU3	I rarely encounter technical problems when using ChatGPT	3.00	0.692
Behavioral Intention	BI1	If given the opportunity, I would continue using ChatGPT	4.43	0.715
	BI2	I plan to incorporate ChatGPT more into my future teaching activities	3.45	1.230
	BI3	Even without external requirements, I would proactively use ChatGPT for lesson planning or instructional design	3.68	1.040
	BI4	I am willing to invest time and effort to learn how to use ChatGPT more efficiently in teaching	3.47	1.160

4.3 Preliminary Exploration of Pre-service Teacher User Types

This study applied K-means cluster analysis and ultimately identified a four-cluster solution with strong explanatory power and theoretical significance. As shown in Fig. 1, the four clusters demonstrated clear differences across indicators such as perceived usefulness (PU), attitude (AT), perceived ease of use (PEU), and behavioral intention (BI). Based on the distribution characteristics of each cluster, this study labeled the four user types as: Resistors (Cluster 1), Cautious Evaluators (Cluster 2), Innovators (Cluster 3), and Pragmatists (Cluster 4):

- **Resistors (10%):** These participants scored significantly low across all indicators related to perceived usefulness and performance expectancy (means approximately −1.5 to −2.2), expressing strong skepticism toward ChatGPT's instructional value. Their behavioral intention (BI1) score was extremely low (−1.715), signaling explicit concerns or resistance to adoption.
- **Cautious Evaluators (28%):** This group exhibited slightly negative mean scores in perceived usefulness and performance expectancy (around −0.2 to −0.5). While they acknowledged ChatGPT's potential, they maintained a reserved and evaluative stance toward its use.
- **Innovators (20%):** These pre-service teachers showed highly positive scores across all dimensions, especially performance expectancy (means around 0.9 to 1.1). They demonstrated high usage frequency and a broad range of instructional applications, actively exploring the teaching potential of ChatGPT.
- **Pragmatists (42%):** This group showed mixed evaluations, with some variables slightly positive (e.g., PEU2 = 0.503) and others slightly negative (e.g., AT2 = −0.459). Notably, they scored relatively low on future integration (BI2 = −0.738), yet displayed a strong inclination toward self-initiated exploration (BI3 = 0.747), reflecting a selective and utilitarian approach to adoption.

Further analysis revealed differences in cluster distribution based on academic background. Participants with STEM backgrounds were more likely to be classified as Innovators or Pragmatists, while those from non-STEM fields were more frequently categorized as Cautious Evaluators. Quantitative analysis confirmed that pre-service teachers who reported higher usage frequency of ChatGPT also had significantly higher scores in perceived usefulness, ease of use, and behavioral intention ($t = 3.12$, $p < 0.01$). This typology framework effectively captures the diversity in pre-service teachers' acceptance of ChatGPT and provides an empirical foundation for designing differentiated training strategies.

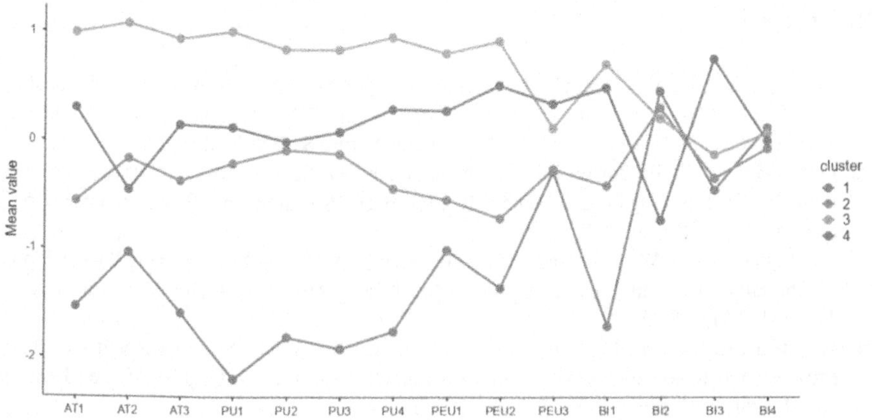

Fig. 1. Mean Scores of Key Variables Across the Four Identified Clusters

5 Conclusion

This pilot study integrated TAM and UTAUT frameworks to preliminarily identify four types of pre-service teachers in their use of ChatGPT: Innovators, Pragmatists, Cautious Evaluators, and Resistors. These groups showed significant differences in perceived usefulness, ease of use, behavioral intention, and ethical concerns, reflecting the diverse attitudes and behaviors pre-service teachers hold toward generative AI in education.

Innovators demonstrated high levels of acceptance and confidence, while Pragmatists used ChatGPT selectively for specific tasks, prioritizing efficiency and usability. Cautious Evaluators were influenced by ethical and pedagogical concerns, and Resistors showed strong skepticism, preferring traditional teaching approaches. Overall, the main concerns expressed by pre-service teachers focused on overreliance, accuracy issues, and the potential weakening of students' independent and critical thinking skills—indicating the value tensions between technological convenience and core educational principles. Based on these differences, this study proposes targeted training strategies tailored to each user type. For Innovators, advanced, inquiry-based learning and peer collaboration projects can deepen their innovative practice and ethical reflection. Pragmatists would benefit from ready-to-use prompt templates and typical instructional scenarios to help them build efficient, structured workflows. For Cautious Evaluators, phased implementation and case-based learning may help reduce uncertainty and build trust. Resistors may respond better to training grounded in educational values and teacher professionalism, with an emphasis on human–AI collaboration and non-substitutive use cases, supported by hands-on experiences in controlled environments. These differentiated strategies address the specific needs and characteristics of each group and offer practical guidance for designing AI literacy curricula within teacher education programs.

As an exploratory study, this research is limited by its small sample size and participant composition. Future studies are encouraged to expand the sample, adopt longitudinal designs, and further develop technology acceptance models tailored to educational settings, to better understand the decision-making processes behind teachers' adoption of AI technologies.

References

1. Li, P.-H., Lee, H.-Y., Cheng, Y.-P., Starčič, A.I., Huang, Y.-M.: Solving the Self-regulated Learning Problem: Exploring the Performance of ChatGPT in Mathematics. In: Innovative Technologies and Learning, pp. 77–86. Springer Nature Switzerland (Year)
2. Dimas, D., et al.: Exploring Pre-Service Teachers' Difficulties of ChatGPT as a Tool for Planning The Learning Process. Innovative: Journal Of Social Science Research **5**, 5906–5922 (2025)
3. Ma, J., Pengcheng, W., Benqian, L., Tian, W., Shan, P.X., Wang, D.: Exploring User Adoption of ChatGPT: A Technology Acceptance Model Perspective. Int. J. Human-Comp. Interact. **41**, 1431–1445 (2025)
4. Wu, T.-T., Lee, H.-Y., Li, P.-H., Huang, C.-N., Huang, Y.-M.: Promoting Self-Regulation Progress and Knowledge Construction in Blended Learning via ChatGPT-Based Learning Aid. J. Educat. Comput. Res. **61**, 3–31 (2023)
5. Lee, H.-Y., Chen, P.-H., Wang, W.-S., Huang, Y.-M., Wu, T.-T.: Empowering ChatGPT with guidance mechanism in blended learning: effect of self-regulated learning, higher-order thinking skills, and knowledge construction. Int. J. Educ. Technol. High. Educ. **21**, 16 (2024)
6. Lee, G.G., Zhai, X.: Using ChatGPT for Science Learning: A Study on Pre-service Teachers' Lesson Planning. IEEE Trans. Learn. Technol. **17**, 1643–1660 (2024)
7. Davis, F.D.: Perceived Usefulness, Perceived Ease of Use, and User Acceptance of Information Technology. MIS Q. **13**, 319–340 (1989)
8. Venkatesh, V., Morris, M.G., Davis, G.B., Davis, F.D.: User acceptance of information technology: toward a unified view. MIS Q. **27**, 425–478 (2003)
9. Islamoglu, H., Kabakci Yurdakul, I., Ursavas, O.F.: Pre-service teachers' acceptance of mobile-technology-supported learning activities. Education Tech. Research Dev. **69**, 1025–1054 (2021)
10. Guan, L., Zhang, Y., Gu, M.M.: Pre-service teachers preparedness for AI-integrated education: An investigation from perceptions, capabilities, and teachers' identity changes. Comp. Educ. Artif. Intell. **8**, 100341 (2025)

Adaptive Auto-Prompting in Inquiry-Based Learning: Enhancing Curiosity and Learning Engagement to Improve Higher-Order Thinking

Pin-Hui Li[1], Kinshuk[2], and Yueh-Min Huang[1](✉)

[1] Department of Engineering Science, National Cheng Kung University, Tainan City, Taiwan
huang@mail.ncku.edu.tw

[2] College of Information, University of North Texas, Denton, USA
kinshuk@unt.edu

Abstract. In inquiry-based learning, curiosity is the key factor driving students to actively explore and engage in deep learning, while the cultivation of higher-order thinking skills is a core objective. However, some students may lose interest and motivation due to difficulties or uncertainties encountered during the learning process, which can negatively impact learning outcomes and limit the full benefits of inquiry-based learning. Therefore, providing timely and adaptive prompts has become an essential strategy for enhancing learning engagement and cognitive development. This study developed an Auto-Prompt Learning Aid (APLA), which dynamically adjusts prompt content based on students' learning states and behavioral patterns to provide targeted learning support. The results indicate that APLA significantly enhances students' curiosity across three dimensions: joyful exploration, sensitivity to gaps, and tolerance for uncertainty. Additionally, it effectively strengthens both cognitive and emotional engagement, encouraging students to immerse themselves more deeply in learning. Moreover, APLA contributes to the development of students' higher-order thinking skills, particularly in problem-solving and critical thinking, demonstrating that adaptive prompts can reinforce students' inquiry abilities and cognitive growth. The findings of this study validate the application value of APLA in inquiry-based learning and suggest that adaptive prompt systems help maximize the benefits of inquiry-based learning, fostering the development of higher-order thinking skills while optimizing students' learning experiences and cognitive growth.

Keywords: Inquiry-based learning · Curiosity · Learning Engagement · Higher-Order Thinking

1 Introduction

Inquiry-Based Learning (IBL) is a crucial direction in contemporary educational reform, aiming to cultivate students' self-directed learning abilities, critical thinking, and problem-solving skills [1]. This learning model emphasizes active exploration and hands-on practice as the foundation for knowledge construction, rather than relying solely

W.-S. Wang et al. (Eds.): ICITL 2025, LNCS 15913, pp. 121–130, 2026.
https://doi.org/10.1007/978-3-031-98185-2_14

on direct instruction from teachers. However, this highly autonomous approach places higher demands on students' attention, learning strategies, and self-regulation skills. During the learning process, many students may experience confusion, helplessness, or frustration due to a lack of background knowledge, ineffective problem-solving strategies, or inadequate learning guidance. In such cases, the advantages of inquiry-based learning may not be fully realized [2].

To address these challenges, numerous studies have highlighted that timely scaffolding and guidance in inquiry-based learning can significantly enhance learning outcomes, reduce cognitive load, and boost students' motivation and confidence [3]. In this process, teachers play a critical role by designing developmentally appropriate learning tasks and providing targeted guidance at key moments to help students clarify problems, construct knowledge, and develop problem-solving skills. However, in traditional classrooms, the limited number of teachers makes it difficult to provide personalized support for every student in real time, hindering the effective implementation of individualized instruction. This is where educational technology demonstrates its significant value—by leveraging intelligent systems and digital tools. Real-time and personalized learning support can be provided, compensating for the shortage of human resources and further enhancing the effectiveness of inquiry-based learning [4].

In inquiry-based learning, students exhibit differences in background knowledge and learning progress, necessitating adaptive and personalized guidance mechanisms to maximize learning effectiveness. The core of individualized instruction lies in providing appropriate learning resources and challenges based on students' needs. For example, students with insufficient foundational knowledge require supplementary background information and fundamental concepts to establish a solid learning foundation, enabling them to engage in inquiry activities successfully [5]. On the other hand, students who progress faster or have already completed the learning activity should be provided with more challenging problems, open-ended inquiries, or extension activities to deepen exploration, foster higher-order thinking, and enhance creativity [6]. Such differentiated instructional designs ensure that all students can engage in inquiry within their appropriate zone of proximal development, thereby increasing their interest, engagement, and motivation for self-directed learning while minimizing frustration or disengagement caused by tasks that are too difficult or too easy.

To effectively enhance students' motivation for active learning, this study designed an adaptive learning support mechanism that provides tiered instructional guidance to align learning content and support strategies with the needs of different learners. By offering personalized scaffolding, students' engagement and interest in exploration are heightened, ultimately leading to improved learning outcomes. Based on this framework, this study developed an Auto-Prompt Learning Aid (APLA) that integrates Generative AI (ChatGPT) and image recognition technology (YOLOv8) to dynamically adapt to students' learning behaviors and provide real-time, individualized support. The system analyzes students' behavioral patterns using image recognition technology and generates adaptive prompts via ChatGPT to help students overcome learning difficulties, maintain motivation, and engage in deeper thinking. The research aims to address the following questions:

1. How can the APLA effectively enhance students' curiosity and learning engagement in an inquiry-based learning environment?
2. How can the APLA effectively promote the development of students' higher-order thinking skills in an inquiry-based learning environment?

2 Related Work

To establish the theoretical foundation of this study, this section reviews and analyzes literature related to three core dimensions of inquiry-based learning: curiosity, learning engagement, and higher-order thinking skills. Curiosity pertains to the stimulation of students' learning motivation and their drive for sustained exploration; learning engagement involves students' behavioral, emotional, and cognitive involvement throughout the inquiry process; and higher-order thinking skills represent the central objective of inquiry-based learning, encompassing critical thinking, problem-solving, and creativity. Through the examination of these three dimensions, this section aims to clarify their theoretical underpinnings and practical challenges, serving as the basis for the system design and intervention strategies proposed in this study.

2.1 Curiosity in Inquiry-Based Learning

Curiosity is the fundamental driving force that motivates individuals to explore the unknown, construct knowledge, and develop innovative thinking, playing a crucial role in the learning process [7]. When students develop curiosity about learning content, their intrinsic motivation is stimulated, prompting them to actively engage in learning activities, continuously explore, and solve problems to deepen their understanding of knowledge [8]. However, if the learning environment lacks appropriate stimuli or challenges, students may resort to passive learning due to a lack of interest or experience frustration from excessive cognitive load, ultimately diminishing their motivation for continued exploration [9].

Therefore, educational design should focus on creating a learning environment that fosters curiosity by incorporating open-ended questions, adaptive challenges, and personalized learning support to enhance students' interest in learning and encourage active participation. Additionally, the integration of technology-assisted tools, particularly generative artificial intelligence and learning analytics, enables real-time adaptation to students' learning behaviors and provides dynamic support, further strengthening their learning motivation and higher order thinking development. Consequently, effectively cultivating and sustaining students' curiosity in inquiry-based learning settings is not only key to improving learning outcomes but also a significant issue in contemporary educational research.

2.2 Learning Engagement in Inquiry-Based Learning

Learning engagement refers to the degree of involvement students demonstrate during the learning process, encompassing behavioral, emotional, and cognitive dimensions. In inquiry-based learning, learning engagement plays a decisive role in learning outcomes, as students must actively explore, formulate hypotheses, and solve problems to construct knowledge. However, due to the highly autonomous nature of inquiry based learning, some students may feel lost or frustrated if they lack effective learning strategies or appropriate guidance, leading to decreased engagement. Therefore, adaptive learning support, such as automated prompting tools or intelligent learning systems, can provide real-time guidance based on students' learning behaviors to ensure their sustained engagement in inquiry activities and maintain their motivation [10].

Furthermore, when the learning environment offers moderate challenges, encourages students to ask questions and reflect, and integrates technology-assisted adaptive learning, it can enhance students' engagement in inquiry-based learning, further promoting the development of their higher-order thinking skills and knowledge construction abilities [11].

2.3 Higher Order Thinking in Inquiry-Based Learning

Inquiry-based learning is widely recognized in the field of education as a key strategy for cultivating higher-order thinking skills. Its core objective is to develop learners with deep thinking and innovative abilities through processes of self-directed exploration, problem-solving [12], and knowledge construction [13]. However, despite the widely recognized educational value of inquiry-based learning, its implementation faces several challenges that may affect learning outcomes and prevent some students from fully realizing their potential in higher-order thinking.

One of the greatest challenges in inquiry-based learning is the variation in students' self-directed learning abilities. Since the inquiry process requires students to engage in independent thinking and exploration, some may struggle with open-ended problems due to a lack of learning strategies or prior knowledge, leading to confusion or helplessness that negatively impacts their motivation and engagement. Additionally, the difficulty in providing real-time individualized guidance is another major challenge in inquiry-based learning. In traditional classroom settings, teachers often need to manage multiple students simultaneously, making it difficult to respond promptly to each student's learning needs. As a result, some students may not receive the necessary support during the learning process, which further hinders the development of their higher-order thinking skills [14].

To address these challenges, inquiry-based learning requires an adaptive support mechanism to ensure that students can learn within an appropriate level of challenge while receiving real-time, personalized guidance. Therefore, this study developed an Auto-Prompt Learning Aid (APLA), a system capable of monitoring students' learning status in real time and providing contextual inquiry prompts based on their behavioral patterns and learning progress.

3 Auto-Prompt Learning Aid (APLA)

This study adopts the POE (Predict-Observe-Explain) inquiry-based learning model proposed by White and Gunstone [15] as the design framework, aiming to guide students through a systematic inquiry process to develop higher-order thinking skills and deepen their understanding of knowledge.

However, during the implementation of inquiry-based learning, students may feel confused due to a lack of guidance or effective learning strategies, leading to lower engagement and hindering the development of higher-order thinking skills. To stimulate students' curiosity and engagement while maximizing the benefits of inquiry-based learning, this study integrates Generative AI (ChatGPT) and image recognition technology (YOLOv8) to develop an Auto-Prompt Learning Aid (APLA). This system monitors students' behavior in real time and provides adaptive guidance based on their learning progress, ensuring they receive appropriate support throughout the predict, observe, and explain phases.

For instance, when students struggle during the prediction phase, the system can provide relevant background knowledge or guiding questions. During the observation phase, if students fail to record data effectively or overlook key phenomena, the system can issue prompts to refine their observations. In the explanation phase, APLA can offer feedback on students' reasoning, encouraging them to reflect further and refine their conceptual understanding. Figure 1 and Table 1 illustrate the operational mechanism and application context of APLA.

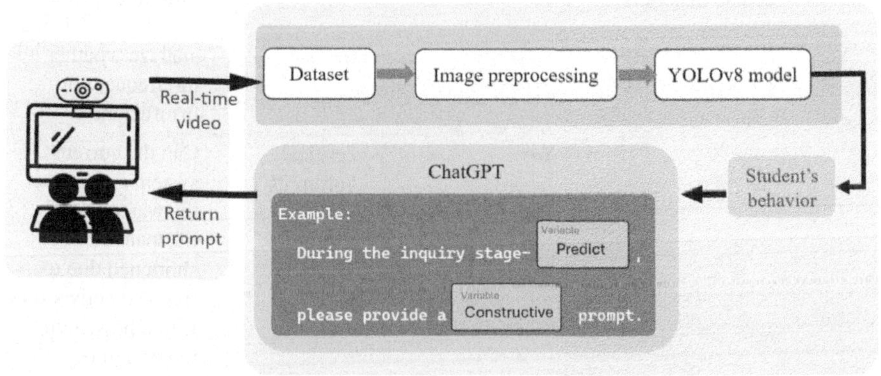

Fig. 1. APLA system architecture diagram.

Table 1. System Judgment, Prompt Types, and Examples for Each POE Stage

POE	System Judgment	Student's Behavior	Prompt Types	Examples
Predict	The student fills out a questionnaire to answer prediction questions. The system determines whether the student has touched the keyboard or mouse	No	constructive prompts	Try drawing a simple flowchart to explain how the system should detect when the soil is dry and automatically activate the irrigation device
		Yes	creative prompts	Besides soil moisture sensors, are there other ways to determine if plants need watering? Can you design a smarter irrigation method?
Observe	The student conducts hands-on operations, and the system determines whether the student has touched relevant course materials	No	constructive prompts	Modify the program code so that it records the time before each watering. This way, we can know how many times the system waters in a day and analyze whether it is too frequent or insufficient
		Yes	critical prompts	Can the current system ensure that the water pump's lifespan is not shortened due to frequent activation? If not, how should the design be improved to prevent this issue?

(continued)

Table 1. (*continued*)

POE	System Judgment	Student's Behavior	Prompt Types	Examples
Explain	The student explains experimental results, and the system determines whether the student has spoken	No	constructive prompts	Based on the test data results, propose at least one way to improve the system. Draw a new design diagram and revise your initial assumptions accordingly
		Yes	creative prompts	If this system were to be used in different environments, how would you adjust its functions to suit different scenarios?

4 Results and Discussion

This study employed ANCOVA (Analysis of Covariance) to examine differences in curiosity, learning engagement, and higher-order thinking skills between groups, assessing the effectiveness of the APLA auto-prompting system. In the analysis, pre-test scores were used as covariates to control initial differences in students' abilities, ensuring the accuracy of group comparisons. The ANCOVA results aimed to reveal the statistical significance of post-test performance differences between the experimental and control groups, further validating whether APLA influences students' learning behaviors and cognitive development. Following this, an in-depth discussion was conducted in this study on variables with significant effects, analyzing key factors that may impact learning outcomes and exploring the applicability and potential improvements of the auto-prompting mechanism in inquiry-based learning environments.

4.1 Does the APLA Effectively Enhance Students' Curiosity and Learning Engagement?

Based on the results in Table 2, regarding the five facets of curiosity, Joyous Exploration, Deprivation Sensitivity, and Stress Tolerance showed significant effects, indicating that the APLA auto-prompting system effectively enhanced students' curiosity in inquiry-based learning. This suggests that students become more willing to explore knowledge, actively seek information, and experience reduced anxiety and stress when facing challenges. However, Social Curiosity and Thrill Seeking did not reach significance, suggesting that the system had limited impact on students' curiosity about peers' learning behaviors or their pursuit of novel and stimulating experiences.

For the three dimensions of learning engagement, Cognitive Engagement and Emotional Engagement demonstrated significant improvements, indicating that the APLA prompting mechanism facilitated deeper learning and problem-solving engagement while also enhancing students' emotional involvement, making them more interested and invested in the learning process. However, Behavioral Engagement did not reach significance, suggesting that the APLA auto-prompting mechanism had limited influence on students' observable learning behaviors, such as class participation and task completion frequency.

The findings suggest that providing timely inquiry prompts in an inquiry-based learning environment can effectively enhance students' curiosity, making them more eager to explore, actively ask questions, and seek more information while also reducing stress when facing learning challenges. Additionally, APLA significantly improved students' cognitive and emotional engagement, encouraging deeper thinking and fostering a stronger sense of involvement in the learning process. However, the system had a limited impact on social curiosity and thrill-seeking behavior, likely because inquiry-based learning primarily focuses on individual knowledge construction rather than social interactions, reducing the emphasis on peer curiosity. Furthermore, the lack of significant changes in behavioral engagement may be attributed to the already motivating learning environment, where students maintained a consistent level of participation regardless of APLA intervention.

Table 2. ANCOVA results for curiosity and learning engagement

Variable	SS	df	Mean Square	F	*p*	Partial η^2
Joyous Exploration	346.1	1	346.1	84.21	**< 0.01****	0.297
Deprivation Sensitivity	236.8	1	236.8	45.78	**< 0.01****	0.157
Stress Tolerance	211.4	1	211.4	23.44	**< 0.05***	0.197
Social Curiosity	124.6	1	124.6	14.15	**0.238**	0.101
Thrill Seeking	97.4	1	97.4	4.64	**0.497**	0.078
Behavioral engagement	115.6	1	115.6	12.14	**0.249**	0.097
Cognitive engagement	587.6	1	587.6	94.12	**< 0.001*****	0.341
Emotional engagement	221.4	1	221.4	74.16	**< 0.01****	0.159

Note. * $p < .05$, ** $p < .01$, *** $p < .001$

4.2 Does the APLA Effectively Promote the Development of Students' Higher-Order Thinking Skills?

According to Table 3, APLA had a significant impact on students' problem-solving and critical thinking skills, but its effect on creativity did not reach statistical significance.

The problem-solving skill analysis showed that APLA significantly improved students' ability to analyze problems, organize information, and develop strategic solutions in inquiry-based learning. Similarly, for critical thinking skills, the analysis indicated that APLA helped students improve their ability to evaluate evidence, engage in logical reasoning, and construct well-supported arguments during inquiry activities. However, regarding creativity, the results were not statistically significant, suggesting that APLA's prompting mechanism had a limited impact on fostering students' creative thinking. This may be because APLA primarily provides constructive and critical prompts based on learning progress, with less emphasis on divergent thinking or innovative problem-solving.

In inquiry-based learning, adaptive prompts can effectively enhance students' problem-solving and critical thinking skills. This is likely because APLA offers targeted inquiry guidance and reflective mechanisms, helping students strengthen their logical reasoning and decision-making abilities, allowing them to systematically analyze problems and evaluate different solutions. However, its lack of significant impact on creativity may be related to the design of the prompting mechanism. Creativity development often requires greater openness, divergent reasoning, and unstructured exploration, whereas APLA primarily focuses on structured inquiry processes. While it is effective in guiding students to understand concepts and develop critical thinking, it appears to have limitations in stimulating innovative ideas and breakthrough thinking.

Although this study incorporated creative prompts, the results indicate limited effectiveness in enhancing students' creativity. This could be due to students' reliance on system-generated prompts, which may restrict their independent exploration and innovative thinking. Future research could improve the prompting mechanism by incorporating more open-ended question designs, encouraging interdisciplinary thinking, or guiding students to engage in self-questioning and reflective inquiry to better support creativity development.

Table 3. ANCOVA results for higher-order thinking skills

Variable	SS	df	Mean Square	F	p	Partial η^2
Creativity	127.1	1	127.1	11.6	0.267	0.174
Problem-solving skill	295.1	1	295.1	75.3	$< 0.001^{***}$	0.249
Critical thinking skill	227.4	1	227.4	56.4	$< 0.01^{**}$	0.213

Note. $^{*}p < .05$, $^{**}p < .01$, $^{***}p < .001$

5 Conclusion

This study confirmed the value of applying APLA in inquiry-based learning environments. Findings showed that APLA significantly enhanced students' curiosity, particularly in joyful exploration, deprivation sensitivity, and stress tolerance. It also improved cognitive and emotional engagement, supporting the development of problem-solving and critical thinking skills. However, its effects on social curiosity, behavioral engagement, and creativity were limited, likely due to the system's focus on individual learning and structured prompts. These results offer practical implications. For teachers, integrating adaptive prompts through AI-assisted tools like APLA can support inquiry processes, reduce anxiety, and deepen engagement. However, they should also provide opportunities for peer interaction and creative exploration. For students, engaging with system prompts and reflecting on their thought processes can strengthen analytical and evaluative thinking skills.

As for future research, expanding the participant pool beyond a single university in Taiwan would help assess the generalizability of the findings. Enhancing APLA with features that promote creativity and social interaction, such as open-ended prompts or collaborative inquiry, could further extend its potential in supporting inquiry-based learning across multiple dimensions.

References

1. Biswal, S., Behera, B.: Enhancing science process skills through inquiry-based learning: A comprehensive literature review and analysis. Int. J. Sci. Res. **12** (2023)
2. Deák, C., Kumar, B., Szabó, I., Nagy, G., Szentesi, S.: Evolution of new approaches in pedagogy and STEM with inquiry-based learning and post-pandemic scenarios. Education Sciences **11**, 319 (2021)
3. MacKinnon, S.L., Archer-Kuhn, B.: Reigniting curiosity and inquiry in higher education: A realist's guide to getting started with inquiry-based learning. Taylor & Francis (2023)
4. Li, P.-H., Lee, H.-Y., Lin, C.-J., Wang, W.-S., Huang, Y.-M.: InquiryGPT: augmenting ChatGPT for enhancing inquiry-based learning in STEM education. J. Educ. Comp. Res. **62**, 2157–2186 (2025)
5. Lu, K., Pang, F., Shadiev, R.: Understanding the mediating effect of learning approach between learning factors and higher order thinking skills in collaborative inquiry-based learning. Education Tech. Research Dev. **69**, 2475–2492 (2021)
6. Khasawneh, E., Hodge-Zickerman, A., York, C.S., Smith, T.J., Mayall, H.: Examining the effect of inquiry-based learning versus traditional lecture-based learning on students' achievement in college algebra. Int. Electr. J. Math. Educ. **18**, em0724 (2023)
7. Wagstaff, M.F., Flores, G.L., Ahmed, R., Villanueva, S.: Measures of curiosity: A literature review. Hum. Resour. Dev. Q. **32**, 363–389 (2021)
8. Goupil, L., Proust, J.: Curiosity as a metacognitive feeling. Cognition **231**, 105325 (2023)
9. Ten, A., Kaushik, P., Oudeyer, P.-Y., Gottlieb, J.: Humans monitor learning progress in curiosity-driven exploration. Nat. Commun. **12**, 5972 (2021)
10. Orosz, G., Németh, V., Kovács, L., Somogyi, Z., Korom, E.: Guided inquiry-based learning in secondary-school chemistry classes: A case study. Chem. Educ. Res. Pract. **24**, 50–70 (2023)
11. Safitri, E.: A comprehensive of the guided inquiry learning model in education: a review. J. Digi. Learn. Dist. Educ. **2**, 622–626 (2023)
12. Santana-Vega, L.E., Feliciano-García, L., Suárez-Perdomo, A.: Inquiry-based learning in the university context: a systematic review. Revista Espanola de Pedagogia **78**, 9 (2023)
13. Abdurrahman, M.S., Halim, A.A., Sharifah, O.: Improving polytechnic students' high-order-thinking-skills through inquiry-based learning in mathematics classroom. Int. J. Evaluat. Res. Educ. **10**, 976–983 (2021)
14. Liu, C., Zowghi, D., Kearney, M., Bano, M.: Inquiry-based mobile learning in secondary school science education: A systematic review. J. Comput. Assist. Learn. **37**, 1–23 (2021)
15. White, R., Gunstone, R.: Prediction-observation-explanation. Probing Understanding **4**, 44–64 (1992)

ChatGPT-Assisted Escape Room: Preservice Teacher Preparation for Generative Artificial Intelligence Enhanced Instructional Design

Andreja Istenič[1,2(✉)], Monika Frania[3], and Žiga Turk[1]

[1] Faculty of Education, University of Primorska, Koper, Slovenia
andreja.istenic7@gmail.com, ziga.turk@fgg.uni-lj.si
[2] Faculty of Civil and Geodetic University of Ljubljana, Ljubljana, Slovenia
[3] Faculty of Social Sciences, University of Silesia, Katowice, Poland
monika.frania@us.edu.pl

Abstract. Escape rooms are used in didactic settings, forming learning environments from an angle of learning connected to authentic context, authentic activity and authentic students' interactions. Didactic setting consisting of learning objectives, instructional/didactic strategies, and learning methods reflects game design. Learning objectives are transformed into game design, the instructional/didactic strategy is transformed in game strategy and learning methods are transformed into game mechanisms (challenges and puzzles). The study examined preservice teachers' design of a digital escape room for early STEM learning. ChatGPT was utilized for lesson planning and escape room scenario and design. The digital escape room design was a part of the educational technology course for classroom teachers in modernising pedagogical study programmes in 2024/25. Students' evaluations of the escape room instructional design supported by generative artificial intelligence are presented.

Keywords: Generative Artificial Intelligence · ChatGPT · Escape room · Exit game · Instructional design · Preservice teachers · STEM

1 Introduction

With the technology development of instruction has been constantly changing. Escape rooms have gained popularity as innovative educational tools, offering immersive experiences that promote critical thinking, problem-solving, and teamwork [1–3]. These game-based learning environments are being implemented across various disciplines, with educators adapting the concept to suit different pedagogical goals [4]. In the period of COVID-19, the need for online and blended learning fostered innovative strategies, and the escape room was utilized in preservice teacher education [5], enabling diverse strategies or combining strategies. Digital escape rooms, in particular, are being explored as a means to break down barriers in STEM education and create more engaging learning experiences [3]. Studies have shown that DERs can enhance students' problem-solving abilities and learning motivation in science education [6]. While escape rooms show

W.-S. Wang et al. (Eds.): ICITL 2025, LNCS 15913, pp. 131–141, 2026.
https://doi.org/10.1007/978-3-031-98185-2_15

promise in fostering 21st-century skills and increasing student motivation, there is a need for more structured research to evaluate their effectiveness and develop best practices for implementation [1, 2, 4] and especially escape rooms in teacher education require attention. In Gonzales and Alez-Munoz study [7] pre-service teachers expressed high overall satisfaction with the virtual educational escape room (VEER) experience, and this satisfaction was not significantly affected by their gender or age. Participants had a highly favorable perception of game-based learning (GBL), both from the perspective of being current students and as future teachers. They perceived a high level of soft skills utilization during the VEER intervention, particularly in the areas of collaboration, problem-solving, and team management. In the study by Makri [8] the DEERs were identified innovative, promising, immersive, active, and collaborative instructional approaches that can enhance learning more than traditional methods. Results showed that DEERs have a positive impact on students' cognitive, behavioral, and affective learning outcomes. In the study were also identified the key design characteristics and best practices for developing effective DEERs include team size, time frame, puzzle structure, and use of digital technologies. As the use of escape rooms in education continues to grow, educators are encouraged to align game mechanics with pedagogical approaches and focus on achieving educational goals through gameplay [1].

1.1 The Role of Educational Technology in Teacher Education

In the initial teacher education, the instructional design prepares preservice teachers in the field of educational technology. The field is influenced by technology developments. In the early 20th Century, educational technology had a supportive role in instruction as an aid, device or resource within the visualisation movement with the technological development of telecommunications, sound transmission, radio, television, and film [9]. The development of communication theories, the conception of educational technology transits from audiovisual materials to a conveyor or mediator of instruction [10]. The rise of the psychology of instruction enhances the instructional design-based models of instruction [11]. With the proliferation of computers and the Internet, the role of educational technology shifts and expands from a structural component (tool or resource) to a process component supporting the process of instruction [12]. The rapid technological developments with artificial intelligence open issues in teachers' roles and competences [13]. Educational technology is recognised as essential in setting a learning environment and forms one of fundamental areas in the framework in the P21 [14] for the 21st Century learning, enabling Information, Media and Technology skills which are connected with learning and Innovation; Life and Career skills and Core subjects and themes (Standards and Assessment), Curriculum and Instruction, Professional development, Learning environment).

European Educational systems address issues in technology developments affecting society by the development of teacher and learner competence for sustainable development [15], digital competences [16], artificial intelligence literacy [17], and all of the mentioned should address the teacher's readiness in the complex issue of ethics. Ethical issues related to technological developments and applications in society and education reflect sustainable development. Mouta et al. [18] examined blind spots of ethics in their review of artificial intelligence through the potential disparities in terms of access, pedagogical quality and ownership and rights to data and resources and how ethics regulations are being put in place. Providing pedagogical quality in the integration of generative artificial intelligence in education requires the preparation of teachers and students. As indicated in P21 [14], learning and innovation are intertwined with Information, media and technology skills, and teachers need training to utilise deep learning models employed by artificial intelligence for enhanced learning outcomes, personalization and educational data analysis. ChatGPT by OpenAI can be integrated into traditional instruction. Van den Berg and Plessis [19] examine ChatGPT in teachers' lesson planning for creating course material, designing real-life scenarios for discussions, case studies and critical reasoning in the classroom, arguing for increased creativity, critical thinking, and problem solving.

1.2 The Instructional Strategies in Escape Room Game Design

De Lope and Medina-Medina [20] present a comprehensive taxonomy of serious games based on criteria: game development, game platform, game design, game use, game users, and business model. Analysing game design, authors list: genre, narrative, interactivity, context of use and application areas. Authors use Herz's categorization of genres from 1997 that involves action, adventure, fight, logic, simulation, sport, and strategy. For the escape room design, let us indicate the following genres: Blended (interacting with physical objects triggering digital response (Scanning QR codes)/ Narrative-driven (Character in a plot) / Puzzle-focused / Team-building / Mobile/ Virtual reality / Outdoor / Board games.

Instructional strategies (didactic strategies) involve diverse levels and engagements of students depending on learning objectives, methods and students' preferences and abilities [21]. Hus and Grmek [21] list a behaviour (work)-oriented lesson, experience-oriented lesson, team lesson, project lesson, problem lesson, research lesson.

Learning methods taxonomy by Valenčič Zuljan and Kalin [22] highlights Verbal method (explanation and conversation), Documentation methods (textual), Demonstration, Operationally practical methods (inquiry, practical work, physical activity, writing, drawing, play). The verbal method of explanation is elaborated further [22], and among indicated categories, storytelling is of special interest. In the instruction, teaching and learning stream to approach the authenticity of a learner by forming a learning environment from the angle of learning connected to authentic context, authentic activities, authentic students' life and interactions [12]. In setting a learning environment, a didactic setting utilizes storytelling to establish context known to a child. As Istenič [12] summarizes, storytelling represents a child's reality, enabling the establishment of a child's meaning, and is, according to Bruner [23], narrative thinking. Storytelling exploits imagination, which a child utilizes as an essential tool [24]. Storytelling is an integral part of perception and interpretation [25], therefore forming didactic reality. The escape room is a learning environment structured by a storyline within a physical, online or blended space, to play towards objectives according to the rules. The design of an escape room could be aligned with the instructional design from the angles of objectives, strategies, and methods accompanying activities (Fig. 1).

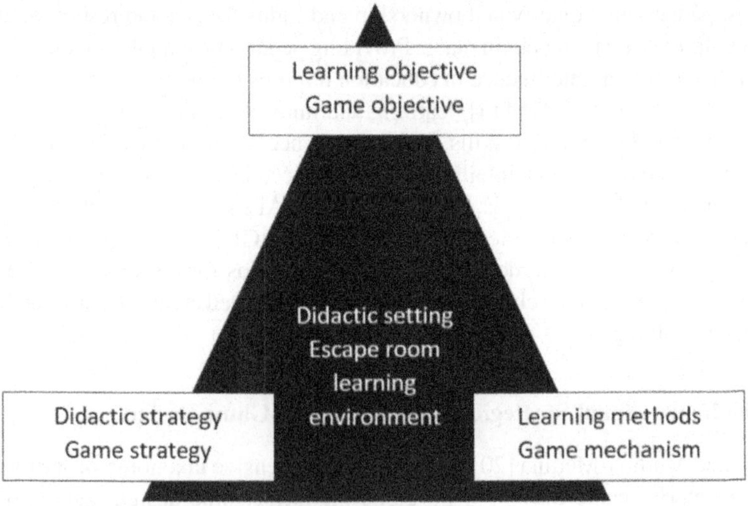

Fig. 1. CAP The model of Escape Room learning environment (Figure owned by authors)

Escape rooms are used in didactic settings, forming learning environments from an angle of learning connected to authentic context, authentic activity and authentic students' interactions. Didactic setting consisting of learning objectives, instructional/didactic strategies, and learning methods reflects game design. Learning objectives are transformed into game design, the instructional/didactic strategy is transformed into game strategy, and learning methods are transformed into game mechanisms (challenges and puzzles). The escape room or breakout room enables the withdrawal from a busy day-to-day context into a room, the environment designed for full engagement. In instruction, the escape room enables a setting of didactic reality according to the learners' developmental level and preferences. Designing an escape room requires innovative, creative thinking when considering curriculum objectives and content and streamlining it into the didactic setting of escape room learning environments. Generative artificial intelligence supports a process of lesson planning and design by generating ideas generation and designing learning material [19]. Haramina et al. [26] applied ChatGPT to generate virtual reality escape room puzzles.

2 Methods and Materials

The study was conducted to examine preservice teachers' design of a digital escape room for early STEM learning. The digital escape room design was a part of the educational technology course for classroom teachers in 2024/25 as a part of the project "Modernisation of pedagogical study programmes - Modernisation of the NOO PSP" co-funded by the Ministry of Education (MoE) and The European Commission NextGenerationEU. The course objectives consist of concepts, theories and taxonomies in the field of educational technology, psychological-developmental and societal-cultural factors of implementing educational technology and media in classroom teaching, developing instructional competency of teacher based on the TPACK framework (technology, pedagogy, content knowledge), utilizing computational thinking, artificial intelligence literacy, and multiliteracy. The didactic principles, formats and methods in the work with educational technology in inclusive learning environments are conducted with project work on didactic strategies and learning methods, feedback and assessment in face-to-face, online and blended learning environments. The course covers social, ethical, health-related, and legal aspects of the use of educational technology, artificial intelligence, and learning analytics. The sustainable development objectives were highlighted in a course as a part of "the Modernisation study".

In the academic year 2024/25 the project work included escape rooms in collaboration of the course leader A. Istenič and visiting professor M. Frania, who presented escape room experiences from Poland [5]. During the lectures, the theory and practice of escape rooms were presented before tutorials, during the design of escape rooms in tutorials and after projects were completed. The study started in November 2024 and ended in January 2025.

The course is conducted by lectures and tutorials. 46 students participated (4 males and 42 females) in the case study conducted in the course Educational technology. Students were informed about the study and presentation of analysis and evaluation results in research articles. The study is aligned with ethical standards of the Helsinki Declaration and its later amendments or comparable ethical standards. Students' project work was conducted in groups of 5–6 students in three groups during tutorials. Preparation and final reflections took place in lectures with all students participating. All student groups applied the Genially escape room application [27]. One group applied ChatGPT in the escape room design, and two groups were working without generative intelligence. The new technology and application integration by service and preservice teachers depends on their readiness for educational technology integration. After the escape room design, students responded to an evaluation questionnaire assessing the skills developed and their perception of escape room design and utilization of digital tools.

Research questions:

RQ1: How do students evaluate the escape room design and its effect on their competences?

RQ2: How do students evaluate the digital tools and ChatGPT for designing escape rooms?

Instruments for the study consisted of a pre- and post-test, a questionnaire during and at the end of the project work. In this paper, the results presenting students' evaluation of escape rooms are presented (N = 30). Descriptive statistics is presented for students' evaluations of the escape room instructional design supported by generative artificial intelligence (Fig. 2).

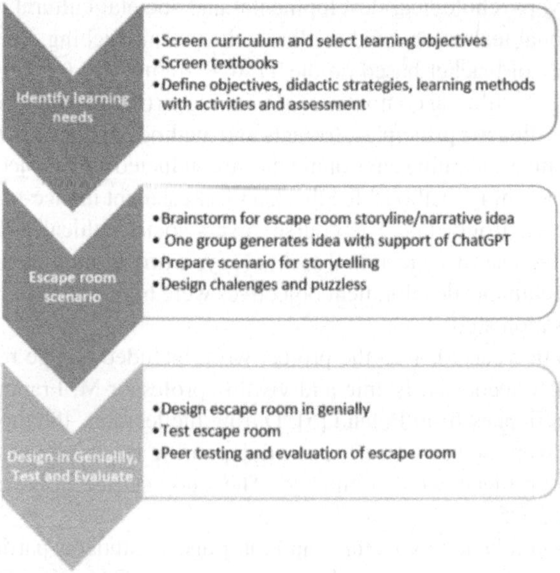

Fig. 2. Escape room design in four stages (authors' own figure)

3 Result and Discussion

3.1 Students' Evaluation of Escape Room Design and Its Effect of Competences

The perception of innovative instruction with digital technology integration depends on teacher's perception of technology usability and contribution to instruction. Research proves escape rooms in innovative instruction for the development of 21st Century skills [1–3, 6]. Preservice teachers reported that the design of escape rooms, on Fig. 3, fulfilled the anticipation of having fun according to the edutainment idea, discovering something new and engaging in a creative way. They were more critical to the clarity of project objectives, having difficulty to understand the multidimensional task of escape room design following curricular objectives integrating instructional/didactic strategy, selecting learning methods utilizing challenges and puzzles. They rated well the use of digital tools however; the team collaboration was rated lower with more students marked neutral (3). Students rated skills development (Fig. 4), highly the use of escape rooms for engaging classes for children, preparation for their future jobs and opportunity for collaboration. In the assessment of the creative problem solving, critical thinking, logical thinking, and digital proficiency, and design of a lesson plan, more students marked neutral (3). Students presented their learning satisfaction with the stages of the escape room design process (Fig. 5). Students expressed high satisfaction with designing educational puzzles and searching for a theme for an escape room, and also establishing a storyline. Regarding the level of difficulty, the most difficult stages (Fig. 6) were for students also most satisfying (Fig. 5). Creative engagement was needed for those stages, the searching for a theme of an escape room, designing a narrative and designing puzzles.

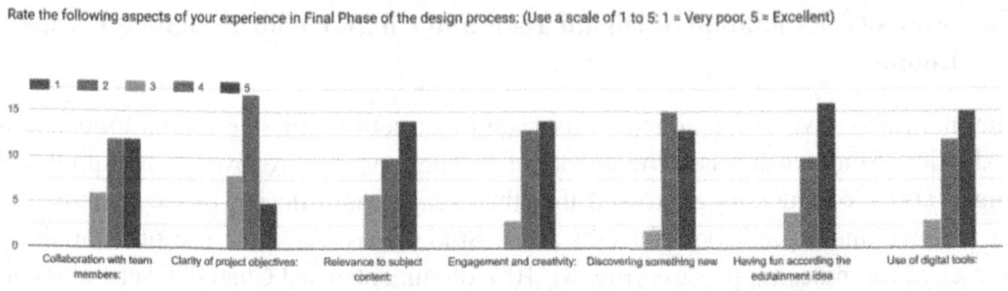

Fig. 3. Final evaluation of a design process (authors' own figure)

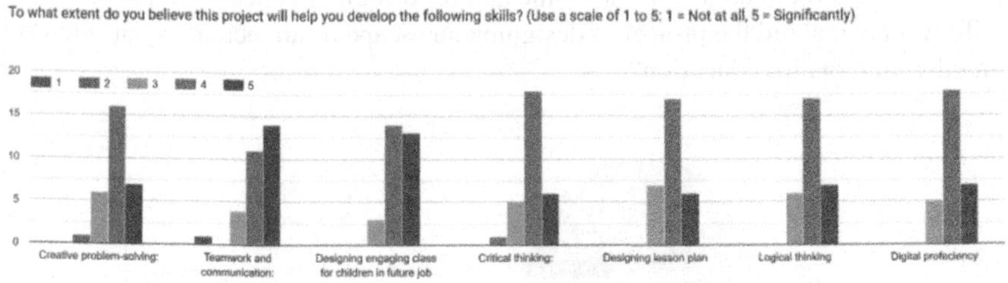

Fig. 4. Skills development in a design process (authors' own figure)

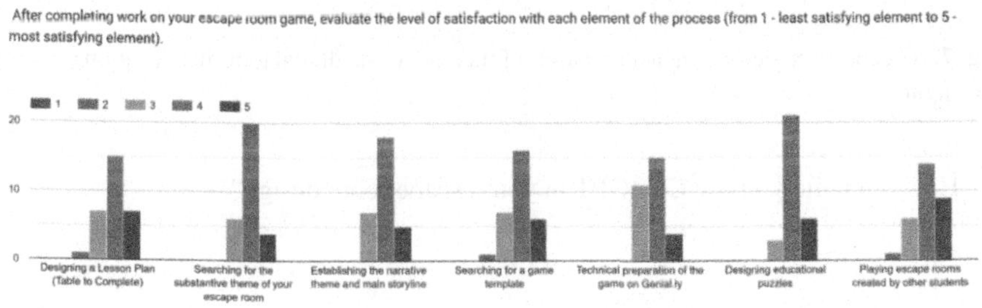

Fig. 5. Evaluation of the stages of the escape room design process (authors' own figure)

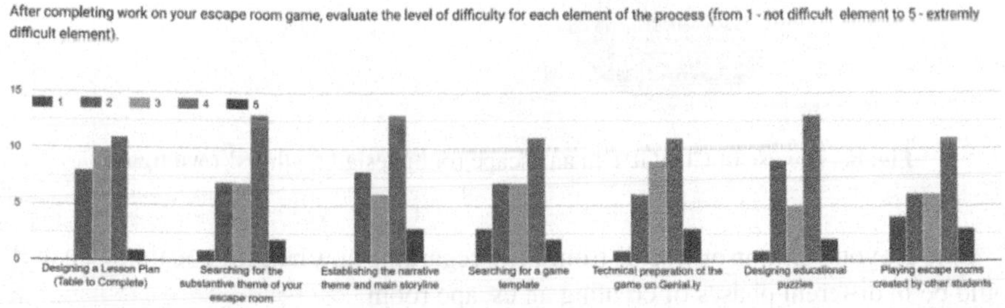

Fig. 6. Evaluation difficulty of the stages of the escape room design process (authors' own figure)

3.2 Students' Evaluation of Digital Tools and ChatGPT for Designing Escape Rooms

The main objective in the course is to design instruction utilizing digital tools and its evaluation. Students assessed the impact of escape room for creative use of digital tools (Fig. 7).60% of students expressed that the escape room design raised their interest for creative and digital tools for education. Students assessed the use of ChatGPT in an escape room design process (Fig. 8). 10% of students used ChatGPT very often and 16.7% did not use it at all. Students assessed the usability of ChatGPT in an escape room design (Fig. 9). Students believe that ChatGPT is useful for searching and generating ideas for escape room theme, for storyline and for design of educational puzzles.

To what extent did the project of designing an escape room increase your interest in using digital tools for education?

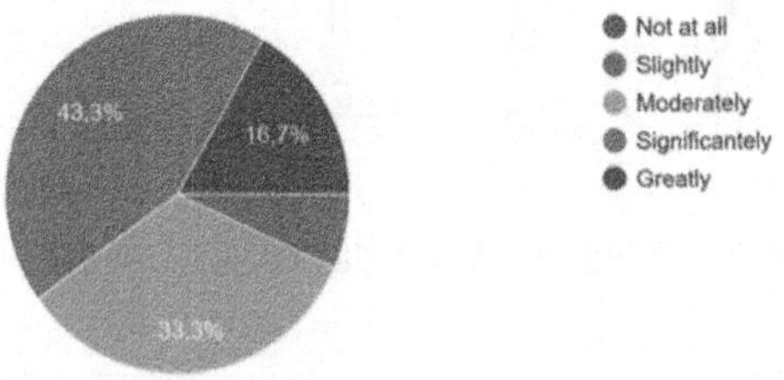

Fig. 7. Escape room design impact on interest for creative and digital tools in education (authors' own figure)

How often did you use ChatGPT in your escape room design?

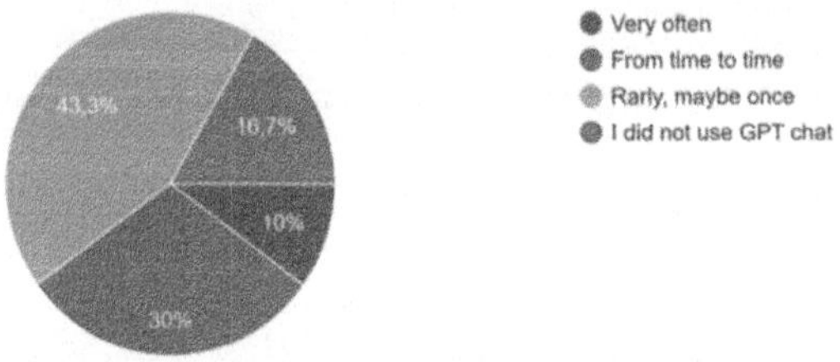

Fig. 8. The use of ChatGPT in an escape room design (authors' own figure)

Express your opinion on a scale from 1 to 5 regarding how helpful you think ChatGPT could be in different phases of creating an escape room.

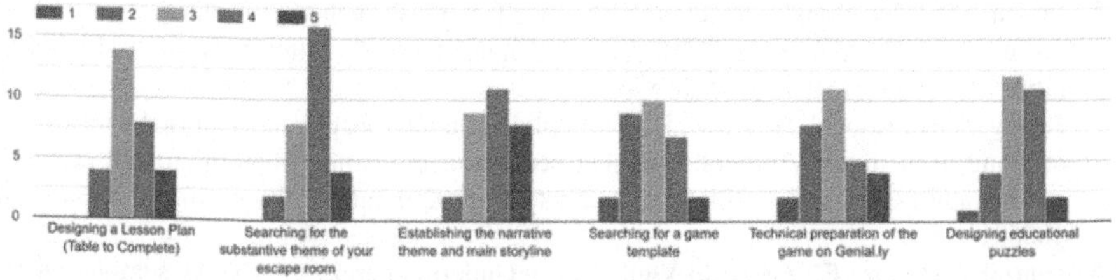

Fig. 9. Usefulness of ChatGPT in a stages of an escape room design (authors' own figure)

4 Conclusion

This is a small-scale study in an educational technology course exploring and preparing preservice students for educational use of generative artificial intelligence while lesson planning and designing a course material and tasks. It requires high level of creativity, critical thinking and problem-solving in establishing a theme for a game and designing engaging challenges and puzzles. The escape room design was aiming at innovative instructional design utilizing digital tools and generative artificial intelligence, taking into account an educational system, considering complex factors. Preservice teachers will be facing challenges of rapid technology developments and will act as a change agent, reducing and overcoming the potential disparities in access, pedagogical quality, the ownership and rights to data and resources and contribute in setting ethics regulations. Providing pedagogical quality in the integration of generative artificial intelligence in education requires the preparation of preservice teachers.

Funding. The project "Modernisation of pedagogical study programmes - Modernisation of the NOO PSP" is co-funded by the Ministry of Education and The European Commission NextGenerationEU). University of Ljubljana is implementing the project in a consortium with the University of Maribor and the University of Primorska; The ARIS P2–0210; The scientific fellowship of Monika Frania at the University of Primorska the „Research Excellence Initiative - Mobility Component" (3rd Ed., 2024), by the University of Silesia in Katowice, Poland.

References

1. Veldkamp, A., van de Grint, L., Knippels, M.C.P.J., van Joolingen, W.R.: Escape education: A systematic review on escape rooms in education. Educational Research Review **31** (2020). https://doi.org/10.1016/j.edurev.2020.100364
2. Veldkamp, A., Daemen, J., Teekens, S., Koelewijn, S., Knippels, M.C.P., van Joolingen, W.R.: Escape boxes: Bringing escape room experience into the classroom. Br. J. Edu. Technol. **51**(4), 1220–1239 (2020)
3. Sidekerskiene, T., Damaševičius, R.: Out-of-the-box learning: digital escape rooms as a metaphor for breaking down barriers in STEM education. Sustainability **15**, 7393 (2023). https://doi.org/10.3390/su15097393
4. Taraldsen, L.H., Haara, F.O., Lysne, M.S., Jensen, P.R., Jenssen, E.S.: A review on use of escape rooms in education – touching the void. Education Inquiry **13**(2), 169–184 (2022). https://doi.org/10.1080/20004508.2020.1860284

5. Frania, M.: Educational e-escape room as an educational method of media literacy training for future teachers during the COVID-19 pandemic. Media Education **17**(3), 452–459 (2021). https://doi.org/10.13187/me.2021.3.452
6. Huang, S.-H., Kuo, Y.-H., Chen, H.-C.: Applying digital escape rooms infused with science teaching in elementary school: Learning performance, learning motivation, and problem-solving ability. Thinking Skills and Creativity **37** (2020). https://doi.org/10.1016/j.tsc.2020.100681
7. González-Muñoz, E., Gallardo-Vigil, M.Á., Gutiérrez-Pérez, J.: The Mysterious Disappearance: assessment of a sustainability-themed virtual educational escape room in higher education. Journal of Applied Research in Higher Education (2024)
8. Makri, A., Vlachopoulos, D., Martina, R.A.: Digital escape rooms as innovative pedagogical tools in education: a systematic literature review. Sustainability **13**, 4587 (2021). https://doi.org/10.3390/su13084587
9. Reiser, A.R., Ely, D.P.: The field of educational technology as reflected through its definition. Education Tech. Research Dev. **45**(3), 63–72 (1997)
10. 1Blažič, M., Ivanuš Grmek, M., Strmčnik, F.: Didaktika. Novo mest: Visokošolsko središče Novo mesto (2003)
11. Reiser, R.A.: A history of instructional design anIstenič, A.: d technology: Part II: A history of Instructional media. Educational Technology Research and Development **49**(1), 53–64 (2001) (2019)
12. Istenič, A.: Educational technology and the construction of authentic learning environments. Ljubljana: ULFGG (2020). https://repozitorij.uni-lj.si/Dokument.php?id=141497&lang=slv
13. Istenič Starčič, A.: Human learning and learning analytics in the age of artificial intelligence. Br. J. Edu. Technol. **50**(6), 2975–2976 (2019). https://doi.org/10.1111/bjet.12879
14. Partnership for 21st Century Skills (P21) & American Colleges of teacher education (AACTE). (2010). 21st century knowledge and skills in educator preparation White paper. https://files.eric.ed.gov/fulltext/ED519336.pdf
15. Bianchi, G., Pisiotis, U., Cabrera Giraldez, M.: GreenComp – The European sustainability competence framework. In: Bacigalupo, M., Punie, Y. (eds.) European Commission, Joint Research Centre. Publications Office of the European Union, Luxembourg (2022). https://doi.org/10.2760/13286
16. Redecker, C.: European Framework for the Digital Competence of Educators: DigCompEdu. In: Punie, Y. (ed.) EUR 28775 EN. Publications Office of the European Union, Luxembourg (2017). https://doi.org/10.2760/159770, JRC107466
17. Sperling, K., et al.: In search of artificial intelligence (AI) literacy in teacher education: A scoping review. Computers and Education Open 100169 (2024)
18. Mouta, A., Pinto-Llorente, A.M., Torrecilla-Sánchez, E.M.: Uncovering blind spots in education ethics: Insights from a systematic literature review on artificial intelligence in education. Int. J. Artif. Intell. Educ. **34**(3), 1166–1205 (2024)
19. van den Berg, G., du Plessis, E.: ChatGPT and generative AI: Possibilities for its contribution to lesson planning, critical thinking and openness in teacher education. Education Sciences **13**(10), 998 (2023)
20. De Lope, R.P., Medina-Medina, N.: A Comprehensive taxonomy for serious games. Journal of Educational Computing Research **55**(5), 629–672 (2016). https://doi.org/10.1177/0735633116681301(Originalworkpublished2017)
21. Hus, V., Ivanuš Grmek, M.: Didactic strategies in early science teaching. Educational Studies **37**(2), 159–169 (2011). https://doi.org/10.1080/03055698.2010.506336
22. Valenčič Zuljan, M., Kalin, J.: Učne metode in razvoj učiteljeve metodične kompetence. PEF, Ljubljana (2020)
23. Bruner, J.: Life as narrative. Social research **71**(3), 691–710 (2004)

24. Vigotsky, L.S.: Mind and society. Harvard University Press, The development of higher psycological process. Cambridge (1978)
25. Zupan Sosič, A.: Zgodba, pripoved in pripovedovanje v dvoravninski in troravninski koncepciji pripovedi. Primerjalna književnost **26**(3), 61–83 (2013)
26. Haramina, E., et al.: Learning algorithms concepts in a virtual reality escape room. In: 2024 47th MIPRO ICT and Electronics Convention (MIPRO), pp. 2057–2062. IEEE (2024)
27. Genially Retrieved from https://Genially.com/templates/games/escape-room/

STEMChat: Investigating Student Perceptions of ChatGPT-Based Mobile Instant Messaging in Collaborative STEM Learning

Hsin-Yu Lee and Ting-Ting Wu(✉)

Graduate School of Technological and Vocational Education, National Yunlin University of Science and Technology, Yunlin 640, Taiwan, R.O.C.
ttwu@yuntech.edu.tw

Abstract. The integration of ChatGPT into mobile instant messaging (MIM) for STEM education addresses significant collaboration challenges such as information overload and limited support for complex problem-solving. This study developed STEMChat, a ChatGPT-enhanced MIM tool with real-time question-answering and conversation summarization capabilities, which was implemented with twenty-five undergraduate engineering students over 6 weeks for group projects. Data collected through semi-structured interviews based on an extended Technology Acceptance Model revealed favorable perceptions across multiple dimensions: perceived usefulness (76% positive), perceived ease of use (82% positive), and behavioral intention to use (78% positive). Two additional constructs—Perceived AI Support and Perceived STEM Learning Enhancement—demonstrated how AI-enhanced communication addressed domain-specific collaborative challenges. Students particularly valued STEMChat's capacity to clarify technical terminology, facilitate structured problem decomposition, and maintain coherent documentation of complex design processes. These findings provide valuable insights for developing AI-enhanced collaborative tools specifically tailored to address the unique challenges of collaborative problem-solving and knowledge construction in STEM education contexts.

Keywords: ChatGPT · Mobile instant messaging · STEM education · Technology Acceptance Model · Collaboration · Student perceptions

1 Introduction

The integration of digital technologies has significantly transformed STEM (Science, Technology, Engineering, and Mathematics) education, particularly in facilitating collaborative learning experiences [1, 2]. In STEM fields, collaborative problem-solving represents a fundamental skill that students must develop to address complex, real-world challenges [3]. As educational institutions increasingly implement online and hybrid approaches to STEM instruction, the need for effective digital collaboration tools has become paramount [4].

W.-S. Wang et al. (Eds.): ICITL 2025, LNCS 15913, pp. 142–151, 2026.
https://doi.org/10.1007/978-3-031-98185-2_16

Mobile Instant Messaging (MIM) applications have emerged as essential tools for supporting educational communication and collaboration due to their ubiquity, immediacy, and accessibility [5]. However, when applied specifically to STEM education contexts, traditional MIM tools reveal significant limitations that can impede effective collaboration. STEM discussions often involve complex technical concepts, mathematical notations, and intricate problem-solving processes that can be difficult to communicate effectively through text-based messaging alone [6]. Additionally, the information density characteristic of STEM discussions can lead to cognitive overload, as students struggle to track multiple threads of technical reasoning simultaneously [7].

A critical challenge in STEM collaborative learning is maintaining both depth and coherence in discussions [8]. When students collaborate on engineering design problems or scientific investigations, conversations frequently branch into multiple technical considerations, making it difficult to maintain a holistic understanding of the problem space [9]. Traditional MIM platforms offer limited support for organizing these complex discussion pathways or synthesizing key insights across extended collaborative sessions [10].

The emergence of Large Language Models (LLMs) such as ChatGPT presents a promising opportunity to address these STEM-specific collaboration challenges. While research has explored ChatGPT's applications in education broadly [11, 12], limited attention has been paid to how it might enhance collaborative learning specifically within STEM disciplines. The integration of ChatGPT capabilities into MIM platforms could potentially provide contextual support for technical discussions, help synthesize complex problem-solving threads [13, 14], and facilitate more effective knowledge construction in collaborative STEM settings.

This study introduces STEMChat, a ChatGPT-enhanced mobile instant messaging tool designed specifically to support collaborative learning in STEM education. STEMChat incorporates two key features to address the identified challenges: (1) real-time technical question answering to maintain discussion flow when conceptual clarification is needed, and (2) conversation summarization to help students synthesize complex technical discussions and maintain coherence in problem-solving processes.

Unlike previous research that has primarily focused on comparing ChatGPT-enhanced and traditional communication tools across various metrics, this pivot study concentrates specifically on understanding student perceptions of STEMChat in supporting STEM collaboration. By employing an extended Technology Acceptance Model (TAM) framework with domain-specific constructs, we aim to elucidate how students perceive the value, usability, and impact of AI-enhanced communication tools in addressing the unique challenges of collaborative STEM learning.

This research addresses the following question: How do students perceive STEMChat in terms of its usefulness, ease of use, and impact on collaborative learning in STEM education contexts? By focusing on student perceptions, we aim to provide insights into the design and implementation of effective AI-enhanced collaborative tools specifically tailored to the needs of STEM education.

2 STEMChat System Design

To address the unique challenges of collaborative STEM learning, we developed STEMChat, a ChatGPT-enhanced mobile instant messaging tool designed to support technical discussions and collaborative problem-solving. STEMChat integrates with LINE, a widely-used messaging platform in our research context, ensuring familiarity and accessibility for students. The system is specifically designed to facilitate STEM collaboration through two key features: real-time technical question answering and conversation summarization with problem-solving support.

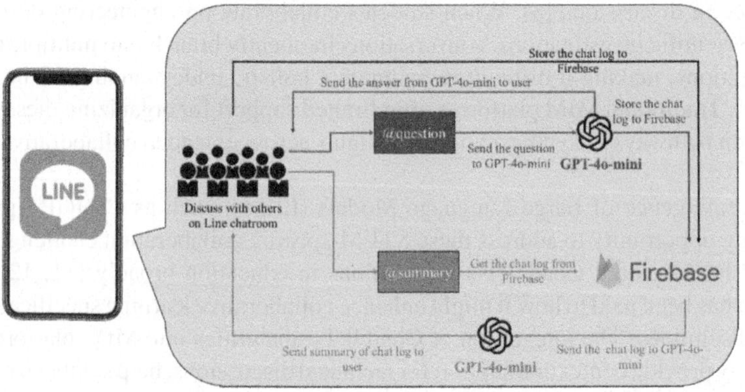

Fig. 1. The operational flow of STEMChat

As illustrated in Fig. 1, STEMChat employs a client-server architecture that integrates the LINE messaging platform with GPT-4o-mini and a Firebase database. The system is designed to support collaborative STEM problem-solving through seamless integration into students' existing communication workflows. When students encounter technical questions during their discussions, they can invoke STEMChat's assistance by typing "@question" followed by their inquiry. This command triggers the system to process the query through GPT-4o-mini, which then provides a response directly in the chat interface. Simultaneously, this interaction is logged in Firebase, creating a retrievable history of technical clarifications that supports the iterative nature of STEM problem-solving.

The system's conversation summarization feature is activated when students type "summary" during their collaborative sessions. This command prompts STEMChat to retrieve recent chat logs from Firebase and process them through GPT-4o-mini with a specialized prompt designed for STEM problem-solving contexts. The resulting summary identifies key technical concepts, maps relationships between ideas, highlights decision points, and organizes information according to standard problem-solving frameworks relevant to STEM disciplines. This functionality directly addresses the challenge of maintaining coherence and structure during complex technical discussions.

STEMChat's implementation includes carefully crafted prompts to optimize ChatGPT's performance for STEM collaboration contexts. For the question-answering function, GPT-4o-mini is configured with the prompt: "*You are an AI assistant supporting*

STEM students in collaborative problem-solving. Please answer the following technical question concisely, accurately, and with appropriate STEM terminology: [User's question]." The model's parameters (temperature = 0.7, frequency_penalty = 0.0) balance technical precision with conversational tone.

For the summarization feature, the system retrieves the 500 most recent messages and processes them with a STEM-oriented prompt: "*Summarize the key technical points of this STEM discussion in a structured format. Identify: (1) Primary concepts and principles discussed, (2) Problem statements and constraints, (3) Proposed solutions and their technical justifications, (4) Decision points and outcomes, (5) Next steps or open questions: [500 messages].*" The parameters (temperature = 0.3, frequency_penalty = 0.5) ensure concise, technically accurate summaries.

3 Methodology

3.1 Participants and Setting

This pivot study employed a qualitative approach to investigate student perceptions of STEMChat in supporting collaborative STEM learning. Twenty-five undergraduate engineering students (14 males, 11 females, aged 20–23 years, Mage = 21.6, SD = 0.9) participated in the study. Participants were enrolled in a course on Networks Embedded.

System and Application at a university in Taiwan and were selected based on their prior experience with collaborative STEM projects and familiarity with mobile messaging applications.

The study was conducted over a 6-week period during which participants used STEMChat to support their collaborative work on engineering design projects. These projects required sustained team communication, technical problem-solving, and documentation of design processes—activities that align with the collaborative challenges STEMChat was designed to address. The engineering design projects focused on developing sustainable energy solutions, requiring students to collaborate on technical analyses, prototype designs, and implementation strategies.

All participants provided informed consent, and the study was approved by the university's Research Ethics Committee. Data collection and analysis focused exclusively on students' perceptions of the STEMChat system rather than evaluating their academic performance, aligning with the pivot study approach.

3.2 Data Collection

Semi-structured interviews served as the primary data collection method, allowing for in-depth exploration of students' perceptions of STEMChat. The interview protocol was developed based on an extended Technology Acceptance Model (TAM) framework, incorporating additional constructs specifically relevant to AI-enhanced STEM collaboration.

The interview guide was structured around the following constructs:

Perceived Usefulness (PU): "How did STEMChat enhance your performance in collaborative STEM problem-solving?".

Perceived Ease of Use (PEOU): "What challenges did you encounter while using STEMChat during your engineering design project?".

Attitude Towards Use (ATU): "What are your overall thoughts on using STEMChat for collaborative engineering work?".

Behavioral Intention to Use (BIU): "Would you use STEMChat in future STEM collaborative activities? Why?".

In addition to these core TAM constructs, we included two domain-specific constructs:

Perceived AI Support (PAS): "How did the AI features of STEMChat support technical aspects of your collaborative engineering work?" This construct was adapted from [15], who introduced the concept of perceived AI support in educational contexts. We modified this construct to specifically address the AI-powered support for STEM-specific tasks and communication needs.

Perceived STEM Learning Enhancement (PSLE): "In what ways did STEMChat improve your collaborative learning experience in engineering design?" This construct was based on [15], who used perceived learning enhancement to evaluate technology impact on learning experiences. We adapted this construct to focus specifically on how STEMChat supported STEM-specific learning processes such as technical problem decomposition, systematic analysis, and iterative solution development.

All 25 participants were interviewed individually, with each interview lasting 30–45 min. Interviews were conducted in person, audio-recorded with permission, and later transcribed for analysis. The semi-structured format allowed for consistent coverage of key constructs while providing flexibility to explore unique insights and experiences.

3.3 Data Analysis

Interview transcripts were analyzed using thematic analysis within the extended TAM framework. The analysis process followed these steps:

1. Familiarization with the data through multiple readings of transcripts
2. Initial coding of responses related to each TAM construct
3. Development of themes within each construct
4. Review and refinement of themes
5. Final theme definition and naming
6. Analysis and interpretation of thematic patterns

Two researchers independently coded a subset of the transcripts (20%) to ensure reliability. Cohen's kappa coefficient was calculated to assess inter-rater agreement, yielding a value of 0.84, indicating strong agreement. After establishing reliability, the remaining transcripts were coded by one researcher, with regular consultations to address any ambiguous segments.

For each TAM construct, responses were categorized as positive, neutral, or negative to provide a quantitative overview of perceptions. Additionally, key themes emerging within each construct were identified and analyzed, with particular attention to how students' perceptions related to STEM-specific collaboration challenges.

The analysis also focused on identifying connections between the standard TAM constructs and the domain-specific constructs of Perceived AI Support and Perceived STEM Learning Enhancement. This approach allowed for a more comprehensive understanding of how students perceived STEMChat's value specifically within the context of collaborative STEM learning.

4 Results

4.1 Perceived Usefulness (PU)

Analysis of interview responses revealed that 76% of participants perceived STEMChat as useful for supporting collaborative STEM learning, with 16% expressing neutral perceptions and 8% reporting negative perceptions. Three key themes emerged regarding the system's perceived usefulness.

Technical Clarification and Information Access: Students valued STEMChat's ability to provide immediate clarification of technical concepts during collaborative discussions:

"*During our solar panel efficiency calculations, we encountered unfamiliar terms like 'fill factor.' STEMChat quickly explained the concept and provided the formula, which kept our discussion moving forward rather than stalling while we searched elsewhere.*" (Participant 07).

Problem Decomposition and Structuring: Participants appreciated how STEMChat's summarization feature helped organize complex engineering problems into manageable components, making their collaboration more systematic and structured.

Documentation and Knowledge Management: Students highlighted the value of maintaining a coherent record of technical discussions and decisions, particularly important given the iterative nature of engineering design processes.

Some participants noted limitations regarding domain-specific technical depth, occasionally requiring verification from other sources for advanced concepts.

4.2 Perceived Ease of Use (PEOU)

The analysis showed that 82% of participants found STEMChat easy to use, with 12% expressing neutral perceptions and 6% reporting difficulties. Key usability themes included the system's seamless integration with familiar messaging platforms and appropriate response formatting for technical discussions.

"*I already used LINE for everyday communication, so adding STEMChat functionality felt natural. The '@' commands were intuitive and didn't disrupt our natural conversation flow during technical discussions.*" (Participant 09).

While most participants quickly adapted to the command structure, some suggested improvements for STEM contexts, such as better equation formatting and integration with sketching tools for quick diagrams.

4.3 Attitude Towards Use (ATU)

Overall, 72% of participants expressed positive attitudes toward STEMChat, with 20% neutral and 8% negative. Students valued the enhancement of collaborative efficiency and appreciated how the system complemented rather than replaced human collaboration:

"*STEMChat felt like having an additional team member who could provide quick technical input and help organize our discussions. It made our collaboration more efficient and focused.*" (Participant 02).

Several participants connected their use of STEMChat to future professional practice, noting its relevance to industry environments where structured technical communication is essential. Some concerns were expressed about potential overdependence affecting independent research skills.

4.4 Behavioral Intention to Use (BIU)

Analysis revealed that 78% of participants intended to use STEMChat in future STEM collaborative activities. Students indicated that project complexity was a key determinant in their intention to use the system, with greater likelihood for complex engineering projects requiring sustained collaboration. Many expressed interest in enhanced functionality, particularly integration with computational tools or visualization support.

"*Beyond course projects, I see myself using this for student engineering competitions, research collaborations, and potentially in industry internships. Any situation requiring structured technical discussion would benefit from these features.*" (Participant 12).

4.5 Perceived AI Support (PAS)

This domain-specific construct revealed that 74% of participants positively evaluated STEMChat's AI capabilities for STEM collaboration. Key themes included technical vocabulary clarification, multi-perspective technical input, and consistency in technical communication:

"*Engineering discussions use specialized terminology that not everyone in the group may understand equally. STEMChat helped level the playing field by providing quick clarification of technical terms, which made our collaboration more inclusive.*" (Participant 05).

Students particularly valued how the AI support helped standardize technical language and introduce alternative approaches to engineering problems, expanding their thinking during design processes.

4.6 Perceived STEM Learning Enhancement (PSLE)

Regarding learning impact, 70% of participants believed STEMChat enhanced their STEM learning experience. Students appreciated support for systematic engineering problem-solving approaches, connections between theory and application, and documentation of iterative design processes:

"The summaries organized our discussions according to a systematic engineering design framework–problem definition, requirements analysis, solution generation, and evaluation. This reinforced good engineering practice." (Participant 10).

Participants noted that STEMChat made their technical reasoning processes more visible, helping them develop more rigorous analytical skills and reflect on how their thinking evolved through design iterations.

5 Discussion and Conclusion

This study investigated student perceptions of STEMChat, a ChatGPT-enhanced mobile messaging tool designed to support collaborative learning in STEM education. The findings provide key insights into how AI-enhanced communication tools can address specific challenges in STEM collaboration and how students perceive their educational value.

5.1 Addressing STEM-Specific Collaboration Challenges

Results demonstrate that STEMChat effectively addresses several key challenges in STEM collaboration identified in previous research. The system's question-answering feature mitigates the interruptions in technical discussions that Tang and Hew [10] identified as detrimental to collaborative flow. By providing immediate clarification of technical concepts, STEMChat maintains momentum in problem-solving sessions.

Information overload in technical discussions [15] is addressed through the summarization feature, helping students manage complex information and maintain coherence across extended collaborative sessions. Students' positive response to this functionality aligns with research by Wang, Chia-Ju, Hsin-Yu, Yueh-Min and and Wu [12] on the importance of reflection and knowledge organization in STEM learning.

The findings also support Lee, Wu, Lin, Wang and Huang [16]'s emphasis on systematic problem decomposition in STEM education, with students valuing STEMChat's ability to organize discussions according to engineering design frameworks.

5.2 Implications and Future Directions

This study offers several implications for AI-enhanced tool design in STEM education. First, the findings highlight the importance of integrating AI capabilities into existing communication platforms rather than creating standalone systems, reducing adoption barriers. Second, domain-specific AI enhancements should be tailored to the specific communication and cognitive processes of STEM disciplines. Third, AI tools should balance support with student agency, scaffolding rather than supplanting student-led problem-solving processes.

Limitations of this study include its focus on perceptions rather than learning outcomes, the relatively short implementation period, and the specific sample of engineering students. Future research should employ mixed-methods approaches to correlate perception data with objective measures of collaborative effectiveness and learning gains. Longitudinal studies could provide insights into how perceptions evolve with extended use. Additionally, research is needed on how such tools can be adapted to different STEM disciplines and interdisciplinary collaboration.

5.3 Conclusion

This study provides evidence that students perceive ChatGPT-enhanced mobile messaging tools favorably for supporting collaborative learning in STEM education. STEMChat addresses specific challenges in STEM collaboration through features that maintain discussion flow, manage information complexity, and support systematic problem-solving approaches.

The findings contribute to our understanding of how AI can be effectively integrated into collaborative STEM learning environments, highlighting the importance of domain-specific design, seamless integration with existing platforms, and appropriate balance between AI support and student agency. As educational institutions continue to explore innovative approaches to STEM education, AI-enhanced collaborative tools like STEMChat offer promising avenues for supporting the complex technical communication and problem-solving processes central to these disciplines.

References

1. Lee, H.-Y., Cheng, Y.-P., Wang, W.-S., Lin, C.-J., Huang, Y.-M.: Exploring the learning process and effectiveness of STEM education via learning behavior analysis and the interactive-constructive-active-passive framework. J. Educ. Comp. Res. **61**, 951–976 (2023)
2. Lin, C.-J., Lee, H.-Y., Wang, W.-S., Huang, Y.-M., Wu, T.-T.: Enhancing reflective thinking in STEM education through experiential learning: The role of generative AI as a learning aid. Education and Information Technologies (2024)
3. Lin, C.-J., Wang, W.-S., Lee, H.-Y., Huang, Y.-M., Wu, T.-T.: Recognitions of image and speech to improve learning diagnosis on STEM collaborative activity for precision education. Educ. Inf. Technol. **29**, 13859–13884 (2024)
4. Kier, M.W., Johnson, L.L.: Exploring How Secondary STEM Teachers and Undergraduate Mentors Adapt Digital Technologies to Promote Culturally Relevant Education during COVID-19. Education Sciences **12**, 48 (2022)
5. Lee, H.-Y., Huang, Y.-M.: Bridging STEM Education and Ubiquitous Learning: A Case Study on Developing a LINE Chatbot with Google's Gemini for Virtual Peer Collaboration. In: Innovative Technologies and Learning, pp. 237–246. Springer Nature Switzerland, (Year)
6. Walsh, L., Ross, A.B.: The Visual Invention Practices of STEM Researchers: An Exploratory Topology. Sci. Commun. **37**, 118–139 (2015)
7. Iammartino, R., Bischoff, J., Willy, C., Shapiro, P.: Emergence in the U.S. Science, Technology, Engineering, and Mathematics (STEM) workforce: an agent-based model of worker attrition and group size in high-density STEM organizations. Complex & Intelligent Systems **2**, 23–34 (2016)
8. Crippen, K.J., Antonenko, P.D.: Designing for Collaborative Problem Solving in STEM Cyberlearning. In: Dori, Y.J., Mevarech, Z.R., Baker, D.R. (eds.) Cognition, Metacognition, and Culture in STEM Education: Learning, Teaching and Assessment, pp. 89–116. Springer International Publishing, Cham (2018)
9. Lin, K.-Y., Yu, K.-C., Hsiao, H.-S., Chu, Y.-H., Chang, Y.-S., Chien, Y.-H.: Design of an assessment system for collaborative problem solving in STEM education. Journal of Computers in Education **2**, 301–322 (2015)
10. Tang, Y., Hew, K.F.: Effects of using mobile instant messaging on student behavioral, emotional, and cognitive engagement: a quasi-experimental study. Int. J. Educ. Technol. High. Educ. **19**, 3 (2022)

11. Li, P.-H., Lee, H.-Y., Cheng, Y.-P., Starčič, A.I., Huang, Y.-M.: Solving the Self-regulated Learning Problem: Exploring the Performance of ChatGPT in Mathematics, pp. 77–86. Springer Nature Switzerland (Year)
12. Wang, W.-S., Chia-Ju, L., Hsin-Yu, L., Yueh-Min, H., Wu, T.-T.: Integrating feedback mechanisms and ChatGPT for VR-based experiential learning: impacts on reflective thinking and AIoT physical hands-on tasks. Interact. Learn. Environ. **33**, 1770–1787 (2025)
13. Wu, T.-T., Lee, H.-Y., Li, P.-H., Huang, C.-N., Huang, Y.-M.: Promoting self-regulation progress and knowledge construction in blended learning via ChatGPT-based learning aid. Journal of Educational Computing Research **61**, 3–31 (2024)
14. Lee, H.-Y., Chen, P.-H., Wang, W.-S., Huang, Y.-M., Wu, T.-T.: Empowering ChatGPT with guidance mechanism in blended learning: effect of self-regulated learning, higher-order thinking skills, and knowledge construction. Int. J. Educ. Technol. High. Educ. **21**, 16 (2024)
15. Huang, Y.-M., Chen, P.-H., Lee, H.-Y., Sandnes, F.E., Wu, T.-T.: ChatGPT-Enhanced Mobile Instant Messaging in Online Learning: Effects on Student Outcomes and Perceptions. Computers in Human Behavior 108659 (2025)
16. Lee, H.-Y., Wu, T.-T., Lin, C.-J., Wang, W.-S., Huang, Y.-M.: Integrating Computational Thinking Into Scaffolding Learning: An Innovative Approach to Enhance Science, Technology, Engineering, and Mathematics Hands-On Learning. J. Educ. Comp. Res. **62**, 431–467 (2023)

Enhancing the Development of Higher Order Thinking in Beginners Through Creative Guided GPT

Shu-Chen Wang[1], Jiann-Liang Chen[2], and Yueh-Min Huang[1](✉)

[1] Department of Engineering Science, National Cheng Kung University, Tainan City, Taiwan
huang@mail.ncku.edu.tw

[2] Department of Electrical Engineering, National Taiwan University of Science and Technology, Taipei, Taiwan
Lchen@mail.ntust.edu.tw

Abstract. Creative learning emphasizes student-driven exploration, collaborative communication, and multifaceted thinking. For novice learners from non-major disciplines, the desire for exploration stimulated during the process of acquiring new knowledge can effectively enhance intrinsic motivation, encouraging diverse attempts and deepening understanding, thereby promoting the development of higher-order thinking skills. However, beginners often struggle to connect knowledge and concepts, facing difficulties in identifying boundaries during the transition between convergent and divergent thinking. Appropriate guidance and prompts are necessary to help them achieve balance between these modes of thinking. This study developed an instructional assistant system called Innovation Spark GPT (InnoSparkGPT), aimed at supporting non-major students in creative collaborative projects. By simulating real-world scenarios, the system enhances students' conceptual connections and employs prompt engineering aligned with various stages of the Creative Problem Solving (CPS) model. Specifically, InnoSparkGPT applies suitable constraints to students' responses while providing creative guidance and suggestions to facilitate flexible transitions between divergent and convergent thinking. This mechanism not only stimulates creative ideation but also assists students in developing and refining problem-solving strategies to complete collaborative project development. Furthermore, the system encourages students to share diverse perspectives during discussions, thereby refining and enhancing their ideas to generate more appropriate solutions. This research explores the potential of leveraging emerging technologies to inspire creative thinking among non-major learners. By integrating stage-based learning strategies, it aims to assist them in tackling complex tasks, providing effective methods and insights for the development of higher-order thinking skills in beginners.

Keywords: Creative Problem Solving · Higher Order Thinking · Learning engagement · ChatGPT

W.-S. Wang et al. (Eds.): ICITL 2025, LNCS 15913, pp. 152–161, 2026.
https://doi.org/10.1007/978-3-031-98185-2_17

1 Introduction

In the current era of information explosion and emphasis on interdisciplinary integration for diverse skill development, individuals must possess critical thinking and problem-solving abilities to identify the most suitable solutions among numerous options. The ability to grasp key concepts and extend them into innovative thinking is essential for adapting to various real-world scenarios. Such competencies not only enhance adaptability but also serve as critical factors in strengthening competitiveness within modern society. Consequently, higher-order thinking (HOT) is recognized as an indispensable core skill today. HOT emphasizes learners' in-depth analysis of problems to grasp the underlying core concepts, promoting continuous self-reflection, evaluating the feasibility of solutions, and experimenting with diverse problem-solving strategies. The process of learning programming effectively fosters students' higher-order thinking skills. Through programming, students develop the ability to abstract concepts from concrete problems and use creativity to design algorithms for solution development. Furthermore, critically evaluating these solutions requires students to apply foundational knowledge and progress toward more advanced cognitive skills.

For students from non-computer science disciplines, their foundational programming knowledge is often underdeveloped, leading to a learning process heavily reliant on memorization and imitation. This dependence hinders their ability to connect syntax with logical concepts, making it difficult for them to approach new programming concepts or problem scenarios [1] Non-computer science students often perceive programming as irrelevant to their field of study, resulting in decreased learning motivation. These issues limit their opportunities to develop higher-order thinking skills, particularly creativity. Creativity is typically driven by intrinsic motivation and built upon solid knowledge construction. It emerges from rich life experiences that inspire creative ideas, followed by deep thinking that connects knowledge and experiences to generate diverse solutions. Developing creativity involves multiple iterations of divergent and convergent thinking. However, students often struggle to find the balance between these processes, necessitating substantial guidance to facilitate the iterative switching between divergent and convergent thinking, which is essential for creativity cultivation. Traditional teaching methods are often constrained by limited human resources, making it difficult for instructors to provide timely, individualized feedback and guidance that addresses each student's learning needs. This limitation adversely affects students learning motivation and engagement, In response to the challenges of fostering creative thinking within conventional instruction, technological interventions offer opportunities to transcend existing pedagogical frameworks, enhancing learning effectiveness and promoting the development of higher-order thinking skills [6].

This study proposes that integrating ChatGPT into creativity-oriented learning strategies is a feasible and effective approach to fostering HOT in beginners. Providing students with clear learning objectives helps guide their cognitive processes and enhance learning outcomes. Based on this premise, this study developed the Innovation Spark GPT (InnoSparkGPT) system, aimed at strengthening students' conceptual connections through simulated real-life scenarios. Following the phased instructional strategy of Creative Problem Solving (CPS), the system assists students in deconstructing.

complex problems and provides real-time guidance throughout the transition between divergent and convergent thinking. This process aims to stimulate students' creative thinking and expressive abilities. This study seeks to answer the following research question: Does creativity-guided GPT improve students' higher-order thinking skills?

2 Related Work

2.1 Phased Strategies for Creative Problem Solving

Creative learning emphasizes student-centered, self-directed exploration and problem identification. It involves applying accumulated life experiences and knowledge construction to conduct comprehensive analysis, fostering open-mindedness and developing solutions. However, without structured objectives, students' creative ideas may lack feasibility, and the problem-solving process may become excessively divergent. Therefore, creative learning requires extensive attempts and repeated practice. Creative Problem Solving (CPS) is a structured approach aimed at stimulating creativity to address complex problems. It provides students with clear learning objectives and guidance in shifting between different modes of thinking. Treffinger defines CPS as a six-stage process [10]:

1. **Mess-Finding.** The objective of this phase is to clarify the current confusion and uncertainties by systematically exploring the contextual framework, identifying potential core issues, and establishing a critical foundation for subsequent processes.
2. **Data-Finding.** To understand the essence of the core problem, conducting an in-depth exploration by gathering various relevant information is essential. Utilizing progressive methods such as the "5 Whys" technique effectively uncovers the underlying root causes behind surface-level issues, thereby enhancing the accuracy and specificity of problem definition.
3. **Problem-Finding**. In the CPS process, a critical stage involves clarifying ambiguous problem situations and transforming them into specific, actionable research directions. Reframing the problem using a "How might we…?" framework helps to focus on the core issue and provides concrete, promising avenues for innovative exploration.
4. **Idea-Finding.** Breaking existing cognitive limitations by drawing on experiences and practices from other contexts or fields, engaging in analogy and recombination to generate diverse and innovative ideas and potential solutions.
5. **Solution-Finding.** After the creative brainstorming phase, consolidate the various potential solutions generated and evaluate them based on key criteria such as feasibility, innovation, and effectiveness. Select the optimal solution accordingly.
6. **Acceptance-Finding.** The designed solution will be implemented and applied in practice, followed by in-depth discussions and feedback exchanges with participants to evaluate its feasibility and effectiveness. The practical outcomes will be critically reflected upon and validated to further clarify the solution's suitability and identify potential areas for improvement.

CPS emphasizes a thorough understanding and analysis of the problem's essence before generating creative ideas, followed by inference and verification. This process requires both cognitive flexibility and logical thinking to integrate diverse perspectives into problem-solving solutions. It contributes to developing students' abilities in decomposing complex problems, critical thinking, and creative thinking skills [8].

2.2 Higher Order Thinking Ability in Creative Problem Solving Strategies

Higher Order Thinking (HOT) originates from Bloom's taxonomy of cognitive domains, which categorizes thinking into six levels: remembering, understanding, applying, analyzing, evaluating, and creating. HOT refers to cognitive processes built upon foundational levels of memory and understanding, emphasizing higher-level thinking skills such as analysis, evaluation, and creation. These skills are essential components of the CPS process. CPS extends beyond generating novel ideas; it emphasizes students' ability to flexibly apply knowledge, redefine problems, generate diverse solutions, and critically assess options to select the most appropriate approach in complex and uncertain contexts. Recent studies have examined the impact of CPS on fostering higher-order thinking in novices, revealing that structured frameworks for HOT development enhance the efficiency of generating creative solutions. Additionally, guided feedback plays a crucial role in offering broader perspectives, ensuring learners remain oriented throughout the learning process [7].

2.3 ChatGPT

CPS emphasizes a student-centered learning process that involves dynamic shifts between various thinking modes to address problems. Throughout this process, students require continuous, real-time, and targeted guidance to effectively complete tasks. As a natural language processing-based AI conversational tool, ChatGPT provides immediate interactive learning support. Its guidance functions help students clarify problem nature, deconstruct tasks, and identify core concepts. During the ideation phase, interactive dialogues with ChatGPT facilitate brainstorming activities, offering diverse perspectives and innovative suggestions [3], which promote creative thinking by breaking away from conventional frameworks. Additionally, ChatGPT can simulate various roles according to different contexts, providing contextualized feedback that allows students to critically examine and refine their ideas, enhancing critical thinking and reflective skills, thereby improving their overall problem-solving competence. This study will design ChatGPT prompts aligned with the six stages of CPS (Mess Finding, Data Finding, Problem Finding, Idea Finding, Solution Finding, Acceptance Finding) to develop a learning assistant aimed at training students' CPS skills. By simulating real-world scenarios and constraining student responses to ensure that their own ideas lead the process, this approach will provide stage-specific guidance and feedback to ensure that students have clear objectives at each stage.

3 Method

3.1 Guided Creative Problem Solving GPT Assistant (InnoSparkGPT)

The process of fostering creativity involves multiple shifts between divergent and convergent thinking. However, students often struggle to identify the boundaries between these modes, requiring real-time guidance to provide clear direction from chaos, thereby enhancing their ability to leverage creativity to solve complex problems. To address this, this study employs the CPS teaching strategy combined with ChatGPT-designed prompts to develop a learning assistant that aids students in completing CPS tasks. By introducing controlled chaos within specific topics and providing guided questioning and idea suggestions, students are trained to switch between divergent and convergent thinking repeatedly, evaluating the rationale to ensure the objectives of each CPS stage are met. Concurrently, the approach aims to cultivate students' higher-order thinking skills. The system is implemented using Flask and integrated with the ChatGPT API. The following sections will elaborate on the specific operational process.

3.2 The Design of InnoSparkGPT Assistant

During the Mess Finding and Data Finding stages, students assume the role of a BMI calculator sales manager. Through InnoSparkGPT, they engage with simulated scenarios reflecting real-life demands for BMI calculators. Students are prompted to identify potential customer groups, explain their reasons for needing BMI calculators, and conduct research on customer segments, needs, and motivations. After group discussions, they submit their findings to InnoSparkGPT, which assesses whether the descriptions of customer groups and needs are reasonable and coherent. Throughout the brainstorming process, InnoSparkGPT provides guidance to help students focus on the core issues of the scenario (see Fig. 1).

In the Problem Finding stage, students will further explore the target audience and their needs based on their responses, generating more detailed problem descriptions. For example, "If we want to sell a BMI calculator to them, how can we make this product distinctive? Please list three specific ideas." This question aims to guide students in developing initial creative solutions. InnoSparkGPT will evaluate the feasibility of each proposal and suggest additional features for consideration. Students can then critically assess their proposed solutions, fostering critical thinking skills (see Fig. 2).

During the Idea Finding and Solution Finding stages, InnoSparkGPT first presents demonstration examples based on the students' proposed system features. It then prompts students to list three aspects of their system planning, including the system name, all functionalities, and detailed descriptions. Additionally, InnoSparkGPT assesses the feasibility of the proposed system and provides recommendations. This process helps students select the final project idea to be implemented using App Inventor (see Fig. 3).

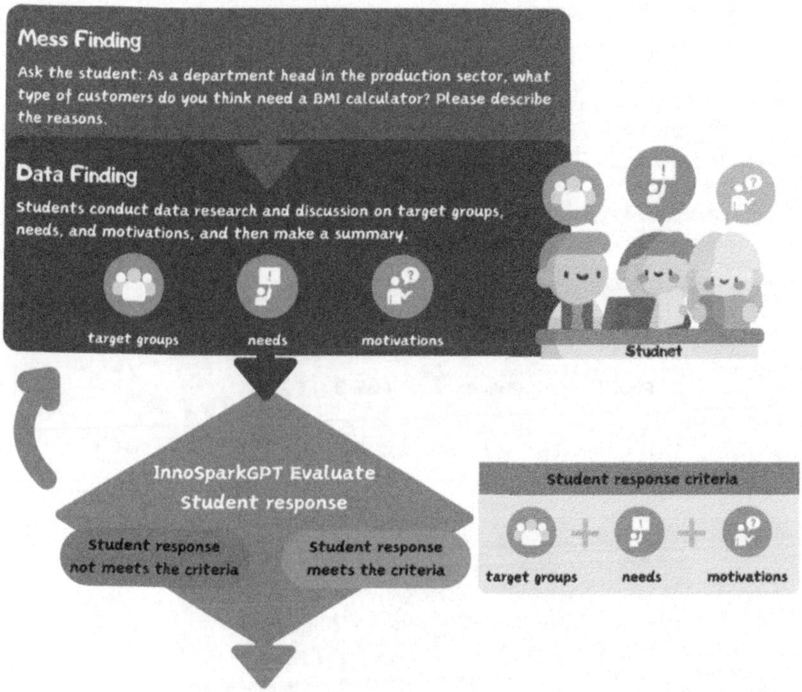

Fig. 1. InnoSparkGPT Mess & Data Finding Stages.

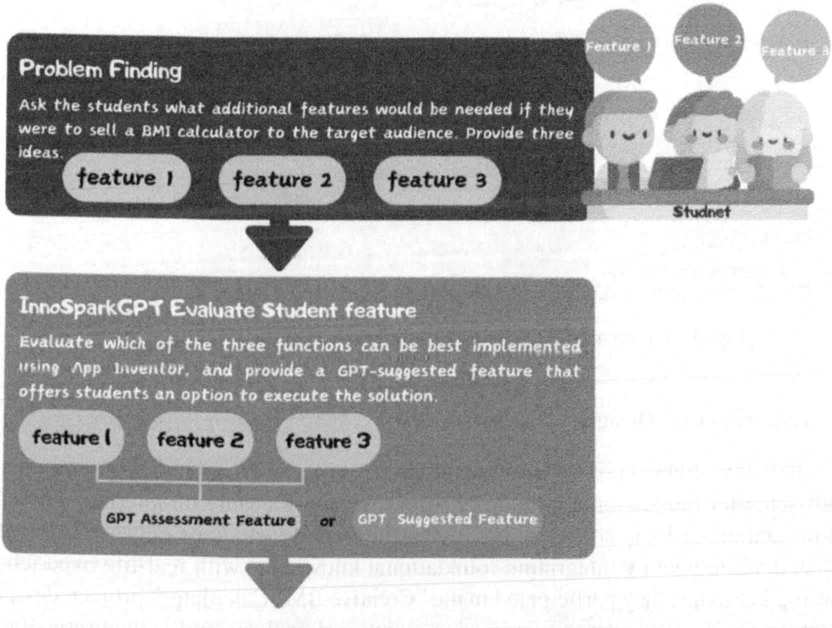

Fig. 2. InnoSparkGPT Problem Finding Stage.

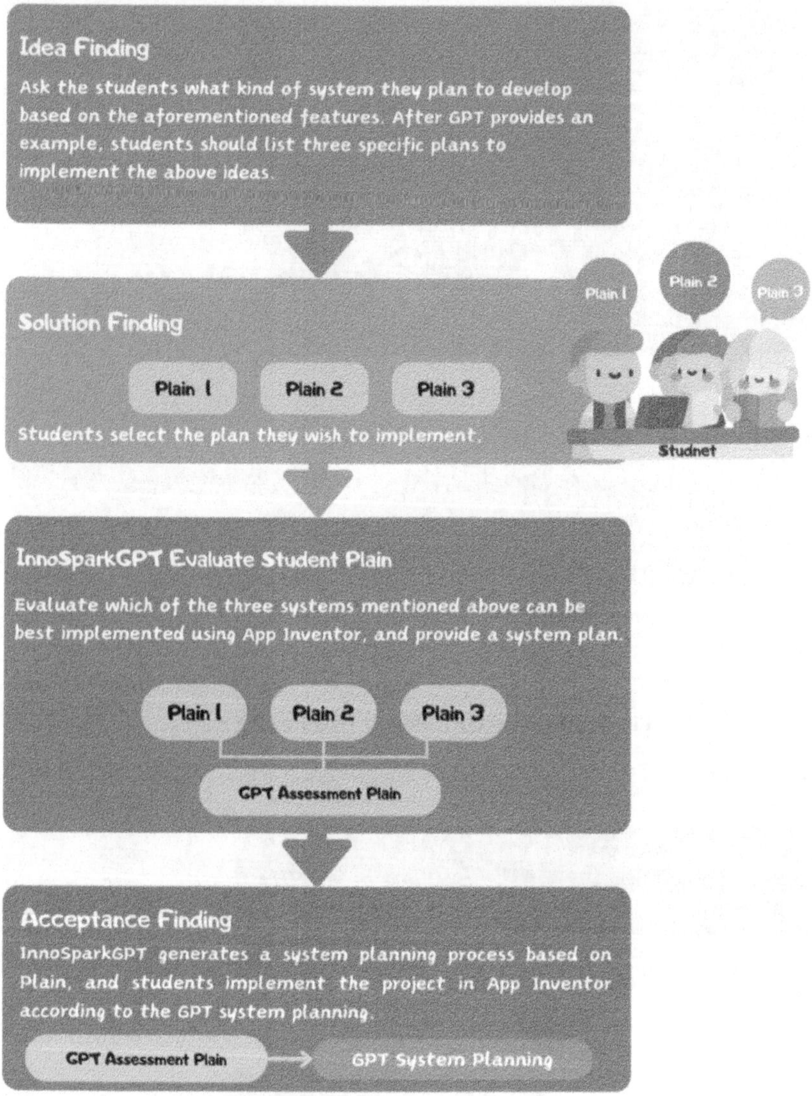

Fig. 3. InnoSparkGPT Idea & Solution & Acceptance Finding Stages.

3.3 Experimental Design

This study investigated non-major undergraduate students (N = 41) who participated in a half-semester foundational training on App Inventor, focusing on interface operation and programming logic concepts. Following the training, students engaged in creative project development by integrating foundational knowledge with real-life experiences. Working in groups, they participated in the "Creative BMI Calculator" project, designed to simulate real-world scenarios requiring situational analysis and collaborative brainstorming to generate diverse problem-solving solutions. The experimental group (n = 20) utilized InnoSparkGPT for project development assistance, while the control group (n = 21) employed traditional ChatGPT. The primary aim of this study was to assess whether InnoSparkGPT effectively facilitates students' cognitive flexibility between divergent and convergent thinking to foster creative solutions. Furthermore, the study evaluated whether this learning process significantly enhances students' higher-order thinking skills. The assessment of higher-order thinking was based on a modified version of [2] scale, comprising three dimensions: creativity, critical thinking, and problem-solving skills. A five-point Likert scale was used to measure these aspects, with data collected through pre- and post-tests.

4 Results and Discussion

This study employed a one-way independent samples ANCOVA to examine whether there were significant differences in higher-order thinking skills between students using InnoSparkGPT and those using traditional ChatGPT for creative collaboration projects. To ensure the data met the homogeneity of regression slopes assumption, a homogeneity test of regression coefficients was conducted in advance. The interaction term (Group * Pre-test Score) resulted in $F = 0.017$, $p = 0.898 > 0.05$, indicating non-significant differences between regression slopes across groups, thus satisfying the assumption and allowing for ANCOVA analysis. Descriptive statistics indicated statistically significant differences in creativity ($F = 10.681$, $p = .002$) and critical thinking ($F = 4.706$, $p = .036$). Problem-solving ability was near significance ($F = 3.858$, $p = .057$), as shown in Table 1. The experimental group demonstrated higher mean scores in creativity (M = 4.16, SD = 0.77), critical thinking (M = 4.13, SD = 0.6), and problem-solving ability (M = 4.18, SD = 0.65) compared to the control group's creativity (M = 3.73, SD = 0.82), critical thinking (M = 3.89, SD = 0.71), and problem-solving ability (M = 3.86, SD = 0.77), as shown in Table 2. These results suggest that using InnoSparkGPT for creative collaboration projects effectively enhances students' creativity and critical thinking. Although the difference in problem-solving ability was not statistically significant, the experimental group still achieved higher post-test scores compared to the control group.

Table 1. Descriptive Statistics of the Higher-Order Thinking Scale

	EG (N = 20)				CG (N = 21)			
	Pre test		Post-test		Pre-test		Post-test	
	M	SD	M	SD	M	SD	M	SD
Creativity	4.14	0.6	4.16	0.77	3.92	0.71	3.73	0.82
Critical thinking	4.05	0.69	4.13	0.6	3.7	0.77	3.89	0.71
Problem solving	4.1	0.76	4.18	0.65	3.8	0.83	3.86	0.77

Table 2. Descriptive Statistics of the Higher-Order Thinking Scale

Variable	SS	df	MS	F	*p*	Partial η^2
Creativity	135.143	1	135.143	10.681	.002**	.219
Critical thinking	20.727	1	20.727	4.706	.036*	.110
Problem solving	82.592	1	82.592	3.858	.057	.092

Note. *p < .05, **p < .01

This study focuses on guiding non-major students to complete creative collaborative projects using the CPS learning strategy. The development of the InnoSparkGPT learning assistant aims to simulate scenarios and implement prompt engineering to strengthen connections between disciplinary knowledge and real-life experiences. Clear tasks and objectives are provided at each stage, allowing non-major students to accomplish programming-related creative projects under systematic guidance. The study evaluates the impact of this system on higher-order thinking skills during the project completion process. The findings indicate that designing staged tasks effectively reduces students' cognitive load and enhances their engagement with the problem context. Providing appropriate guidance during the process of cognitive shifts enables students to concentrate more on creative ideation and problem-solving. Striking a balance between free exploration and structured guidance at each stage is crucial for fostering creativity [9].

Furthermore, this research emphasizes a dual-guidance model that integrates AI interaction and interpersonal collaboration. By offering diverse perspectives and continuously examining their thought processes, students, through iterative discussions with ChatGPT, adjust their learning strategies and enhance critical thinking skills [4]. This approach not only prevents over-reliance on AI tools but also encourages students to refine their hypotheses, evaluate feedback, and reflect on their ideas and theories, thereby achieving higher-level knowledge construction. However, the results indicate no significant difference in problem-solving ability between students assisted by InnoSparkGPT and those using traditional ChatGPT during classroom tasks. Nonetheless, both groups demonstrated improved post-test scores compared to pre-test scores. This suggests that once students establish a solid foundation of disciplinary knowledge, they can independently tackle tasks using ChatGPT. The integration of emerging technologies not only stimulates forward-thinking and innovative ideas but also offers concrete and practical solutions that effectively address real-world needs, thereby supporting students in accomplishing programming-related tasks [5].

5 Conclusion

This study designs experimental activities specifically for non-major university students, utilizing the learning assistant InnoSparkGPT to effectively stimulate creativity and facilitate task completion. However, university students often face limitations in creative thinking due to prior educational or life experiences, resulting in habitual thinking patterns. Therefore, future research aims to apply this approach to students in the knowledge construction stage (e.g., elementary and middle school students) to explore whether technological guidance across various subjects can foster more innovative ideas and lead to more effective learning outcomes. The design of InnoSparkGPT aims to support students in completing creative collaborative projects by employing prompt-based guidance that helps them focus on learning objectives without overly relying on AI-generated answers. This approach enhances problem-solving abilities and programming skills. InnoSparkGPT functions not only as a technical support tool but also as a bridge connecting disciplinary knowledge with real-world experiences. Through phased task guidance and continuous reflection mechanisms, it assists students in developing higher-order thinking skills, improving learning outcomes, and cultivating interdisciplinary competencies.

References

1. Bettin, B., Jarvie-Eggart, M., Steelman, K.S., Wallace, C.: Preparing first-year engineering students to think about code: a guided inquiry approach. IEEE Trans. on Educ. **65**, 309–319 (2022)
2. Chai, C.S., Deng, F., Tsai, P.-S., Koh, J.H.L., Tsai, C.-C.: Assessing multidimensional students' perceptions of twenty-first-century learning practices. Asia Pac. Educ. Rev. **16**, 389–398 (2015)
3. Hernaus, T., Nikolina, D.e., Hauff, S.: The necessity of job design for employee creativity and innovation: nothing happens without supervisor support. European Journal of Work and Organizational Psychology **33**, 583–598 (2024)
4. Lee, H.-Y., Chen, P.-H., Wang, W.-S., Huang, Y.-M., Wu, T.-T.: Empowering ChatGPT with guidance mechanism in blended learning: effect of self-regulated learning, higher-order thinking skills, and knowledge construction. Int. J. Educ. Technol. High. Educ. **21**, 16 (2024)
5. Lee, H.-Y., Lin, C.-J., Wang, W.-S., Chang, W.-C., Huang, Y.-M.: Precision education via timely intervention in K-12 computer programming course to enhance programming skill and affective-domain learning objectives. Int. J. STEM Educ. **10**, 52 (2023)
6. Li, P.-H., Lee, H.-Y., Lin, C.-J., Wang, W.-S., Huang, Y.-M.: InquiryGPT: Augmenting ChatGPT for Enhancing Inquiry-Based Learning in STEM Education. J. Educ. Comp. Res. **62**, 2157–2186 (2025)
7. Lim, C., Han, H.: Development of instructional design strategies for integrating an online support system for creative problem solving into a University course. Asia Pac. Educ. Rev. **21**, 539–552 (2020)
8. Lin, Y.-N., Hsia, L.-H., Hwang, G.-J.: Developing students' creative problem-solving strategies in the context of blended sports education. Br. J. Edu. Technol. **56**, 190–207 (2025)
9. Rosen, Y., Stoeffler, K., Simmering, V.: Imagine: Design for Creative Thinking, Learning, and Assessment in Schools. J. Intelligence **8**, 16 (2020)
10. Treffinger, D.J.: Creative Problem Solving: Overview and educational implications. Educ. Psychol. Rev. **7**, 301–312 (1995)

Exploring the Impact of Using GenAI Applications on MIS Students' Learning in System Analysis

Yen-Wei Huang and Wei-Tsong Wang(✉)

Department of Information Management, National Cheng Kung University, Tainan City, Taiwan
r78131024@gs.ncku.edu.tw, wtwang@mail.ncku.edu.tw

Abstract. This study aims to explore the impact of varying levels of cognitive load on students' learning behaviors when using ChatGPT in generative AI-assisted instructional settings. Grounded in Cognitive Load Theory, the research involves the design of an instructional module on "Systems Analysis and Design" within the field of Information Management. An experimental approach was employed to examine the mechanisms through which ChatGPT influences extraneous cognitive load, intrinsic cognitive load, and students' continued intention to use the tool. It is hypothesized that both intrinsic and extraneous cognitive load experienced by students in ChatGPT-assisted learning environments negatively affect their willingness to continue using the tool. To test this hypothesis, Structural Equation Modeling was utilized for data analysis. The results reveal that both intrinsic and extraneous cognitive load exert significant negative effects on continued usage intention. This suggests that excessive cognitive load during the learning process may reduce students' willingness to adopt ChatGPT as a learning tool in the future. Overall, this study provides both theoretical and practical implications for the integration and design of generative AI tools in educational settings.

Keywords: ChatGPT · Cognitive Load Theory · System Analysis and Design · Continued Intention

1 Introduction

The advancement of Artificial intelligence (AI) is ushering education into a new era, elevating computer-assisted instruction to unprecedented levels. On one hand, generative AI offers the potential to personalize learning experiences by tailoring content and dynamically adjusting instructional strategies based on individual student progress. This enables highly individualized learning pathways. However, the swift evolution of such technologies introduces significant challenges, including the risk of generating biased or inaccurate information and the potential for students to become overly reliant on AI, thereby hindering the development of critical thinking and autonomous learning skills [1]. Scholars [2] have emphasized the importance of appropriate guidance to ensure the ethical and effective use of generative AI tools in educational settings. Teachers play a crucial role in fostering responsible and critical use of these tools, particularly

W.-S. Wang et al. (Eds.): ICITL 2025, LNCS 15913, pp. 162–170, 2026.
https://doi.org/10.1007/978-3-031-98185-2_18

by encouraging student independence and reflective evaluation of AI-generated content. Furthermore, the quality of generative AI output is highly dependent on the design of effective prompts to produce content aligned with learning objectives and support students in developing core competencies.

In the area of information management education, the ability to actively analyze, evaluate, and integrate information not only enables students to critically assess theories and data, but also equips them to make informed decisions within the complex environments of modern education and workplaces. Systems analysis and design represent a fundamental and central component of systems engineering, serving as a practical application of systems theory. Within the software development lifecycle, the process of requirements elicitation is particularly critical, as it ensures that the developed system accurately aligns with user needs and business objectives. In essence, the goal of requirements elicitation is to thoroughly comprehend, and accurately articulate user or client needs to ensure that the subsequent development process can fulfill these needs while maintaining requirement stability throughout the project lifecycle [3].

Based on the discussion above, this study aims to explore the effectiveness of generative AI to learning skills/knowledge of "Systems Analysis" course. The objective is to investigate whether such technologies can effectively enhance students' acceptance of the technology and their intention to use it continuously. The research findings can offer useful information provided of generative AI as an instructional aid.

2 Literature Review

2.1 Generative Artificial Intelligence

The rapid development of generative AI is profoundly reshaping traditional educational paradigms. As an innovative tool, generative AI offers highly personalized learning content tailored to individual needs, enabling real-time adjustments in learning pace and strategy to support personalized learning experiences. Moreover, generative AI serves as a powerful support tool for educators. Teachers can leverage AI-assisted tools such as automated grading systems, content generation platforms, and real-time feedback mechanisms to reduce their work loads. This allows educators to devote more time to creative and interactive instructional activities. Additionally, AI's analytical capabilities enable teachers to more accurately identify students' learning difficulties, thereby facilitating targeted interventions and personalized support.

However, the integration of AI into education also presents significant challenges. For instance, AI-generated information may be biased or inaccurate, potentially undermining students' critical thinking skills and capacity for independent learning [4, 5].

Another key concern is that students may become overly reliant on AI-generated content, diminishing their intrinsic motivation for self-directed learning. The accuracy and educational value of AI-generated content is another critical issue that requires close scrutiny by researchers and educators.

In conclusion, while the application of generative AI in digital education holds immense potential to enhance learning experiences and teaching efficiency, its design and deployment must be approached with careful consideration of equity, ethics, and long-term implications to ensure that its benefits are accessible for all learners.

2.2 Cognitive Load Theory

Cognitive Load Theory (CLT) [6] argues that human cognitive architecture primarily consists of long-term memory (LTM) and working memory (WM) [7].

Building on prior research, cognitive load is typically categorized into two types: intrinsic cognitive load and extraneous cognitive load. Each type exerts distinct influences on learning performance. Intrinsic cognitive load is determined by the inherent complexity of the learning material and the learner's prior knowledge [8]. To effectively manage intrinsic load, instructional strategies may include simplifying the content or enhancing the learner's background knowledge, thereby enabling them to better comprehend complex material.

Extraneous cognitive load, by contrast, arises from additional cognitive demands imposed by instructional design. This type of load reflects cognitive resources expended on non-essential elements, often resulting from poor instructional design or redundant information [9]. Reducing extraneous load allows learners to allocate more working memory capacity to process the intrinsic aspects of the learning task, thereby improving overall learning efficiency.

Therefore, it is essential that instructional design concurrently addresses both intrinsic and extraneous cognitive load. By minimizing unnecessary cognitive demands while supporting learners in managing the complexity of the core material.

2.3 Systems Analysis and Design

In the core curriculum of Information Management, the "Requirements Elicitation" unit within the Systems Analysis and Design course plays a pivotal role in equipping students with the skills necessary to accurately identify and analyze user needs, and to translate those needs into actionable system design specifications.

Therefore, students are trained to engage effectively with diverse stakeholders, including end users, business units, and technical teams. This course not only teaches the techniques for identifying requirements but also familiarizes students with common challenges in the requirements analysis process, including inconsistencies, evolving needs, and ambiguities, via using analytical tools, such as use case diagrams, flowcharts, and requirements matrices, to clearly define functional and non-functional requirements.

Moreover, students are expected to master the ability to transform vague or abstract requirements into concrete, measurable technical specifications. This ensures that the system design aligns with user expectations and meets established objectives.

During this process, it is essential to develop an in-depth understanding of the business context, identify operational challenges, and define the problems that the system is expected to address in order to ensure that all requirements are specific, feasible, and aligned with user expectations. The requirement specification documents can then serve as a reference for all subsequent system development activities [10].

In summary, requirements elicitation is the foundation of any systems development project. It enables students to strengthen their analytical thinking, master data collection techniques, improve technical writing and communication skills, and develop adaptability and systems thinking. Beyond gaining a theoretical understanding of systems analysis, students also enhance their practical competencies in problem-solving, collaboration, and communication—laying a solid foundation for future roles in system development and information management.

2.4 Intention to Continue Use

The theoretical foundation for understanding users' continuance intention is grounded in three major frameworks: Technology Acceptance Model (TAM), the Expectation Confirmation Theory (ECT), and the Self-Determination Theory (SDT). According to TAM, perceived ease of use and perceived usefulness affect users' behavioral intention. If students perceive ChatGPT as easy to learn and operate, and if it effectively enhances their efficiency, their intention to continue using the tool increases [11]. ECT posits that when users' expectations are confirmed or exceeded, satisfaction is achieved, which in turn fosters a greater intention to continue use [12]. SDT emphasizes both intrinsic and extrinsic motivation, suggesting that interactive systems, such as ChatGPT, can enhance continued usage if they provide users with a sense of challenge and accomplishment [13]. Considering these factors properly can significantly improve ChatGPT's ability to attract and retain users in educational and professional settings.

3 Research Methodology

3.1 Course Context

In the "Systems Analysis and Requirements Determination" course, students are trained to collect, analyze, organize, and define user requirements to ensure that the designed system effectively addresses real-world problems and meets user needs. The course places particular emphasis on techniques and methodologies such as requirements elicitation, the formulation of requirement specifications, construction of use cases, and management of requirement changes. These competencies are essential for future careers in system development and project management.

ChatGPT has the potential to serve as a valuable supplementary tool in this context, supporting students in several key areas: (1) eliciting and analyzing requirements, (2) drafting use cases and requirement specifications, (3) managing requirement changes, and (4) problem-solving and providing real-time guidance. Through the integration of generative AI tools like ChatGPT, students may be better equipped to develop accurate, well-structured system requirements, while also fostering critical thinking and autonomous learning.

3.2 Research Hypotheses

With the increasing maturity of contemporary digital learning environments, generative artificial intelligence (AI) tools—such as ChatGPT—have been progressively integrated into higher education to enhance students' learning efficiency and depth of understanding. This is particularly relevant in courses such as Systems Analysis, which emphasize logical reasoning and problem-solving. In such contexts, students are often required to process large volumes of abstract and structured information, which can lead to significant cognitive load challenges.

If students are appropriately guided in using ChatGPT as a learning aid, for instance, for clarifying concepts, receiving real-time feedback, or simulating requirement-gathering interviews, this may help to reduce their mental burden and, in turn, improve their learning outcomes. However, if students perceive the tool as difficult to operate, find its responses overly abstract, or are unable to obtain timely and practical learning support, the tool may instead increase their cognitive load. Such negative experiences could reduce students' acceptance and willingness to continue using the tool.

According to Cognitive Load Theory, learners possess limited cognitive resources, and excessive intrinsic or extraneous cognitive load can hinder information processing and undermine learning motivation. Extraneous cognitive load refers to the additional cognitive burden resulting from factors such as unfriendly interface design, unclear prompts, or overly complex operational procedures during interaction with ChatGPT. Additionally, intrinsic cognitive load refers to the difficulty and psychological pressure students experience when trying to comprehend core course content, such as programming syntax, system structure, and analytical processes. Building on this theoretical foundation, two research hypotheses are proposed:

H1: Extraneous cognitive load has a negative impact on students' intention to continue using ChatGPT.
H2: Intrinsic cognitive load has a negative impact on students' intention to continue using ChatGPT.

To conclude, this study aims to clarify the mechanisms by which different types of cognitive load influence students' willingness to adopt generative AI tools in learning contexts, thereby offering empirical insights and optimization recommendations for the design and application of AI tools in digital learning environments (see Fig. 1).

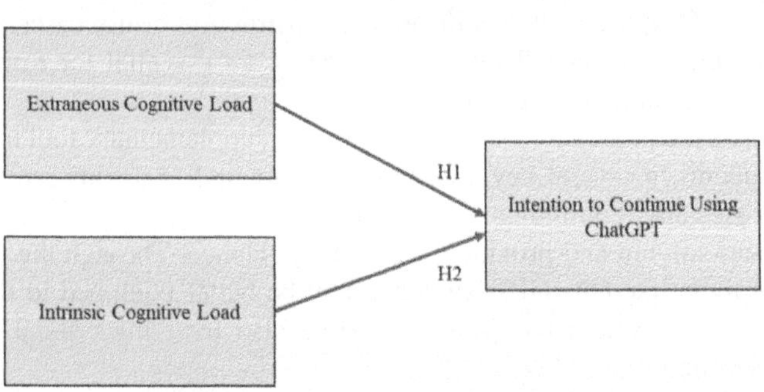

Fig. 1. Research Hypothesis Diagram

3.3 Research Procedure

This study employed an online experimental approach to enhance accessibility and reduce logistical costs. A total of 35 participants engaged in a structured learning activity based on instructional videos. The activity included viewing tutorial content and prompt strategy demonstrations, interacting with the generative AI tool ChatGPT (GPT-4 version), and completing relevant questionnaires.

The participants were restricted to a maximum interaction time of 15 min with GPT-4. In addition, the task scope was deliberately constrained to comply with token limitations applicable to free-tier GPT users, thereby ensuring consistent operational conditions across all participants (see Fig. 2).

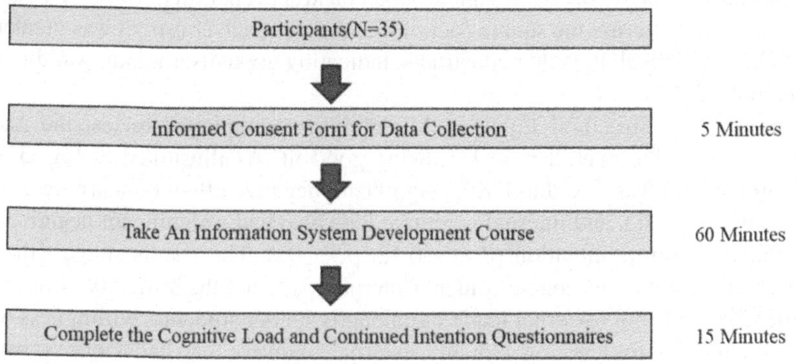

Fig. 2. Experimental Design

3.4 Questionnaire Design

This study employed a questionnaire survey to collect data, with the instrument developed and refined based on the research objectives, hypotheses, and relevant literature. The final questionnaire comprised 26 items, covering two primary constructions: cognitive load and the intention to continue using ChatGPT. To enhance measurement sensitivity and ensure the reliability and validity of the instrument, the questionnaire underwent multiple rounds of revision and pilot testing.

The measures of intrinsic and extraneous cognitive loads were adapted from the instrument developed by [14], and were contextualized to fit the learning environment of an information management course. Intrinsic cognitive load refers to students' perceived difficulty of the learning task itself, as reflected in statements such as, "I find the content of the 'requirements elicitation' topic very difficult." Extraneous cognitive load, pertains to the complexity of how information is presented, such as, "I find the explanation style in the 'requirements elicitation' section difficult to understand." Additionally, measures of the intention to continue using ChatGPT was adapted from the framework proposed by [15]. Although originally developed to assess service quality, this framework has since been widely applied in studies related to learning motivation and behavioral intention. All items were rated using a 7-point Likert scale, ranging from 1("strongly disagree") to 7 ("strongly agree") to ensure the. Internal consistency and structural validity of the measures used [16].

4 Results

This study employed Structural Equation Modeling (SEM) for analysis, with the results presented in Fig. 3. To ensure the measurement model of the latent variables exhibited good reliability and validity, Confirmatory Factor Analysis (CFA) was conducted. The results indicated that the Composite Reliability (CR) values for all constructs were greater than 0.80, and the Average Variance Extracted (AVE) for each construct exceeded 0.50, demonstrating strong convergent validity and construct reliability. Moreover, based on Fornell-Larcker criterion the square root of the AVE for each construct was greater than its correlations with all the other constructs, indicating good discriminant validity of the measured used.

Subsequently, Structural Equation Modeling was employed to test the research hypotheses, with the overall model showing good fit. As illustrated in Fig. 3, external cognitive load was found to have a significant negative effect on learning intention ($\beta = -0.67$, $p < .01$), and internal cognitive load also had a significant negative effect on continued learning intention ($\beta = -0.52$, $p < .01$). The results suggest that both challenges inherent in the course content (internal load) and the difficulty of interacting with the ChatGPT tool (external load) significantly hinder students' willingness to continue using the tool for learning. Notably, external cognitive load had a more substantial impact, indicating that, when designing and applying AI tools in teaching, reducing system complexity and enhancing usability is key to improving students' continuous learning intentions.

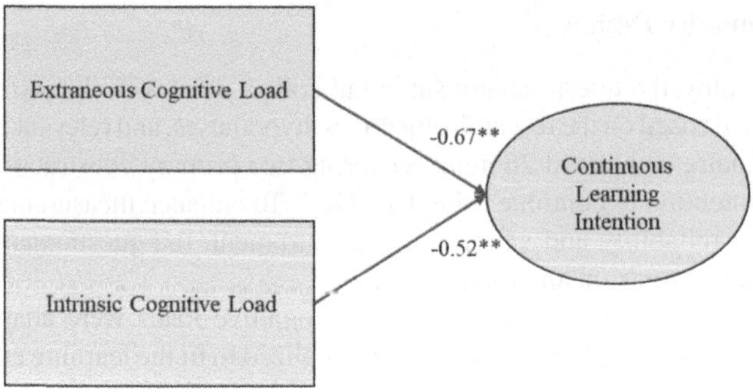

Fig. 3. Experimental Results

5 Discussion

The findings of this study indicate that learning tasks that requires high cognitive demands due to task complexity or improper tool design tend to lead to a significant negative impact on students' intention to continue learning. Specifically, in learning contexts involving generative AI tools, if the user interface is not intuitive, feedback is overly complex, or clear guidance is lacking, learners are likely to experience additional cognitive pressure, which subsequently reduces their acceptance of the tool and their motivation to use it [17].

Overall, this study confirms the negative impact of cognitive load on learning intention and further explains its potential disruptive effects on learning behavior. Particularly in today's era of increasingly widespread digital learning tools, designers and educators should prioritize optimizing the user experience. By reducing unnecessary external cognitive load and enhancing system usability and interactivity, it is possible to promote greater learner engagement and sustained use intentions, thereby achieving an effective and sustainable AI-assisted learning.

6 Conclusion

This study aims to explore the application of generative AI to Management Information Systems (MIS) courses and its impact on students' learning process in "System Analysis," using ChatGPT as an example. The results indicate that when students experience excessive information processing demands, whether from the content of the course or the system's operational complexity, their acceptance and motivation to use the tool may decrease. This study not only validates the core concept of cognitive load theory but also highlights the importance of carefully assessing learners' cognitive capacity when integrating generative AI tools into educational settings.

Future research could further explore multiple aspects, including how teaching design optimization, user-friendly interfaces, prompt guidance strategies, and personalized learning support can effectively reduce cognitive load and improve overall learning experiences and tool acceptance. Such studies will not only contribute to the theoretical framework of generative AI tools in higher education but also provide valuable insights for the practical application and strategic design of these tools in teaching, thereby fostering the collaborative development of AI technologies and educational goals.

References

1. Kong, S.-C., Yang, Y.: A human-centered learning and teaching framework using generative artificial intelligence for self-regulated learning development through domain knowledge learning in k–12 settings. IEEE Trans. Learn. Technol. **17**, 1562–1573 (2024). https://doi.org/10.1109/TLT.2024.3392830
2. Crawford, J., Cowling, M., Allen, K.-A.: Leadership is needed for ethical ChatGPT: character, assessment, and learning using artificial intelligence (AI). J. Univ. Teach. Learn. Pract. **20**, 1–19 (2023)
3. Browne, G.J., Ramesh, V.: Improving information requirements determination: a cognitive perspective. Information & Management **39**, 625–645 (2002)
4. Kasneci, E., et al.: ChatGPT for good? On opportunities and challenges of large language models for education. Learn. Individ. Differ. **103**, 102274 (2023)
5. Bhutoria, A.: Personalized education and artificial intelligence in the United States, China, and India: a systematic review using a human-in-the-loop model. Comput. Educ.: Artific. Intell. **3**, 100068 (2022)
6. Sweller, J., Van Merrienboer, J.J., Paas, F.G.: Cognitive architecture and instructional design. Educ. Psychol. Rev. **10**, 251–296 (1998)
7. Sweller, J., Sweller, S.: Natural information processing systems. Evol. Psychol. **4**, 147470490600400130 (2006)

8. Sweller, J., Van Merriënboer, J.J., Paas, F.: Cognitive architecture and instructional design: 20 years later. Educ. Psychol. Rev. **31**, 261–292 (2019)
9. Klepsch, M., Schmitz, F., Seufert, T.: Development and validation of two instruments measuring intrinsic, extraneous, and germane cognitive load. Front. Psychol. **8**, 1997 (2017)
10. Davis, G.B.: Strategies for information requirements determination. IBM Syst. J. **21**, 4–30 (1982)
11. Venkatesh, V., Morris, M.G., Davis, G.B., Davis, F.D.: User acceptance of information technology: toward a unified view. MIS Q. **27**(3), 425–478 (2003). https://doi.org/10.2307/30036540
12. Hossain, M.A., Quaddus, M.: Expectation–confirmation theory in information system research: a review and analysis. Informat. Syst. Theory: Explain. Predict. Digit. Soc. **1**, 441–469 (2012)
13. Deci, E.L., Ryan, R.M.: Self-determination theory. Handbook Theories Soc. Psychol. **1**, 416–436 (2012)
14. Leppink, J., Paas, F., Van der Vleuten, C.P., Van Gog, T., Van Merriënboer, J.J.: Development of an instrument for measuring different types of cognitive load. Behav. Res. Methods **45**, 1058–1072 (2013)
15. Cronin, J.J., Jr., Taylor, S.A.: Measuring service quality: a reexamination and extension. J. Mark. **56**, 55–68 (1992)
16. Krieglstein, F., Schneider, S., Beege, M., Rey, G.D.: How the design and complexity of concept maps influence cognitive learning processes. Educ. Tech. Research Dev. **70**, 99–118 (2022)
17. Patac, L.P., Patac, A.V., Jr.: Using ChatGPT for academic support: Managing cognitive load and enhancing learning efficiency–A phenomenological approach. Soc. Sci. Human. Open **11**, 101301 (2025)

AI-Supported Summative Reflection to Foster Motivation and Teamwork in STEM: An Application of the 6E+R Framework

Chia-Ju Lin[1], Margus Pedaste[2], and Yueh-Min Huang[1(✉)]

[1] Department of Engineering Science, National Cheng Kung University, Tainan, Taiwan
huang@mail.ncku.edu.tw

[2] I, nstitute of Education of the University of Tartu, Tartu, Estonia

Abstract. This study explores the integration of artificial intelligence (AI) in reflective learning processes within STEM education. Based on the 6E+R learning model, an AI-supported summative reflection tool was implemented in a collaborative problem-solving (CPS) activity to examine its effects on students' learning motivation, teamwork competency, and reflective content. A total of 28 high school students participated in a one-day Micro:bit autonomous vehicle workshop and were randomly assigned to either an experimental or control group. The experimental group used an AI-powered reflection tool that employed large language models (LLMs) to automatically generate structured summaries and feedback, while the control group engaged in traditional reflThis is to inform you that corresponding author has been identified as per the information available in the Copyright form.ection by manually recording and reviewing their learning experiences. Results indicated that the experimental group significantly outperformed the control group in both learAs Per Springer style, both city and country names must be present in the affiliations. Accordingly, we have inserted the city names in all affiliations. Please check and confirm if the inserted city names are correct. If not, please provide us with the correct city names.ning motivation and teamwork competency, with medium effect sizes. Topic modeling using BERTopic revealed that the experimental group's reflections focused more on strategy adjustment, logical reasoning, and conceptual understanding, whereas the control group's reflections were more descriptive and operational. These findings suggest that AI-supported structured feedback can enhance the quality of student reflections, increase learning engagement, and improve collaborative interactions. This study demonstrates the practical value and effectiveness of AI-assisted reflection within the 6E+R instructional model, offering new directions for reflective design in STEM collaborative learning and expanding the potential of generative AI in educational settings.

Keywords: STEM Education · AI-Supported Reflection · Collaborative Problem Solving · Learning Motivation · Teamwork Competency

W.-S. Wang et al. (Eds.): ICITL 2025, LNCS 15913, pp. 171–180, 2026.
https://doi.org/10.1007/978-3-031-98185-2_19

1 Introduction

STEM education aims to cultivate students' problem-solving skills, critical thinking, and interdisciplinary knowledge integration [1]. The 6E Learning byDeSIGN™ model [2], comprising six phases—Engage, Explore, Explain, Engineer, Enrich, and Evaluate—has been widely adopted to support inquiry-based and hands-on STEM learning [3], and has shown positive impacts on student motivation, STEM skills, and learning performance [4].

However, learners may become overly focused on task completion, neglecting reflection and strategic learning. To address this, Lin, Lee, Wang, Huang and Wu [3] proposed extending the 6E model into the 6E+R framework by embedding a "Reflection" phase. This addition encourages students to review their learning process, assess team dynamics, and critically evaluate their learning strategies. Empirical findings suggest that structured reflection helps learners identify knowledge gaps, enhance collaborative behavior, and improve problem-solving competence [5].

Nevertheless, conventional reflection methods often rely heavily on students' ability to self-regulate and independently review their experiences, which may be hindered by cognitive overload or limited metacognitive skills. This challenge is particularly salient in collaborative problem-solving (CPS) contexts, where learners engage in teamwork to construct knowledge and develop solutions [6]. In CPS activities, collaboration and interaction play key roles in facilitating knowledge integration and strategic reflection [7]. Moreover, the effectiveness of learning strategies depends on how students apply them behaviorally, which significantly affects learning outcomes [8]. Traditional evaluation methods such as self-report questionnaires and observations often fail to capture the nuances of these cognitive and social processes, highlighting the need for more comprehensive data analysis approaches.

Recent advances in artificial intelligence (AI) have enabled novel forms of learning support, particularly in the domain of reflective practice. AI-based tools that automatically summarize student discussions through natural language processing (NLP) and semantic analysis can offer real-time, structured feedback that enhances learning reflection [9, 10]. Despite these advancements, there remains a lack of empirical research on how AI-supported summative reflection influences CPS behaviors and learning outcomes within the 6E + R framework.

To bridge this gap, the present study investigates the implementation of AI-supported summative reflection in CPS activities guided by the 6E + R model. In this context, conventional reflection refers to student-led reviews of the learning process, relying on personal awareness and manual summarization of team discussions. In contrast, AI-supported summative reflection leverages large language models (LLMs) to automatically analyze CPS discussions and generate structured feedback that supports systematic reflection and strategy refinement. This study seeks to answer the following research questions:

1. Does AI-supported summative reflection enhance students' learning motivation in CPS activities?
2. Does AI-supported summative reflection improve students' teamwork competency?
3. How do the reflective themes differ between students using AI-supported summative reflection and those using conventional reflection?

2 Related Work

2.1 Collaborative Problem Solving in STEM Education

Collaborative learning and hands-on practices are central to effective STEM education, as they facilitate the application of knowledge in real-world contexts and enhance knowledge transfer [11]. As a pedagogical strategy, CPS is effective in fostering student motivation, engagement, and teamwork [12], but novice learners often struggle with applying interdisciplinary concepts [14]. In structured domains like programming and engineering, learning bottlenecks are common without proper support [13].

Without appropriate guidance, they may experience learning bottlenecks that negatively impact both performance and engagement [1, 14]. To support learners in these contexts, instructional scaffolding has been proposed as an essential strategy to foster cognitive engagement and conceptual development [15]. Well-designed scaffolding can not only deepen students' understanding of abstract concepts but also enhance their motivation and active participation in CPS tasks.

Reflection mechanisms help students revisit their learning experiences, identify obstacles, and refine their collaborative strategies to improve problem-solving outcomes [16]. However, integrating structured reflection into CPS activities remains a challenge in STEM education. The question of how to systematically support learners' reflective processes within CPS frameworks has become an important research issue.

2.2 6E + R Model and AI-Supported Reflection

The 6E model, derived from the 5E framework, adds an "Engineer" phase to strengthen design thinking [17]. Studies have shown that STEM instruction based on the 6E model can significantly enhance students' academic achievement, higher-order thinking skills, and positive attitudes toward STEM learning [18]. Moreover, it has been shown to promote students' creativity and integrated learning competencies.

Despite its pedagogical strengths, the 6E model lacks a built-in reflective mechanism and does not provide technological support to facilitate systematic learning review and self-adjustment [19]. Reflective learning has been widely recognized as a key component in developing students' metacognition, enabling deeper knowledge construction and better transfer of learning [20]. To address this limitation, Lin, Lee, Wang, Huang and Wu [3] extended the model to include a seventh phase—Reflection, thereby proposing the 6E+R model. This enhanced model encourages students to evaluate their learning process, consider group collaboration dynamics, and adjust their learning strategies based on reflective insights.

This study, therefore, aims to examine how AI-supported summative reflection—enabled by large language models—can enhance students' learning motivation, teamwork competency, and reflective depth within the context of a one-day CPS-based STEM workshop using the 6E+R framework. The findings are expected to contribute to the growing body of literature on AI-enhanced reflective learning and offer practical implications for instructional design in STEM education.

3 Methodology

3.1 Participants

28 high school students from Taiwan voluntarily participated in a one-day STEM workshop focused on developing autonomous vehicles using Micro:bit. Informed consent was obtained from all participants and their guardians, and all data were anonymized for academic use only.

Students were randomly assigned to either an experimental group or a control group (n = 14 each). Both groups received identical instruction based on the 6E + R learning model, with the only difference being the reflection method. The experimental group used an AI-supported reflection tool powered by large language models (LLMs) to generate structured feedback based on CPS discussions. The control group engaged in conventional reflection, manually reviewing and recording their learning experiences without AI assistance.

3.2 Experimental Design

This study adopted a quasi-experimental design to investigate the application and impact of AI-supported reflection in collaborative problem solving (CPS) activities within a STEM context. The learning content focused on fundamental autonomous vehicle development using Micro:bit. All participants engaged in hands-on STEM activities and received identical instructional content and curriculum design, grounded in the 6E + R learning model (i.e., the 6E learning model with Reflection). The key distinction between the two groups lay in the type of reflective strategy employed during the final phase of the learning process.

Students in the experimental group utilized an AI-Supported Summative Reflection approach. They interacted with a custom-developed AI Summative Tool, which used large language model (LLM) technology to automatically analyze the transcripts of their CPS discussions. The tool generated structured learning summaries and provided personalized feedback, as illustrated in Fig. 1. This feedback highlighted key discussion points and offered actionable suggestions to help students revise strategies and conduct systematic reflection. In contrast, the control group adopted a conventional reflection approach, in which students manually reviewed their learning process and team discussions without technological assistance. They were responsible for individually or collaboratively recording and organizing their reflections, relying solely on their own cognitive awareness and summarization skills.

The CPS learning activity lasted one full day and was facilitated by the same instructor for all participants to ensure instructional consistency. The course content covered key areas such as system architecture of autonomous vehicles, sensor control, programming logic, and data processing techniques. The learning activities were structured based on the 6E+R instructional model, which followed six core phases—Engage, Explore, Explain, Engineer, Enrich, and Evaluate—and incorporated collaborative problem solving (CPS) strategies. Students worked in teams to complete project-based tasks and concluded the session with presentations and reflective discussions, as shown in Table 1.

Upon completing their projects, teams presented their outcomes and engaged in reflective discussions.

To assess the impact of AI-supported reflection on students' learning outcomes, participants in the experimental group first used the AI Summative Tool to synthesize their discussion content, followed by a reflection process enriched by the AI-generated summaries and suggestions. Meanwhile, students in the control group conducted open-ended reflections through group discussions and self-recording, without any form of AI assistance.

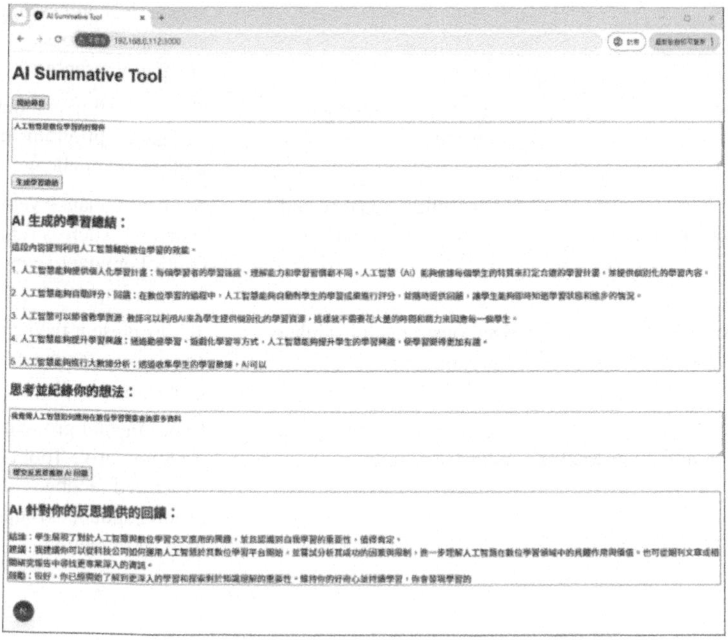

Fig. 1. Illustration of the AI-Supported Summative Reflection Tool.

Table 1. CPS Learning Activities Based on the 6E + R Model.

6E+R Phase	Learning Objectives	Learning Activities
Engage (Motivation)	Stimulate interest in Micro:bit autonomous vehicles	The instructor introduces applications of Micro:bit vehicles and guides students to explore obstacle-avoidance design ideas

(*continued*)

Table 1. (*continued*)

6E+R Phase	Learning Objectives	Learning Activities
Explore (Concept Exploration)	Understand basic hardware and sensors	Students test core functions of Micro:bit vehicles, including motors, ultrasonic sensors, and line-tracking modules
Explain (Concept Construction)	Develop programming logic	The instructor explains MicroPython coding and sensor data processing; students write basic navigation programs
Engineer (Design and Implementation)	Design and implement solutions	Teams develop and optimize navigation programs based on a racetrack challenge
Enrich (Extension and Innovation)	Extend functionality and explore innovation	Students enhance vehicle functions, such as remote control or adaptive navigation, and test improvements
Evaluate (Performance Assessment)	Demonstrate and validate outcomes	Teams present their projects and receive feedback from the instructor and peers
Reflect (Reflection and Adjustment)	Consolidate learning and adjust strategies	Experimental group uses the AI Summative Tool to receive structured feedback; control group conducts group-based manual reflection

3.3 Instruments and Data Analysis

To examine whether AI-supported summative reflection enhances students' learning motivation and teamwork competency during collaborative problem-solving (CPS) activities, this study employed two validated instruments.

Students' learning motivation was assessed using a questionnaire adapted from Wang and Chen [21], consisting of six items designed to measure students' interest, engagement, and perceived value of learning during the CPS activity. Additionally, students' teamwork competency was evaluated using the Teamwork Scale for Youth developed by Lower, Newman and Anderson-Butcher [22], which contains ten items targeting students' perceptions of team interaction, contribution, and collaboration quality. Both instruments used a five-point Likert scale ranging from 1 (strongly disagree) to 5 (strongly agree).

Given the limited sample size and potential non-normal distribution of the data, non-parametric statistical methods were adopted. The Mann–Whitney U test was used to compare the differences between the experimental and control groups in terms of learning motivation and teamwork competency.

In addition to the quantitative analysis, the study also investigated differences in students' reflection content between the two groups. Student-generated reflective texts, originally written in Chinese, were analyzed using BERTopic, a topic modeling technique that combines transformer-based embeddings and clustering algorithms to identify thematic structures in textual data. All reflections were translated into English for consistency in topic extraction and visualization. Keyword clouds were generated to illustrate the dominant themes emerging from each group's reflections, providing further insight into the cognitive depth and focus of students' reflective thinking.

4 Results

4.1 Learning Motivation

To determine the impact of AI-supported summative reflection on students' learning motivation, a Mann–Whitney U test was conducted on the post-test scores of both groups. The results indicated that students in the experimental group ($M = 4.28$, $SD = 0.43$) scored significantly higher than those in the control group ($M = 3.76$, $SD = 0.61$), $U = 59.0$, $p = .035$. The effect size ($r = .40$) suggests a moderate effect. These findings indicate that structured feedback generated by the AI tool effectively enhanced students' motivation during the CPS activity by clarifying learning goals and promoting focused engagement, as shown in Table 2.

Table 2. Mann–Whitney U Test Results for Learning Motivation.

Group	*N*	*Mean*	*SD*	*U*	*p*	*r*
Experimental group	14	4.28	0.43	59.0	.035*	0.4
Control group	14	3.76	0.61			

Note. * $p < 0.05$

4.2 Teamwork Competency

To evaluate differences in teamwork competency between the two groups, a Mann–Whitney U test was applied to the post-test scores obtained from the Teamwork Scale for Youth. The results showed that students in the experimental group ($M = 4.18$, $SD = 0.39$) performed significantly better than those in the control group ($M = 3.71$, $SD = 0.54$), with $U = 57.5$, $p = .027$. The effect size ($r = .42$) indicates a moderate effect. These findings suggest that AI-generated summaries facilitated students' understanding of group dynamics, enhanced their communication confidence, and increased their recognition of team contributions, thereby improving overall collaboration quality, as shown in Table 3.

Table 3. Mann–Whitney U Test Results for Teamwork Competency.

Group	*N*	*Mean*	*SD*	*U*	*p*	*r*
Experimental group	14	4.18	0.39	57.5	.027*	0.42
Control group	14	3.71	0.54			

Note. * $p < 0.05$

4.3 Reflection Topic Analysis

To further explore the cognitive focus and depth of student reflections, BERTopic was used to extract and visualize key themes from the reflective texts of both groups. As illustrated in Fig. 2, the experimental group's reflections centered on strategic and conceptual terms such as "summary," "observation," "inference," "adjustment," and "logic," indicating deeper levels of reflective thinking. In contrast, Fig. 3 shows that the control group's reflections were dominated by operational and surface-level terms such as "fail," "reboot," "error," and "unclear." These differences suggest that the AI-supported tool helped guide students toward more meaningful and structured reflections, as shown in Figs. 2 and 3.

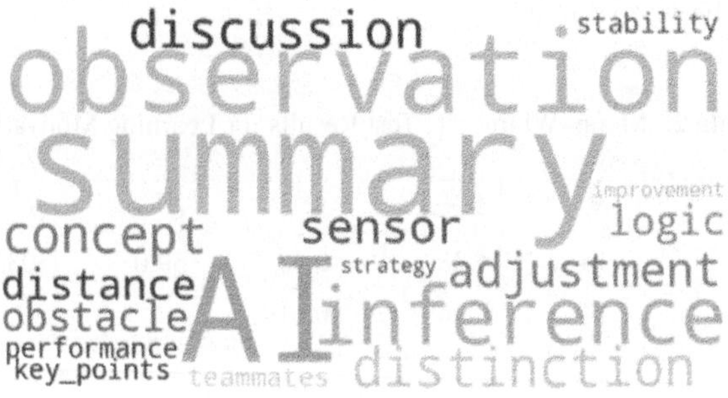

Fig. 2. Keyword cloud of reflective topics generated by the experimental group.

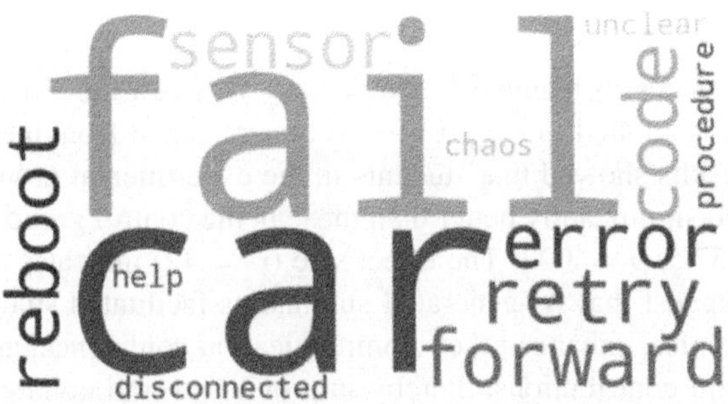

Fig. 3. Keyword cloud of reflective topics generated by the control group.

5 Results

This study examined the effects of AI-supported summative reflection within a STEM-based collaborative problem-solving (CPS) activity using the 6E + R learning framework. The results demonstrated that students who used AI-generated reflective feedback outperformed those engaging in conventional reflection in terms of learning motivation, teamwork competency, and the depth of reflective content.

For learning motivation, students in the experimental group showed significantly higher scores. The structured feedback generated by the AI tool clarified learning goals and promoted sustained engagement, supporting prior findings on the role of timely and targeted feedback in enhancing motivation.

In terms of teamwork competency, the AI-supported group reported greater awareness of team dynamics and contributions. The ability to revisit structured summaries appeared to strengthen collaboration and improve the quality of team communication.

Topic modeling analysis further revealed that reflections in the AI group focused more on strategic thinking and concept understanding, while the control group's reflections centered on technical issues and procedural descriptions. This suggests that AI-supported reflection can help shift students' focus toward higher-order thinking [23].

Overall, the findings confirm that AI-assisted reflection enhances both individual learning and group collaboration in CPS settings. Integrating AI tools into reflective learning offers a practical way to support metacognition and engagement in STEM education. This study also provides empirical support for the 6E + R framework, highlighting the value of embedding structured reflection supported by AI to improve learning outcomes.

References

1. Nugraha, M.G., Kidman, G., Tan, H.: Interdisciplinary STEM education foundational concepts: Implementation for knowledge creation. Eurasia J. Math. Sci. Technol. Educ. **20**, em2523 (2024)
2. Burke, B.N.: THE ITEEA 6E Learning by DeSIGN Model. Technol. Eng. Teacher **73**, 14–19 (2014)
3. Lin, C.-J., Lee, H.-Y., Wang, W.-S., Huang, Y.-M., Wu, T.-T.: Enhancing STEM collaboration through reflective strategies in the 6E learning model: insights from voice recognition analysis. Educ. Inf. Technol. **30**(4), 4251–4276 (2024). https://doi.org/10.1007/s10639-024-12957-9
4. Lin, K.-Y., Hsiao, H.-S., Williams, P.J., Chen, Y.-H.: Effects of 6E-oriented STEM practical activities in cultivating middle school students' attitudes toward technology and technological inquiry ability. Res. Sci. Technol. Educ. **38**, 1–18 (2020)
5. Cohn, C., Snyder, C., Fonteles, J.H., T. S, A., Montenegro, J., Biswas, G.: A multimodal approach to support teacher, researcher and AI collaboration in STEM+C learning environments. British J. Educ. Technol. **56**, 595–620 (2025)
6. Lin, K.-Y., Yu, K.-C., Hsiao, H.-S., Chu, Y.-H., Chang, Y.-S., Chien, Y.-H.: Design of an assessment system for collaborative problem solving in STEM education. J. Comput. Educ. **2**, 301–322 (2015)
7. Chen, L., Taniguchi, Y., Shimada, A., Yamada, M.: Exploring behavioral and strategic factors affecting secondary students' learning performance in collaborative problem solving-based STEM lessons. SAGE Open **14**, 21582440241251640 (2024)

8. Zimmerman, B.J.: Becoming a self-regulated learner: an overview. Theory Into Practice **41**, 64–70 (2002)
9. Lin, C.-J., Lee, H.-Y., Wang, W.-S., Huang, Y.-M., Wu, T.-T.: Enhancing reflective thinking in STEM education through experiential learning: The role of generative AI as a learning aid. Educ. Inform. Technol. **30**(5), 6315–6337 (2024). https://doi.org/10.1007/s10639-024-13072-5
10. Lindqvist, M.H., Arvidsson, C.: Exploring student and AI generated texts: reflections on reflection texts. Electron. J. e-Learn. **22**, 52–59 (2024)
11. Roberts, T., Maiorca, C., Jackson, C., Mohr-Schroeder, M.: Integrated STEM as problem-solving practices. Invest. Math. Learn. **14**, 1–13 (2022)
12. Chen, L., et al.: Direction of collaborative problem solving-based STEM learning by learning analytics approach. Res. Pract. Technol. Enhanced Learn. **14**(1), 1–28 (2019). https://doi.org/10.1186/s41039-019-0119-y
13. Jimmy, Zambrano R., Kirschner, F., Sweller, J., Kirschner, P.A.: Effects of prior knowledge on collaborative and individual learning. Learn. Instruct. **63**, 101214 (2019)
14. Picton, C., Kahu, E.R.: 'I knew I had the support from them': understanding student support through a student engagement lens. High. Educ. Res. Dev. **41**, 2034–2047 (2022)
15. Li, P.-H., Lee, H.-Y., Lin, C.-J., Wang, W.-S., Huang, Y.-M.: InquiryGPT: augmenting ChatGPT for enhancing inquiry-based learning in STEM education. J. Educ. Comput. Res. **62**, 2157–2186 (2024)
16. Wang, W.-S., Lin, C.-J., Lee, H.-Y., Huang, Y.-M., Wu, T.-T.: Integrating feedback mechanisms and ChatGPT for VR-based experiential learning: impacts on reflective thinking and AIoT physical hands-on tasks. Interact. Learn. Environ. 1–18 (2024)
17. Yazıcı, Y.Y., Hacıoğlu, Y., Sarı, U.: Entrepreneurship, STEM attitude, and career interest development through 6E learning byDeSIGN™ model based STEM education. Int. J. Technol. Des. Educ. **33**, 1525–1545 (2023)
18. Li, X., Ma, H., Liu, H., Li, X., Hu, Y., Jing, B., Feng, C.: Effects of 6E-based learning on students' academic achievement, higher-order thinking skills, and attitudes towards STEM. Res. Sci. Educ. (2024)
19. Bi, J., Bigdeli, H., Izadpanah, S.: The effect of the flipped classroom on reflective thinking, academic self-efficacy, and achievement motivation in language learners in intermediate level. Educ. Inf. Technol. **28**, 11589–11613 (2023)
20. Huang, Y.-M., Wang, W.-S., Lee, H.-Y., Lin, C.-J., Wu, T.-T.: Empowering virtual reality with feedback and reflection in hands-on learning: effect of learning engagement and higher-order thinking. J. Comput. Assist. Learn. **40**, 1413–1427 (2024)
21. Wang, L.C., Chen, M.P.: The effects of game strategy and preference-matching on flow experience and programming performance in game-based learning. Innov. Educ. Teach. Int. **47**, 39–52 (2010)
22. Lower, L.M., Newman, T.J., Anderson-Butcher, D.: Validity and reliability of the teamwork scale for youth. Res. Soc. Work. Pract. **27**, 716–725 (2015)
23. Lee, H.-Y., Chen, P.-H., Wang, W.-S., Huang, Y.-M., Wu, T.-T.: Empowering ChatGPT with guidance mechanism in blended learning: effect of self-regulated learning, higher-order thinking skills, and knowledge construction. Int. J. Educ. Technol. High. Educ. **21**, 16 (2024)

The Impact of Generated AI-Supported Learning on Elementary Students' Writing Skills

Hsin-Chin Chen[1](✉), Jin-Yu Chuang[2], Yueh-Min Huang[2], Kai-Huang Chen[1], and Yao-Chin Wang[1]

[1] Department of Electronic Engineering, Cheng Shiu University, Kaohsiung City, Taiwan
{0662,5977,0644}@gcloud.csu.edu.tw

[2] Department of Engineering Science, National Cheng Kung University, Tainan City, Taiwan
n98121020@gs.ncku.edu.tw, huang@ncku.edu.tw

Abstract. This study aims to explore the potential of integrating generative artificial intelligence (GAI) into writing instruction to enhance students' writing abilities. By using AI-generated visual images as writing prompts, the approach stimulates learners' writing inspiration. The study adopts a quasi-experimental design to evaluate the impact of generative AI tools on writing performance and cognitive abilities, with data collected through pre- and post-tests as well as classroom observations. The results show that AI-generated images significantly improve students' narrative structure, creative idea generation, and writing fluency. These findings highlight the potential of AI-generated visuals as an innovative instructional tool that offers personalized and context-rich learning experiences with practical applications in education.

Keywords: Generated AI · Writing Skills · Elementary Education

1 Introduction

Writing is a foundational skill in elementary education, playing a crucial role in students' academic success and personal development. It enables learners to articulate their thoughts, communicate effectively, and connect ideas across various disciplines [1]. Beyond academic purposes, writing supports cognitive growth by helping students organize their thoughts, express creativity, and engage deeply with complex concepts. It also serves as a medium for self-expression and emotional reflection, allowing students to build confidence and develop a sense of identity. Writing promotes lifelong learning by teaching essential skills such as planning, revising, and synthesizing information, all of which are critical for adapting to future challenges. Given its profound importance, prioritizing the development of strong writing abilities in elementary education is essential to equipping students with the tools they need for academic, social, and professional success [2].

Elementary students often face significant challenges in transforming abstract thoughts into coherent text, particularly during descriptive or creative writing tasks.

W.-S. Wang et al. (Eds.): ICITL 2025, LNCS 15913, pp. 181–188, 2026.
https://doi.org/10.1007/978-3-031-98185-2_20

This difficulty stems from the complex processes involved in writing, which require idea generation, organization, and the effective use of language mechanics. Research has shown that insufficient support and limited engagement with writing activities can further exacerbate these struggles, leaving students feeling frustrated and unmotivated to improve their skills [3]. Traditional instructional methods, while beneficial for some, often fail to address the unique needs of individual learners, limiting opportunities for personalized and meaningful learning experiences. This lack of tailored support can hinder students' ability to explore their creativity and express their ideas effectively [4]. As a result, many elementary students struggle to develop confidence and competence in writing, highlighting the need for more innovative and supportive teaching strategies.

AI-powered educational technologies (AI-EdTech) are increasingly being adopted to automate and enhance learning activities, offering personalized and innovative solutions. For example, educational recommender systems suggest tailored learning resources, providing reminders, real-time feedback, and study recommendations to support student performance [5]. Despite their potential, these tools may exhibit unpredictable behaviors, posing challenges for classroom integration. The rise of K-12 AI education highlights the importance of equipping students with AI literacy to navigate the rapid social and technological changes of the 21st century [6]. Among AI concept and technologies, some educational tools help make AI concepts more concrete and easier to understand for young learners [7, 8].

The integration of educational technologies, such as visual materials, offers effective solutions to enhance elementary students' writing process. These tools scaffold the writing process, bridge the gap between abstract thinking and written expression [9, 10]. To enhance students' in writing skills, this study leverages image-based AI tools as an intervention in elementary education. By providing personalized and context-specific visuals, AI tools inspire students' ideas, support content organization, and encourage critical thinking. A quasi-experimental design will be conducted to evaluate the effectiveness of this approach. The experimental group will use AI-generated visuals during writing tasks, while the control group will follow traditional methods. Therefore, the study aims to determine whether integrating AI-generated images can significantly improve students' writing performance.

2 Related Studies

2.1 Elementary Education on Writing Skill

In the context of elementary education, the development of students' writing skills constitutes a fundamental objective within language instruction. Writing is regarded not merely as a cognitive activity but as a critical mode through which learners articulate their thoughts and emotions. To effectively foster writing proficiency, it is essential to employ appropriate pedagogical strategies and instructional tools that support students in gradually acquiring writing competence and confidence. As noted by Taylor et al. [11], teachers implement differentiated scaffolding approaches tailored to students' developmental needs, incorporating resources such as mentor texts, graphic organizers, and individualized feedback to facilitate the writing process. Furthermore, systematically integrated instruction has been demonstrated to enhance both reading and writing outcomes among students [12]. The integration of educational technologies into writing tasks enables learners to engage in more creative and cognitively demanding activities, thereby promoting improved written expression. Within this framework, teachers play a pivotal role in curriculum design, guiding students through reflective and generative processes that reinforce the practical application of writing skills in meaningful contexts [13].

2.2 AI-Assisted Learning on Writing

In recent years, artificial intelligence (AI) technologies have gradually emerged in the field of elementary education, demonstrating broad potential in the development of writing skills. Liu et al. [14] proposed an artificial intelligence-supported English writing approach that incorporates a reflective thinking promotion mechanism to enhance learners' reflective thinking and improve their English writing quality. Similarly, Li et al. [15] conducted a study assessing the effectiveness of ChatGPT versions 3.5 and 4 in enhancing English as a Foreign Language (EFL) writing assessments within classroom settings. These technologies also enable teachers to more effectively track students' writing progress and implement personalized instruction. However, some scholars further highlighted that excessive dependence on AI could lead to various challenges, such as ethical concerns, technical and connectivity issues, and doubts regarding the accuracy and trustworthiness of AI-generated content [16]. Therefore, AI should serve as a supportive tool rather than the primary instructional method, and the role of teacher guidance and pedagogical strategies remains indispensable.

3 Research Method

The study aims to evaluate the role of generated AI in enhancing elementary students' writing skills. The research focuses on implementing AI-generated visual tools to support students in bridging abstract thinking and written expression, fostering creativity, and promoting writing cognitive processes. The study includes a quasi-experimental design, where students engage in writing tasks with AI-generated visuals to stimulate their imagination and organize their ideas. Additionally, assessments of students' writing performance will be conducted. The activities conducted are as follows:

3.1 Participants

The participants were fifth-grade elementary school students, consisting of 19 students in the experimental group and 17 students in the control group. While students had prior experience using ChatGPT, this experiment marked their first exposure to the AI image-generation feature of DALL•E.

3.2 Experimental Activity

The experimental design that integrates AI-generated image tools into the writing process to enhance students' writing performance and cognitive development, as shown in Fig. 1. The figure outlines a step-by-step process, starting with a pre-test for writing performance (Weeks 1–2), followed by dividing students into a control group and an experimental group (Weeks 3–7). The control group practiced conventional writing, while the experimental group utilized AI-generated visuals as part of their writing activities. Finally, a post-test for writing performance (Weeks 8).

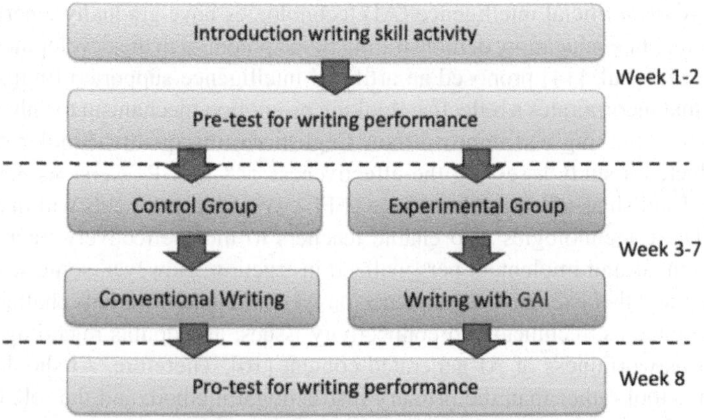

Fig. 1. Experimental procedure.

During the writing process, students in the experimental group used AI-generated tools to transform textual descriptions into visual representations, which were shared on a collaborative digital whiteboard. This collaborative discussion allowed for peer feedback, enriching creativity and story development. Additionally, DALL•E-generated four-panel comics served as reflective tools, helping students evaluate and revise their compositions. By incorporating this process into the creative writing task, titled "The Treasure Hunt of ___," students demonstrated cognitive skills, such as analyzing visuals, synthesizing ideas, and generating arguments, as reflected in Fig. 2. This framework highlights how AI tools scaffolded the writing process, ensuring a balance of autonomy and teacher guidance, while promoting deeper engagement and fostering advanced cognitive development.

Fig. 2. The AI-generated image for writing skill.

3.3 Data Collection

To measure improvements in writing skills, various assessments will be employed. The Taiwan National Education Counseling Team's Elementary School Counseling Group has developed an "Elementary School Composition Scoring Rubric Combined with Junior High School Academic Writing Assessment." This rubric evaluates compositions across four dimensions: "Idea and Material Selection," "Structure and Organization," "Word Choice and Sentence Construction," and "Spelling, Format, and Punctuation." Each dimension includes six levels, and the combined scores across all dimensions constitute the overall composition scale score.

4 Result and Discussion

Before the experiment began, a pre-test on writing ability was conducted for both the experimental and control groups to confirm whether there were any significant differences in students' baseline abilities. According to the statistical analysis results shown in Table 1, the average score of the control group was 9.82 (SD = 3.96), while the experimental group scored an average of 8.68 (SD = 1.84). The independent samples t-test result yielded there was no significant difference in writing ability between the two groups at the pre-test stage. This suggests that the students' writing abilities were generally comparable. This ensures that any differences observed in writing performance during the subsequent experiment can be attributed to the integration of AI-generated image tools in the teaching process.

Table 1. Writing Performance of Pre-Test

Group	N	Mean	SD	*t*	*p*
Experimental	19	8.68	1.84	−1.08	0.289
Control	17	9.82	3.96		

Note: $*p < 0.05$, $**p < 0.01$

As shown in Table 2, this study conducted a T-test analysis on post-test writing scores to control for the influence of pre-test scores and further examine differences in writing performance between the experimental and control groups. The analysis showed a p-value of 0.035 ($p < 0.05$), reaching statistical significance. This indicates that even when accounting for the influence of pre-test scores, the post-test writing scores of the experimental group were significantly higher than those of the control group. Specifically, the mean score of the experimental group was 12.15 (SD = 4.55), which was noticeably higher than the control group's mean of 9.20 (SD = 3.48). These results suggest that using AI-generated image tools in writing instruction positively influenced student performance. This further validates the effectiveness of AI-generated image tools as instructional aids that can help students enhance their writing skills, especially in areas such as content organization, narrative structure development, and creative thinking.

Table 2. Writing Performance of Post-Test

Group	N	Mean	SD	*t*	*p*
Experimental	19	12.15	4.55	2.19	*0.035
Control	17	9.20	3.48		

Note: $*p < 0.05$, $**p < 0.01$

The findings from this study reveal the significant impact of AI-generated image tools on enhancing students' writing performance. The use of AI-generated visuals as writing prompts facilitated richer and more detailed compositions by helping students bridge the gap between abstract ideas and textual expression. Students incorporated vivid descriptions, coherent storylines, and creative elements into their writing, aligning with findings by Smeda et al. [9], which emphasize the role of visual stimuli in improving narrative skills. These tools also increased motivation, particularly among novice writers, by providing visual scaffolding and reducing cognitive barriers, supporting similar conclusions by [17].

The integration of AI-generated image tools in writing instruction provides educators with innovative strategies to scaffold learning and foster creativity. These tools can assist students in transforming abstract ideas into coherent text, particularly those who struggle with generating or organizing ideas. Research by [7] and Wang & Lester [8] highlights how AI technologies can inspire creativity and encourage deeper engagement with learning tasks. Teachers can design collaborative writing activities, leveraging AI-generated visuals as shared prompts to stimulate peer discussions and critical analysis. Additionally, such tools have potential applications beyond writing, supporting interdisciplinary learning and creative problem-solving tasks in contexts such as history, science, and art.

This study acknowledges several limitations. The sample size was relatively small, limiting the generalizability of findings to broader educational contexts. The study also focused on specific AI tools and features, such as image generation, which may not fully represent the potential of other AI applications. Variations in students' familiarity with technology and writing skills may have influenced the results, as seen in prior studies [5]. Additionally, the short duration of the intervention restricted the ability to measure long-term impacts on writing performance.

5 Conclusion

This study demonstrates that AI-generated image tools can provide students with concrete visual guidance in writing instruction, effectively enhancing their ability to conceptualize and express ideas. This not only validates the potential of AI technology in educational settings but also highlights its value in promoting personalized learning and increasing students' motivation to write. Through visual support, students are able to transform abstract ideas into concrete content, producing richer and more detailed compositions. AI-generated image tools show great promise in fostering creativity, collaboration, and engagement, offering educators innovative strategies for scaffolding learning. However, the study is limited by a small sample size and a short intervention duration. Therefore, future research should include long-term follow-up studies to further examine the sustained impact of AI tools on writing and critical thinking.

References

1. Graham, S., Tavsanli, O.F., Kaldirim, A.: Improving writing skills of students in Turkey: a meta-analysis of writing interventions. Educ. Psychol. Rev. **34**(2), 889–934 (2022)
2. Yang, G., Chen, Y.T., Zheng, X.L., Hwang, G.J.: From experiencing to expressing: a virtual reality approach to facilitating pupils' descriptive paper writing performance and learning behavior engagement. Br. J. Edu. Technol. **52**(2), 807–823 (2021)
3. Graham, S.: Changing how writing is taught. Rev. Res. Educ. **43**(1), 277–303 (2019)
4. Troia, G.A.: Evidence-based practices for writing instruction (Document No. IC-5). University of Florida, Collaboration for Effective Educator, Development, Accountability, and Reform Center. Development, Accountability, and Reform Center (2014)
5. Bodily, R., Verbert, K.: Review of research on student-facing learning analytics dashboards and educational recommender systems. IEEE Trans. Learn. Technol. **10**(4), 405–418 (2017)
6. Ng, D.T.K., Lee, M., Tan, R.J.Y., Hu, X., Downie, J.S., Chu, S.K.W.: A review of AI teaching and learning from 2000 to 2020. Educ. Inf. Technol. **28**(7), 8445–8501 (2023)
7. Kim, K., Kwon, K.: Tangible computing tools in AI education: Approach to improve elementary students' knowledge, perception, and behavioral intention towards AI. Educ. Inform. Technol. 1–32 (2024)

8. Wang, N., Lester, J.C.: K-12 education in the age of AI: a Call to action for K-12 AI literacy. Int. J. Artif. Intell. Educ. **33**(2), 228–232 (2023)
9. Smeda, N., Dakich, E., Sharda, N.: The effectiveness of digital storytelling in the classrooms: a comprehensive study. Smart Learn. Environ. **1**, 1–21 (2014)
10. Yamaç, A., Ulusoy, M.: The effect of digital storytelling in improving the third graders' writing skills. Int. Electron. J. Elementary Educ. **9**(1), 59–86 (2017)
11. Taylor, K.S., Keane, K., Silverman, R.D., Levine, S.: Elementary Teachers' Scaffolding in Writing Instruction. Literacy Res. Instruct. 1–21 (2024)
12. Kim, Y.S.G., Zagata, E.: Enhancing reading and writing skills through systematically integrated instruction. Read. Teach. **77**(6), 787–799 (2024)
13. Pella, S. M.: Learning to teach writing in the age of standardization and accountability; toward an equity writing pedagogy. Teaching/Writing: J. Writing Teacher Educ. **4**(1), 1 (2015)
14. Liu, C., Hou, J., Tu, Y.F., Wang, Y., Hwang, G.J.: Incorporating a reflective thinking promoting mechanism into artificial intelligence-supported English writing environments. Interact. Learn. Environ. **31**(9), 5614–5632 (2023)
15. Li, J., Huang, J., Wu, W., Whipple, P.B.: Evaluating the role of ChatGPT in enhancing EFL writing assessments in classroom settings: a preliminary investigation. Humanit. Soc. Sci Commun. **11**(1), 1–9 (2024)
16. Chen, C., Gong, Y.: The role of AI-assisted learning in academic writing: a mixed-methods study on Chinese as a second language students. Educ. Sci. **15**(2), 141 (2025)
17. Höffler, T.N., Leutner, D.: Instructional animation versus static pictures: a meta-analysis. Learn. Instr. **17**(6), 722–738 (2007)

Computational Thinking in Education

A Study on the Effectiveness of Integrating Innovative Learning Strategies into Computational Thinking in Programming Learning for Non-CS Major Students

I-Fan Liu(✉)

Department of Allied Health Education and Digital Learning, National Taipei University of Nursing and Health Sciences, No. 365, Ming-Te Road, Taipei City, Taiwan
ifliuG@gmail.com

Abstract. Given the rise of the AI era, learning programming languages is no longer exclusive to students in information-related disciplines. However, non-CS major students often encounter challenges when taking programming courses, such as unclear learning objectives, complex course materials, and a lack of learning motivation. The primary aim of this study is to examine the effectiveness of computational thinking in programming learning for non-CS major students by introducing innovative learning strategies. This study employs a quasi-experimental design involving 59 non-CS major students from a university in Taiwan. The findings indicate that the control group (CG) and the experimental group (EG) significantly improved post-test scores across all computational thinking units. Moreover, among the six units, the EG group outperformed the CG group in all but the algorithms unit, where no significant difference was observed. This study suggests that future liberal arts curricula should be tailored to non-CS major students and incorporate more forward-thinking courses and learning methods to align with the talent development needs of the AI era.

Keywords: Computational Thinking · Collaborative Task-Oriented Learning · Programming Learning for Non-CS Major Students · Liberal Arts Education

1 Introduction

According to a research report by the World Economic Forum [16], in the next decade, most existing human jobs will be replaced by automation, robotics, and artificial intelligence (AI), but there will also be 60% to 70% of new types of jobs created in response, and the operational processes of businesses will be drastically changed to reduce the cost of labor. In order to respond to the future demand for digital talents, the Ministry of Education in Taiwan, in its Comprehensive Blueprint for Information Education (2016–2020) plan, has a vision of "Deep Learning and Digital Citizenship," which aims to cultivate students who can effectively make good use of information technology (IT), apply it to the learning of different subject areas, and solve the problems faced in the

W.-S. Wang et al. (Eds.): ICITL 2025, LNCS 15913, pp. 191–198, 2026.
https://doi.org/10.1007/978-3-031-98185-2_21

future from it [8]. In addition, in the new syllabus of the 2019th school year, the 12-year national education will integrate programming education in junior and senior high schools, which means that students' basic education will cover a part of computational thinking. In the future, they can articulate with the information field courses in higher education when they enter colleges or universities.

In recent years, the trend of digital information has changed dramatically due to the rapid development of technologies such as big data, the Internet of Things (IoT), mobile devices, and cloud technologies. For example, automobiles, humanoid robots, and drones are all AI-enabled inventions that require robust information systems and mobile computing to complete, and they rely on the operation of applications and computational thinking. US President Obama once said, "It is time to learn the ABCs and colors at the same time you learn to write programs" [13]. Kenichi Ohmae, a Japanese trendsetter, said, "All counselors should learn to write codes because it makes their logic better" [9]. Programming is a relatively inexpensive way for students to develop their thought processes and practical, creative experiences, and it is one of the ways students can develop their self-learning skills [6].

Taiwan's Ministry of Education will implement a new 12-year national education curriculum in 2019, aiming to have 50% of all college students take programming courses by 2022 to enhance their competitiveness in the future workplace. In response to this initiative, universities and colleges offer programming courses for non-CS major students. The learning objectives of the courses emphasize the cultivation of basic programming literacy, logical thinking, practical skills, and the ability to define problems and propose solutions. In the past, most programming courses were offered by university information technology-related departments, such as the Department of Computer Science, Information Engineering, and Information Management. It is worth mentioning that some tertiary institutions do not have any information-related departments. In order to reach the threshold of 50% of the university students who have taken the program courses, most of them have made the programming language a mandatory course in liberal arts education and hired teachers with information technology expertise to support the courses for non-CS major students [1].

However, non-CS major students can only passively accept the arrangement of the school policy without any right to choose. While taking the course, they often encounter problems such as unclear learning objectives, complex course materials, and a lack of learning motivation [3]. Therefore, the primary aim of this study is to examine the effectiveness of computational thinking in programming learning for non-CS major students by introducing innovative learning strategies.

2 Literature Review

2.1 The Role of Information Technology in Liberal Arts Education

Professional disciplines primarily train students to become specialists in a specific field. In contrast, liberal arts education equips them to engage with knowledge across diverse domains, approach issues from multiple perspectives, and develop a comprehensive personal knowledge system. The uniqueness of Liberal Arts lies in the development of independent learning and interdisciplinary thinking skills, with special emphasis on cultivating a broad base of knowledge that enables students to understand contemporary issues affecting individuals, society, the nation, or global, and to be able to think critically, reflexively, and independently. As the times continue to evolve, especially with the wave of digitization sweeping across the globe, educators should cultivate in students the ability to take a macro view and make good use of IT to solve problems. Further, problem-solving requires the integration of interdisciplinary and cross-field knowledge and skills so that IT can play a complementary role in promoting students' thinking, wisdom, and humanistic care in liberal arts education [17].

With the current IT development, not everyone needs to be a professional programmer, although programming skills are increasingly valued. Therefore, instead of simply cultivating excellent programming skills, IT education should further emphasize critical thinking and problem-solving skills, which is known as Computational Thinking (CT). CT is not only about programming but also involves core competencies such as abstraction, algorithmic design, and systematic analysis, which develop an individual's ability to effectively respond to and solve problems in multiple contexts [6]. Wing [15] proposed five CT components: decomposition, algorithmic thinking, abstraction, generalization, and evaluation. CT is defined as a problem-solving method that is not limited to basic computer science concepts to solve problems or design systems. Therefore, effective and accurate problem-solving is a skill everyone should learn and use. Papert first introduced the concept of CT in 1980, believing that in the future, computers would no longer be exclusive to information engineers but would change thinking [10]. Students in any field could combine computational skills with critical thinking to construct solutions to problems. However, such an avant-garde idea has been criticized at that time when computers were not widely available. Due to the rapid development of today's digital society, CT has been widely mentioned in many literatures in the context of the growing importance of computer science education. However, the conceptualization is slightly different due to the different temporal and spatial contexts [7]. Therefore, this study will also focus on incorporating a liberal arts perspective into planning CT learning activities when reconfiguring the programming language curriculum.

2.2 Collaborative Task-Oriented Learning

In general, task-oriented learning is widely utilized in modern classroom activities. To effectively enhance students' learning motivation and achieve better learning outcomes, instructors must meticulously design task-based problems. Willis [11] proposed six types of learning tasks, one of which is problem solving. For this type of task, learners must first analyze the tasks open-mindedly to find ways and means to solve the problems. Dolmans et al. [2] suggested the principle of task design, which should be designed so that students can connect with their prior knowledge and experience. The level of difficulty of the tasks is recommended to be designed progressively. The complexity of the process should be moderate but not so much that it exceeds the cognitive load of the learning process. Meanwhile, it is important to think about configuring tasks in such a way as to stimulate students' interest in finding solutions. This drives motivation and collaborative team-based learning and enhances the full range of knowledge and skills that lead to good learning effectiveness [11].

In contrast, collaborative task-oriented learning is based on achieving a goal and task, where members participate in an activity together. Group members communicate and coordinate with each other and accomplish goals through interaction and collaboration. According to past research, collaborative task-oriented learning in group settings can improve the learning effectiveness of programming and the understanding of CT among group members [5]. In addition, collaborative task-oriented learning can increase students' achievement motivation, which allows students to become more motivated to study and have a longer-term memory of what they have learned [4].

3 Methods

Currently, most university students in Taiwan possess mobile devices, with nearly everyone owning a smartphone. Mobile apps on smartphones, tablets, and other mobile devices provide various popular information services among students. Students use apps to engage in various activities, including socializing (e.g., Instagram, Facebook), entertaining, getting information, and even learning in the course, such as using ChatGPT and generative AI to assist learning. Therefore, using smartphones as the carrier of programming learning will be a more direct and immediate learning experience.

In addition, considering that students do not have a background in the field of information technology, the course focuses on training programmatic CT so that students do not need to have any foundation in a programming language but only need basic logical thinking skills to learn. Meanwhile, we adopted APP Inventor, a platform developed by the Massachusetts Institute of Technology (MIT), as the foundation for introductory programming learning. This platform utilizes a block-based, drag-and-drop approach to program development, allowing students to construct applications by assembling predefined components. With an extensive library of built-in components, even students with no prior programming experience can quickly develop functional and robust apps.

This study used a quasi-experimental design in which the same instructor taught an introductory programming course in liberal arts education to two classes. The lessons were mainly taught in the physical classroom, while some chapters were taught online as asynchronous pre-recorded lessons. In terms of content, the instructor integrated logic and CT learning units [12], including decomposition, algorithms, abstraction, debugging, generalization, and iteration, into the programming curriculum of the two classes. At the same time, logic training is integrated into some chapters, such as variables and operators, sequences, choices, loops, and arrays. Since this part of logic and CT may be abstract and complex for non-CS major students, it is important to emphasize the importance of logic and CT in these chapters. Therefore, before taking these learning units, the instructor will allow students to read the designated materials online, such as case studies or story scenarios, to make it easier for the students to learn. The materials include animated stories, videos, speeches, and MOOCs. The content is the same for both classes.

In addition, in terms of learning strategies, the control group (CG) class adopts a task-oriented learning method. In the classroom, the instructor assigns learning tasks based on the content of the learning units, and students must complete the CT problem-solving tasks within a specified period and upload the files. The content of the files varies according to the learning tasks. It is presented in various ways, including source code, concept maps, answers to problems (e.g., international CT Bebras tests), and content writing on CT-related scenarios. This is intended to help students understand the basic logic and CT of the code in a more concrete manner. The experimental group (EG) class adopts the collaborative task-oriented learning method, in which students are divided into randomized groups (two students as a group) to complete the problem-solving tasks through teamwork at the teaching site.

4 Results

A total of 59 students from a university in Taiwan were the participants of this study, including 28 students in the experimental group and 31 students in the control group. The basic demographics of the participants included 21 male students (35.6%) and 38 female students (64.4%) with backgrounds from nursing school, the College of Healthcare, and the College of Human Development of Health. The average age was 20.1. Less than 6% of the students had studied programming in the past. Of those students who had studied programming, nearly 60% were interested in a programming learning experience. None of the participants had any previous experience with CT.

In order to understand the integration of different learning strategies into CT in the programming course, Table 1 shows the results of the two groups' performance on the CT pre-test and post-test. For the CG group, there was a significant difference between the pre-test and post-test (t = -2.996, *Sig.* = .005, $p < 0.05$), and the mean score of the post-test (M = 56.45) was significantly higher than that of the pre-test (M = 50.16). Similarly, for the EG group, there was also a significant difference between the pre-test and post-test (t = -8.792, *Sig.* = .000, $p < 0.05$), and the mean score of the post-test (M = 70.43) was significantly higher than that of the pre-test (M = 52.32). Therefore, CG and EG groups significantly improved the post-test scores through different learning strategies in the CT chapter.

Table 1. The paired-sample t-test on the Learning Effectiveness of CT

Group	*n*	CT Pre-test		CT Po-test		*t*	*Sig*
		Mean	SD	Mean	SD		
CG group	31	50.16	15.356	56.45	9.327	-2.996	.005*
EG group	28	52.32	16.526	70.43	13.412	-8.792	.000*

There are six learning units in CT, including decomposition, algorithms, abstraction, debugging, generalization, and iteration. Each unit is graded from 0 to 100, with a score below 60 being a failing grade. Table 2 shows the performance (post-test) of different learning strategies in each unit of CT. Except for the algorithms unit, where no significant difference was found between the two groups (t = −1.666, Sig. = .101, p > 0.05), the EG group significantly outperformed the CG group in all other units.

Furthermore, this study found that the EG group, which adopted the collaborative task-oriented learning method, achieved an average score above the passing threshold (60) on the CT post-test for all units except for the algorithms unit. These findings suggest that for non-CS major learners, employing a task-oriented learning strategy combined with collaborative teamwork enhances CT development more effectively than individual task-oriented learning.

This suggests that non-CS major learners significantly benefit from peer collaboration, interaction, discussion, and the collective process of identifying and solving problems as part of their CT development. Notably, the algorithms unit primarily aims to cultivate students' algorithmic thinking, requiring them to design logical and structured instructions to solve problems. These instructions encompass four key subcategories: algorithm design, parallel processing, efficiency, and automation. This aspect of learning generally necessitates prior programming knowledge and foundational skills, presenting notable challenges as well as opportunities for growth among non-CS major learners.

Table 2. The independent-sample t-test on the Learning Effectiveness of CT (post-test)

CT Units	CG group ($n = 31$)		EG group ($n = 28$)		*t*	*Sig*
	Mean	SD	Mean	SD		
Decomposition	63.23	17.490	74.29	10.157	−3.004	.004*
Algorithms	48.06	13.643	54.64	16.663	−1.666	.101
Abstraction	52.10	14.421	67.68	13.228	−4.310	.000*
Debugging	52.74	13.530	66.07	11.891	−4.001	.000*
Generalization	62.74	14.424	80.89	11.308	−5.338	.000*
Iteration	59.52	17.905	78.93	10.746	−5.104	.000*

5 Conclusion

Integrating computational thinking into programming learning aims to cultivate logical reasoning and problem-solving skills. For non-CS major students, implementing the innovative learning strategy proposed in this study significantly improved computational thinking learning outcomes in both the control and experimental groups. Furthermore, adopting a collaborative task-oriented learning method enhances the logical training process of computational thinking across different units, including decomposition, abstraction, debugging, generalization, and iteration. The students must engage in interactive discussions, collaborative problem-solving, and shared decision-making with their peers to accomplish learning tasks.

Liberal arts education upholds the mission of cultivating fundamental competencies among university students. In the era of AI, fostering interdisciplinary information literacy requires greater participation from non-CS major students. The vision of integrating programming-related courses into liberal arts is to establish programming language as a gateway for engaging with technology—similar to essential literacy skills such as listening, speaking, reading, and writing. The goal is not to train the students to become programming experts but rather to develop their logical reasoning, problem-solving competencies, and the ability to establish standard operating procedures (S.O.P.) through programming logic. This study suggests that future liberal arts curricula should explore more forward-thinking courses like AI and incorporate innovative and diverse learning methods. These courses should be tailored to the needs of non-CS major students to ensure accessibility and relevance. Developing such curricula represents the future work of this research.

Acknowledgements. This work was supported by the National Science and Technology Council of Taiwan under contract numbers NSTC 109-2511-H227-006, and NSTC 110-2511-H227-004. The authors would like to thank all the people who took part in this study.

Disclosure of Interests. There are no competing interests.

References

1. Hsu, C.-Y., Hwang, F.-N., Chen, T.-Y., Chang, C.-H.: ICCE 2023 learning outcomes of computer programming and information technology - integrated courses for non-computer science majors: case study of a public research university in Taiwan. Int. Conf. Comput. Educ. (2023). https://doi.org/10.58459/icce.2023.4801
2. Dolmans, D.H., Snellen-Balendong, H., van der Vleuten, C.P.: Seven principles of effective case design for a problem-based curriculum. Med. Teach. **19**(3), 185–189 (1997). https://doi.org/10.3109/01421599709019379
3. Echeverría, L., Cobos, R., Machuca, L., Claros, I.: Using collaborative learning scenarios to teach programming to non-CS majors. Comput. Appl. Eng. Educ. **25**(5), 719–731 (2017). https://doi.org/10.1002/cae.21832
4. Kexin, D., Buang, N.A.: Relationship between effectiveness of flipped classroom, blended learning and task-oriented teaching methods on academic achievement among vocational college students in an OBE IT system environment. J. Digitainab. Realism Mastery **3**(04), 26–40 (2024). https://doi.org/10.56982/dream.v3i04.228
5. Kielstra, J., Molenaar, I., van Steensel, R., Verhoeven, L.: Supporting socially shared regulation during collaborative task-oriented reading. Int. J. Comput.-Support. Collab. Learn. **17**(1), 65–105 (2022). https://doi.org/10.1007/s11412-022-09365-x
6. Lai, X., Wong, G.K.W.: Collaborative versus individual problem solving in computational thinking through programming: a meta-analysis. Br. J. Edu. Technol. **53**(1), 150–170 (2022). https://doi.org/10.1111/bjet.13157
7. Lodi, M., Martini, S.: Computational thinking, between papert and wing. Sci. Educ. **30**(4), 883–908 (2021). https://doi.org/10.1007/s11191-021-00202-5
8. Ministry of Education: The Comprehensive Blueprint for Information Education (2016–2020) (2016). https://ws.moe.edu.tw/001/Upload/3/relfile/6315/46563/65ebb64a-683c-4f7a-bcf0-325113ddb436.pdf
9. Ohmae, K.: Marketing Strategy for Value Exploration. In: Marketing for Competitiveness: Asia to the World—In the Age of Digital Consumers, p. 175 (2016). https://doi.org/10.1142/9789813201972_0001

10. Papert, S.A.: Mindstorms: Children, Computers, and Powerful Ideas. Basic Books (2020)
11. Race, P.: Task-based learning. Med. Educ. **34**(5), 335–336 (2000)
12. Shute, V.J., Sun, C., Asbell-Clarke, J.: Demystifying computational thinking. Educ. Res. Rev. **22**, 142–158 (2017). https://doi.org/10.1016/j.edurev.2017.09.003
13. White House: President Obama Is the First President to Write a Line of Code (2014). https://obamawhitehouse.archives.gov/blog/2014/12/10/president-obama-first-president-write-line-code
14. Willis, J.: A flexible framework for task-based learning. In: Challenge and Change in Language Teaching, pp. 52–62 (1996)
15. Wing, J.M.: Computational thinking. Commun. ACM **49**(3), 33–35 (2006)
16. World Economic Forum: The Future of Jobs Report 2018. World Economic Forum, Geneva, Switzerland (2018). http://www3.weforum.org/docs/WEF_Future_of_Jobs_2018.pdf
17. Yamada, R.: Thoughts on the trends in 21st-century liberal arts education: seeking possibility of collaboration between universities and industry. Korean J. General Educ. **18**(6), 13–19 (2024). https://doi.org/10.46392/kjge.2024.18.6.13

Design and Framework of Learning Systems

Which Students Collaborate? Unsupervised Identification of Team Structures from Individual Reports Documenting Groupwork

Frode Eika Sandnes(✉)

Oslo Metropolitan University, 0130 Oslo, Norway
frodes@oslomet.no

Abstract. Groupwork is believed to have positive effects on learning. This study addresses a practical use-case where students solve assignments in groups yet demonstrate their learning outcomes through a portfolio of individual reports. When grading such coursework, it is beneficial to collectively examine the individual report written by all the group members. However, students often make mistakes when declaring their group composition, while others forget or refuse to disclose their team. This can be particularly challenging with anonymized portfolios. This paper presents a simple, accurate, and computationally efficient unsupervised algorithm for detecting group structures based on the contents of the reports. Tests on 2151 reports by approximately 500 students showed that a large portion of groups could be identified successfully (33%–88%), with a mean similarity of 63%–94%, mean precision of 83%–97%, and mean recall of 70%–97%. The approach thus holds potential as a pragmatic tool for administering coursework assessments. Details on how to adjust the approach for three additional use cases are presented, namely the matching of final and former reports by the same students, identifying potential plagiarism cases for manual screening, and identifying incorrectly submitted reports.

Keywords: examination support tools · groupwork · plagiarism detection · anomaly detection · bag-of-words · anonymization

1 Introduction

This study is framed in an educational context where students learn by working on three practical projects covering the main parts of the syllabus. The first project is individual where students demonstrate their ability to work independently, while the second and third projects are solved in groups with the intention to enhance students' collaboration skills, harvest group learning effects, and experience collective intelligence [1]. Many educators believe that groupwork can have a positive effect on motivation and learning [2]. To further stimulate motivation two of the three projects are on a freely selected topic (free task) to pursue their individual interests, obviously within certain constraints, and

W.-S. Wang et al. (Eds.): ICITL 2025, LNCS 15913, pp. 201–211, 2026.
https://doi.org/10.1007/978-3-031-98185-2_22

one fixed topic assigned by the teacher (fixed task) to ensure exposure to key parts of the syllabus. Learning outcomes are assessed by examining each students' portfolio at the end of the semester. The benefits of traditional exams versus portfolio exams have been extensively discussed [3, 4]. My justification for choosing portfolios was to eliminate exam anxiety and encourage active learning.

Each portfolio thus comprises three reports. Many educators implement similar regimes where groupwork is documented in one group report. This choice is attractive as fewer reports reduce the grading load but also introduces problems such as free riders [5]. Instead, students are required to write individual accounts of the groupwork. The goal is to make each student accountable for the groupwork and prevent free riders. Students are invited to submit an optional complete draft during the course to receive feedback (*formative reports*), allowing students to implement corrections and improvements before submitting the portfolio (*final reports*) for assessment.

On the downside, individual reports increase the feedback and grading load threefold. The laborious and often mundane examination task therefore needs to be well-organized and systematic. One coping strategy is to read the individual reports of the group members collectively. This gives a complete impression of the groupwork but also insight into the learning outcomes of the individual group members.

Several learning management systems and exam systems can handle groupwork but assume one group report (or artefact). They are not designed to handle individual accounts of groupwork. Coursework anonymization, usually implemented to achieve fair grading [6], can further complicate the problem. To solve this in practice each student is required to declare their group members. However, some students forget to make these declarations, make mistakes (as discussed in [7], or refuse to disclose their collaborators. Such anomalies can lead to a significant additional workload.

Previously, an attempt was made to solve this problem using document similarity based on word bigrams [8], but the low success rates were too low for the approach to be applicable in practice. Besides this previous attempt there are seemingly few related works addressing this particular use case. This work thus documents a new attempt using a bag-of-words approach. Three other practical use-cases are also explored employing the same paradigm, formative vs final version matching, screening for possible plagiarism [9, 10], and identifying incorrectly submitted portfolios.

2 Unsupervised Coursework Analysis

2.1 Identifying Student Groups

It is assumed that student groups comprise 1 to 5 students. Some students are unable to find collaborators and there are situations that prevent students from participating in groupwork. These students are allowed to work alone. The limit of 5 members was set to stimulate healthy group dynamics, encourage learning, and prevent free riders.

The input to the algorithm is a report set, one report per student. Each report is first sanitized by removing non-textual characters and then split into individual words. Next, word sets are created using the word sequences. These sets represent unique words used in each of the reports. These sets are illustrated as sets *a*, *b*, and *c* in Fig. 1 (a) representing unique words used by student *a*, *b*, and *c*.

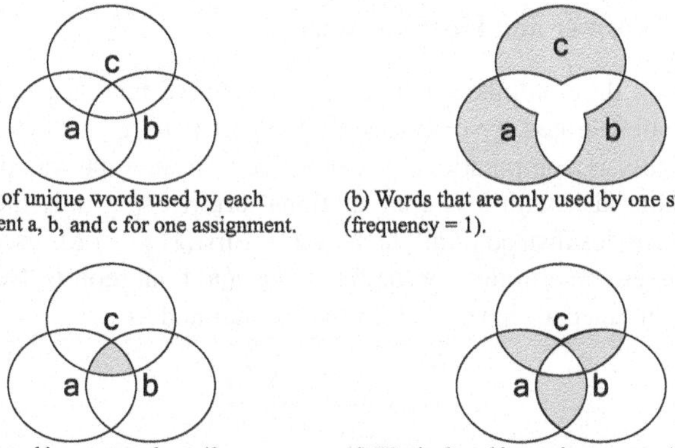

(a) Sets of unique words used by each student a, b, and c for one assignment.

(b) Words that are only used by one student (frequency = 1).

(c) Words used by most students (frequency > 8).

(d) Words shared by student groups (1 < frequency < 9).

Fig. 1. Analyzing unique words in student reports.

Next, a list of unique words used in all the texts is found by combining all the words in the individual sets into a list. This list is used to compute a word histogram denoting how many reports that include a particular word. Solo words (frequency of one) are only used by a single student (often typos) and are discarded. Solo words are illustrated in Fig. 1 (b) as the set difference between the words of each student and the set of all other words. Common words (high frequency) used by many students (analogous to stop words) were also discarded. Common words used by (most) students are illustrated in Fig. 1 (c) as the intersection of all the word sets.

The algorithm keeps words with a frequency between 2 and 8, i.e., words that are used by at least two students, but not more than eight students. The upper limit of 8 was found experimentally through trial and error. Figure 1 (d) illustrates the set of words shared by some students (intersections). These words of interest are used to identify potentially collaborating student pairs. For each word the list of students using this word is identified (by probing the word set membership). The list of students is then used to record all the possible student pairs. For example, if the list has two students, there will only be one pair. If the list has three students *a*, *b*, and *c*, there will be three pairs *ab*, *ac*, and *bc*, and so forth.

Finally, the groups are identified using a collaboration pair histogram computed from the detected student pairs. This histogram is processed in descending order of frequency. For each student pair, if neither of the students are assigned a group yet a new group is established with the two students as members. If just one of the students in the pair is assigned a group, the unassigned student is also added to this group, unless the maximum group size is reached or the drop in frequency is large in which case the unassigned student is simply marked as assigned. A large drop was defined as the larger frequency being more than twice as large as the smaller frequency. Unassigned students are classified as solo groups.

2.2 Matching Former and Final Versions

In previous work the automatic matching of formative reports and final reports was successfully demonstrated by comparing all report pairs using the bigram similarity [8]. However, this is computationally expensive. An attempt was therefore made to perform the same task with less computational effort using only the small subset of solo word frequencies instead of all the bigrams. First, solo words used by each student (see Fig. 1(b)) were determined for the formative and final reports. Next, each pair was matched using the Jaccard index (set similarity), defined as

$$J(A, B) = \frac{|A \cap B|}{|A \cup B|}$$

where A and B are the set of words for the two reports. For each final report, the former report with the highest similarity is considered the match.

2.3 Identifying the Most Similar Reports

Plagiarism detection involves comparing the similarity of a document against a document database. It can be relevant to perform a local plagiarism check within a class to identify students plagiarizing peers. This is relevant when students are tasked to write individual accounts of groupwork activities. Group members less confident in writing may be tempted to borrow phrases and snippets from classmates. Typically, such comparisons involve computing the similarity between each document pair which can be computationally intensive (O(N2)).

For each report, the five (arbitrarily chosen) word pairs with the highest frequency (see Fig. 1 (d)) were tagged as contenders. Each report is then compared to each of five contenders using a traditional document similarity measure ($O(N)$).

2.4 Identifying Incorrectly Submitted Reports

An exam system may be configured with several upload widgets, one for each of the reports of a portfolio. Some students submit their project portfolio incorrectly, especially if they are under late-minute stress to meet formal submission deadlines. For instance, the student may accidentally submit one of the reports twice or accidentally swap the upload category, say upload report 1 as report 2 and vice versa. Although such cases are rare (about 1%) and quite noticeable, it can be useful to identify such mistakes early allowing early corrective action.

We start with a set of portfolios, each containing three reports. The approach involves first identifying (solo) words only used in each of the respective assignments (assignment signature), and then comparing each submitted report with the three (assignment signature) sets. These assignment solo words were identified by considering all words in all the reports of each assignment, respectively. Figure 1 (a) illustrates this, although A, B, and C denote assignments aggregated for all students instead of individual students. The set of words only used in the three assignments is found by computing the set differences:

$$A' = A - (B \cup C)$$
$$B' = B - (A \cup C)$$
$$C' = C - (B \cup A)$$

The intersection between the set of unique words for each report and each of the assignment unique word sets A′, B′ and C′ is computed, and the largest intersection is considered a match. Anomalies are thus detected if the assignment match does not equal the actual assignment category.

3 Experimental Evaluation

The algorithms were implemented in JavaScript. These were evaluated using a curated dataset (see Table 1). This set comprises assignments across two years, including a formative (draft) version submitted for feedback and final version submitted for assessment. Of the N reports in each set only the ones (N′) with more than 2 pages were included in the analysis as reports with less than 3 pages are often incomplete. Self-declared group structures were available as ground-truth.

Table 1. The dataset used in the analysis.

Id	Year	Version	Mode	Task	N	N′	Mean pages	Mean words
1	2023	former	Individual	Free	155	151	6.5	1392
2			Group	Fixed	126	125	10.2	2327
3			Group	Free	145	145	7.4	1778
4		final	Individual	Free	224	223	6.7	1506
5			Group	Fixed	222	222	10.8	2448
6			Group	Free	222	221	7.9	1872
7	2024	former	Individual	Free	163	159	6.5	1401
8			Group	Fixed	130	129	10.1	2196
9			Group	Free	137	137	8.0	1732
10		final	Individual	Free	209	205	6.8	1491
11			Group	Fixed	210	206	10.6	2319
12			Group	Free	208	205	8.6	1891

The Jaccard index was used for quantifying the similarity of a detected group A of students in a group (set) against the ground truth B of actual students in a group (set). In addition, the precision, recall and F-values were computed, defined as:

$$precision = \frac{tp}{tp + fp} = \frac{|A \cap B|}{|A \cap B| + |A - B|}$$

$$recall = \frac{tp}{tp + fn} = \frac{|A \cap B|}{|B|}$$

$$F = 2\frac{precision \times recall}{precision + recall}$$

where tp is the true positives, fp the false positives, and tn the false negatives. Only aggregated mean results are presented. To explore the effects of anonymization a sanitized derivative dataset was created. The reports were processed group-wise. A list of individual text tokens with the personal information about each group member (different name parts and student numbers) was established. All instances matching the tokens within the group members' reports were removed.

4 Results

The experiments were run on a Lenovo Yoga laptop PC with modest specifications, namely a 2.3 GHz 2 core Intel i5-6200U CPU with 8 aGb of RAM. The total processing took about 30 s.

4.1 Identifying Student Groups

Figure 2 shows the weighted sum of the success rates for all groupworks. Success was defined as identified groups that exactly matched the ground truth. Groups were easier to detect when the reports included personal info as the success rate is systematically lower with anonymized reports. Second, the formative reports were associated with higher success rates than the final reports. Third, reports based on freely chosen topics had higher group identification rates than fixed topics set by the teacher.

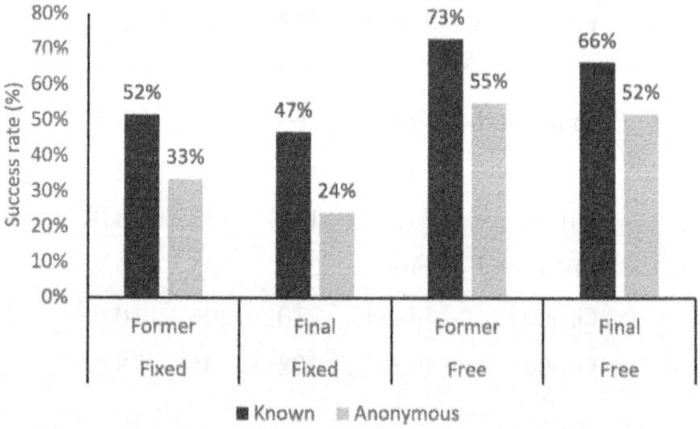

Fig. 2. Successfully detected groups (exact matches).

Although not identical, an identified group may still be quite similar to the ground truth. Figure 3 shows the weighted mean similarity with the ground truth across the different conditions. These results show that the differences are small when compared to the ground truth. Yet, the pattern is identical, that is, that anonymization, final, and fixed assignments yield lower similarities, while known, formative and free assignments are associated with comparatively higher similarities. Table 2 lists the results in more detail. Precision, recall and F values are also included for reference.

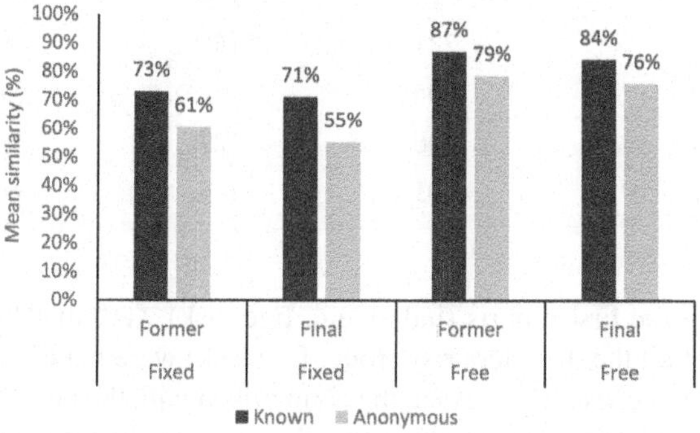

Fig. 3. Mean similarity of detected groups with the ground truths.

Table 2. Student identification results. K! = known, X? = anonymous

Id	Task	Success		Mean similarity		Mean precision		Mean recall		Mean F	
		K!	X?	K!	X?	K!	X?	K!	X?	K!	X?
2	Fixed	0.66	0.46	0.82	0.68	0.93	0.88	0.88	0.77	0.87	0.76
8		0.37	0.21	0.65	0.54	0.83	0.75	0.77	0.70	0.74	0.66
5		0.59	0.24	0.79	0.56	0.90	0.85	0.86	0.65	0.85	0.67
11		0.33	0.24	0.63	0.55	0.86	0.88	0.70	0.60	0.73	0.66
3		0.88	0.56	0.94	0.80	0.97	0.88	0.97	0.90	0.96	0.86
9	Free	0.58	0.54	0.80	0.77	0.86	0.91	0.92	0.84	0.86	0.84
6		0.73	0.55	0.88	0.78	0.96	0.91	0.91	0.83	0.92	0.84
12		0.60	0.49	0.81	0.74	0.94	0.92	0.86	0.80	0.87	0.81

4.2 Matching Former and Final Versions

Table 3 lists the results of matching report versions. These only apply to the subset of students that submits both versions. The results show high success rates in the range from 96.1% to 99.3%.

4.3 Identifying the Most Similar Reports

Table 4 lists the aggregated results obtained identifying the most similar reports. The results show that the rate of exact matches varies greatly with the type of submission.

Table 3. Version matching results

Ids	N (formative)	N (final)	N (both)	Success (%)
1, 4	151	223	147	98.6%
2, 5	125	222	124	99.2%
3, 6	145	221	145	98.6%
7, 10	159	205	155	96.1%
8, 11	129	206	127	98.4%
9, 12	137	205	136	99.3%

Less than 15% of the first reports (individual, free task) were matched exactly, while more than 81% of all the third reports (group, free task) were matched exactly.

Although the matches are not exact, the comparison with the benchmarks shows that these are relatively similar. An algorithm based on full document matching using word bigrams [8] was used as a benchmark. Note that there were no plagiarism cases in the datasets.

Table 4. Identifying the most similar reports.

Project	N	Exact match	Benchmark difference
1: individual, free	738	14.6%	1.2%
2: group, fixed	682	54.7%	0.6%
3: group, free	708	81.9%	0.4%

4.4 Identifying Incorrectly Submitted Reports

The experiments showed that the algorithm was successfully able to identify the incorrectly submitted reports, without false positives (see Table 5).

Table 5. Identifying incorrect submissions.

Year	Version	Individual, free	Group, fixed	Group, free
2023	Formative			1
2024				1
2023	Final		4	4
2024			2	2

5 Discussion

5.1 Identifying Student Groups

The group identification results support an explanation where the likelihood of successfully detecting the groups is related to the availability of unique information. An anonymized text has less information than one that includes names and student numbers. Moreover, tasks where students freely choose the topic results in more diverse texts with more unique words that leads to higher group identification rates. One explanation for final reports having lower group identification rates than formative reports is that students submitting the formative reports are more on top of things than students that only submit the final reports. Students that only submit the final report may be finishing at the last minute and fail to follow the submission instructions. The proposed detection of groups from the text content may therefore be a useful fallback for teachers that rely on students' group declarations.

The anonymization procedure attempted to remove all personal identifiers. In anonymized exams students are often given a unique running number that will connect specific exam results with specific students yet hide the student identities from the examiners. Such running numbers would serve the same function as personal information in identifying the groups. Hence, the approach may hold potential for identifying group structures even with anonymous reports.

The unique keywords identified for each group potentially can be used to get an impression about the content of the groupwork especially for free tasks. Manually inspecting the sets of unique keywords shared by groups revealed that a fraction of these were indeed terms that signal the content of the work, some of the words where personal information such as names and student numbers (with the dataset that was not anonymized) and most of the other words were more unusual words that did not give any valuable clues to the project contents. The weighted mean number of unique words was 28, and the most keywords identified was 279. A mean of 28 words seems acceptable if teachers rapidly need to get an overview through visual inspection. Some of the (one person) groups had no unique keywords.

5.2 Matching Former and Final Versions

Table 3 shows that the success rate is higher for the last two reports compared to the first report. This is as observed in [8] which was attributed to students having more time to revise the first report. This assumes that the assignments are given at different points of time throughout the semester, while the final portfolio is due at the end of the semester.

5.3 Identifying the Most Similar Pairs

The approach may be a promising alternative for identifying suspicious cases than more elaborate algorithms, thus reducing the computational burden. The exact match rate will most likely increase if the candidate set is increased from 5. It must be noted that the exact match is relative to the chosen benchmark. This benchmark is not a universal truth. Document similarity depends on the chosen measure used.

5.4 Identifying Incorrectly Submitted Reports

Identifying incorrectly submitted reports is perhaps a trivial issue. However, it may be useful to screen portfolios immediately after the formal deadline. Students can then be notified about problems, typically arising from unintentional mistakes, and given a chance to rectify the issue before the examination commences. Assessments can thus be made on more representative grounds.

5.5 General Discussion

Although the detected groups do not fully match the ground truth, they may provide sufficient information to be useful and can thus supplement a regime where students self-declare group memberships. The unsupervised group information can be used to corroborate the self-group declarations and provide useful clues for teachers in situations where the self-group declarations are missing. The approach also holds potential for regimes without self-declared group information or with anonymous submissions. However, trials are needed to assess the practicality of this use-case.

A potential byproduct of this work is the anonymization of student reports. Indeed, various information can be linked despite being anonymous [11]. The unique keywords for each student or group can be manually inspected to identify and remove sensitive information that has been missed by the algorithm. Obviously, this implies that the texts do not describe personal information.

6 Conclusion

A simple bag-of-words method for automatically detecting group structures from work was presented. Experimental results show that groups could be identified at a sufficiently high rate to be useful in practice. Several by-products of the method were illustrated for version matching, plagiarism detection, and incorrect submission detection. An implementation is available at https://github.com/frode-sandnes/grouping.

References

1. Meza, J., Jimenez, A., Mendoza, K., Vaca-Cárdenas, L.: Collective intelligence education, enhancing the collaborative learning. In: Proceedingsof the ICEDEG, pp. 24–30. IEEE (2018)
2. Sainsbury, E., Walker, R.: Motivation, learning and group work–the effect of friendship on collaboration. In: Proceedings of The Australian Conference on Science and Mathematics Education (2009)
3. Forenc, K.M., Eriksson, F.M., Malhotra, B.: Medical students' perspectives on an assessment of reflective portfolios [letter]. Adv. Med. Educ. Pract. **11**, 463–464 (2020). https://doi.org/10.2147/AMEP.S266849
4. Richardson, J.T.: Coursework versus examinations in end-of-module assessment: a literature review. Assess. Eval. High. Educ. **40**(3), 439–455 (2015)
5. Hall, D., Buzwell, S.: The problem of free-riding in group projects: Looking beyond social loafing as reason for non-contribution. Act. Learn. High. Educ. **14**(1), 37–49 (2013)

6. Brennan, D.J.: University student anonymity in the summative assessment of written work. High. Educ. Res. Dev. **27**(1), 43–54 (2008)
7. Sandnes, F.E.: FLINK: an educator's tool for linking inaccurate student records. In: Huang, Y.-M., Rocha, T. (eds.) Innovative Technologies and Learning: 6th International Conference, ICITL 2023, Porto, Portugal, August 28–30, 2023, Proceedings, pp. 143–152. Springer Nature Switzerland, Cham (2023). https://doi.org/10.1007/978-3-031-40113-8_14
8. Sandnes, F.E.: On portfolio assessment, group work, and quasi-anonymization: what structural information do anonymized reports reveal? In: International Conference on Innovative Technologies and Learning, pp. 149–158. Springer Nature, Cham (2024)
9. Jian, H.L., Sandnes, F.E., Huang, Y.P., Cai, L., Law, K.M.: On students' strategy-preferences for managing difficult course work. IEEE Trans. Educ. **51**(2), 157–165 (2008)
10. Sandnes, F.E., Tollefsen, M., Herstad, J., Knarlag, K.A.: Should student coursework be universally designed? universal design requirements may prevent academic cheating. In: Universal Design 2024: Shaping a Sustainable, Equitable and Resilient Future for All, pp. 158–165. IOS Press (2024)
11. Sandnes, F.E.: HIDE: short IDs for robust and anonymous linking of users across multiple sessions in small HCI experiments. In: Extended Abstracts of the 2021 CHI Conference on Human Factors in Computing Systems, pp. 1–6. ACM (2021)

Exploring the Factors Affecting Student's Online Assessing Peers' Ability - Continuance Intention as the Mediator

Chi-Cheng Chang, Wan-Hsuan Yen(✉), and Jing-Yuan Wu

National Taiwan Normal University, Taipei 106, ROC
gordonwyen@gmail.com

Abstract. Online peer assessment helps students better understand the subject of the course and evaluation standards but also develops critical thinking skills. However, previous research focused mainly on verifying the benefits of online peer assessment and rarely systematically explored the factors affecting its validity. In some qualitative studies, online assessing peers' ability has been found to be an essential factor influencing the effectiveness of assessment. Therefore, this study aimed to sort out the factors that affect online assessing peers' ability under the theory of planned behavior (TPB) while clarifying whether attitudes and perceived behavioral control of assessing peers online would positively influence continuance intention and learners' online assessing peers' ability. We retrieved 221 valid samples and employed JASP software to conduct SEM analysis on data. We found that attitudes and perceived behavioral control of assessing peers positively affected continuance intention. Continuance intention mediated the relationship between attitudes, online assessing peers' ability, and perceived behavioral control and online assessing peers' ability. It is recommended that participants' attitudes and continuance intention toward assessment be assessed before the implementation of online peer assessment. When students report that peer assessment is unfair, poorly trained assessors, and unclear assessment criteria, teachers must address these issues promptly to prevent a vicious cycle. Future research could look at other factors interfering with online peer assessment, such as course familiarity and teacher feedback on ratings.

Keywords: Theory of Planned Behavior (TPB) · Peer Assessment · Self-assessment · Attitude · Perceived Behavioral Control

1 Introduction

In present-day teaching, emphasis is placed on learner-centered approaches, which aim to design environments where students have opportunities to explore and think critically [1]. Online assessment is one such approach that not only allows students to take on more responsibility in their learning process, but also facilitates a better understanding of the topic, assessment criteria and personal values [2–4].

However, most studies have focused on exploring the effectiveness of online self-assessment and peer assessment, or comparing the strengths and weaknesses of both

W.-S. Wang et al. (Eds.): ICITL 2025, LNCS 15913, pp. 212–221, 2026.
https://doi.org/10.1007/978-3-031-98185-2_23

approaches and their impact on each other [5–7]. For instance, high-quality peer assessment can help expand cognition, while self-assessment can serve as a complementary role, compensating for the aspects that peer assessment may lack [8].

Peer assessment has been found to be more effective than self-assessment, but it is also possible that there are both advantages and disadvantages [9]. This is due to factors such as peers lacking expertise, insufficient assessment skills leading to low-quality feedback, or conflicting advice from peers, which may not benefit students [10, 11]. Therefore, it can be inferred that the reasons for the reduced effectiveness of peer assessment vary, and "assessing peers' ability" is the most commonly mentioned factor. Thus, this study aimed to focus on identifying the elements that affect it.

Online peer assessment has often approached the perspectives from Social Learning Theory, Social Constructionism, or Metacognition, to explain why students can learn from the assessment process. However, these theories cannot further assist this study in clarifying the relationships between influencing factors. Therefore, the theory of planned behavior (TPB) [12] was chosen as the basis for exploration, to clarify the process of developing abilities from the root of behavior. The concept of this theory is that an individual's attitude toward a certain behavior, perceived subjective norms, and perceived behavioral control can affect their continuance intention and actual behavior performance [13, 14].

The behavior referred to the theory is whether an individual actually performs the behavior or the quality of the ability. Therefore, the actual behavior performance that this study aimed to investigate is "assessing peers' ability". In addition, since the subjective norms in the online assessment environment will be influenced by teachers and peers at the same time, the connotation is relatively complicated. This study is for the purpose of preliminary exploration, so this variable will be reserved for follow-up research for further discussion.

In sum, the purpose of this study was to explore the factors influencing assessing peers' ability through TPB. The research question is whether online peer assessment attitudes and perceived behavioral control will positively affect the intention to continue, and further influence online assessing peers' ability.

2 Literature Review and Hypothesis Development

2.1 Online Peer Assessment

Online assessment has been increasingly used in the teaching field in recent years, encouraging students to take more responsibility in the learning process. However, Li et al. pointed out that the effectiveness of peer feedback had pros and cons [9]. The benefits include enriching students' understanding of the content, improving subjective judgment, and facilitating deeper self-reflection in self-assessment. On the other hand, the drawbacks may arise due to the lack of trust among peers, tense communication, competition, and lack of preparation for peer learning, which can affect the effectiveness of assessment [3].

In addition, Stančić mentioned that students may feel worried about their own assessing peers' ability and the responsibility of peer grading, but by meeting their basic psychological needs, these initial concerns can be transformed into learning motivation [15].

Therefore, there are many reasons that can affect the effectiveness of peer assessment, among which the ability to assess peers is the most frequently mentioned. Improving this ability can help enhance the benefits of assessment for students.

2.2 Theory of Planned Behavior (TPB)

The theory of planned behavior (TPB) was proposed by Ajzen [12]. Subsequently, many studies have applied TPB to explore different fields and provide more comprehensive feedback to the theory. Therefore, after collecting multiple suggestions, Ajzen proposed the latest framework [16], which argues that an individual's attitude toward a behavior, perceived subjective norms, and perceived behavioral control will be influenced by the individual's beliefs. These three elements will affect an individual's continuance intention and their behavior performance. Actual behavioral control will also affect the positive relationship between intention and behavior performance.

TPB has been widely applied in the fields of management, healthcare, and marketing [17–20], but there were various results in these fields. For example, Wu and Lin found that subjective norms did not influence the intention to share knowledge, while other causal relationships held true [21]. However, Tarigan et al. indicated that both attitudes and subjective norms had a significant impact on the intention to engage in green consumption behavior for an online store, while the positive relationship between perceived behavioral control and intention was not significant [22].

This study aimed to explore online assessing peers' ability, the characteristics differ from other online settings, including anonymity, passive participation in assessment activities, the prolonged execution of assessment activities, etc. These differences may result in different relationships between factors and are worth further clarification.

2.3 The Correlation Between TPB and Online Assessing Peers' Ability

Attitudes Toward Online Assessing Peers' Behavior (Att). According to TPB, intention is influenced by attitudes, which means that an individual's evaluation of a specific behavior will affect whether they want to perform that behavior [23]. As Seifert and Feliks found, online peer assessment contributes to improving students' assignment quality and assessment abilities, which in turn affects their attitudes toward assessment [2]. However, some students believed that an assessment was a waste of time, and poor feedback quality and conflicting assessments from peers left them without any gains [4]. Therefore, the first research hypothesis is as follows:

Hypothesis 1. Attitudes toward online assessing peers' behavior positively influence continuance intention of online assessing peers.

Perceived Behavioral Control in Online Assessing Peers' Behavior (Con). The second factor that influences behavioral intention is perceived behavioral control, which requires an understanding of both internal and external factors that may facilitate or impede the behavior [24]. This involves assessing the extent to which individuals have the necessary resources and ability to overcome potential barriers to the behavior [16]. In the initial model, perceived behavioral control was assigned a moderating role in the relationship between attitudes and subjective norms on intentions, but empirical studies mostly found only main effects [12]. Therefore, subsequent research has placed perceived behavioral control as a preceding variable to intention [25]. So we proposed:

Hypothesis 2. Perceived behavioral control in online assessing peers' behavior positively influence continuance intention of online assessing peers.

Continuance Intention of Online Assessing Peers' Behavior (Int). Behavioral intention is determined by three factors: attitudes, subjective norms and perceived behavioral control. The direct precursor of behavior is the continuance intention to perform the behavior, and consequently, the stronger the intention, the more likely the behavior will follow [26]. Because the subjective norms will be influenced by teachers and peers, the facet is complicated. Therefore, this study focused on the influence of the other two variables, and the subjective norms will be further explored in subsequent studies.

Actual Behavior Performance: Online Assessing Peers' Ability (Ability). Ajzen stated that people may not necessarily act according to their intentions [16]; therefore, intention and actual behavior scales need to have discriminant validity to avoid unclear concepts. Sheeran found that only 50% of participants who intended to engage in a behavior actually did so [27]. In this study, the "difference between the average assessing peers score given by students and teachers" was used as a basis for measurement to avoid potential confusion in measuring actual behavior and to reflect a more accurate representation of online peer assessment. The hypotheses formulated based on the structure of the TPB are as follows:

Hypothesis 3. Continuance intention of online assessing peers' behavior positively influence online assessing peers' ability.

Hypothesis 4. Continuance intention of online assessing peers' behavior have a mediating effect on the relationship between attitudes toward online assessing peers' behavior and online assessing peers' ability.

Hypothesis 5. Continuance intention of online assessing peers' behavior have a mediating effect on the relationship between perceived behavioral control in online assessing peers' behavior and online assessing peers' ability.

Online Assessing Peers' Experience (Exp). Individuals' online self-assessment and peer assessment experiences can influence their attitudes toward online assessment [8]. Seifer and Feliks [2] have pointed out that past assessment experiences can affect one's judgment of their own assessment ability, representing perceived behavioral control. Kyndt et al. [28] also found a negative correlation between employees' qualifications and their willingness to learn. Therefore, the quantity and quality of online peer assessment experiences may affect students' attitudes, perceived behavioral control, and continuance intentions toward online assessing peers. This study included online assessing peers' experiences as a control variable to avoid interference with the relationship among other variables.

3 Methods

This study applied convenience sampling, conducting a questionnaire survey as well as field data collection. We retrieved 221 master and doctoral students from the same university, who used the same online assessment platform. These adult learners were capable of undertaking peer assessment tasks [29]. During the semester, students conducted self-assessment and peer assessment activities for their own and peers' reports. At the end of the semester, participants completed a questionnaire on gender, online assessing peers' experience, attitudes, perceived behavioral control and continuance intention of online assessing peers' behavior.

Since exploring online peer assessment with TPB is a new research topic, there are no relevant scales to reference. However, Ajzen provided a questionnaire template because he believed that TPB is applicable in different fields, and suggested designing it with a reflective approach [30]. Therefore, this study referred to the scale examples to design items for attitude, perceived behavioral control, and continuance intention that are suitable for the online peer assessment context. There are total 11 items, and some examples included: (1) Att: I really like the online assessing peers' activity. (2) Con: I believe I can do well in the online assessing peers' task. (3) Int: I hope to continue using the online assessing peers' system in the future.

The targets of the online assessment activity are oral expression and presentation quality of the presenter, with 4 items each, totaling eight items. The assessment scale is from 1 to 5, with a data interval of 0.25, such as 4.75, 3.25, 2.5, etc. The "online assessing peers' ability" was "difference between the average assessing peers score given by students and teachers". For example, a student evaluates the average of peers as M, and the teacher evaluates the average of peers as T. The gap between the two is $|M-T|$. The smaller the value is, the better the assessing ability is. So the assessing ability needed to be reversely scored as $5-|M-T|$. If $M = 4.2$, $T = 4.3$, the assessing ability is $5-|M-T| = 5-|-0.1| = 4.9$.

4 Results

4.1 Confirmatory Factor Analysis (CFA)

In this study, the confirmatory factor analysis (CFA) was conducted using JASP software to validate the scales on peer attitude, perceived behavioral control, and continuance intention toward online assessing peers. The results indicated that the factor loading of each item is greater than .7 and significant based on the t-test [31], indicating the reliability of each item (latent variable). The composite reliability (CR) is greater than .7, which meets the standard criteria [32], and the average variance extracted (AVE) is greater than .5, which satisfies the requirements of Fornell and Larcker for convergent validity, indicating good overall convergence validity [31]. The results are shown in Table 1.

The results of discriminant validity analysis in this study are shown in Table 2, and the confidence intervals do not include one, indicating that the variables in this study have discriminant validity.

Table 1. Results of confirmatory factor analysis.

	Factor loading	z	CR	AVE
Att1	.77	13.53***	.88	.66
Att2	.86	16.01***		
Att3	.88	16.58***		
Att4	.73	12.55***		
Con1	.92	18.02***	.92	.79
Con2	.88	16.72***		
Con3	.86	16.17***		
Int1	.84	15.67***	.95	.81
Int2	.86	16.42***		
Int3	.96	19.74***		
Int4	.95	19.35***		

*** $p < .001$

Table 2. Results of the discriminant validity.

	Estimate	95% Confidence Interval
Att ↔ Con	0.46	[0.34, 0.57]
Att ↔ Int	0.85	[0.79, 0.91]
Con ↔ Int	0.48	[0.38, 0.58]

4.2 Structural Equation Model (SEM)

Structural equation modeling analysis can be performed with a sample size of over 200. SEM was conducted by means of JASP software to obtain confidence intervals for indirect effects, in order to test the hypotheses regarding the mediating effects. The results showed that CFI = 0.93, NFI = 0.92, and IFI = 0.94, indicating good fit of the measurement model [33]. The summary of the indirect effects is shown in Table 3 and the SEM analysis results are presented in Fig. 1.

Table 3. Results of the indirect effects.

	Estimate	β	95% Confidence Interval
Att → Int → Ability	0.09	0.32*	[−0.00, 0.24]
Con → Int → Ability	0.01	0.04+	[−0.01, 0.10]

$^{+}p < .1$;* $p < .05$

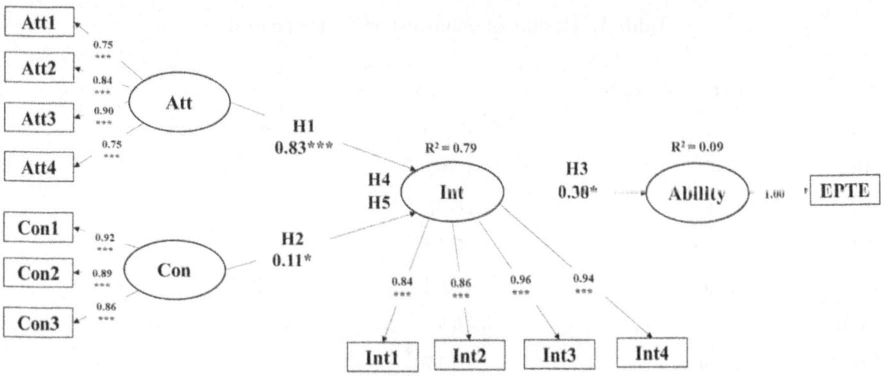

Fig. 1. Results of the SEM.

The results showed that the confidence interval for the direct effect of attitudes toward online assessing peers' behavior on continuance intention didn't include zero, indicating a significant direct effect [34], supporting H1 ($\beta = 0.83$, $p < .001$). The direct effect of continuance intention on online assessing peers' ability was significant ($\beta = 0.38$, $p < .05$), supporting H3. The mediating effect of continuance intention on attitudes and ability was significant ($\beta = 0.32$, $p < .05$), supporting H4.

The confidence interval of the direct effect of perceived behavioral control on continuance intention didn't include zero, indicating a significant direct effect ($\beta = 0.11$, $p < .05$), and H2 was supported. The mediating effect of continuance intention on perceived behavioral control and ability was boundary significant ($\beta = 0.04$, $p < .1$), marginally supporting H5.

5 Conclusion

5.1 Discussion

Mediating Effect of Continuance Intention of Online Assessing Peers' Behavior on the Relationship Between Attitudes and Ability. When students have a high continuance intention, the tension and competition in the feedback process may become more significant, which affects the accuracy of assessing peers' ability. Therefore, teachers need to pay attention to the learners' attitude and participation in the assessment, especially when students respond to issues such as an unfair assessment and inadequate training of assessors [10], timely handling is required to avoid a vicious cycle.

Mediating effect of Continuance Intention of Online Assessing Peers' Behavior on the Relationship Between Control and Ability. Panadero and Alqassab [35] mentioned that if peer assessment adopts an anonymous system, it affects the content of peer feedback, the accuracy of peer assessment scores, and students' perceptions of peer assessment. Therefore, the characteristics of online peer assessment environments may lead to differences in individual perceived behavioral control and the demonstration of online peer assessment abilities. For example, if peers consistently give high scores, individuals may also tend to give higher scores in self-assessment and peer assessment. Coupled with the inherent tendency for individuals to give higher self-assessment scores, this may result in overall averages being higher than what they should be. This also corresponds to the results of this study, where perceived online peer assessment behavioral control has a positive impact on continued intent, but actually has no significant impact on online peer assessment ability. Therefore, educators should be mindful of this phenomenon. Students who have a continued intent to participate still need to be attentive to the cultivation of their online peer assessment abilities.

5.2 Limitations and Suggestions for Future Research

Online Assessing Peers' Experiences. Since the number of students enrolled in each class is different, the number of peer assessments required during a single semester varies as well. It is recommended that future research investigate the long-term development of assessing peers' ability, such as grouping individuals based on their online assessing peers' experience, and determining if there are differences [36].

Data Source Adjustment: Online Assessing Peers' Ability. Research on TPB often uses self-reported measures, which may have common method variance (CMV) and raise questions about the representativeness of the data [19]. To avoid these issues, this study adjusted the sources of data for ability. In the future, we can expand with a larger sample size or evaluated for applicability in other contexts.

References

1. Blum-Smith, S., Maxwell, M.Y., Karen, B.: Stepping back and stepping in: facilitating learner-centered experiences in MOOCs. Comput. Educ. **160**, 104042 (2021). https://doi.org/10.1016/j.compedu.2020.104042
2. Seifert, T., Feliks, O.: Online self-assessment and peer-assessment as a tool to enhance student-teachers' assessment skills. Assess. Eval. High. Educ. **44**(2), 169–187 (2019). https://doi.org/10.1080/02602938.2018.1487023
3. To, J., Panadero, E.: Peer assessment effects on the self-assessment process of first-year undergraduates. Assess. Eval. High. Educ. **44**(6), 920–932 (2019). https://doi.org/10.1080/02602938.2018.1548559
4. Wanner, T., Palmer, E.: Formative self-and peer assessment for improved student learning: the crucial factors of design, teacher participation and feedback. Assess. Eval. High. Educ. **43**(7), 1032–1047 (2018). https://doi.org/10.1080/02602938.2018.1427698
5. Chien, S., Hwang, G., Jong, M.S.: Effects of peer assessment within the context of spherical video-based virtual reality on EFL students' English-Speaking performance and learning perceptions. Comput. Educ. **146**, 103751 (2020). https://doi.org/10.1016/j.compedu.2019.103751
6. Double, K.S., McGrane, J.A., Hopfenbeck, T.N.: The impact of peer assessment on academic performance: a meta-analysis of control group studies. Educ. Psychol. Rev. **32**, 481–509 (2020). https://doi.org/10.1007/s10648-019-09510-3
7. Iglesias Pérez, M.C., Vidal-Puga, J., Pino Juste, M.R.: The role of self and peer assessment in Higher Education. Stud. Higher Educ. **47**(3), 683–692 (2022). https://doi.org/10.1080/03075079.2020.1783526

8. Cheong, C.M., Luo, N., Zhu, Z., Lu, Q., Wei, W.: Self-assessment complements peer assessment for undergraduate students in an academic writing task. Assess. Eval. High. Educ. **48**(1), 135–148 (2023). https://doi.org/10.1080/02602938.2022.2069225
9. Li, H., Xiong, Y., Hunter, C.V., Guo, X., Tywoniw, R.: Does peer assessment promote student learning? A meta-analysis. Assess. Eval. High. Educ. **45**(2), 193–211 (2020). https://doi.org/10.1080/02602938.2019.1620679
10. Lin, Y., Yu, Z.: A bibliometric analysis of peer assessment in online language courses. Languages **8**(1), 47 (2023). https://doi.org/10.3390/languages8010047
11. Pidduck, T.M., Bauer, N.: Perceptions of online self-and peer-assessment: accounting students in a large undergraduate cohort. J. Appl. Res. High. Educ. **14**(4), 1480–1495 (2022). https://doi.org/10.1108/JARHE-03-2021-0120
12. Ajzen, I.: From intentions to actions: a theory of planned behavior. In: Kuhl, J., Beckmann, J. (eds.) Action Control, pp. 11–39. Springer Berlin Heidelberg, Berlin, Heidelberg (1985). https://doi.org/10.1007/978-3-642-69746-3_2
13. Hagger, M., Hamiltion, K.: Progress on theory of planned behavior research: advances in research synthesis and agenda for future research. J. Behav. Med. (2025). https://doi.org/10.1007/s10865-024-00545-8
14. Li, J., Lin, Y., Yang, Y.: Extending the theory of planned behavior model to explain people's behavioral intentions to follow China's AI generated content law. BMC Psychol. **12**, 367 (2024). https://doi.org/10.1186/s40359-024-01824-4
15. Stančić, M.: Peer assessment as a learning and self-assessment tool: a look inside the black box. Assess. Eval. High. Educ. **46**(6), 852–864 (2021). https://doi.org/10.1080/02602938.2020.1828267
16. Ajzen, I.: The theory of planned behavior: frequently asked questions. Human Behav. Emerg. Technol. **2**(4), 314–324 (2020). https://doi.org/10.1002/hbe2.195
17. Choi, D., Johnson, K.K.P.: Influences of environmental and hedonic motivations on intention to purchase green products: an extension of the theory of planned behavior. Sustain. Product. Consumpt. **18**, 145–155 (2019). https://doi.org/10.1016/j.spc.2019.02.001
18. Hagger, M.S., Cheung, M.W.-L., Ajzen, I., Hamilton, K.: Perceived behavioral control moderating effects in the theory of planned behavior: a meta-analysis. Health Psychol. **41**(2), 155–167 (2022). https://doi.org/10.1037/hea0001153
19. Lin, N., Roberts, K.R.: Using the theory of planned behavior to predict food safety behavioral intention: a systematic review and meta-analysis. Int. J. Hosp. Manag. **90**, 102612 (2020). https://doi.org/10.1016/j.ijhm.2020.102612
20. Ulker-Demirel, E., Ciftci, G.: A systematic literature review of the theory of planned behavior in tourism, leisure and hospitality management research. J. Hospitality Tourism Manag. **43**, 209–219 (2020). https://doi.org/10.1016/j.jhtm.2020.04.003
21. Wu, S., Lin, T.-C.: Exploring knowledge sharing behavior of is personnel with theory of planned behavior (in Chinese). J. Inf. Manag. **14**(2), 75–110 (2007). https://doi.org/10.6382/JIM.200704.0075
22. Tarigan, E.D.S., Putri, Y.S., Sabrina, H.: Green buying behavior using theory of TPB in online shop in Medan city. Int. J. Sci. Technol. Manage. **2**(3), 604–607 (2021)
23. Berisha, F., Vula, E., Gisewhite, R., McDuffie, H.: The effectiveness and challenges implementing a formative assessment professional development program. Teacher Dev. **28**(1), 19–43 (2024). https://doi.org/10.1080/13664530.2023.2210533
24. Li, L., Wang, K., Chen, J.: Effects of learner factors on the scorer reliability of self- and peer-assessment of Chinese college students' EFL writing. Innov. Educ. Teach. Int. (2024). https://doi.org/10.1080/14703297.2024.2305936
25. Albayati, H., Alistarbadi, N., Rho, J.J.: Assessing engagement decisions in NFT Metaverse based on the Theory of Planned Behavior (TPB). Telematics Inform. Reports **10**, 100045 (2023). https://doi.org/10.1016/j.teler.2023.100045

26. Ajzen, I.: The theory of planned behavior. Organ. Behav. Hum. Decis. Process. **50**(2), 179–211 (1991). https://doi.org/10.1016/0749-5978(91)90020-T
27. Sheeran, P.: Intention—behavior relations: a conceptual and empirical review. Eur. Rev. Soc. Psychol. **12**(1), 1–36 (2002). https://doi.org/10.1080/14792772143000003
28. Kyndt, E., Dochy, F., Onghena, P., Baert, H.: The learning intentions of low-qualified employees: a multilevel approach. Adult Educ. Q. **63**(2), 165–189 (2013). https://doi.org/10.1177/0741713612454324
29. Fenwick, T., Tennant, M.: Understanding adult learners. In: Foley, G. (ed.) Dimensions of Adult Learning, pp. 55–73. Routledge (2020)
30. Ajzen, I.: Constructing a theory of planned behavior questionnaire (2006). http://www-unix.oit.umass.edu/~aizen/pdf/tpb.measurement.pdf
31. Fornell, C., Larcker, D.F.: Structural equation models with unobservable variables and measurement error: algebra and statistics. J. Mark. Res. **18**(3), 382–388 (1981)
32. Hair, E., Halle, T., Terry-Humen, E., Lavelle, B., Calkins, J.: Children's school readiness in the ECLS-K: predictions to academic, health, and social outcomes in first grade. Early Childhood Res. Q. **21**(4), 431–454 (2006). https://doi.org/10.1016/j.ecresq.2006.09.005
33. Kline, R.B.: Principles and Practice of Structural Equation Modeling. Guilford Publications (2015)
34. MacKinnon, D.P., Fairchild, A.J., Fritz, M.S.: Mediation analysis. Annu. Rev. Psychol. **58**, 593–614 (2007). https://doi.org/10.1146/annurev.psych.58.110405.085542
35. Panadero, E., Alqassab, M.: An empirical review of anonymity effects in peer assessment, peer feedback, peer review, peer evaluation and peer grading. Assess. Eval. High. Educ. **44**(8), 1253–1278 (2019). https://doi.org/10.1080/02602938.2019.1600186
36. Joh, J., Plakans, L.: Peer assessment in EFL teacher preparation: a longitudinal study of student perception. Lang. Teach. Res. **29**(1), 338–362 (2025). https://doi.org/10.1177/13621688211060776

Web Scraping and Its Use for Teaching in Course Information Systems in Tourism

Radim Dolak(✉) and Patrik Kajzar

School of Business Administration in Karvina, Silesian University in Opava, 733 40 Karvina, Czechia
{dolak,kajzar}@opf.slu.cz

Abstract. This paper discusses the use of web scraping in the Information Systems in Tourism course, highlighting its potential to enhance students' understanding of data management and analysis in the tourism industry. It also explores its application in the hotel industry and reputation management, highlighting the use of tools such as for example Apify, Browse.AI or Outscraper for data extraction and analysis that is preparing students for future careers in the tourism and hospitality sectors. The use of web scraping tools for educational purposes related to hotel industry analysis will also be discussed in this paper. By adding web scraping into the curriculum, students can acquire hands-on experience collecting and analysing real-world data, preparing them for future careers in tourism. This will provide students a hands-on experience understanding how data may be collected and used for decision-making in the tourism business.

Keywords: web scraping · data extraction · information systems in tourism · hotel industry · teaching

1 Introduction

This paper deals with using web scraping and its use for teaching in the course Information Systems in Tourism. Web scraping is a valuable tool for extracting data from websites, which can be utilized to enhance students' understanding of data management and analysis in the context of tourism. By incorporating web scraping into the curriculum, students can gain practical experience in collecting and analysing real-world data, preparing them for future careers in the field of Information Systems in Tourism. This will provide students with a hands-on approach to understanding how data can be collected and utilized for decision-making within the tourism industry. Additionally, exploring the applications of web scraping in the hotel industry will offer students insight into specific data sources and analysis techniques relevant to their future careers.

The use of web scraping tools for educational purposes related to hotel industry analysis will also be discussed in this paper with practical examples of available cloud-based services such as Apify, Browse.AI or Outscraper. This will allow students to gain practical experience in utilizing these tools for data extraction and analysis. By familiarizing themselves with these tools, students will be better prepared to tackle real-world challenges in the field of tourism and hospitality.

W.-S. Wang et al. (Eds.): ICITL 2025, LNCS 15913, pp. 222–230, 2026.
https://doi.org/10.1007/978-3-031-98185-2_24

2 Web Scraping

Web scraping is a crucial technique in the realm of data extraction, enabling the transformation of unstructured web data into structured formats suitable for analysis. This process is particularly significant in various fields, including computer science, data science, and psychology, as it facilitates the collection of large datasets from diverse online sources. There will be mention as first state of art dealing with web scraping principles and ethical consideration. We will mention also literature overview about possible using of web scraping for hotel prices and reviews analysis and for hotel reputation management.

2.1 Web Scraping Principles and Ethical Considerations

Understanding the principles of web scraping is essential for effectively harnessing its capabilities. At its core, web scraping involves the automated extraction of data from web pages, typically formatted in HTML. This transformation allows for the conversion of unstructured data into structured datasets that can be stored in databases or spreadsheets for further analysis [5]. The process is not only efficient but also significantly reduces the time and effort required compared to traditional data collection methods, such as manual copy-and-paste techniques [7]. For instance, web scraping can be utilized to gather information from job postings, product prices, or social media interactions, thereby providing valuable insights into trends and patterns across various domains [17].

The principles of web scraping encompass several methodologies and technologies. Common techniques include HTML parsing, DOM parsing, and the use of APIs for data extraction [5]. These methods allow for the systematic collection of data, ensuring that the extracted information is relevant and organized. Additionally, web scraping can be integrated with other technologies, such as natural language processing (NLP), to enhance data analysis capabilities [2]. For example, combining web scraping with NLP can facilitate the extraction of sentiment from social media posts, providing deeper insights into public opinion on various topics [14].

2.2 Web Scraping and Its Use for Hotel Prices and Reviews Analysis

Web scraping has emerged as a critical tool for collecting prices and reviews in the hotel industry, enabling stakeholders to gain detailed insights into market dynamics and customer sentiment. This automated data extraction method allows hotel managers, pricing analysts, and marketers to monitor competitors effectively, strategize pricing, and enhance service offerings based on real-time consumer feedback.

One of primary using of web scraping in the hotel sector is to gather customer reviews and pricing information from various online travel agencies (OTAs) and review platforms. Research has shown that the relationship between hotel prices and online ratings is significant—higher-rated hotels generally command higher prices due to the perceived value associated with quality customer experiences [1]. For instance, a study utilizing data from Booking.com indicates that factors such as a hotel's star rating and customer reviews significantly influence its pricing structure [11]. Moreover, ongoing analysis of online reviews enables hotels to adapt their operational policies and improve customer satisfaction. A survey revealed that 95% of tourists consider online reviews crucial in their booking decisions, thereby emphasizing the impact of reviews on consumer behaviour [20]. This highlights a vital connection between pricing strategy and online reputation; hotels that leverage web scraping to analyse trends in reviews can adjust their service delivery and pricing strategies to remain competitive [10]. For instance, when hotels identify frequently mentioned grievances in guest reviews, they can implement targeted improvements, thereby justifying price adjustments based on enhanced consumer satisfaction [21].

2.3 Web Scraping and Its Use for Hotel Reputation Management

Web scraping plays a pivotal role in the online reputation management of hotels by enabling the collection of customer feedback, reviews, and other user-generated content from various platforms. As the hotel industry increasingly moves towards a digital-first approach, the ability to monitor and analyse online sentiments has become not only advantageous but essential for maintaining competitive edge and enhancing service offerings.

Firstly, online reviews significantly influence hotel reputation and consumer decision-making processes. Research indicates that travellers are heavily swayed by online ratings and reviews, with a substantial percentage stating they reconsider hotel bookings based on the presence or absence of reviews. For example, a study found that 53% of respondents stated they would not book a hotel that does not have any reviews, and 87% indicated that online reviews help them feel more confident in their travel decisions [16]. Furthermore, positive guest reviews can elevate a hotel's status, leading to increased bookings and repeat customers, making it vital for hotel managers to actively manage their online presence and respond to guest feedback [8, 19]. Web scraping can streamline this process by automating the collection and analysis of reviews from multiple platforms, allowing for a comprehensive view of customer sentiment.

Secondly, online reputation management strategies, such as responding to reviews and engaging with customers on social media, have been shown to enhance brand image and foster loyalty [9, 18]. For instance, positively interacting with reviewers can enhance hotel reputation and foster customer loyalty. Research emphasizes that effective communication and timely engagement can influence customer perceptions positively [13, 15]. Web scraping tools can facilitate these interactions by providing hoteliers with real-time insights into customer opinions, enabling them to tailor their responses and engagement strategies accordingly [12].

3 Web Scraping Tools

Web scraping is a multifaceted technique that plays a significant role in data extraction and analysis across various disciplines. Its principles, methodologies, and ethical considerations are essential for anyone looking to leverage the power of web data.

Table 1. Web scraping cloud-based services.

Tool name	Website	Free Testing	Prebuild Robots
Apify	https://www.apify.com	YES	4000 +
Brighdata	https://brightdata.com	YES	100 +
Browse.AI	https://www.browse.ai	YES	200 +
Octoparse	https://www.octoparse.ai	YES	400 +
Outscraper	https://outscraper.com	YES	20 +

There is a variety of tools and technologies that are available for web scraping, each offering unique functionalities that cater to different user needs. From programming libraries in Python and R to user-friendly applications and cloud-based services such as Apify, Browse.AI or Outscraper. These tools empower users to efficiently collect and analyse data from the web. We will mention only web scraping cloud-based services that we have tested for teaching purposes (Table 1).

Apify stands out as a specialized platform that simplifies web scraping through a user-friendly interface and powerful back-end capabilities, making it accessible for both technical and non-technical users. Apify is the largest ecosystem where developers build, deploy, and publish web scrapers, AI agents, and automation tools. They call them actors. There are now about more than 4000 different prebuild robots called in this solution as a actors [3].

Actor consists of source code and various settings. You can think of an Actor as a cloud app or service that runs on the Apify platform. The run of an Actor is not limited to the lifetime of a single HTTP transaction. It can run for as long as necessary, even forever. Basically, Actors are programs packaged as Docker images, which accept a well-defined JSON input, perform an action, and optionally produce an output [4]. There many actors accessible through Apify store for hotel industry analysis. The most popular Apify actors for Booking.com that was tested and used for teaching purposes are listened in the following Table 2.

Table 2. Most popular Apify actors for Booking.com

Actor name	Description	Monthly users	Price	Rating
Booking Scraper	Scrape Booking with this hotels scraper and get data about accommodation on Booking.com. You can crawl by keywords or URLs for hotel prices, ratings, addresses, number of reviews, stars. You can also download all that room and hotel data from Booking.com with a few clicks: CSV, JSON, HTML, and Excel	370	$5.00 for 1,000 results	4,4 from 5

(continued)

Table 2. (*continued*)

Actor name	Description	Monthly users	Price	Rating
Fast Booking Scraper	Scrape Booking with this hotel scraper and get data about accommodation on Booking.com. Extract data by keywords or URLs for hotel prices, ratings, location, number of reviews, stars. Scrape and download data from Booking.com in JSON, Excel, HTML and CSV	59	$2.00 for 1,000 results	4,0 from 5
Booking Reviews Scraper	Scraper to get reviews from hotels, apartments and other accommodations listed on the Booking.com portal. Extract data using hotel URLs for review text, ratings, stars, basic reviewer info, length of stay, liked/disliked parts, room info, date of stay and more. Download in JSON, HTML, Excel, CSV	191	$2.00 for 1,000 reviews	4,7 from 5

4 Web Scraping and Its Use for Teaching in Course Information Systems in Tourism

We will start with a brief description about our university course called Information Systems in Tourism, then we will summarise our practical experience with web scraping and its use for teaching purposes in this course. Finally, we will discuss limitations and future research.

4.1 Course Information Systems in Tourism

The aim of the course Information Systems in Tourism is to acquaint students with the use of IT/ICT in tourism and tourism with a particular focus on booking and demand systems, systems for supporting the management and operation of accommodation and catering facilities and geographic information systems. Attention will also be paid to current development trends in the use of IS/ICT in tourism and tourism. Important is emphasis on current trends, such as E-tourism and mobile applications, with the aim of preparing students to work with technologies that emphasize efficiency and quality of services.

Requirements for the student are the following: minimum 50% attendance at seminars, preparation and presentation of seminar work, involvement in project teaching. Evaluation methods: preparation of seminar work (30% evaluation), involvement in project teaching (30% evaluation), written examination (40% evaluation).

4.2 Web Scraping and Its Use for Teaching in Course Information Systems in Tourism

Web Scraping and its use for teaching in course Information Systems in Tourism is possible in many ways. The most important and relevant source for hotel industry analysis is for our course global portal Booking.com.

Global portal Booking.com is available in 43 languages and offers more than 28 million total reported accommodation listings, including over 6.6 million listings alone of homes, apartments and other unique places to stay. No matter where you want to go or what you want to do, Booking.com makes it easy and backs it all up with 24/7 customer support [6].

What are the possibilities for utilizing data obtained from Booking.com through web scraping technics? There are several advantages for the travel sector with specialization for hotel industry analysis that can be identified.

- We can easy track the prices of products and services. This is important for staying informed about the optimal price to maintain competitiveness.
- The utilization of AI in the travel sector facilitates dynamic price adjustments and the personalization of offers through real-time market analysis, thereby providing a competitive advantage and enhanced consumer satisfaction.
- We can easy track reviews for different hotels created by their customers and this analysis is connected with the reputation management.

As part of the teaching, we tried out working with the following cloud-based service with the students: Apify, Browse.AI and Outscraper.

Task number 1: work with Apify prebuild robot called "Booking Scraper" for extracting web data – accommodation ratings and prices. First you will sign up on online forms for one specific region from the list of the regions of the Czech Republic or Slovakia and the task will be to download data from Booking.com. You will filter out accommodation for 1 night for one room for 2 people in a given country/region/type of accommodation according to the selection in the table. Max results per destination or URL is 1000 records, set the currency to EURO. Then download 2× the resulting file in Excel (overview and all fields) and name it so that the country name, region name, facility type and file type are visible.

Task number 2: work with a Browse.ai tool for extracting website data – accommodation reviews and prices. Find your name in the online shared table and for the given country and tourist destination (for example Turkey, Alanya) and type of accommodation facility (hotel or apartment) and you will download data from Booking.com (price will be during 31.7.2025–01.08.2025 and you will filter accommodation for 1 night for one room and for 2 people according to the destination selected in the table and select the filter for the type Hotel or Apartment. Maximum limit is 500 records in trial version. Download the resulting file in CSV format and name it as, so that the name of the country, region and type of facility is visible.

Task number 3: work with Outscraper tool for extracting website data – reviews for one specific hotel. The goal was to download detailed reviews from selected hotels with a 3-star standard within the Czech Republic. You will use prebuild robot called "booking-reviews" with free limit of 500 reviews records for one specific hotel.

Our recommendation about using cloud-based web services for education purposes connected with for hotel industry analysis are the following.

- it is often necessary for students to divide the tasks into smaller parts for their teamwork (according to regions, districts or hotel quality (2-star, 3-star, 4-star, 5-star).
- multiple access by many students from the university network may lead to blocking of the service functionality by provider and it is then necessary for students to complete their individual tasks independently at home.

4.3 Limitations and Future Research

There are many limitations and questions for future research. The most significant restriction is that trial accounts for cloud-based web scraping services only permit a monthly download limit of a specific quantity of data. This can be restrictive for users who require large amounts of data or frequent updates. Upgrading to a paid account may be necessary for those with higher data needs. In order to offer subscription monthly licensing of cloud-based web scraping services, we must set up a university funding mechanism.

Furthermore, we need to prepare a comprehensive assessment that shows how web scraping activities improve students' understanding of how to use global hotel reservation systems for analysis based on actual datasets. This important study should be based on surveys from pre- and post-activity assessments to measure the acquisition of knowledge and the development of skills. Through this assessment, we hope that we will be able to obtain the funds required to give students access to the cloud-based prepaid web scraping services.

Web scraping limitations also include potential legal issues related to data privacy and copyright infringement. Additionally, relying solely on scraped data may not provide a comprehensive understanding of the market dynamics and consumer behaviour in the travel sector. It is important to use web scraping ethically and ensure compliance with regulations to avoid legal consequences. Furthermore, supplementing scraped data with other research methods can offer a more holistic view of the market landscape and consumer preferences.

Future research in the travel sector should focus on integrating web scraping with traditional research methods to gain a more accurate and nuanced understanding of industry trends. By combining data from multiple sources, researchers can make more informed decisions and predictions about the future of the travel sector. This approach can also help in identifying emerging patterns and opportunities that may not be evident through web scraping alone. Additionally, incorporating qualitative research methods such as surveys and interviews can provide valuable insights into consumer behaviour and preferences within the travel industry.

5 Conclusion

Leveraging web scraping for collecting prices and reviews is not only beneficial but crucial for hotels aiming to enhance their market strategies and improve customer relations. By effectively analysing and utilizing this data, hotel managers can strategically position their services and offerings, leading to improved profitability and competitive advantage in the hospitality industry.

Web scraping also serves as a critical tool in the hotel industry's reputation management landscape, providing vital insights and enabling timely responses to customer feedback. As reliance on online feedback continues to grow, hotels that leverage web scraping can enhance their reputation, drive guest loyalty, and ultimately improve overall performance metrics.

Incorporating web scraping tools into the curriculum of Information Systems in Tourism courses can provide students with valuable skills and knowledge that are directly applicable to the hotel industry. By understanding how to effectively use these tools for data extraction and analysis, students can enhance their problem-solving abilities and be better equipped for success in their future careers in the tourism and hospitality sector.

Acknowledgments. This paper was supported by the Ministry of Education, Youth and Sports within the Institutional Support for long-term Development of a Research Organization Silesian University in Opava in 2025.

Disclosure of Interests. The author has no competing interests to declare that are relevant to the content of this article.

References

1. Abdirazakov, N.M., Kushebayev, Z.T., Numanova, F.A., Orynbet, P.Z., Myltykbayeva, G.E.: Understanding the relationships between hotel variables in Almaty, Kazakhstan: an investigation using Booking.com data. Bull. Karaganda Univ. Econ. Ser. **112**(4), 7–18 (2024)
2. Anglin, K.: Gather-narrow-extract: a framework for studying local policy variation using web-scraping and natural language processing. J. Res. Educ. Effect. **12**(4), 685–706 (2019)
3. APIFY Homepage: https://apify.com. Last accessed 2 Feb 2025
4. APIFY Documentation: https://docs.apify.com. Last accessed 2 Feb 2025
5. Arjunan, T.: Building business intelligence data extractor using NLP and Python. Int. J. Res. Appl. Sci. Eng. Technol. **10**(10), 23–28 (2022)
6. Booking.com Homepage: https://www.booking.com/content/about.en-gb.html,last. Accessed 10 Feb 2025
7. Bradley, A., James, R.: Web scraping using R. Adv. Methods Pract. Psychol. Sci. **2**(3), 264–270 (2019)
8. Gabbard, D.: The impact of online reviews on hotel performance. J. Modern Hospit. **2**(1), 26–36 (2023)
9. Garrido-Moreno, A., Morales, V., Lockett, N., King, S.: The missing link: creating value with social media use in hotels. Int. J. Hosp. Manag. **75**, 94–104 (2018)
10. Gaur, L., et al.: Capitalizing on big data and revolutionary 5G technology: extracting and visualizing ratings and reviews of global chain hotels. Comput. Electr. Eng. **95**, 107374 (2021)
11. Han, S., Anderson, C.: Web scraping for hospitality research: overview, opportunities, and implications. Cornell Hospit. Q. **62**(1), 89–104 (2020)
12. Khan, A., Khan, N., Bodla, A.: The after-shock effects of high-performers turnover in hotel industry: a multi-level study. Int. J. Contemp. Hosp. Manag. **33**(10), 3277–3295 (2021)
13. Kothari, S., Professor, A.: Online reputation management strategies in hospitality industry: a cross-sectional study. PNE **55**(1) (2023)

14. Lan, H., et al.: Covid-scraper: an open-source toolset for automatically scraping and processing global multi-scale spatiotemporal covid-19 records. IEEE Access **9**, 84783–84798 (2021)
15. Mukolwe, E., Rotich, D., Mapelu, I., Ipara, H.: Marketing crisis management and hotel performance: evidence from hotels in Mombasa county, Kenya. J. Hospit. Tourism **3**(2), 76–94 (2023)
16. Nicoli, N., Papadopoulou, E.: Tripadvisor and reputation: a case study of the hotel industry in Cyprus. EuroMed. J. Bus. **12**(3), 316–334 (2017)
17. Park, Y., Shin, Y.: Novel scratch programming blocks for web scraping. Electronics **11**(16), 2584 (2022)
18. Peco-Torres, F., Peña, A., Frías-Jamilena, D.: How to enhance online reputation? an empirical study from a joint customer–firm perspective. J. Vacat. Mark. **31**(1), 67–82 (2023)
19. Phillips, P., Barnes, S., Zigan, K., Schegg, R.: Understanding the impact of online reviews on hotel performance. J. Travel Res. **56**(2), 235–249 (2016)
20. Priyantina, R., Sarno, R.: Sentiment analysis of hotel reviews using latent Dirichlet allocation, semantic similarity and LSTM. Int. J. Intell. Eng. Syst. **12**(4), 142–155 (2019)
21. Višković, K., Rašan, D., Prevolšek, D.: Content analysis of Tripadvisor online reviews: the case of Valamar riviera hotels in Dubrovnik, pp. 307–319 (2023)

Extending eMath4All Platform to Broaden Applicability, Enrich Learning Experience and Enhance Teacher Support

Teo-Christian Ion and Elvira Popescu(✉)

Computers and Information Technology Department, University of Craiova, Craiova, Romania
ion.teo.n3d@student.ucv.ro, elvira.popescu@edu.ucv.ro

Abstract. This paper presents an enhanced version of the eMath4All platform, a specialized distance learning and teaching tool, primarily intended for middle school mathematics education. The platform has been expanded to support high school mathematics, as well as physics and chemistry, thereby broadening its applicability. Additionally, this paper introduces two novel software modules: a curriculum scheduling tool that automates the process of planning and organizing educational content over a specified timeframe, initially tailored to meet the needs of teachers in Romania; and a new set of features that enables the integration and creation of interactive applications and games within the platform, further enhancing its functionality. The extended platform was evaluated through a private tutoring scenario, which lasted for three months and provided valuable insights into its usability and effectiveness.

Keywords: E-learning platform · STEM education · Virtual whiteboard · Curriculum scheduling · Interactive apps

1 Introduction

The rapid advancement of digital technologies and internet has fundamentally transformed education [10], enabling innovative learning strategies through electronic devices and fostering knowledge acquisition. The proliferation of online learning platforms is particularly noteworthy, with many institutions and educators leveraging these tools to enhance instruction. The recent pandemic further accelerated this shift, forcing many countries to temporarily adopt online-only instruction [1]. Research suggests that technology integration can increase student engagement [8] and improve academic outcomes. The internet also facilitates synchronous communication which could address the limitations of asynchronous communication [2] and also expands access to educational resources. While many courses have successfully transitioned to online formats, mathematics presents unique challenges [4]. General online platforms often lack the specific features required for effective mathematics instruction. The unique characteristics of the subject [11], namely the algebraic notation and geometric figures inherent to mathematics cannot be easily represented using a standard keyboard, hindering online learning.

W.-S. Wang et al. (Eds.): ICITL 2025, LNCS 15913, pp. 231–240, 2026.
https://doi.org/10.1007/978-3-031-98185-2_25

Mathematics is a foundational subject [7] that fosters critical thinking skills [6] and supports understanding in other disciplines. However, many students struggle with mathematics, which can lead to decreased motivation and negatively impact their academic performance across all subjects. Researchers are investigating technology-enhanced learning environments as a way to alleviate the difficulties educators and students encounter in mathematics education. While technology offers potential solutions, concerns exist about its exclusive reliance [12]. Many instructors therefore adopt a blended approach, integrating technology with traditional methods, often using specialized applications for tasks like graph plotting and geometric visualizations. Research also explores the intersection of robotics and mathematics, with studies demonstrating the impact of this combination on students [3].

In this context, we proposed eMath4All, an online platform designed to deliver mathematics instruction remotely while relying on traditional teaching methods [9]. It allows teachers to utilize familiar instruments and techniques, adapting them for a virtual environment where teachers and students are not physically present together. Built initially for middle school mathematics, eMath4All focuses on addressing the specific needs of both students and teachers. Its development prioritized user-friendliness and ease of adoption, incorporating feedback from teachers and students throughout the process to ensure intuitive functionality and minimize the learning curve.

The eMath4All platform offers several key features. First, it facilitates real-time synchronous communication with virtual webcams and a collaborative virtual whiteboard. Integrated into the whiteboard is a mathematical keyboard, designed for middle school level, allowing users to easily insert mathematical symbols and functions using shortcuts, mimicking writing on a real notebook. A geometry shape tool enables users to collaboratively construct geometric shapes, visible to all connected participants. Second, the platform includes a virtual library where teachers can share, tag, and categorize files. Students can also create private document archives, such as homework or worksheets, accessible for teacher review and analysis. Third, teachers can create and launch assessments, viewing student responses in real-time using the integrated mathematical editor, which supports algebraic expressions and geometric shapes. Finally, each student has a personal profile page to track their progress and view other relevant statistics.

In the current paper, we report on the extension of the eMath4All platform, designing and implementing several new features, which were subsequently tested in an online private tutoring scenario. The rest of the paper is structured as follows: Sect. 2 discusses the development of the platform to support high school mathematics, chemistry, and physics; Sect. 3 presents a new module that automates curriculum scheduling for teachers; Sect. 4 introduces a new library section that enables teachers to develop and publish apps for students; Sect. 5 presents the testing and evaluation of the platform, along with the results obtained; Sect. 6 concludes the paper, highlighting the key findings and implications for future research and development.

2 Extending the eMath4All Virtual Whiteboard

Our first goal was to expand the eMath4All platform to support not just math instruction at middle school level, but also at high school level, as well as physics and chemistry. As such, to better support the specific needs of high school students in mathematics, we extended the virtual keyboard to include essential symbols such as the integral, definite integral, and nth root. We also developed a comprehensive symbol set that encompasses the necessary notations for physics and chemistry, including Greek symbols and other frequently used symbols in an intuitive layout. The keyboard design allows students to focus on learning and understanding complex concepts rather than struggling with notation. The refined virtual keyboard is shown in Fig. 1.

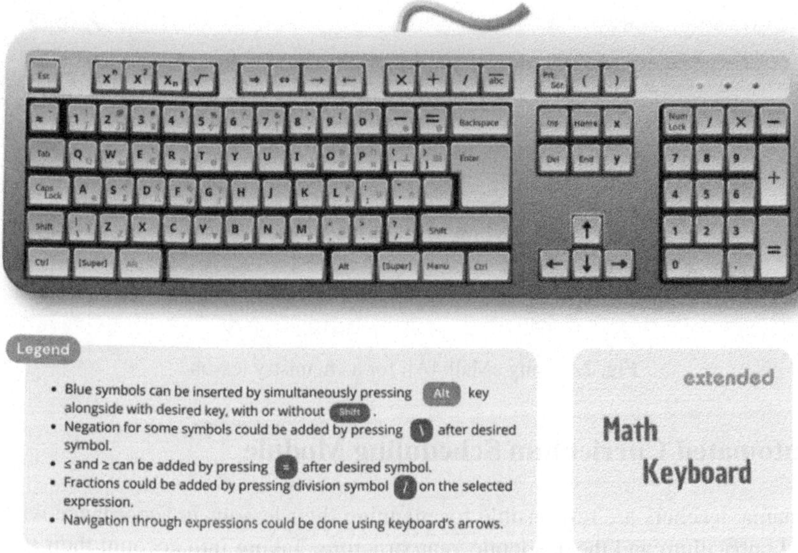

Fig. 1. Extended eMath4All virtual keyboard

The eMath4All virtual whiteboard was also upgraded to allow the insertion of pictures in real-time, enabling the platform to integrate external visual elements for users instantaneously. Thus, the features of the refined virtual whiteboard, including the virtual keyboard, geometry tools, and image embedding, are suitable for teaching several subjects, such as mathematics, physics and chemistry. Figure 2 shows an example of the advanced whiteboard being used for a chemistry lesson.

All the enhancements were developed using the modular codebase of eMath4All, which is based on JavaScript and web technologies, as presented in [9]. The extensions were built modularly, allowing for future improvements. The platform's intuitive and user-friendly interface ensures easy integration of new functionalities without affecting existing workflows. Overall, eMath4All can provide a comprehensive learning environment for both middle school and high school students, supporting their needs in mathematics, physics, and chemistry.

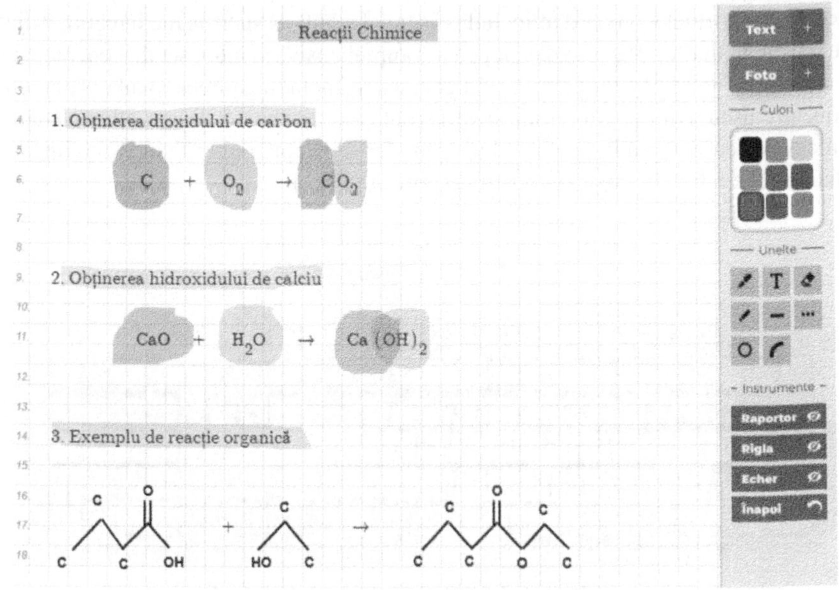

Fig. 2. Using eMath4All for a chemistry lesson

3 Automated Curriculum Scheduling Module

In Romania, teachers are responsible for planning their lessons in accordance with the national curriculum and the academic year structure. Taking into account their weekly teaching hours, teachers must divide the curriculum into manageable segments, allocating sufficient time to each section and subsection to ensure thorough coverage. This planning also necessitates adapting to specific classroom needs, designing student assessments, and accounting for school holidays to effectively utilize the entire academic year. Our goal was to offer teachers a simple tool to help them generate the curriculum scheduling documents automatically; we therefore designed and implemented a dedicated module in eMath4All virtual library.

While designed for Romanian teachers and pre-loaded with the Romanian national curriculum (organized by class and level), this module is adaptable. It can be tailored to different timelines and curricula as this information is provided as a structured text file. Figure 3 illustrates the required text file structure, which includes chapters, sections, competency codes, and an importance score for each section.

A separate text file contains a list of competency identification codes and their corresponding descriptions. This file, pre-populated according to the national curriculum, serves as a default database. However, teachers can customize it to align with the school curriculum or for other purposes, such as planning private tutoring sessions, where specific needs and goals require a focused timeline.

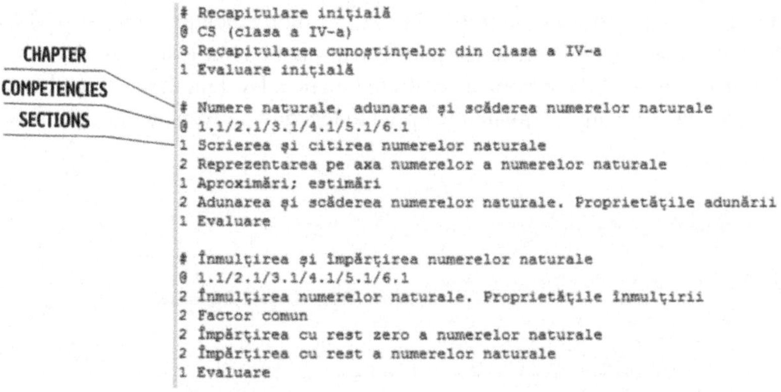

Fig. 3. Sample content file for the curriculum scheduling module

To allow for accurate scheduling, a configuration file enables teachers to define both vacancy periods and time intervals dedicated to non-traditional activities. In the Romanian educational system, these activities include periods like ecology-focused initiatives (so called "Green week") or practical skills training outside of regular instruction (so called "Alternative school" week). Instead of being marked as vacancies, the schedule should reflect these periods as dedicated time for these specific activities.

The system automatically generates four printable tables. The first table provides a timeline view of the curriculum content, displaying the weekly hours allocated to each chapter and section, as illustrated in Fig. 4; vacancies and other activities are also included in this table.

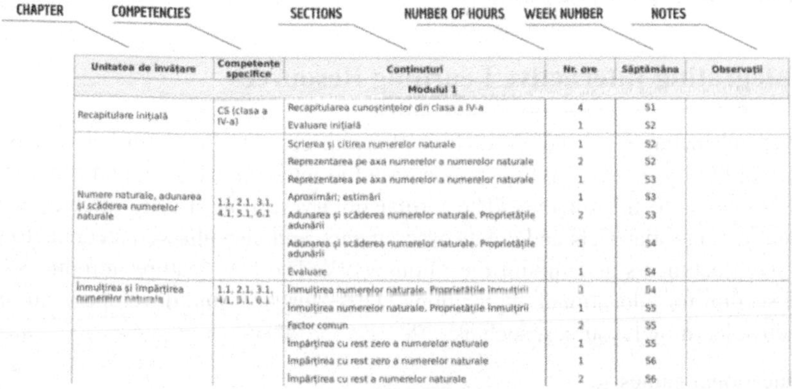

Unitatea de învățare	Competențe specifice	Conținuturi	Nr. ore	Săptămâna	Observații
		Modulul 1			
Recapitulare inițială	CS (clasa a IV-a)	Recapitularea cunoștințelor din clasa a IV-a	4	S1	
		Evaluare inițială	1	S2	
Numere naturale, adunarea și scăderea numerelor naturale	1.1, 2.1, 3.1, 4.1, 5.1, 6.1	Scrierea și citirea numerelor naturale	1	S2	
		Reprezentarea pe axa numerelor a numerelor naturale	2	S2	
		Reprezentarea pe axa numerelor a numerelor naturale	1	S3	
		Aproximări; estimări	1	S3	
		Adunarea și scăderea numerelor naturale. Proprietățile adunării	2	S3	
		Adunarea și scăderea numerelor naturale. Proprietățile adunării	1	S4	
		Evaluare	1	S4	
Înmulțirea și împărțirea numerelor naturale	1.1, 2.1, 3.1, 4.1, 5.1, 6.1	Înmulțirea numerelor naturale. Proprietățile înmulțirii	3	S4	
		Înmulțirea numerelor naturale. Proprietățile înmulțirii	1	S5	
		Factor comun	2	S5	
		Împărțirea cu rest zero a numerelor naturale	1	S5	
		Împărțirea cu rest zero a numerelor naturale	1	S6	
		Împărțirea cu rest a numerelor naturale	2	S6	

Fig. 4. Excerpt of a sample schedule generated by eMath4All

The second table outlines the school year's structure, or alternatively, the specific timeframe designated by the teacher (similar to a personalized tutoring schedule). It also highlights the periods allocated to supplementary activities. The third table details the number of hours students spend on coursework or studying for each chapter in the curriculum; it also identifies the time allocated to supplementary activities. The fourth table outlines the key competencies emphasized throughout the learning process. Figure 5 provides an example of these competencies in practice. By default, the module alerts the instructor when there are too many materials to teach in a given amount of time.

COMPETENTE SPECIFICE

Cod	Descriere
1.	**Identificarea unor date, mărimi și relații matematice, în contextul în care acestea apar**
1.1.	Identificarea numerelor naturale în contexte variate
1.2.	Identificarea fracțiilor ordinare și zecimale în contexte variate
1.3.	Identificarea noțiunilor geometrice elementare și a unităților de măsură în diferite contexte
2.	**Prelucrarea unor date matematice de tip cantitativ, calitativ, structural, cuprinse în diverse surse informaționale**
2.1.	Efectuarea de calcule cu numere naturale folosind operațiile aritmetice și proprietățile acestora
2.2.	Efectuarea de calcule cu fracții folosind proprietăți ale operațiilor aritmetice
2.3.	Utilizarea instrumentelor geometrice pentru a măsura sau pentru a construi configurații geometrice
3.	**Utilizarea conceptelor și a algoritmilor specifici la diverse contexte matematice**
3.1.	Utilizarea regulilor de calcul pentru efectuarea operațiilor cu numere naturale și pentru divizibilitate
3.2.	Utilizarea de algoritmi pentru efectuarea operațiilor cu fracții ordinare sau zecimale
3.3.	Determinarea perimetrelor, a ariilor (pătrat, dreptunghi) și a volumelor (cub, paralelipiped dreptunghic) și exprimarea acestora în unități de măsură corespunzătoare
4.	**Exprimarea în limbajul specific matematicii și informațiilor, concluziilor și demersurilor de rezolvare pentru o situație dată**
4.1.	Exprimarea în limbaj matematic a unor proprietăți referitoare la comparări, aproximări, estimări și ale operațiilor cu numere naturale
4.2.	Utilizarea limbajului specific fracțiilor/procentelor în situații date
4.3.	Transpunerea în limbaj specific a unor probleme practice referitoare la perimetre, arii, volume utilizând transformarea convenabilă a unităților de măsură

Fig. 5. Competencies table, including code and description (generated by eMath4All)

The module was built using HTML, CSS & JavaScript, with PHP driving the schedule generation process. This allowed seamless integration of the module into the existing eMath4All platform, specifically as a supplementary button within the personal library for teachers. The generated schedules are displayed in HTML tables optimized for printing on landscape A4 or Letter paper sizes. The printable page includes an open-source WYSIWYG editor, enabling teachers to further customize the automatically generated schedule to their specific needs.

4 Integrating Interactive Learning Resources

Another enhancement of the eMath4All platform consisted in a further extension of the virtual library module, aiming to increase the interactivity level and provide additional resources to the students. The virtual library section already allowed teachers to share learning materials and create assessments, and also allowed students to create and share documents and submit their homework. The new feature introduces a dedicated section for educational applications, where teachers and developers can upload interactive learning resources, such as:

- Educational games
- Geometric visualization tools
- Dynamic apps that can run on the web (via WebAssembly)
- Virtual laboratories
- Embedded public web applications (such as games, graph plotting tools, etc.)

These applications can be created by teachers and developers, and once created, they are accessible to the entire platform. All applications should be based on web technologies and consist of a few files, using the following structure (with a minimum of two files required for an app to run):

- *app.json*: This is the configuration file of an app, which has a default template available for developers. This file includes the name of the app, a description, the filename of the icon, and the type of application. Here, the developer or teacher can specify whether the app is standalone (with all necessary files uploaded by the developer to the server) or embedded (in which case the developer or teacher only needs to specify the URL location of the app).
- *app.php*: This is the main file of the application, containing the scripts that will be executed when students open the application.
- an unlimited number of other files, which could be modules of the *app.php* file or distinct pages of the app that can be navigated by the user.
- The key features of this new module of the virtual library include:
- The ability to embed external web pages and web applications using iFrames
- The ability to embed applications that use browser plugins (such as Java or Unity)
- Built-in support for Macromedia (Adobe) Flash applications and games through the open-source Flash Player emulator Ruffle
- An integrated code editor for developers to develop applications directly through the eMath4All platform
- Support for WebAssembly, which allows the integration of a vast array of applications (including emulators for operating systems)
- Access to the library's existing files and the student's private library through the platform's API, where, for example, an application can save progress while a student is working with it.

From a student's perspective, it is easy to use an application, as they can launch it by simply clicking on its icon. Thus, the newly added module provides enhanced interactivity and diverse educational resources without requiring students to exit the eMath4All platform or switch between multiple apps. In addition, it allows developers to create the necessary tools for extending the platform's capabilities with more advanced lessons and resources. The implementation of this module was done using HTML, CSS and JavaScript on the frontend, alongside PHP on the backend, relying on the modularly developed functions of eMath4All.

To showcase the module's capabilities, we developed a simple application that enables students to compile JavaScript code within their web browser, as illustrated in Fig. 6. This app includes a code editor and a virtual console for displaying output, functioning directly in the browser as a coding playground where students can learn programming concepts. This application illustrates how the eMath4All platform could be expanded to incorporate also informatics lessons.

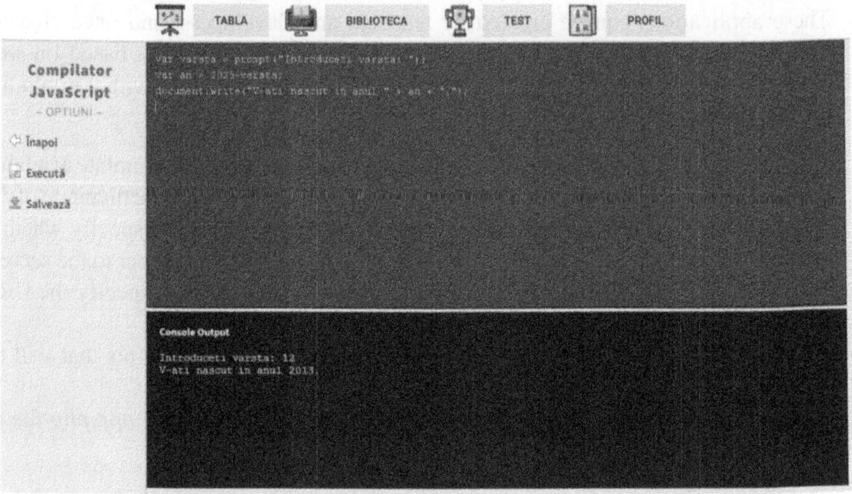

Fig. 6. JavaScript compiler app integrated in eMath4All

5 Platform Testing and Results

In order to test the new features of the eMath4All platform, a private tutoring scenario was used with a group of students. In our study, we utilized the eMath4All platform with its newly developed features, including the JavaScript compiler, which is integrated as a sample application; the virtual whiteboard and video conference system, which enabled real-time communication with the students; and the virtual library with all its features.

The study involved a total of eight students who participated in a private tutoring scenario, with individual private sessions alongside a tutor who helped them learn concepts and solve problems. The students were from different middle and high school grades, with different backgrounds and learning needs. The study unfolded over a three-month period, during which all the students used the eMath4All platform in weekly sessions, each lasting two hours. The tutoring process involved the following activities:

- Three students used eMath4All to learn programming for high school, utilizing the virtual whiteboard, video conference, virtual library, and the JavaScript compiler, which was included as the first interactive app developed for eMath4All.
- Two students used eMath4All to learn chemistry for middle school and high school respectively, using features such as the virtual whiteboard, virtual library, and a sample app that embedded an interactive periodic table.
- Two students used eMath4All to learn high school physics.
- One student used eMath4All to learn high school mathematics.

Data was collected by observing students' interactions with the platform during the tutoring sessions. The students learning informatics praised the JavaScript app, finding it engaging and helpful in improving their programming skills. The extended mathematical keyboard was also appreciated by the students, particularly those using eMath4All for mathematics, physics and chemistry. The positive results obtained in our study suggest that the platform has the potential to support teaching and learning and may contribute to increased student engagement, motivation, and understanding of certain concepts.

Additionally, the System Usability Scale (SUS) [5], a widely recognized tool for usability evaluation, was used to gauge the students' perceptions of the system. The results of the SUS questionnaire are shown in Fig. 7. The average SUS score was 97.5, corresponding to an A + based on the curved grading scale, indicating a high level of usability for the platform, as perceived by the students.

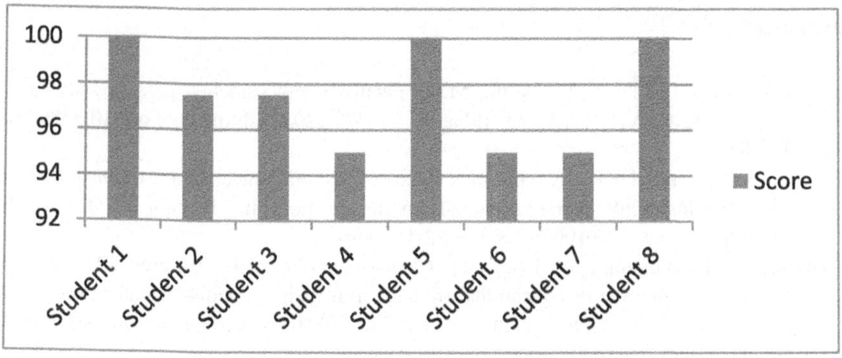

Fig. 7. SUS score results

6 Conclusion

In this paper we presented the enhancement of the eMath4All educational platform with additional modules for both students and teachers. More specifically, we adapted it for high school mathematics instruction and introduced support for physics and chemistry; this involved updating the virtual keyboard with subject-specific symbols and incorporating features like image support, enabling the inclusion of visuals and illustrations.

Secondly, we developed an automatic curriculum scheduler that is adapted to the Romanian school year structure, generating schedules and necessary documents for the teachers. This tool could potentially benefit teachers and tutors beyond Romania by allowing them to schedule and plan content delivery over a specified period, by configuring the input files.

Third, we enhanced the virtual library to offer more than just document sharing, assessment creation, and schedule generation. The updated library now supports applications, making it more interactive and allowing teachers to integrate engaging content like apps, games, and animation files directly into their lessons. This opens the door for adapting eMath4All for use in other disciplines as well. As a first example, we integrated a JavaScript compiler app and used it to teach programming to students, thus expanding the eMath4All platform to include informatics instruction.

The testing phase of eMath4All yielded preliminary findings on its usability and effectiveness. Observations from private tutoring sessions and students' responses to the System Usability Scale (SUS) questionnaire suggest that the extended platform was positively received by the learners. However, it should be noted that the study was limited by a small sample size and the specific context of private tutoring, which may not be representative of broader educational settings. Future research should focus on longitudinal testing with a larger number of participants, in different contexts and instructional scenarios; an in-depth analysis of the collected student data could provide further insights into the learning process supported by eMath4All.

References

1. Almahasees, Z., Mohsen, K., Amin, M.O.: Faculty's and students' perceptions of online learning during COVID-19. Front. Educ. **6**, 638470 (2021). https://doi.org/10.3389/feduc.2021.638470
2. Belt, E.S., Lowenthal, P.R.: Synchronous video-based communication and online learning: an exploration of instructors' perceptions and experiences. Educ. Inf. Technol. **28**(5), 4941–4964 (2023). https://doi.org/10.1007/s10639-022-11360-6
3. Brender, J., El-Hamamsy, L., Bruno, B., Chessel-Lazzarotto, F., Zufferey, J.D., Mondada, F.: Investigating the role of educational robotics in formal mathematics education: the case of geometry for 15-year-old students. In: EC-TEL 2021 Proceedings, pp. 67–81. Springer (2021). https://doi.org/10.48550/arXiv.2106.10925
4. Bringula, R., Reguyal, J.J., Tan, D.D., Ulfa, S.: Mathematics self-concept and challenges of learners in an online learning environment during COVID-19 pandemic. Smart Learn. Environ. **8**(1), 22 (2021). https://doi.org/10.1186/s40561-021-00168-5
5. Brooke, J.: SUS: A Retrospective. Journal of User Experience **8**(2), 29–40 (2013)
6. Cresswell, C., Speelman, C.P.: Does mathematics training lead to better logical thinking and reasoning? A cross-sectional assessment from students to professors. PLoS ONE **15**(7), e0236153 (2020). https://doi.org/10.1371/journal.pone.0236153
7. Department for Education: Research review series: Mathematics. https://www.gov.uk/government/publications/research-review-series-mathematics/research-review-series-mathematics (2021)
8. Hamilton-Hankins, O.J.: The impact of technology integration on the engagement levels of ten second grade students in an English language arts classroom. Doctoral dissertation, University of South Carolina (2017)
9. Ion, T.C., Popescu, E.: An innovative distance learning platform for mathematics education in secondary schools: design, development and preliminary studies. Educ. Inf. Technol. **30**, 5529–5560 (2025). https://doi.org/10.1007/s10639-024-13040-z
10. Ibrahim, I. S., Kenwright, B.: Smart education: Higher education instruction and the internet of things (IoT). arXiv:2207.02585 (2022). https://doi.org/10.48550/arXiv.2207.02585
11. Irfan, M., Kusumaningrum, B., Yulia, Y., Widodo, S.A.: Challenges during the pandemic: Use of e-learning in mathematics learning in higher education. Infinity J. **9**(2), 147–158 (2020). https://doi.org/10.22460/infinity.v9i2.p147-158
12. Zoltan, R.A.G., Magdaş, I.C., Dulamă, M.E.: Using smart board in preuniversity education in Romania. In: Proceedings of the 14th International Conference on Virtual Learning, pp. 86–92 (2019)

Evaluating Cognitive Learning Hierarchies of LLM-Created Assessment Questions in Engineering Education

Christopher Chung Lim Kwan(✉)

The Hong Kong Polytechnic University, Kowloon, Hong Kong SAR
ceclkwan@polyu.edu.hk

Abstract. With the recent popularity of Large Language Model (LLM) applications such as GPT-4o, o3-mini and DeepSeek-R1, subject instructors, class teachers, and educational practitioners generally perceive LLMs as virtual assistants in education, creating multiple types of assessments such as assignments, quizzes, examination papers, marking schemes and suggested solutions in formal and informal settings. The present study is to explore the use of contemporary LLMs such as GPT-4o, o3-mini and DeepSeek-R1 in preparing assessment questions, suggested solutions and marking schemes of Probability and Engineering Statistics in response to research questions on the completeness, correctness, consistency and cognitive levels of assessment questions and solutions. It is found that the LLM-created assessment questions are complete, and the total score of the assessment questions is consistent with that of its marking scheme. The suggested solutions to the questions are complete and mostly correct. Despite arithmetic errors, there are about two-thirds of application-oriented questions, and other hierarchies of cognitive learning questions such as understanding-oriented, analysis-oriented and evaluation-oriented questions in the assessment, aligning with learning outcomes of the subject satisfactorily.

Keywords: Assessment · Revised Bloom's taxonomy · Large language model · Learning outcome · Engineering education

1 Introduction

The evolution of contemporary Large Language Models (LLMs) such as GPT-4o, o3-mini and DeepSeek-R1 has already drawn the attention of educators, teaching practitioners, class teachers, and subject lecturers to their potential applications in education. From the learners' perspective, it is now possible to always use LLMs as personal tutors to support their studies and to assist them in figuring out the structure of reflective and critical thinking-based writing as scaffolding activities [11]. On the other hand, Johri et al. [5] outlined the potential impact of Generative Artificial Intelligence (GAI) and its subset, LLM, on engineering education practices such as question creation, assignment and assessment generation related to teaching and learning. In this regard, subject

W.-S. Wang et al. (Eds.): ICITL 2025, LNCS 15913, pp. 241–250, 2026.
https://doi.org/10.1007/978-3-031-98185-2_26

instructors, class teachers, and educational practitioners generally perceive LLMs as virtual assistants in education, creating multiple types of assessments such as assignments, quizzes, examination papers, marking schemes and suggested solutions in formal and informal settings.

These sorts of formative and summative assessments are traditionally and primarily devised by them to examine student learning and overall performance and to quantitatively measure the achievement of the intended subject learning outcomes for course evaluation and accreditation purposes [2, 4, 12]. In addition, appropriate teaching methodologies are correspondingly used in class to enable students to construct their knowledge, facilitating the achievement of intended subject learning outcomes as per their lesson plans. An assessment with different cognitive levels of learning questions is generally prepared in alignment with the subject curriculum and learning outcomes as per the revised Bloom's Taxonomy [1, 3, 6, 10]. Inevitably, they need to invest much time in preparing assessment questions, solutions, and marking schemes such as assignments, mid-term and final examination papers to have an error-free set after several cross-checking [9].

With the recent popularity of LLM applications, it is most likely to pass some of the engineering subjects with the aid of ChatGPT-4 [11]. Kwan [8] explored ChatGPT-generated assessment scripts, noting deficiencies in high cognitive levels of questions and discrepancies between assessment and solution scripts. High cognitive levels of learning questions are crucial for students to build up reasoning skills, critical thinking and other abilities [7]. There is a genius need to evaluate the completeness, correctness, consistency and cognitive learning hierarchy of the latest LLMs, such as GPT-4o, o3-mini and DeepSeek-R1, in creating assessment questions, solutions, and marking schemes, highlighting the value of the present study of evaluating cognitive learning hierarchies of LLM-created assessment questions.

2 The Context of the Study

The subject curriculum of probability and engineering statistics is designed to enable engineering students to master the principles of probabilistic modelling and statistical inference with relevant applications in civil engineering, as this is a prerequisite for grasping other advanced civil engineering subjects such as construction risk management, water resources, wind and earthquake engineering. They are expected to meet intended subject learning outcomes at the end of the course.

The focus of the study is to evaluate the completeness, correctness, consistency and cognitive learning hierarchy of LLM-created assessment questions of probability and engineering statistics with reference to the revised Bloom's Taxonomy. There are four different knowledge types and six different learning hierarchies within its structure [1, 6]. Four knowledge types are factual, conceptual, procedural and metacognitive knowledge, while six different learning hierarchies are remembering, understanding, applying, analyzing, evaluating and creating. Students are generally expected to demonstrate various abilities from a low cognitive learning hierarchy to a high cognitive learning hierarchy, while grasping conceptual and procedural knowledge of probability and engineering statistics. In this regard, assessments should be carefully devised to ascertain different cognitive learning hierarchies of questions which are in good alignment with the intended subject learning outcomes.

The present study investigates the use of contemporary LLMs such as GPT-4o, o3-mini and DeepSeek-R1 to prepare assessment questions, suggested solutions, and marking schemes of probability and engineering statistics, aiming to address the following research questions:

1. Are the LLM-created assessment questions complete and correct?
2. Is the total score of the LLM-created assessment questions consistent with that of the marking scheme?
3. Are LLM-created solutions to assessment questions complete and correct?
4. What are the cognitive learning hierarchies of LLM-generated assessment questions as per the revised Bloom's Taxonomy?

GPT-4o, o3-mini and DeepSeek-R1 are employed for the present study in response to address the above research questions.

3 Result

Firstly, GPT-4o is prompted to prepare an examination paper of probability and engineering statistics for the first-year civil engineering students. The duration of the generated examination paper is 2 h. There are 8 short questions in total, covering several topics of descriptive statistics, basic probability, conditional probability, discrete and continuous random variables, hypothesis testing, regression analysis and sample correlation in the subject curriculum as shown in Fig. 1. It is found that the GPT-4o-created questions are complete and correct.

Secondly, GPT-4o is prompted to prepare the marking scheme with full solutions of the examination paper. It is also found that the total score of the GPT-4o-created assessment questions is consistent with that of the marking scheme. However, GPT-4o-created solutions to the questions are complete but partially correct. Regarding question 7, an arithmetic error is made from the manipulation of the summation of x time y. The correct summation total is 650 rather than 590. The correct slope and the y-intercept of the regression line should thus be 0.22 and −0.1 respectively rather than 0.1 and 2.9 as depicted in Fig. 2. Similarly, the Pearson correlation coefficient in question 8 should be 0.423 rather than 0.455 as shown in Fig. 2.

Regarding the revised Bloom's Taxonomy, there are one understanding-based, four application-based, two analysis-based and one evaluation-based questions in the GPT-4o-created examination paper. The cognitive learning hierarchies of GPT-4o-generated assessment questions are 10%, 75%, 10% and 5% for understanding, applying, analyzing and evaluating levels respectively.

o3-mini is also chosen to create examination questions of probability and engineering statistics for the first-year civil engineering students. The duration of the generated examination paper is automatically set to be 3 h. There are 8 short questions in total with several sub-questions as shown in Fig. 3. The questions are related to the topics of conditional probability, Bayes' theorem, hypergeometric distribution, Poisson distribution, normal distribution, confidence interval estimation, hypothesis testing and simple linear regression which are covered in the subject curriculum. It is found that the o3-mini-created questions are complete and correct.

Section A: Probability (50 marks)

Question 1: Basic Probability (10 marks)

A construction site has three types of materials: steel, concrete, and wood. The probability of selecting steel is 0.5, concrete is 0.3, and wood is 0.2. If a material is selected at random, what is the probability that it is either steel or wood?

Question 2: Conditional Probability (10 marks)

On a particular day, the probability that it rains is 0.4. The probability that construction work is delayed given that it rains is 0.7. What is the probability that it rains and the construction work is delayed?

Question 3: Discrete Random Variables (15 marks)

A random variable X represents the number of defective beams found in a batch of 10. The probability distribution is given by:

$$P(X = x) = \begin{cases} 0.1 & \text{if } x = 0 \\ 0.2 & \text{if } x = 1 \\ 0.3 & \text{if } x = 2 \\ 0.4 & \text{if } x = 3 \\ 0 & \text{otherwise} \end{cases}$$

Calculate the expected number of defective beams in a batch.

Question 4: Continuous Random Variables (15 marks)

The time T (in hours) taken to complete a certain task on a construction site is modeled by a continuous random variable with the probability density function:

$$f(t) = \begin{cases} 2t & \text{if } 0 \le t \le 1 \\ 0 & \text{otherwise} \end{cases}$$

Find the probability that the task is completed in less than 0.5 hours.

Section B: Engineering Statistics (50 marks)

Question 5: Descriptive Statistics (10 marks)

The following data represents the compressive strength (in MPa) of concrete samples: 25, 30, 28, 32, 27, 29, 31. Calculate the mean and standard deviation of the compressive strength.

Question 6: Hypothesis Testing (15 marks)

A civil engineer claims that the average tensile strength of a new type of steel is 500 MPa. A sample of 10 steel rods is tested, and the average tensile strength is found to be 490 MPa with a standard deviation of 15 MPa. Test the engineer's claim at a 5% significance level.

Question 7: Regression Analysis (15 marks)

A study is conducted to understand the relationship between the load applied (in kN) and the deflection (in mm) of a beam. The following data is collected:

Load (kN)	Deflection (mm)
10	2.1
20	4.3
30	6.5
40	8.7

Perform a simple linear regression analysis to determine the relationship between load and deflection. Calculate the slope and intercept of the regression line.

Question 8: Correlation (10 marks)

Using the data from Question 7, calculate the Pearson correlation coefficient between the load and deflection. Interpret the result.

Fig. 1. GPT-4o-created examination questions of probability and engineering statistics.

o3-mini is further asked to prepare the marking scheme with full solutions of the examination paper. It is also found that the total score of the o3-mini-created assessment questions is consistent with that of the marking scheme. In addition, o3-mini-created solutions to the questions are complete and almost correct. Regarding question 1b, the solution approach is correct but the probability that at most 1 rod is defective in the sample should be rounded off to 0.9462 rather than 0.93.

Question 7: Regression Analysis (15 marks)

Solution:

Calculate the slope (b) and intercept (a) of the regression line $y = a + bx$.

$$b = \frac{n(\sum xy) - (\sum x)(\sum y)}{n(\sum x^2) - (\sum x)^2}$$

$$a = \frac{\sum y - b(\sum x)}{n}$$

Given data:

$$\sum x = 100, \quad \sum y = 21.6, \quad \sum xy = 590, \quad \sum x^2 = 3000, \quad n = 4$$

$$b = \frac{4(590) - (100)(21.6)}{4(3000) - (100)^2} = \frac{2360 - 2160}{12000 - 10000} = \frac{200}{2000} = 0.1$$

$$a = \frac{21.6 - 0.1(100)}{4} = \frac{21.6 - 10}{4} = \frac{11.6}{4} = 2.9$$

Regression line: $y = 2.9 + 0.1x$

Question 8: Correlation (10 marks)

Solution:

Calculate the Pearson correlation coefficient r:

$$r = \frac{n(\sum xy) - (\sum x)(\sum y)}{\sqrt{[n\sum x^2 - (\sum x)^2][n\sum y^2 - (\sum y)^2]}}$$

$$\sum y^2 = 2.1^2 + 4.3^2 + 6.5^2 + 8.7^2 = 4.41 + 18.49 + 42.25 + 75.69 = 140.84$$

$$r = \frac{4(590) - (100)(21.6)}{\sqrt{[4(3000) - 100^2][4(140.84) - 21.6^2]}}$$

$$= \frac{2360 - 2160}{\sqrt{[12000 - 10000][563.36 - 466.56]}}$$

$$= \frac{200}{\sqrt{2000 \times 96.8}} = \frac{200}{\sqrt{193600}} = \frac{200}{440} \approx 0.455$$

Interpretation: There is a moderate positive correlation between load and deflection.

Fig. 2. GPT-4o-generated solutions to questions 7 & 8.

Question 1: Hypergeometric Probability (10 marks)

A quality control test is conducted on a batch of 200 steel rods in which 8 are defective. If 10 rods are randomly selected for inspection:
(a) Write down the hypergeometric probability formula for obtaining exactly k defective rods.
(b) Calculate the probability that at most 1 rod is defective in the sample.
Hint: Use the formula
P(X = k) = [C(D, k) × C(N − D, n − k)] / C(N, n)
where N = total number of rods, D = number defective, n = sample size, and k = number of defectives in the sample.

Question 2: Conditional Probability & Bayes' Theorem (10 marks)

In a factory, beams are produced by two machines:
• 40% of beams come from Machine A with a failure rate of 5%.
• 60% of beams come from Machine B with a failure rate of 10%.
If a beam fails the quality test:
(a) State the event definitions you need.
(b) Use Bayes' theorem to determine the probability that the failed beam came from Machine A.
Show all steps.

Question 3: Normal Distribution (15 marks)

The compressive strength (in MPa) of a certain concrete type is normally distributed with a mean (μ) of 30 MPa and a standard deviation (σ) of 4 MPa.
(a) What is the probability that a randomly selected specimen will have a compressive strength exceeding 35 MPa?
(b) Determine the compressive strength value below which 10% of the observations fall.
Hint: Use standardization and the standard normal table.

Question 4: Confidence Interval Estimation (15 marks)

A civil engineering firm tests the compressive strength of its concrete. A sample of 16 specimens shows:
• Sample mean = 32 MPa
• Sample standard deviation = 3 MPa
Assuming the compressive strengths are normally distributed, construct a 95% confidence interval for the true mean compressive strength.
Clearly state the distribution used and show all calculations.

Question 5: Hypothesis Testing (15 marks)

A manufacturer claims that their new concrete mix design produces a mean compressive strength greater than 35 MPa. To verify this, an independent test is conducted on 25 specimens. The results are:
• Sample mean = 36 MPa
• Sample standard deviation = 4 MPa
At the 5% significance level:
(a) Formulate the null and alternative hypotheses.
(b) Conduct the appropriate t-test. Show the test statistic calculation and degrees of freedom used.
(c) State your conclusion regarding the manufacturer's claim.

Question 6: Simple Linear Regression (15 marks)

A civil engineering laboratory collected data on beams to study the relation between span length (in meters) and midspan deflection (in millimeters). The recorded data are:

Span (x): 2, 3, 4, 5, 6

Deflection (y): 1.2, 1.8, 2.6, 3.2, 3.9

(a) Fit a simple linear regression model of the form y = a + b·x.
(i) Calculate the slope (b) and the intercept (a) using the least squares method.
(ii) Interpret the meaning of the slope and the intercept in the context of this data.
Hint: The slope $b = \Sigma[(x_i - \bar{x})(y_i - \bar{y})] / \Sigma[(x_i - \bar{x})^2]$ and $a = \bar{y} - b \cdot \bar{x}$.

Question 7: Poisson Distribution (10 marks)

At a busy construction site, the number of minor accidents occurring in a day follows a Poisson distribution with an average (λ) of 2 accidents per day.
(a) What is the probability of exactly 3 accidents occurring on a given day?
(b) Find the probability that on a given day there will be at most 1 accident.
Show your work using the Poisson probability formula:

$P(X = k) = (\lambda^k \cdot e^{(-\lambda)}) / k!$ for k = 0, 1, 2, ...

Question 8: Conceptual/Short Essay (10 marks)

(a) Explain the differences between Type I and Type II errors in the context of hypothesis testing.
(b) Provide a brief example from civil engineering (e.g., quality control in concrete production or safety assessments) that illustrates the potential impact of each type of error.
Your answer should demonstrate an understanding of error implications and the importance of balancing risk in engineering decisions.

Fig. 3. o3-mini-created examination questions of probability and engineering statistics.

Among eight created questions, there are five application-based, two analysis-based and one evaluation-based questions in accordance with the revised Bloom's Taxonomy. The cognitive learning hierarchies of o3-mini-generated assessment questions are 12%, 67%, 12% and 9% for understanding, applying, analyzing and evaluating levels respectively.

Probability and Engineering Statistics Examination
Year 1 Civil Engineering
Time Allowed: 2 hours
Total Marks: 100

Instructions

1. Answer **all** questions.
2. Show all calculations clearly.
3. Use appropriate notation and formulas.
4. Statistical tables and a calculator are permitted.

Question 1: Basic Probability (25 marks)
a) A civil engineer tests two concrete mixes. Mix A has a 0.1 probability of failing a strength test, and Mix B has a 0.15 probability. The failures are independent. **Calculate the probability that both mixes fail.** *(5 marks)*
b) The probability of a delivery truck being late to a construction site is 0.2. If three trucks are scheduled today, **find the probability that exactly one is late** (assume independence). *(5 marks)*
c) Reinforced rods are sourced from Supplier X (60%) and Supplier Y (40%). Defect rates are 5% for X and 3% for Y. **Determine the overall defective rate.** *(7 marks)*
d) **Using Bayes' theorem,** find the probability that a defective rod came from Supplier X. *(8 marks)*

Question 2: Probability Distributions (25 marks)
a) Cracks in a highway follow a Poisson distribution with a mean of 2 per kilometer. **Find the probability of at least one crack in a 0.5 km section.** *(5 marks)*
b) Concrete blocks have compressive strengths normally distributed with $\mu = 25$ MPa and $\sigma = 2$ MPa. **What percentage of blocks have strength < 20 MPa?** *(6 marks)*
c) **Determine the strength value that 90% of blocks exceed.** *(7 marks)*
d) If 10 blocks are tested, **find the probability that exactly 3 have strength < 20 MPa** (use the binomial distribution). *(7 marks)*

Question 3: Descriptive Statistics (25 marks)
The maximum load (in tons) for 10 steel beams is:
18, 22, 25, 21, 19, 24, 17, 23, 20, 21
a) **Calculate the mean, median, and mode.** *(6 marks)*
b) **Compute the range, variance, and standard deviation.** *(8 marks)*
c) **Construct a box plot** and identify quartiles (Q1, Q3) and potential outliers. *(7 marks)*
d) **Interpret** what the mean and standard deviation indicate about beam capacity. *(4 marks)*

Question 4: Hypothesis Testing (25 marks)
A manufacturer claims their concrete mix has an average compressive strength of 30 MPa. A sample of 25 mixes yielded $\bar{x} = 28.5$ MPa and $s = 4$ MPa. Test this claim at $\alpha = 0.05$.
a) **State the null (H_0) and alternative (H_1) hypotheses.** *(4 marks)*
b) **Is this a one-tailed or two-tailed test? Explain.** *(5 marks)*
c) **Calculate the t-test statistic.** *(8 marks)*
d) **Determine the critical value and decide whether to reject H_0.** Conclude in context. *(8 marks)*

END OF EXAM

Marking Guidelines

- Correct formulas and logical steps are awarded marks even if arithmetic errors occur.
- Final answers must include units where applicable.
- For hypothesis testing, conclusions must be stated clearly in engineering terms.

Good Luck!

Fig. 4. DeepSeek-R1-created examination questions of probability and engineering statistics.

There are four questions in the DeepSeek-R1-created examination paper, and each question is further subdivided into four sub-questions as shown in Fig. 4. Its duration is 2 h. The total mark is 100, and the mark allocation for each question is 25. After rigorous checking, the DeepSeek-R1-generated examination paper is complete without any missing parts. The questions of the DeepSeek-R1-generated examination paper are logically and grammatically correct.

DeepSeek-R1 is further asked to prepare the marking scheme with full solutions of the examination questions. It is found that each question is worth 25 marks, and four questions have a total of 100 marks. The result indicates that the total score of the DeepSeek-R1-generated assessment script is consistent with that of the marking scheme. The mark distribution is appropriate for each question.

Question 3: Descriptive Statistics (25 marks)

a) Mean, median, mode

Sorted data: $17, 18, 19, 20, 21, 21, 22, 23, 24, 25$

- **Mean:** $\frac{210}{10} = \boxed{21}$
- **Median:** $\frac{21+21}{2} = \boxed{21}$
- **Mode:** $\boxed{21}$

b) Range, variance, standard deviation

- **Range:** $25 - 17 = \boxed{8}$
- **Variance:** $\frac{1}{9}\sum(x_i - 21)^2 = \frac{60}{9} \approx \boxed{6.67}$
- **Standard Deviation:** $\sqrt{6.67} \approx \boxed{2.58}$

c) Box plot

- **Q1:** 18.75, **Q3:** 23.25, **Median:** 21
- **IQR:** $23.25 - 18.75 = 4.5$
- **Outliers:** None (all data within 12.375 to 29.625)

d) Interpretation

- **Mean:** Central capacity is ~21 tons.
- **Std. Dev.:** Variability is ~2.58 tons.

Fig. 5. DeepSeek-R1-generated solutions to question 3.

It is however noted that DeepSeek-R1-generated solutions to the questions are complete but partially incorrect. Regarding DeepSeek-R1-generated solutions, there are arithmetic errors found in question 3c where the first quartile, Q_1, and the third quartile, Q_3, should be 19 and 23 rather than 18.75 and 23.25 as shown in Fig. 5. In fact, the sorted data can be equally partitioned into 4 parts and the demarcation lines represent the 25th, 50th and 75th percentiles respectively. Thus, the correct IQR should be 4 instead.

There are nine application-based subquestions, three analysis-based subquestions and one evaluation-based subquestion among 16 subquestions of four major questions created from DeepSeek-R1. The cognitive learning hierarchies of DeepSeek-R1-generated assessment questions are 13%, 68%, 11% and 8% for understanding, applying, analyzing and evaluating levels respectively.

The percentage distribution of cognitive learning complexities in LLM-created questions is also shown in Fig. 6. The results generally indicate that there are about two-thirds of application-based questions, 12% of understanding-based, 11% of analysis-based questions and 9% of evaluation-based questions in LLM-created examination papers. There are various medium-to-high cognitive levels of learning questions such as application-oriented, analysis-oriented and evaluation-oriented questions in the assessment, aligning with learning outcomes of the subject satisfactorily.

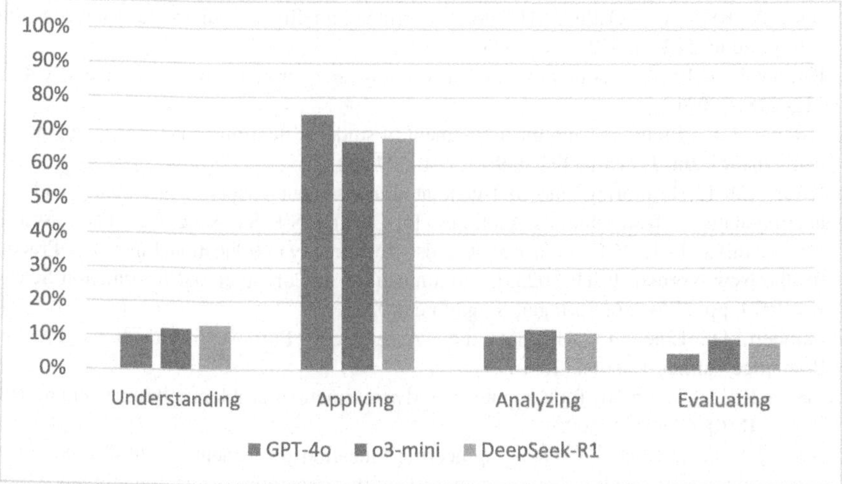

Fig. 6. The percentage distribution of cognitive learning complexities in LLM-created examination questions.

4 Conclusion

The results of the latest LLM-created assessment questions, marking scheme and solutions of Probability and Engineering Statistics are generally satisfactory as the LLM-created questions are complete and correct. The total score of the assessment questions is consistent with that of its marking scheme. The generated solutions to the questions are complete and mostly correct. Despite arithmetic errors found in DeepSeek-R1-generated and GPT-4o-generated solutions, there are about two-thirds of application-oriented questions and other hierarchies of cognitive learning questions such as understanding-oriented, analysis-oriented and evaluation-oriented questions in the assessment, aligning with learning outcomes of the subject satisfactorily.

Disclosure of Interests. The authors have no competing interests to declare that are relevant to the content of this article.

References

1. Anderson, L.W., et al.: A Taxonomy for Learning, Teaching, and Assessing: A Revision of Bloom's Taxonomy of Educational Objectives. Longman, New York (2001)
2. Biggs, J.: Teaching for Quality Learning at University, 2nd edn. Society for Research into Higher Education & Open University Press (2003)
3. Chandio, M.T., Pandhiani, S.M., Iqbal, R.: Bloom's taxonomy: improving assessment and teaching-learning process. J. Educ. Educ. Dev. **3**(2), 203–221 (2016)
4. Hong Kong Institution of Engineers: Professional Accreditation Handbook (Engineering Degrees). Accreditation Board, pp. 1–35 (2013)

5. Johri, A., Katz, A.S., Qadir, J., Hingle, A.: Artificial intelligence and engineering education. J. Eng. Educ. **112**(3), 572–577 (2023)
6. Krathwohl, D.R.: A revision of bloom's taxonomy: an overview. Theory Into Practice **41**(4), 212–218 (2002)
7. Kwan, C.L.C.: Findings from the assessment of students' learning outcomes in engineering mathematics. Int. J. Learn. Teach. **9**(2), 291–297 (2017)
8. Kwan, C.C.L.: Exploring ChatGPT-generated assessment scripts of probability and engineering statistics from bloom's taxonomy. In: Cheung, S.K.S., Wang, F.L., Paoprasert, N., Charnsethikul, P., Li, K.C., Phusavat, K. (eds.) Technology in Education. Innovative Practices for the New Normal. ICTE 2023. Communications in Computer and Information Science, vol. 1974, pp. 275–286. Springer, Singapore (2024)
9. Lambert, D., Lines, D.: Understanding Assessment: Purposes, Perceptions, Practices. Routledge Falmer, London (2000)
10. Mayer, R.E.: A taxonomy for computer-based assessment of problem solving. Comput. Hum. Behav. **18**(6), 623–632 (2002)
11. Nikolic, S., et al.: ChatGPT versus engineering education assessment: a multidisciplinary and multi-institutional benchmarking and analysis of this generative artificial intelligence tool to investigate assessment integrity. Eur. J. Eng. Educ. **48**(4), 559–614 (2023)
12. Sazhin, S.: Teaching mathematics to engineering students. Int. J. Eng. Educ. **14**, 145–152 (1998)

A Learning Analytics Framework for Higher Education in South Africa

Fezile Matsebula[1](✉), Mnkandla Ernest[2], and Themba Masumbuka[1,2]

[1] Sol Plaatje University, Kimberley, Northern Cape, South Africa
fezile.matsebula@spu.ac.za
[2] University of South Africa, Florida Park Roodepoort, Gauteng, South Africa

Abstract. The adoption of Learning Analytics (LA) in higher education has the capacity to improve teaching, learning, and administrative decision-making. Nonetheless, its execution in South African institutions of higher education is constrained by numerous technological, institutional, and socio-cultural obstacles. This research examines the determinants affecting the adoption of Learning Analytics in South African higher education institutions. The research employs a mixed-methods methodology and the Information Systems frameworks to examine the technological readiness, organisational capacity, and environmental forces influencing LA adoption. Qualitative data obtained from stakeholders' interviews are triangulated with quantitative survey data from various institutions to discern trends and obstacles. The results disclose essential insights into infrastructural deficiencies, stakeholder viewpoints, and policy limitations, while emphasising strategies to promote effective adoption. The research enhances the existing knowledge on educational technology adoption and offers practical recommendations for increasing Learning Analytics integration to enhance institutional efficiency and student achievement.

Keywords: Learning Analytics · South Africa · Higher Education · Adoption

1 Introduction

The contemporary higher education landscape is shaped by various significant factors driving its progress and transformation [1]. Key among these factors is addressing the needs of an increasingly diverse student demographic [2, 3], fostering a culture of lifelong learning [4], improving the quality of the student learning experience [5, 6], and broadening access to education [7]. Adapting the requirements of various learners necessitates that institutions modify their pedagogical approaches, curricula, and support services to address students from different cultural, socio-economic, and academic backgrounds.

The emergence of learning analytics (LA) has significantly influenced higher education. Learning analytics include the gathering, examination, and use of data regarding student behaviours, performance, and engagement to enhance teaching and learning [8–13]. This data-centric methodology empowers institutions to improve decision-making, tailor learning experiences, and detect at-risk students for prompt interventions [14].

W.-S. Wang et al. (Eds.): ICITL 2025, LNCS 15913, pp. 251–263, 2026.
https://doi.org/10.1007/978-3-031-98185-2_27

By promoting a more customised and anticipatory educational methodology, LA has emerged as an effective instrument for enhancing student performance, maximising resources, and aligning institutional strategies with the requirements of learners.

According to Marquez, Henríquez, Chevreux, Scheihing, and Guerra, [15] the adoption of LA in higher education has gained traction as institutions seek to harness data to improve student outcomes, personalize learning experiences, and enhance decision-making processes. Despite its transformative potential, the uptake of LA remains uneven, particularly in regions with limited resources and technological infrastructure. Adoption is often influenced by factors such as institutional readiness, stakeholder awareness, and the availability of skilled personnel to manage and interpret complex datasets. While developed countries have made significant strides in embedding LA into their educational systems, many institutions in the Global South, including South Africa, are still grappling with barriers such as funding constraints, lack of training, and ethical concerns related to data privacy.

2 Literature Review

2.1 The South African Higher Education Landscape

South Africa is home to twenty-six public universities, yet digital transformation in most higher education institutions remains inconsistent. While some South African universities boast advanced digital technologies, others lag significantly, resulting in a partially transformed education landscape [1, 16]. In some institutions, digital integration is a work in progress, revealing stark disparities in technological readiness [17]. This uneven digital progression impacts the ability of South African higher education institutions to offer uniform quality education, despite the advancements that digital technologies bring to the academic environment.

The disparate digital change in South African higher education, alongside the exigencies of the post-Covid-19 era and the fourth industrial revolution (4IR), highlights the imperative for specific frameworks to facilitate the integration of new breakthroughs like learning analytics. Although most South African universities have adopted hybrid teaching and learning approaches, the potential of learning analytics to refine existing practices and improve student results is yet little examined. This research aims to fill this gap by creating a learning analytics adoption framework specifically designed for South Africa's higher education context.

2.2 Learning Analytics Adoption Framework

Current frameworks for the implementation of learning analytics are designed to assist institutions in the intricate process of incorporating LA into their operations. These frameworks generally encompass critical domains including technological infrastructure, policy formulation, stakeholder involvement, and ethical considerations [18, 19, 33]. The SHEILA framework [34] offers a systematic methodology for policy formulation in learning analytics, highlighting the need of institutional coherence and stakeholder cooperation. The DELICATE framework [35] also emphasises ethical considerations and the cultivation of trust among stakeholders. Nonetheless, these frameworks frequently presuppose a degree of institutional ability and technological sophistication that may be absent in various circumstances, emphasising the necessity for localised and context-specific strategies adapted to places such as South Africa. These adjustments are crucial for tackling specific difficulties and optimising the advantages of learning analytics across varied educational environments (Table 1).

Table 1. Learning Analytics Dimensions

LA Dimensions	SE	EC&T	TR	IS	OC
Critical Dimensions of Learning Analytics [18]	X	X	X		X
Lets Talk Analytics Framework [19]	X	X			
Dimensions of LA adoption [15]		X	X		X
Ethical Framework for Learning Analytics [23]	X	X			
Maturity Model for Learning Analytics Adoption (MMLA) [24]	X	X	X	X	X
Learning Analytics Readiness Instrument LARI [20]	X		X		
DELICATE List [22]	X	X	X	X	X
SHEILA Framework [21]	X				X
The Learning Analytics for Latin America (LALA) Framework [25]	X	X	X	X	

3 Theoretical Framework

This study is grounded in several theoretical frameworks that provide a foundational lens for understanding the adoption of learning analytics (LA) in higher education, particularly in the context of South Africa. However, to maintain openness to the unique challenges and opportunities presented in this uncharted space, the study intentionally avoids specifying the constructs of these frameworks prior to data collection. This flexible approach ensures that the research remains data-driven, allowing emergent findings to shape and refine the understanding of LA adoption. The adoption of LA in South Africa is a mandatory initiative, which necessitates a theoretical foundation that aligns with studies conducted in similar mandatory adoption contexts. For this reason, the Technology Acceptance Model (TAM), the Information Systems (IS) Success Model, and Task Technology Fit were chosen as they are frequently used in research exploring the adoption of technologies under similar conditions.

4 Methodology

4.1 Sampling

The study employed purposive sampling to capture diverse perspectives on the adoption of learning analytics within South African higher education. Data was collected from 112 students across three universities, each representing distinct institutional contexts:

an urban-based university offering exclusively long-distance education, a university situated in a deep rural area, and a university established post-Apartheid. Additionally, 27 academic staff members from these institutions were surveyed to provide insights into teaching and learning practices influenced by learning analytics. To complement these perspectives, in-depth interviews were conducted with three managerial staff members to explore strategic and operational challenges related to learning analytics implementation. This diverse sampling approach ensures a comprehensive understanding of the unique challenges and opportunities within varied educational environments.

4.2 Data Collection and Analysis

Quantitative data from students and lecturers was gathered using a survey questionnaire designed to capture both numerical and qualitative responses. The questionnaire included a dedicated section for open-ended questions, allowing participants to provide detailed qualitative insights to complement the quantitative data. For senior managers, qualitative data was collected through semi-structured interviews. This approach enabled a deeper exploration of managerial perspectives, fostering rich, context-specific insights into the research topic.

The quantitative data was analysed using statistical tools, including SPSS version 27 for descriptive and inferential statistical analysis. These tools facilitated the identification of trends, relationships, and patterns within the data, providing a robust quantitative foundation for the study.

Qualitative data from the interviews and open-ended questionnaire responses were transcribed and analysed using a combination of inductive and deductive thematic analysis, as outlined by [26]. The researchers adhered to the six phases of thematic analysis: familiarization with the data, generation of initial codes, identification of themes, refinement and consolidation of themes, defining and interpreting the themes, and producing the final report [27]. This systematic process ensured a rigorous exploration of the data, balancing the emergence of new themes with alignment to existing theoretical frameworks. Integrating both quantitative and qualitative analyses provided a comprehensive understanding of the research findings, supporting the study's mixed-methods approach.

5 Research Results

5.1 Students Results

The factor loadings extracted through PLS-SEM allowed the researcher to analyse the degree to which each observed variable (survey item) contributes to its respective latent construct. High loadings indicate that the items strongly reflect the underlying factor, ensuring construct validity. In this study, four primary factors emerged: Service Quality, Perceived Usefulness, User Satisfaction, and Attitude. Each of these factor's groups together items with high loadings, suggesting that they are reliable indicators of their respective constructs. This factor structure provides insights into the dimensions of user experience, laying a foundation for understanding the relationships between constructs and informing potential interventions or improvements (Table 2).

Table 2. Student Factor Loadings

Item	Factor 1 (Service Quality)	Factor 2 (Perceived Usefulness)	Factor 3 (User Satisfaction)	Factor 4 (Attitude)	Uniqueness
Q6_12	0.883				0.258
Q6_9	0.852				0.243
Q6_11	0.846				0.298
Q6_8	0.828				0.221
Q6_10	0.806				0.314
Q6_7	0.725				0.269
Q5_3		0.906			0.275
Q5_6		0.858			0.332
Q5_4		0.846			0.240
Q5_5		0.839			0.209
Q5_2		0.758			0.257
Q5_1		0.715			0.301
Q4_4			0.864		0.317
Q4_3			0.829		0.258
Q4_5			0.816		0.254
Q4_2			0.812		0.388
Q4_1			0.776		0.353
Q4_6			0.769		0.286
Q6_3				0.898	0.233
Q6_2				0.884	0.271
Q6_1				0.780	0.458
Q6_4				0.671	0.362
Q6_5				0.655	0.316
Q6_6				0.619	0.374

5.2 Lecturers Results

Four key components were identified: Service Quality, Perceived Usefulness/Net Benefits, System Quality/Technology, and Perceived Usefulness. Below is a summary of the component loadings and uniqueness values for each item. Moderate factor loadings typically range from 0.30 to 0.60. Factor loadings below 0.30 are generally considered weak, while those above 0.60 are considered strong. However, the interpretation can vary depending on the context and the field of study (Table 3).

Table 3. Lecturers Factor Loadings

Item	Component 1 (Service Quality)	Component 2 (Perceived Usefulness/Net Benefits)	Component 3 (System Quality/Technology)	Component 4 (Perceived Usefulness)	Uniqueess
Q6_2	0.853				0.185
Q6_3	0.835				0.148
Q6_6	0.815				0.272
Q6_8	0.765				0.174
Q6_12	0.749				0.134
Q6_13	0.748				0.168
Q6_7	0.739				0.187
Q6_1	0.708				0.322
Q6_10	0.687				0.329
Q6_11	0.650				0.285
Q6_9	0.581				0.321
Q6_18		0.908			0.104
Q6_19		0.887			0.084
Q6_17		0.851			0.112
Q6_20		0.814			0.109
Q5_1			0.907		0.220
Q5_3			0.880		0.089
Q5_4			0.783		0.230
Q5_2			0.672		0.305
Q6_15			0.487		0.462
Q6_14				0.783	0.181
Q6_16				0.741	0.169
Q6_4				0.715	0.100
Q6_5				0.645	0.330

5.3 Findings Emanating from Qualitative Data

See (Table 4).

Table 4. Themes

Theme	Description
Purpose and Scope	A clear purpose prevents misuse and builds trust by defining data collection goals
Phased Implementation	A step-by-step rollout with pilot projects ensures smooth adaptation and refinement
Data Infrastructure	Investment in LMS, SIS, and data security is essential for reliable analytics
Stakeholder Engagement	Early involvement of staff and students enhances trust and adoption
Transparency & Communication	Regular updates foster confidence and stakeholder support
Ethical Considerations	Data privacy policies must be in place, with regular ethical reviews
Cross-Departmental Collaboration	A task force ensures seamless integration across departments
Budget & Resource Planning	Aligning funding with institutional cycles secures sustainability
Data Literacy Support	Training ensures proper interpretation and use of analytics tools
Feedback & Improvement	Continuous stakeholder feedback refines analytics strategies
Data Management	Clear policies on data collection, storage, and security are crucial
Success Metrics	Defined KPIs (e.g., retention, satisfaction) track analytics impact
External Partnerships	Collaborations enhance institutional capacity and best practices
Institutional Communication	Transparent security policies build student confidence in data protection

6 Learning Analytics Framework Components

This table now integrates all qualitative and quantitative insights into the framework components, covering the themes identified in both the qualitative data (managerial and student feedback) and quantitative data (survey items and factor loadings). This comprehensive view helps provide a clear structure for the effective implementation and ongoing optimization of learning analytics systems. In addition, the existing theories and learning analytics adoption frameworks significantly influenced the naming and shaping of the themes by providing established dimensions and processes that guided their development (Table 5).

Table 5. Learning Analytics Framework for South African Higher Education

Framework Component	Component Description	Adoption Factors	Integrated Framework Description
Strategic Vision and Goals	Purpose and scope: Clear alignment with academic goals. Prevents scope creep. Fosters trust	Perceived usefulness and net benefits: High factor loadings on tangible benefits	Clear goals aligned with institutional objectives. Communicate purpose effectively to all stakeholders to ensure understanding and engagement
Stakeholder Engagement and Education	Early involvement through workshops and feedback. Promoting data literacy for support and understanding	Service quality: High value placed on quality of services/support for adoption	Comprehensive engagement plan: Include training, feedback loops, and continuous education efforts to ensure all stakeholders are educated
Data Governance and Ethics	Data collection and management: Strict guidelines for data storage, access, and privacy. Address ethical concerns	System quality/technology: High reliability and performance critical to user trust	Robust data governance policies ensuring privacy compliance. Transparent communication on data collection, storage, and use
Technological Infrastructure and Integration	Data infrastructure development: Emphasis on system interoperability and scalability	Perceived usefulness and net benefits: Technological capabilities impact system adoption	Infrastructure development strategy with interoperability and scalability. Maintain strong technical capabilities with ongoing support
Implementation Strategy	Phased implementation: Start with pilot programs, scale based on feedback	User satisfaction: Phased approach improves satisfaction by addressing concerns in stages	Phased implementation: Pilot programs for key outcomes, iterating based on feedback to meet user needs and expectations

(*continued*)

Table 5. (*continued*)

Framework Component	Component Description	Adoption Factors	Integrated Framework Description
Transparency and Communication	Institutional communication: Students express concerns about data protection. Clear communication needed	Service quality: Desire for transparency, responsiveness, and clarity in data usage	Transparent communication strategy: Regular updates on analytics, data protection, and progress to build trust among all stakeholders
Continuous Improvement and Evaluation	Feedback and iterative improvement: Regular feedback loops for refining the system	Attitude: Varied perceptions suggest regular evaluation and iteration can foster positive attitudes	Continuous evaluation: Regular feedback collection and iterative improvements to ensure the system aligns with evolving needs and concerns
Cultural and Organizational Integration	Cultural integration: Promote data-informed decision-making, involving faculty, staff, and students	User satisfaction: High satisfaction correlates with perceived tangible benefits of the system	Strategy for data-driven culture: Promote learning analytics benefits, integrate into academic processes, and engage faculty and students
Ethical Data Use and Privacy Assurance	Ethical considerations: Guidelines for safeguarding privacy and accountability	System quality/technology: User trust hinges on data protection and privacy	Ethical data use policies: Establish and communicate strict data protection measures and ethical guidelines. Regular audits to ensure compliance
Stakeholder Trust and Assurance	Institutional communication and assurance: Clear, transparent communication needed regarding data protection measures	Perceived usefulness: Security measures are a key factor in students' perception of system reliability	Build trust: Regular communication regarding data protection, security protocols, and actions taken to protect data privacy. Ensure transparency

(*continued*)

Table 5. (*continued*)

Framework Component	Component Description	Adoption Factors	Integrated Framework Description
Risk Management and Data Security	Students' concerns regarding data breaches and the effectiveness of security measures	Service quality: Security features and risk management play a significant role in ensuring the system meets users' needs	Implement robust security measures: Develop a comprehensive risk management framework to address data breaches and ensure student data protection
Data Partnership and Capacity-Building	External collaborations for best practices and capacity building	Perceived usefulness: Partnerships enhance the utility of the learning analytics system by incorporating external insights	Establish strategic partnerships: Collaborate with external organizations and universities to enhance learning analytics infrastructure and support
Resource Planning and Budget Allocation	Budget allocation for analytics infrastructure and staff development	System quality/technology: Adequate funding is crucial for maintaining technical capabilities	Align budget planning: Ensure sufficient funding for infrastructure, training, and system maintenance to sustain learning analytics initiatives
Faculty and Student Data Literacy Support	Need for data literacy programs to enhance engagement and understanding	Service quality: High-quality educational support improves user engagement and the adoption of analytics tools	Design data literacy initiatives: Provide training for faculty and students on how to interpret and leverage learning analytics for better outcomes
Clear Success Metrics and Reporting	Defining metrics to track success and communicate progress	Perceived usefulness: Clear success indicators drive user satisfaction and show value	Establish clear success metrics: Regularly track and report on key performance indicators to show the value and impact of learning analytics systems

7 Conclusion

The integrated framework for learning analytics, as seen in the table, emphasizes the significance of amalgamating qualitative and quantitative insights to tackle the complex nature of learning analytics adoption in educational institutions. The qualitative insights, emphasising stakeholder engagement, cultural integration, and ethical considerations, yield a nuanced comprehension of the institutional context, whereas the quantitative insights deliver measurable outcomes such as user satisfaction, perceived usefulness, and system performance. By synthesising various viewpoints, the framework guarantees that the learning analytics is both technically robust and contextually pertinent, while also being socially endorsed by all parties involved.

The framework's primary strength is in its emphasis on continual improvement and iterative processes, as demonstrated by the elements of stakeholder interaction, feedback loops, and transparency. The qualitative focus on early engagement and continuous teaching cultivates trust and promotes a culture of data-informed decision-making, essential for ensuring long-term adoption. Quantitative insights, especially regarding system quality, user satisfaction, and definitive success measures, furnish institutions with the necessary data to monitor progress and implement evidence-based modifications. This ongoing feedback loop guarantees that the learning analytics system adapts to the requirements and issues of users, hence improving its efficacy and durability.

The framework highlights the necessity for a systematic, incremental approach to adoption, commencing with pilot initiatives and expanding based on feedback. The framework cultivates an atmosphere of trust and comprehension among stakeholders by emphasising clear objectives, efficient communication, and transparency. The implementation of stringent data governance regulations and security protocols guarantees that the system adheres to ethical norms, safeguarding user data and privacy. The framework provides a thorough and realistic roadmap for institutions to launch and sustain effective learning analytics programs, thereby enhancing educational outcomes and fostering institutional growth.

References

1. Kanyane, M.: Digital Work – Transforming the Higher Education Landscape in South Africa, pp. 149–160. New Digital Work (2023)
2. Krasnoff, B.: Culturally Responsive Teaching. A Guide to Evidence-Based Practices for Teaching All Students Equitably. Education Northwest (2016)
3. Darling-Hammond, L., Cook-Harvey, C., Flook, L., Gardner, M., Melnick, H.: With the Whole Child in Mind: Insights from the Comer School Development Program. ASCD, Alexandria, VA (2018)
4. Roche, S., Yang, J., Schneller, C.: The Role of Higher Education in Promoting Lifelong Learning. UNESCO Institute for Lifelong Learning (2015)
5. Dawson, B.A., Kilgore, W., Rawcliffe, R.M.: Strategies for creating inclusive learning environments through a social justice lens. J. Educ. Res. Pract. **12**, 3–27 (2022)
6. World Economic Forum: Shaping the Future of Learning: The Role of AI in Education 4.0 (2024)
7. Department of Education: Education White Paper 3: A Programme for the Transformation of Higher Education (1997)

8. Johar, N.A., Kew, S.N., Tasir, Z., Koh, E.: Learning analytics on student engagement to enhance students' learning performance: a systematic review. Sustainability **15**, 7849 (2023)
9. Osakwe, I., Chen, G., Whitelock-Wainwright, A., Gašević, D., Cavalcanti, A.P., Mello, R.F.: Towards automated content analysis of educational feedback: a multi-language study. Comput. Educ.: Artific. Intell. **3**, 100059 (2022)
10. Paolucci, C., Vancini, S., Bex, R.T., II., Cavanaugh, C., Salama, C., de Araujo, Z.: A review of learning analytics opportunities and challenges for K-12 education. Heliyon **10**(4), e25767 (2024)
11. Martin, F., Ndoye, A.: Using learning analytics to assess student learning in online courses. J. Univ. Teach. Learn. Pract. **13**(3) (2016)
12. Lee, L.K., Cheung, S.K.S., Kwok, L.F.: Learning analytics: current trends and innovative practices. J. Comput. Educ. **7**, 1–6 (2020)
13. Matsebula, F., Mnkandla, E.: Information Systems Innovation Adoption in Higher Education: Big Data and Analytics. In: International Conference on Advances in Computing and Communication Engineering (ICACCE), pp. 326–329. IEEE, Durban, South Africa (2016)
14. Tsai, Y.-S., Gašević, D.: Learning analytics in higher education—challenges and policies: a review of eight learning analytics policies. In: 7th International Conference on Learning Analytics and Knowledge, pp. 233–242 (2017)
15. Márquez, L., Henríquez, V., Chevreux, H., Scheihing, E., Guerra, J.: Adoption of learning analytics in higher education institutions: a systematic literature review. British J. Educ. Technol. (2023). Ramaila, S., Molwele, A.J.: The role of technology integration in the development of 21st century skills and competencies in life sciences teaching and learning. Int. J. Higher Educ. **11**(5) (2022)
16. Mabidi, N.: A systematic review of the transformative impact of the digital revolution on higher education in South Africa. South African J. Higher Educ. **38**(3), 97–113 (2024)
17. Ramaila, S., Molwele, A.J.: The role of technology integration in the development of 21st century skills and competencies in life sciences teaching and learning. Int. J. Higher Educ. **11**(5) (2022)
18. Greller, W., Drachsler, H.: Translating learning into numbers: a generic framework for learning analytics. Educ. Technol. Soc. **15**(3), 42–57 (2012)
19. West, W., Heath, D., Huijser, H.: Let's talk learning analytics: a framework for implementation in relation to student retention. J. Asynchronous Learn. Netw. **20**(2), 1–21 (2016)
20. Arnold, K.E., Lonn, S., Pistilli, M.D.: An exercise in institutional reflection: the learning analytics readiness instrument (LARI). In: Pardo, A., Teasley, S. (eds.) 4th International Conference on Learning Analytics and Knowledge, pp. 163–167. ACM (2014)
21. Tsai, Y.-S., et al.: The SHEILA framework: informing institutional strategies and policy processes of learning analytics. J. Learn. Anal. **5**(3), 5–20 (2018)
22. Drachsler, H., Greller, W.: Privacy and analytics: it's a delicate issue—a checklist for trusted learning analytics. In: 6th International Conference on Learning Analytics and Knowledge, pp. 89–98 (2016)
23. Slade, S., Prinsloo, P.: Learning analytics: ethical issues and dilemmas. Am. Behav. Sci. **57**(10), 1510–1529 (2013)
24. Freitas, E., et al.: MMALA: developing and evaluating a maturity model for adopting learning analytics. J. Learn. Anal. **11**(1), 67–86 (2024)
25. Sanagustín, MP., et al. Building Capacity to Use Learning Analytics to Improve Higher Education in Latin America (2019)
26. Johnson, B., Christensen, L.: Educational Research: Quantitative, Qualitative, and Mixed Approaches. Sage, Los Angeles (2017)

27. Braun, V., Clarke, V.: Thematic analysis. In: Cooper, H., Camic, P.M., Long, D.L., Panter, A.T., Rindskopf, D., Sher, K.J. (eds.) APA Handbook of Research Methods in Psychology, Vol. 2: Research Designs: Quantitative, Qualitative, Neuropsychological, and Biological, pp. 57–71. American Psychological Association, Washington, DC (2012)
28. Braun, V., Clarke, V.: Using thematic analysis in psychology. Qual. Res. Psychol. **3**(2), 77–101 (2006)

Play My Math: Design and Implementation of a Fraction Generator Tool Within a Mathematical Musician Digital Learning Platform

Eric Roldan Roa[1(✉)], Hongtao Li[1], Juan Carlos Ramos Martinez[1], Doris Kristina Raave[1,2], Erika Berenice Roldan Roa[1], Nina Politimou[3], Tyler Colasante[4], Tina Malti[4], Marcus Specht[5], and Julia Mori[6]

[1] Center for Scalable Data Analytics and Artificial Intelligence (ScaDS.AI) Dresden/Leipzig, Universität Leipzig, Humboldtstr. 25, 04105 Leipzig, Germany
eric.roldan@informatik.uni-leipzig.de
[2] Leipzig University, Augustusplatz. 10, 04109 Leipzig, Germany
[3] University College London, Gower St, London WC1E 6BT, UK
[4] Humboldt Science Center for Child Development (HumanKind), Leipzig University, Jahnallee 59, 04109 Leipzig, Germany
[5] Delft University of Technology, Mekelweg 5, 2628 CD Delft, Netherlands
[6] University of Bern, Hochschulstrasse 4, 3012 Bern, Switzerland

Abstract. In this paper, we present and describe a Fraction Generator tool, which is one of the components of our mathematical musician digital learning platform, Play My Math. Teachers and students can use the Fraction Generator tool to discuss, practice, and reinforce conceptual and procedural knowledge of fractions. To that end, the tool offers customizable settings that randomly render exercises in six different categories (i.e., identifying fractions, identifying notations, comparison of fractions, arithmetic applied to fractions, least common multiple, and quantity of a fraction). Additionally, we offer an extra module called the Worksheet Demonstration that teachers can use to guide the students when working with paper-based worksheets. The rationale for the Fraction Generator came from feedback given by teachers during a study we conducted in Mexico in 2024. For designing our tool, we considered principles of technology-enhanced learning and tangible learning interfaces. Finally, to further develop our Fraction Generator initial design, we analyzed qualitative data coming from UK teachers' feedback as part of an intervention we conducted in the UK primary education context at the beginning of 2025.

Keywords: Mathematical musician curricula · music and mathematics · educational technology · fraction education

1 Introduction

Play My Math (PMM) is a digital learning platform that merges music and mathematics within the same learning space to enhance mathematics education in primary school settings [1, 2]. In a previous design-based research cycle [2], teachers expressed a desire for

W.-S. Wang et al. (Eds.): ICITL 2025, LNCS 15913, pp. 264–273, 2026.
https://doi.org/10.1007/978-3-031-98185-2_28

a dedicated component of the platform for generating exercises to practice and reinforce fractions-based conceptual and procedural knowledge without necessarily using music, as their students would still need to face traditional mathematics tests. To address these teachers' request, we built a prototype Fraction Generator (FG) tool that considered the following subtopics of fractions: equivalence of fractions, translation between graphical bar representation of fractions and different mathematical notations (i.e., algebraic, percentage, and decimal notations), and three least common multiple cases (i.e., same denominator, different denominator but direct multiple, and different denominator but no direct multiple). However, when preparing for research done in the UK, where teachers delivered a ten-week fraction program using PMM, we realized that the FG prototype was insufficient. Hence, we iterated and expanded our FG prototype to cover the list of subtopics of fractions that we describe in detail below.

2 Theoretical Background

2.1 What is a Fraction?

In mathematics education, definitions of a fraction can vary in complexity depending on the audience. Definitions can range from "a piece broken off something" [3] to more technical, such as "a numerical representation indicating the quotient of two numbers" [4]. From a mathematical perspective, a fraction can be defined as any number expressed in an a/b format where both a (i.e., numerator) and b (i.e., denominator) are whole numbers and are not equal to zero. The taxonomy of fractions includes the following types of fractions: unit fraction, proper fraction, improper fraction, and mixed fraction. The latter types of fractions vary depending on the numbers assigned to the numerator and denominator. Additionally, when working with two or more fractions, mathematics education distinguishes between having equivalent or nonequivalent fractions, as well as like or unlike fractions. Regardless of the chosen definition and types, Beyranevand [5] posits that the topic of fractions (belonging to rational numbers) plays five targeted functions students should be able to grasp: parts of a whole, ratios, operators, indicated quotients, and measures.

2.2 Common Students' Misunderstandings About Fractions

Learning fractions is notoriously challenging due to the necessary conceptual reorganization, as understanding fractions requires a significant shift from natural number concepts to more abstract ideas [6]. Common errors in fraction tasks, such as treating fractions as whole numbers or misapplying procedures, indicate deep-seated misconceptions due to a lack of conceptual understanding and procedural knowledge [7]. For example, previous research posits that one of the main challenges in learning fractions is students' tendency to directly transfer their knowledge of procedures and concepts around natural numbers to fractions [7, 8]. For instance, in relation to the parts of a whole function, students tend to attribute more value if the fraction has bigger numbers in the numerator and denominator [9]. Another misunderstanding is in relation to the so-called "density of a fraction", which requires students to understand that there is an infinite number of fractions that are equivalent to a given fraction, and that between two given fractions, there is also an infinite number of fractions [10]. Regarding operations with fractions misconceptions, students tend to apply algorithms from natural numbers that do not necessarily apply when dealing with fractions. For instance, parallel direct addition or subtraction is applied to the numerator and denominator [11], or the understanding bias is that multiplying should make a quantity or number bigger whereas dividing should make it smaller [12]. Regarding the indicating quotient function, this presents less challenge as general division rules are applied. Finally, when fractions function as a measure, the most challenging part is that this function requires students to understand that the fractions could also stand for specific numbers (e.g., when specifying a point in a number line) and not necessarily as a relationship between numbers [5].

2.3 PMM Fraction Generator for Technology-Enhanced Learning as a Tangible User Interface

Our FG tool leverages on technology-enhanced learning (TEL) principles included in the conceptualization of Kirkwood and Price [14] who present three affordances of TEL, namely operational improvement to streamline learning activity, quantitative change to improve students affective and emotional engagement, and qualitative change to improve students' cognitive engagement with the learning activity. For example, leveraging on technology for automated feedback in a reinforcement learning activity can execute such an activity faster and more efficiently (operational improvement), gamification elements of such a reinforcement activity tap into motivational aspects (quantitative change) and the adaptable levels of such an activity support deepening the necessary conceptual and procedural knowledge, bringing qualitative change.

In addition to the general TEL affordances, the FG adopts principles of tangible user interfaces (TUI). In mathematics education, TUIs evolved from tangible physical materials, for which rationale and theory posit that cognition is activated by embodiment, model simulations, and situated actions [15]. For instance, when teachers ask the students to count with their fingers (i.e., situated action), the students' finger movement (i.e., embodied element) serves for them to count a quantity (i.e., model representation). Tangible teaching and learning material aids are vast (e.g., fake coins, Lego bricks, etc.). Piaget advocated for using tangible materials in mathematics education to support the development of students' ability to perceive abstract mathematical concepts [16]. TUIs are built upon the same principles of conventional physical, tangible materials in that both account for the multimodal nature of how humans interact with and make sense of their environment [5]. The factors making a TUI effective for education are physical, social, and emotional affordances [17]. In Sect. 3.1, we explain further how these factors have been considered in our design.

3 Method

Overall, in developing the PMM educational platform, we have been following a design-based research approach, which considers multiple iterations to achieve the intended design goals [18]. Next, we describe the three iterations that lead to the current design and state of the FG.

3.1 First Cycle: An Initial Fraction Generator Prototype

As mentioned in the introduction, we initially conceptualized the FG based on our previous intervention study in Mexico 2024 [2]. Back then, from a focus group analysis, we realized that teachers wanted the possibility of generating fraction exercise so that the students could practice their conceptual and procedural fraction skills without necessarily a musical application (i.e., performing or hearing the musical representation of generated fractions). This necessity was driven by the teachers' concern for preparing their students for traditional and/or standardized mathematics tests. To address this, we designed and implemented a FG covering three main subtopics of fractions that the Mexican students struggled most with: equivalence of fractions, translation between graphical bar representation of fractions and different mathematical notations (i.e., algebraic, percentage, and decimal notations), and three least common multiple cases (i.e., same denominator, different denominator but direct multiple, and different denominator but no direct multiple).

We then moved to account for the factors making a TUI effective for education (i.e., physical, social, and emotional). Regarding the physical factor, we decided to 1) enable teachers and students to manipulate all relevant parameters for generating exercises and 2) incorporate configurable bar models so that the students can connect the abstract concept with a responsive graphical representation when solving the exercises. Regarding the social factor, we decided to 1) enable the teachers to incorporate and save any FG module as part of their lesson planning to engage with their students at the individual, group, or classroom level and 2) enable the students to challenge their peers in the PMM platform by configuring and sending them exercises to advance in their mathematical musician progress as part of PMM's gamification narrative [1, 2]. Finally, on the emotional factor, we hypothesized that students would experience positive emotions as a result of solving the FG exercises collectively or by practicing their math skills in a formative assessment manner (e.g., using the FG to practice and gain confidence/feel calmer before a summative test).

In terms of affordances for TEL, the FG supports operational improvement as teachers can instantly generate a vast number of customized exercises with options for automatic feedback. Qualitative change, in the form of targeted improvement in conceptual and procedural understanding is, in addition to applying the needed knowledge, further supported by different visualizations and representations. Quantitative change is leveraged by the gamification narrative, as well as by diverse instructional designs such as the option of solving the exercises collectively.

3.2 Second Cycle: Expanding the Fraction Generator to Cover 4th Grade Fractions Curricula in the UK

In preparation for ongoing research in collaboration with one primary school in London, teachers shared with us the ten-week fraction learning material (i.e., lesson slides) they normally use for teaching fractions. Next, we list the subtopics of fractions that we used to compare and further expand our first Fraction Generator prototype coverage (Table 1).

Table 1. Our UK Partner School's 10-Week Lesson Plan (Based on UK Curricula Year 4).

Week	Lesson	Learning objectives or key concepts
W1	What is a fraction?	Numerator and denominator
W2	Equivalent fractions part 1	Relating fractions in terms of =, >, or <
W3	Equivalent fractions part 2	Relating fractions in terms of =, >, or <
W4	Fractions greater than 1	Improper and mixed fractions
W5	Counting in fractions	Arithmetic applied to fractions
W6	Add two or more fractions	Arithmetic applied to fractions
W7	Subtract two fractions	Arithmetic applied to fractions
W8	Subtract from whole amounts	Arithmetic applied to fractions
W9	Fractions of a quantity	Arithmetic applied to fractions
W10	Calculate quantities	Arithmetic applied to fractions

3.3 Third Cycle: Teacher's Feedback from Our Ongoing Research in the UK

At the end of January 2025, we began our research collaboration with one UK primary school where two teachers delivered an adapted version of PMM's fraction program to groups of students. To facilitate teachers' delivery of the PMM program, we designed and implemented a Course Creator tool [19]. Using this tool, we created ten lesson templates mirroring the topics listed in Sect. 3.2. Finally, on a weekly basis, we held online meetings with the UK teachers to gather their feedback after delivering the corresponding lesson. Similarly to the Mexican intervention described in Sect. 3.1 and reported in previous work [2], we organized and analyzed the teacher's weekly feedback using thematic analysis to fine-tune the FG tool. To inform the further development of the FG tool, we considered all of the teachers' feedback belonging to the grading and streamline teaching processes category of our thematic analysis (e.g., "… and it would be nice if they could practice or solve exercises with more graphical representation than just bars").

4 Result

The current version of the PMM FG considers the following modules: Identifying Fractions, Identifying Notations, Comparing Fractions, Arithmetic Applied to Fractions, Least Common Multiple, Quantity of a Fraction, and Worksheet Demonstration. The first six modules were built to generate random exercises based on parameters the users (i.e., teachers and students) can adjust to generate exercises on the desired difficulty level and fractions subtopic. The Worksheet Demonstrator module is a module the teachers requested to practically guide their students when working with paper-based worksheets. Finally, in the PMM Course Creator that we described in another paper [19], teachers can design and print exercises or worksheets using any combination of the above-mentioned FG modules. Next, we elaborate on the FG modules.

4.1 Identifying Fractions

The Identifying Fractions module, depicted in Fig. 1, considers two sub-exercise configuration paths: Identify Model and Identify Type. The objective of these exercises' paths is for students to practice fractions functioning as a part of a whole and ratios. The Identify Model settings allow the user to configure and generate random exercises with a variety of graphical representations (i.e., bars, circles, collections of objects) using the denominator range and numerator percentage, while incorporating/varying improper and mixed fractions, multiple choice answers, and number of exercises. When multiple choice is not selected, the students need to input the corresponding fraction. The Identify Type path is a multiple-choice, pre-configured exercise generator where users can select among unit, proper, improper, and mixed fractions.

4.2 Identifying Notations

The Identifying Notation module, depicted in Fig. 1, objective is for users to configure and generate exercises to practice translating between graphical representations of fractions and the following notations: numerator/denominator (n/d), algebraic (where the variable S stands for silence), decimal, percentage, and music notation. We decided to keep the music notation exercise generation option for the teachers to decide on incorporating (or not). To that end, the user can configure the number of bars, the denominator range, the numerator percentage, select among the above-mentioned notation options, and the number of exercises to be rendered.

4.3 Comparing Fractions

The Comparing Fractions module, depicted in Fig. 1, considers three sub-exercise configuration paths: Comparison, Identify Equivalent, and Create Equivalent. The objective of these exercises' paths is for students to practice fractions functioning as a part of a whole and ratios when comparing two or more fractions. All three exercise paths allow the users to configure and generate random exercises using the denominator range, numerator percentage, and number of exercises. The Comparison path exercises require the user to select between =, <, and > when comparing a pair of fractions. The Identify Equivalent path requires the user to answer exercises in two steps. First, selecting the equivalent fractions among three different bar configurations, and then writing all three fractions in an n/d notation format. Finally, in the Create Equivalent path, users are given a fraction with its graphical bar configuration as well as either the numerator or numerator on a second configurable bar. Then, users need to find the missing value with the factor needed to create the equivalent fraction.

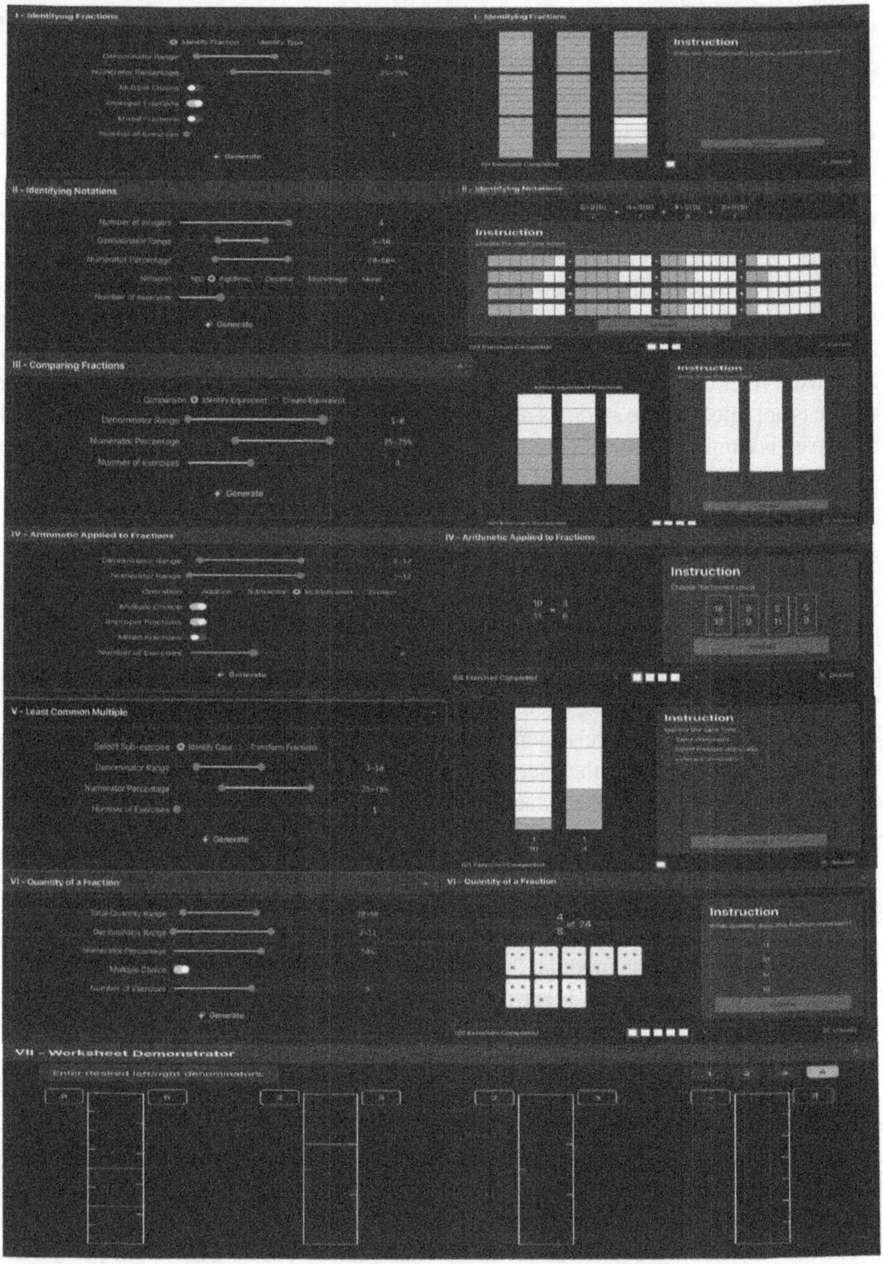

Fig. 1. PMM Fraction Generator modules examples.

4.4 Arithmetic Applied to Fractions

The Arithmetic Applied to Fractions module, depicted in Fig. 1, allows the user to configure and generate random exercises for practicing fractions using addition, subtraction, multiplication, and division. The configurable settings are similar to those of the Identifying Fractions module. When multiple choice is not selected, the students need to input the resulting fraction in a numerator and denominator notation (n/d). To support students with their procedural knowledge, we added a help button they can refer to for remembering procedural considerations when solving these types of exercises.

4.5 Least Common Multiple

The Least Common Multiple module, depicted in Fig. 1, considers two sub-exercise configuration paths: Identify Case and Transform Fractions. The objective of these exercises' paths is for students to practice finding equivalence between two given fractions using their least common multiple. Both types of paths allow the user to configure and generate random exercises using the denominator range, numerator percentage, and number of exercises. The Identify Case is a pre-configured multiple choice exercise generator where users need to identify the correct least common multiple cases when two fractions are given (i.e., same denominator, different denominator but direct multiple, different denominator but no direct multiple). The Transform Fractions path requires the users to input the corresponding fractions resulting from finding the least common multiple from two given fractions.

4.6 Quantity of a Fraction

The Quantity of a Fraction module, depicted in Fig. 1, allows users to practice fractions functioning as an operator and measure. The users can configure and generate random exercises using the quantity range values, denominator range, numerator percentage, multiple choice answer, and number of exercises options. When multiple choice is not selected, the students need to input the quantity the given fraction stands for. In this module, the randomized quantity range value is rendered as small circles that get distributed in the generated denominator. Then, the user needs to answer how many objects (i.e., small circles) the numerator stands for in the presented fraction. The teachers can use this graphical analogy to work with different measuring cases.

4.7 Worksheet Demonstrator

The Worksheet Demonstrator module, depicted in Fig. 1, is a practical and effective way for teachers to guide students when using physical PMM worksheets. This module allows users to work with up to four bars where each bar can have two desired denominators (left and right) with a partial dividing line. Then, teachers can decide which partial line of the respective denominator to complete.

5 Discussion, Conclusion and Future Work

In this paper, we described the iterative design and implementation of the FG tool of our PMM mathematical musician educational technology. The tool comprises seven modules (i.e., Identifying Fractions, Identifying Notations, Comparing Fractions, Arithmetic

Applied to Fractions, Least Common Multiple, Quantity of a Fraction, and Worksheet Demonstration) with teaching and learning affordances to cover subtopics of fractions. The teachers can use this tool to showcase fraction functions (i.e., part of a whole, ratios, operators, indicated quotients, and measures) [5], generate exercises for students to practice their conceptual and procedural knowledge of fractions, and engage in class discussions about common misunderstandings coming from natural number generalizations in the context of fractions [6–12]. As a next step, we are analyzing pre-post data from a research collaboration with one public school in London. In this study, two teachers delivered a ten-week fraction program using the latest PMM platform including the FG iterations described herein (i.e., experimental condition), while three other groups received the standard school fractions program (i.e., control conditions). We expect the FG tool to, in part, positively contribute to students' learning outcomes; however, we acknowledge that it will not be possible to differentiate between the effects resulting from students experiencing mathematics with music from the specific effects of interacting with the FG tool. Future studies are needed to contrast the unique contributions of distinct PMM components.

Acknowledgments. This study was partially funded by Validierungsförderung 2021-2027 (100737267) and by the British Academy's BA/Leverhulme Small Research Grants Programme (grant reference number: SRG2324\241835).

Disclosure of Interests. The authors have no competing interests to declare that are relevant to the content of this article.

References

1. Roldan-Roa, E., et al.: Play my math: first development cycle of an edtech tool supporting the teaching and learning of fractions through music in algebraic notation. In: Ferreira Mello, R., Rummel, N., Jivet, I., Pishtari, G., Ruipérez Valiente, J.A. (eds.) European Conference on Technology Enhanced Learning 2024, LNCS, vol. 14786, pp. 241–246. Springer, Krems (2024)
2. Roldan-Roa, E., et al.: Play my math: second development cycle of an EdTech tool supporting the teaching and learning of fractions through music in algebraic notation. In: Cheng, Y.-P., Pedaste, M., Bardone, E., Huang, Y.-M. (eds.) International Conference on Innovative Technologies and Learning 2024, LNCS, vol. 14786, pp. 44–53. Springer, Tartu (2024)
3. Schwartzman, S.: The Words of Mathematics: An Etymological Dictionary of Mathematical Terms in English, vol. 17. American Mathematical Society (1999)
4. Merriam-Webster.: Fraction. In: Merriam-Webster.com dictionary. https://www.merriam-webster.com/dictionary/fraction. Last accessed 5 May 2025
5. Beyranevand, M.L.: Quick reads: the different representations of rational numbers: a good idea in a small package. Math. Teach. Middle School **19**(6), 382–385 (2014)
6. Gabriel, F., Coché, F., Szucs, D., Carette, V., Rey, B., Content, A.: A componential view of children's difficulties in learning fractions. Front. Psychol. **4**, 715 (2013)
7. Eichelmann, A., Narciss, S., Schnaubert, L., Melis, E.: Typical errors for fraction addition and subtraction—a review of empirical error analysis. J. Math.-Didakt. **33**, 29–57 (2012)

8. Moseley, B., Okamoto, Y.: Identifying fourth graders' understanding of rational number representations: a mixed methods approach. Sch. Sci. Math. **108**(6), 238–250 (2008)
9. Christou, K.P., Vamvakoussi, X.: Natural number bias on evaluations of the effect of multiplication and division: the role of the type of numbers. Math. Educ. Res. J. **35**(3), 427–443 (2023)
10. Önal, H., Yorulmaz, A.: The errors made by primary school fourth graders on fractions. J. Res. Educ. Soc. **4**(1), 98–113 (2017)
11. Markovits, Z., Sowder, J.: Developing number sense: an intervention study in grade 7. J. Res. Math. Educ. **25**(1), 4–29 (1994)
12. Stafylidou, S., Vosniadou, S.: The development of students' understanding of the numerical value of fractions. Learn. Instr. **14**(5), 503–518 (2004)
13. Vamvakoussi, X., Van Dooren, W., Verschaffel, L.: Naturally biased? In search for reaction time evidence for a natural number bias in adults. J. Math. Behav. **31**(3), 344–355 (2012)
14. Kirkwood, A., Price, L.: Technology-enhanced learning and teaching in higher education: what is 'enhanced' and how do we know? A critical literature review. Learn. Media Technol. **39**(1), 6–36 (2014)
15. Barsalou, L.W.: Grounded cognition. Annu. Rev. Psychol. **59**(1), 617–645 (2008)
16. Piaget, J.: Child's Conception of Space: Selected Works, vol. 4. Routledge (2013)
17. Zhou, Y., Wang, M.: Tangible user interfaces in learning and education. Int. Encyclopedia Soc. Behav. Sci. **2**, 20–25 (2015)
18. Easterday, M.W., Lewis, D.R., Gerber, E.M.: Design-Based Research Process: Problems, Phases, and Applications. International Society of the Learning Sciences, Boulder, CO (2014)
19. Roldan-Roa, E., et al.: Play My Math: Design and Implementation of a Course Creator Tool Within a Mathematical Musician Digital Learning Platform (In review)

Experiences with a Pragmatic Student Attendance Management Scheme

Evelyn Eika and Frode Eika Sandnes(✉)

Oslo Metropolitan University, 0130 Oslo, Norway
{Evelyn.Eika,frodes}@oslomet.no

Abstract. In some educational contexts it is necessary to record student attendance, yet the technical infrastructures for registration management may not be available. The goal of this work was to develop a tool to reduce the manual registration management effort. The tool was iteratively developed and tested in six courses over a period of four years. Analyses which were found to be particularly useful included attendance status overviews, individual attendance timelines, and anomalous registrations. The reports generated by the tool can be used to facilitate the formative dialogue between the students and the teacher during the learning process. The proposed scheme is different from most of the previous approaches in that it requires minimal setup and no dedicated infrastructure.

Keywords: Attendance · Class management · Cheating detection · Privacy

1 Introduction

The degree to which students have mandatory attendance requirements varies. In some courses, voluntary inspirational lectures may provide useful background for further self-study, while in others they require mandatory on-campus activities. With small classes of up to 20 students, it is straightforward to identify who is present using roll calls. However, with more students the task of administering attendance requires more effort. One approach used by the authors was to circulate a sheet of paper during each class for the students to sign. This approach is not too disruptive, but some students may sign for their absent friends. Sometimes the lists would be "stuck" if unalert students did not pass the sheet on to the next student. Reviewing the handwritten attendance lists at the end of the semester was tedious and difficult. It was not practical to provide students with updated attendance status during the semester.

Motivated by this, we have been developing a scheme for simple and fast in-class attendance recording procedure and a tool for analyzing these attendance registrations. The goals were to reduce the time diverted away from learning activities, to ensure that the registered individuals were present, to allow continuous status reports to be generated on-the-fly, for the tool to be easily shared with other educators, to be deployable without any need for specific infrastructures, and for students' privacy to be protected.

Our scheme assumes that all the students have access to the Internet during class. At some point during a class, the instructor will call for the students to register their

W.-S. Wang et al. (Eds.): ICITL 2025, LNCS 15913, pp. 274–283, 2026.
https://doi.org/10.1007/978-3-031-98185-2_29

attendance using a unique keyword. Their name and the keyword are registered using a simple online form. Unlike most other studies on attendance management systems, our system was deployed, tested, and evolved over time. Insight into the practical needs of such a system from the perspectives of both students and teachers was gained.

2 Related Work

The underlying reasons for attendance have been widely studied [1]. O'Sullivan et al. [2] argued that students' attendance is regulated by contextual factors such as the pedagogical approaches used and the students' perceptions of the usefulness of the classes. Bati et al. [3] observed that the most compelling reason to attend lectures was the chance to ask questions, while the most common reasons for absence were sleeplessness, health issues, and inefficient lectures. Leufer and Cleary-Holdforth [4] argued that there are valid reasons for absence and warned against policies. Macfarlane [5] argued that attendance rules "further infantilise students rather than developing their capacity to make informed choices as adults thereby failing to respect their academic freedom".

Distance education addresses students that are unable to participate in class physically, thereby having to rely on virtual presence and proxies [6]. Mörtsell [7] identified three approaches for detecting distance attendance, namely video roll calls, attendance performance such as participating in discussions, and "click-like" responses. The negative effects recorded lectures have on physical attendance have been discussed for more than 50 years, from audio tape recordings [8] to more recent video recordings [9].

Many attendance management proposals have been made, yet few have been tested in practice. Garcia et al. [10] proposed a system where students register their attendance in class by inputting a digit-based session passcode using their smartphones. Bhalla et al. [11] proposed the use of Bluetooth for attendance management. Attendance management with radio frequency identification (RFID) technology involves students carrying unique RFID tags, which are detected by an RFID reader in class [12]. Near Field Communication (NFC) is a related technology where students register attendance using their NFC-enabled smartphones on an NFC-reader in class [13]. Several proposals describe the student scanning of quick response (QR) codes shown by the teacher [14]. Attendance systems based on face recognition [15], iris recognition [16], and fingerprints [17] have also been proposed. Systems that rely on biometrics can be quite problematic in terms of privacy and ethics. Noor et al. [18] described a system where the teachers use their smartphones to scan the barcode of the students' identification cards. A similar experimental bar-code system is offered by the authors' university where the teacher logs into a national web portal to manually confirm the presence for a given student for a specific class. The manual nature of this system renders it impractical for large classes as the teacher becomes a bottleneck burdened with the manual registrations. This system also includes functionality comparable to that described by Guevarra and Corpuz [19] where the students scan their ID cards in class using an infrared barcode reader. This barcode reader is attached to the teacher's computer which must be logged into the national portal.

Our literature review revealed few accounts of actual classroom practice. Therefore, a series of blogs for educators were explored. Manual attendance registration seems common using paper or simple spreadsheets. One approach is to ask random students from the list questions during the class. Another approach is to conduct quizzes or polls. Attendance information can also be extracted using the analytics modules in the learning management systems. Several writings discuss the use of Google Forms to take attendance, or using specific attendance apps such as K12 attendance, MyClass Attendance, Chalk Attendance, TeacherKit, Attendance Manager, and Attendink.

3 Method

We have developed and evaluated the proposed attendance tool in six classes across four iterations during a four-year period. During each iteration (semester), the current version of the scheme was deployed in class and students' responses were noted along with our observations and experiences. We reflected on these experiences and used the new insight to adjust the implementation and prepare for the next iteration.

The semesters lasted 12–13 weeks. The bachelor courses were run in two-hour slots twice weekly, while the master courses were one weekly four-hour slot. A formal attendance requirement of 80% was defined for both courses.

All the courses were run physically. All the students studied technology and engineering. Students brought their own devices to class and had Wi-Fi access. Attendance and on-campus presence was a relevant issue as most students had part-time work, and in some cases held full-time positions. A substantial portion of students also had parental responsibilities.

3.1 Attendance Registration Procedure

During each class the instructor chose a suitable time to announce the keyword and ask students to register using an online form. The form had two fields, one for the students' name, and the other for the keyword. The keywords were easy to comprehend and spell (e.g., "rain" and "grace"). A new unique keyword was used with each class. The times of registration were arbitrarily chosen. The link to a registration form was published within the learning management system (Canvas). Information about the purpose of the form and data deletion procedure was provided together with the link. The same registration link was used for each group of students each time to avoid confusion.

4 The Attendance Analysis Tool

Attendance information was collected using an institutionally approved form service that adheres to privacy regulations (nettskema.no). This service recorded the exact time of each response. After each class the teacher retrieved a spreadsheet with all the accumulated registrations, which was uploaded to a local instance of the attendance tool running in the browser. Next, the teacher indicated which three columns contain the timestamps, names, and in-class codes as the tool was thus not bound to a specific spreadsheet format. Once set up, the tool showed an overview of student attendance statistics. The teacher could publish this list within the learning management allowing students to track progress and confirm their attendance.

Students could easily circumvent the attendance scheme by obtaining the code from a fellow student. Such students could typically register later than the other students. Two views were particularly useful for analyzing late registrations. A last registrations-view was typically used after a class, while the teacher could still recall the class, to see which students registered late. The second view showed students that systematically registered late. "Late" was defined as "more than 30 min".

Figure 1 shows a view for helping identify and resolve situations where students use different name variations. The first row shows that the student with the full name "Barbara Elizabeth Jennifer Miller" has been registered with "Barbara Elizabeth Jennifer" and "Barbara Miller". Sometimes name variations are too different to be automatically detected. A view was thus added to inspect all the unique name variations. The list of all unique names can be useful for detecting "missing" registrations in situations where students have used very different names to register attendance.

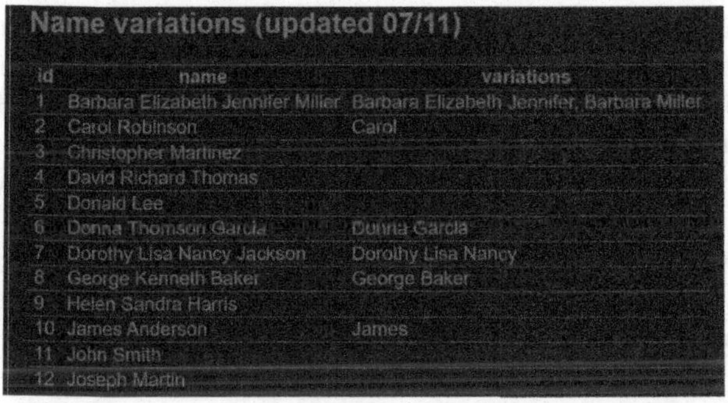
Name variations (updated 07/11)

id	name	variations
1	Barbara Elizabeth Jennifer Miller	Barbara Elizabeth Jennifer, Barbara Miller
2	Carol Robinson	Carol
3	Christopher Martinez	
4	David Richard Thomas	
5	Donald Lee	
6	Donna Thomson Garcia	Donna Garcia
7	Dorothy Lisa Nancy Jackson	Dorothy Lisa Nancy
8	George Kenneth Baker	George Baker
9	Helen Sandra Harris	
10	James Anderson	James
11	John Smith	
12	Joseph Martin	

Fig. 1. Automatically associated name variations (pseudonyms).

To facilitate specific enquiries for individual students, a student timeline is provided (see Fig. 2). The timeline lists all the registrations associated with the student in chronological order. This timeline is useful for pinpointing the exact nature of potential discrepancies. Here "David" was absent in the first class and once towards the end of the semester and was granted a valid exemption for the second class, and registered late twice.

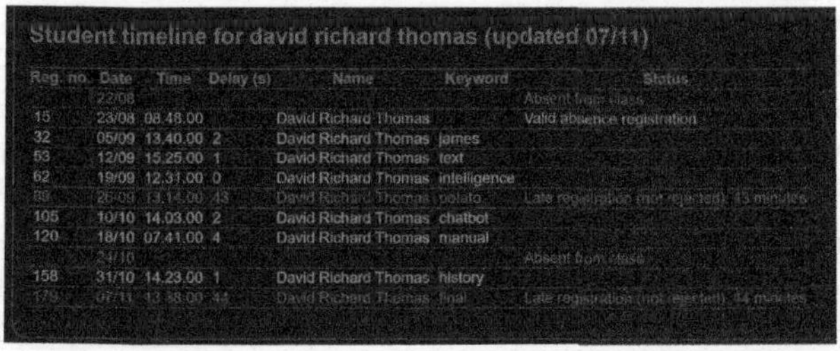
Student timeline for david richard thomas (updated 07/11)

Reg. no.	Date	Time	Delay (s)	Name	Keyword	Status
	22/08					Absent from class
15	23/08	08.48.00		David Richard Thomas		Valid absence registration
32	05/09	13.40.00	2	David Richard Thomas	james	
53	12/09	15.25.00	1	David Richard Thomas	text	
62	19/09	12.31.00	0	David Richard Thomas	intelligence	
89	26/09	13.14.00	43	David Richard Thomas	potato	Late registration (not rejected): 43 minutes
105	10/10	14.03.00	2	David Richard Thomas	chatbot	
120	18/10	07.41.00	4	David Richard Thomas	manual	
	24/10					Absent from class
158	31/10	14.23.00	1	David Richard Thomas	history	
179	07/11	13.38.00	44	David Richard Thomas	final	Late registration (not rejected): 44 minutes

Fig. 2. Detailed registration timeline for individual students (pseudonym).

4.1 Implementation Details

The analysis module was written in vanilla JavaScript. The first step of the analysis involved establishing the probable class dates. This was done by creating a histogram based on all the registered dates. All dates with a frequency above a threshold of 10% were considered a valid class date. This threshold ensured that certain invalid registrations and test registrations are omitted. The delay of each valid registration was computed as a proxy measure of reliability.

To identify the correct keyword used in class on a given date, a frequency histogram was created for all the keywords entered on that given date. The most frequently occurring keyword was recorded as the official keyword for that date. To compensate for potentially incorrectly spelled keywords, the registrations on the given date were checked using approximate string (dice threshold of 0.5).

The attendance tool needed to be robust to name variations and errors. First, all the name variations were identified and sorted in decreasing order according to length. Each name variation was compared to the already processed name variations using approximate string matching. If there were matches above a similarity threshold of 0.8, the current name variation was added as a variant of the one with the highest match. If there were no matches, the current name was established as a new unique name. This approach ensured that the shorter name variations were associated with the longest variation.

Besides compensating for spelling errors and name variations, a check was also performed to see if any participants accidentally swapped the input fields, i.e., entered the keyword into the name field and the name into the keyword field.

5 Results

5.1 Iteration 1: Summative Analysis

One goal of the first iteration was to avoid handwritten sheets of paper that are easily lost. The online form was deployed throughout the semester at a suitable time during each class. We attempted to avoid registering at the very beginning or at the end of the class as some students would arrive late or leave early due to valid responsibilities. We found it practical to conduct the registration in the transition between different activities. On occasions when the instructors forgot to issue the code, the students reminded the instructors. Many students used the learning management system app on their smartphones to register attendance.

The electronic registrations opened the possibility of attendance analysis. Therefore, a simple Java application was written to analyze the exported registration spreadsheets. The implementation was informed by the following observations:

First, several students registered their names inconsistently, incompletely, and/or erroneously. Examples included varying name order (family name first, family name last), only first names, short forms of their first names, nicknames, just family names, unofficial family names, different name parts on different occasions, varying use of spaces, hyphens, and commas, and/or misspellings of their names. One person used seven different variations of his name. This student's name comprised four parts appearing in different orders with varying omissions. A few students misheard or misspelt the keywords. Example variations included "oracle" transcribed as "oracel" (misspelling), "praise" as "price", "raise" as "rice", "eternal" was transcribed as "iteral" (mishearing). Several students inserted a space at the end of the keyword, such as "might". A handful of students used the keyword field to communicate explanatory messages, such as, "I haven't shown up to class, because I was sick" and "perhaps mistaken on the last submission". Next, the name and keyword were erroneously swapped on three occasions. Finally, some students registered much later than the time of registration, some even on a different day.

A fraction of the students regularly contacted the course instructor regarding their attendance. Despite formal descriptions of the attendance requirements, several students expressed uncertainty about what constituted valid attendance. Moreover, several students queried about the status of their accumulated attendance, and others wanted to explain reasons for not attending and obtain concessions. It was not possible to address student queries about attendance during the semester since the analysis was conducted on the collected registrations after the teaching had finished.

This iteration confirmed that attendance analysis reports could be used to successfully identify students that satisfied the minimum attendance requirements, those that did not, and students on the borderline. The consequent communication with a couple of students revealed that they were seemingly unaware of the formal attendance requirements. Moreover, the automatic detection of class dates also eliminated the need for a teacher to keep track of classes, cancelled classes, and moved classes.

5.2 Iteration 2: Formative Feedback Through Timely Updates

The goal of the second iteration was to achieve timely attendance updates. Our initial idea involved a server-based concept. We implemented a simple server-based prototype which would send aggregated analysis reports to the teacher once a week via email.

The weekly attendance reports were perceived as convenient. The teacher was able to answer students' queries during the semester. It seems that the electronic attendance registration scheme led to more requests as students may expect electronically collected information to be timely processed. Consequently, there was a noticeable increase in student-teacher correspondence related to absences and requests for exemptions, most notably due to medical reasons, especially COVID-19 infections during 2021. The teacher had to handle several such requests nearly every week.

Consequently, a simple exemption mechanism was implemented allowing the teacher to manually grant exemptions upon request. This was achieved by the teacher registering the student manually in the form using a passphrase only known to the teacher (e.g., "exepmt2024"). The analysis script was adjusted to compensate for these registrations. This simple addition greatly reduced the load on the teacher as there was no need to administer dedicated exemption lists.

After receiving automatically generated attendance reports after each class for nearly an entire semester, it became obvious that two parts of the report were particularly useful, i.e., the overall attendance statistics and the list of the five last attendance registrations. In several instances the last five attendance registrations for a class revealed anomalies used to engage in dialogue with the respective students.

5.3 Iteration 3: Local Analysis in the Browser

The server application was replaced with a client-side analysis application. The application ran locally in the browser where the teacher loads a spreadsheet for analysis.

In the bachelor class, the students were asked to use a unique first name instead of their full name to increase the students' privacy. We defined a first name as part of a personal name that distinguishes each student from the other students in class. The test showed that most students followed this advice, but some students still used their full names. Some students also used different names at different times which led to some misidentifications. These had to be manually resolved by the instructor. We concluded that simply using a first name is not practical in a large class.

For the master class, the teacher published an updated attendance list every week in the learning management system. A consequence of publishing the attendance statistics to the students was that students would contact the instructor to query about missing registrations. The students expressed satisfaction with having access to this report.

With just 20 students, the teacher also noticed that some students had registered although not being present in class. These students were also the last to register. Some were a couple of hours late or a minimum of 30 min late, and in some cases a few days late. It seemed some of the students shared the code or registered their fellow students on their behalf. Four cases of absentees registering attendance were uncovered. The late registrations provided the instructor with a basis for establishing a dialogue with these students with the objective of understanding their situation and explaining expectations and formalities. Several of the "false" registrations were justifiable. For instance, one student reported being ill but did not know the expected procedure of contacting the instructor directly to get a valid attendance exemption. Instead, the student asked a fellow student for the code so as not to bother the teacher.

Moreover, a traditional roll call was conducted as a random spot check. The signal effect of the roll call had a seemingly preventive effect on attendance and ghost registrations. On the downside, the teacher had to manually register the students.

To facilitate the discussion with individual students, an additional view was implemented which lists all registrations rejected along with the reason for the rejection. However, this global view was later replaced with an individual timeline view with information more relevant for a specific student. This timeline shows the chronological order of annotated student registrations. The timeline overview allowed issues to be quickly resolved.

One some occasions the teacher was late in publishing the updated attendance summary in the learning management system. In these cases, the teacher would receive emails from students reminding the teacher to update the list. Several of the students admitted that they used the list to see how many classes they could miss without getting below the minimum limit due to their family or work-related obligations.

5.4 Iteration 4: Relevant Aggregations

In the revised version of the analysis tool, a view showing all the registration delays for all the students across all classes was replaced with a histogram view only showing the students with late registrations. An aggregated summary proved easier to interpret than a view with all the information. The aggregated registration delay view helped reveal temporal attendance patterns and potential ghost registrations. This view proved particularly useful in the bachelor class due to its large size. Partial roll calls were conducted in-class only for the students appearing on top of this list. Hence, time was saved, not having to call the entire class.

Weekly status updates were published in both courses. The teachers noticed an increased amount of communication with students throughout the semester regarding missing attendances and requests for exemptions. A positive effect was that this communication was conducted during the course instead of at the end.

5.5 General Observations

We observed several positive effects of publishing the attendance lists during the course. Several students contacted the teachers to resolve misunderstandings during the semester. Moreover, there were no attendance enquiries after the end of teaching. Further, the students became seemingly more aware of the attendance requirements. In contrast, leaving the attendance tally towards the end of the semester led to a burst in enquires as the low attendance counts seemingly came as a surprise to several students.

The updated attendance list also led to fewer name variations. This is documented in Fig. 3 showing the ratio of unique name registrations per student for the six courses. Without published lists there were close to three name variations per student, while these ratios were nearly halved with lists. It seems that the regularly published list helped students register their names more consistently by choosing the name variation already appearing on the list. Several students erroneously entered their email address or password instead of the in-class keyword.

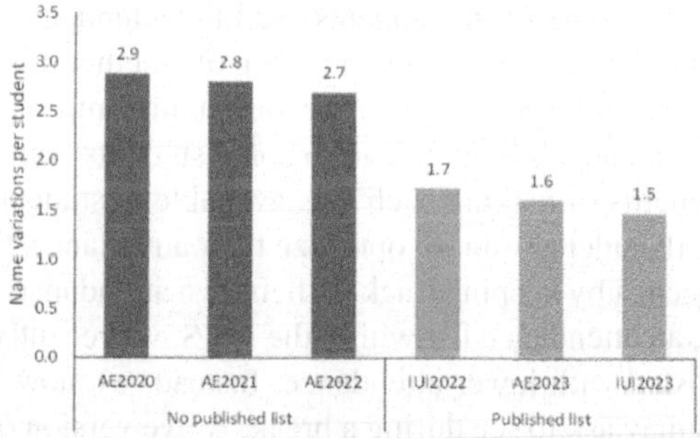

Fig. 3. Name variations per student without published lists (dark grey) and with published lists (light grey).

None of the students raised any concerns or reservations regarding the attendance registration approach. Although several students opposed the mandatory attendance requirements, none of the comments were critical regarding the registration scheme itself.

The in-class discussion of the draft course evaluation report revealed valuable insights about the students' perception of the scheme. Several students commented that obligatory attendance should be abolished. However, the discussion revealed that several students argued in favor of keeping the scheme as it had a positive effect on attendance. In a course where students present papers to their peers and discuss the results, attendance is important for the motivation of the students presenting. Without the attendance requirements, these students expressed that the class would be too sparse to function effectively and foster meaningful discussions.

6 Conclusion

We presented experiences with a pragmatic scheme for registering and managing class attendance. Experiences with the tool over a period of four years were documented herein of which most are positive. From the instructors' perspective, it was straightforward to run the scheme. The tool successfully detected the actual class times, holidays, and cancellations. Some students also registered late for the course, others dropped out in the middle of the semester, and the dynamic nature of the tools meant that no specific action needed to be taken for students who enrolled late or aborted their studies.

One obvious criticism of the proposed approach is that students can easily circumvent the scheme. Without random spot checks a student may simply register their absent friends. Such cases can be difficult to detect. One may speculate that most students first think about themselves and ensure that their own attendance is registered. Sharing a code on request is probably perceived as less problematic and burdensome than actively registering for someone else. One possible remedy is to utilize a student authentication mechanism. If a student is logged into a learning management system, the identity of the registrant could be automatically recorded.

The observation that some of the students used the attendance statistics to balance their attendance with obligations raises the question of whether updated attendance lists may lead to reduced attendance (close to the minimum limit as opposed to 100%). Although updated attendance lists may lead to some students "optimizing" their attendance, the overall benefits of making such lists available to students may outweigh the drawbacks. Besides, if students want to optimize their attendance, they can easily do so without the attendance list by keeping track of their own attendance. Despite the positive effects of publishing an attendance list within the LMS, we recently abolished this idea to protect students listed with lower attendance. Instead, we now bring a paper list to class which students may ask to see during a break. A live version of the analysis tool is available at https://github.com/frode-sandnes/ATTENDANCE.

References

1. Moores, E., Birdi, G.K., Higson, H.E.: Determinants of university students' attendance. Educ. Res. **61**(4), 371–387 (2019)
2. O'Sullivan, S., McMahon, L., et al.: "I did not miss any, only when i had a valid reason" accounting for absences from sociology classes. Teach. Sociol. **43**(1), 15–26 (2015)

3. Bati, A.H., Mandiracioglu, A., Orgun, F., Govsa, F.: Why do students miss lectures? A study of lecture attendance amongst students of health science. Nurse Educ. Today **33**(6), 596–601 (2013)
4. Leufer, T., Cleary-Holdforth, J.: Reflections on the experience of mandating lecture attendance in one school of nursing in the Republic of Ireland. AISHE-J **2**(1), (2010)
5. Macfarlane, B.: The surveillance of learning: a critical analysis of university attendance policies. High. Educ. Q. **67**(4), 358–373 (2013)
6. Ishak, C., Neustaedter, C., Hawkins, D., Procyk, J., Massimi, M.: Human proxies for remote university classroom attendance. In: Proceedings of the CHI 2016, pp. 931–943, ACM (2016)
7. Mörtsell, S.: Sociomaterial explorations of attendance practices in 'schooling without schools.' Learn. Media Technol. **47**(4), 512–523 (2022)
8. Menne, J.W., Hannum, T.E., Klingensmith, J.E., Nord, D.: Use of taped lectures to replace class attendance. AV Commun. Rev. **17**(1), 42–46 (1969)
9. Traphagan, T., Kucsera, J.V., Kishi, K.: Impact of class lecture webcasting on attendance and learning. Educ. Technol. Res. Dev. **58**(1), 19–37 (2010)
10. Garcia, E., Rivera, H., Ponder, N., et al.: Efficient and cost-effective class attendance management with a smartphone-based system. In: Proceedings of the SITE 2017, pp. 965–972, AACE (2017)
11. Bhalla, V., Singla, T., Gahlot, A., Gupta, V.: Bluetooth based attendance management system. IJEIT **3**(1), 227–233 (2013)
12. Arulogun, O.T., Olatunbosun, A., Fakolujo, O.A., Olaniyi, O.M.: RFID-based students attendance management system. IJSER **4**(2), 1–9 (2013)
13. Mazumdar, A.T.I., JosephNg, P.S., Eaw, H.C., Phan, K.Y., Yeck, Y.P.: JomNFCsignIn: seamlessly register your class attendance. In: Al-Emran, M., Al-Sharafi, M.A., Al-Kabi, M.N., Shaalan, K. (eds.) Proceedings of International Conference on Emerging Technologies and Intelligent Systems: ICETIS 2021 (Volume 1), pp. 207–216. Springer International Publishing, Cham (2022). https://doi.org/10.1007/978-3-030-82616-1_19
14. Talip, B.A., Zulkifli, M.Z.: Mobile attendance system using QR codes technology. JTeC **3**(1), 1–3 (2018)
15. Chintalapati, S., Raghunadh, M.V.: Automated attendance management system based on face recognition algorithms. In: IEEE ICCIC 2013, pp. 1–5. IEEE (2013)
16. Kadry, S., Smaili, M.: Wireless attendance management system based on iris recognition. Sci. Res. Essays **5**(12), 1428–1435 (2013)
17. Shakil, M., Nandi, R.N.: Attendance management system for industrial worker using finger print scanner. GJCST **13**(6), 17–22 (2013)
18. Noor, S.A.M., Zaini, N., Latip, M.F.A., Hamzah, N.: Android-based attendance management system. In: Proceedings of the ICSPC 2015, pp. 118–122. IEEE (2015)
19. Guevarra, B.S., Corpuz, F.T.: Development of a class attendance monitoring system using barcode with SMS notification. SFS **10**(1S), 3518–3525 (2023)

Bridging the Digital Divide: User Interface Design Principles for Enhancing Elderly Learners' Engagement with Educational Technology

Wanwisa Wannapipat(✉) and Wanpen Wiersma

International College, Khon Kaen University, 123 Mitraphap Road, Mueang, Khon Kaen 40002, Thailand
wanwwa@kku.ac.th

Abstract. This examines how user interface (UI) design affects elderly users' engagement with educational technology. Through mixed-methods research with adults aged 65–80 (n = 300), we identified critical UI elements that significantly impact learning outcomes. Statistical analysis revealed that font size, navigation clarity, and information organization were strong predictors of learning outcomes (R2 = 0.65, $p < 0.001$), with digital literacy being the most influential factor ($\beta = 0.42$, $p < 0.001$). Factor analysis identified three key dimensions of UI experience: Usability, Visual Design, and Accessibility, accounting for 70% of variance. Qualitative data uncovered themes of cognitive overload and "design disqualification," where participants felt excluded by interfaces created primarily for younger users. These findings demonstrate the direct relationship between interface accessibility and learning opportunities for older adults. We propose evidence-based design guidelines for age-inclusive digital environments that promote digital literacy and lifelong learning, with significant implications for technology developers, educators, and policymakers seeking to create more inclusive learning environments.

Keywords: Andragogy · Geragogy · User interface design · Elderly users · Digital literacy · Educational technology · Social media

1 Background of Study

Educational technology is crucial in modern learning, yet older adults face significant barriers. Approximately 46% of seniors engage with social media, but many struggle with interfaces designed for younger users. These challenges are exacerbated by age-related physiological and cognitive changes. Complicated digital environments hinder their full participation in educational activities and affect their social connectivity and well-being. These issues highlight the need for equitable access to education in an aging society. Neglecting diverse user abilities in technology marginalizes certain populations, undermining educational effectiveness. This research aims to refine user interface designs for

W.-S. Wang et al. (Eds.): ICITL 2025, LNCS 15913, pp. 284–293, 2026.
https://doi.org/10.1007/978-3-031-98185-2_30

elderly learners, addressing their specific challenges with educational technology. By doing so, it seeks to provide evidence-based recommendations for more inclusive digital environments. Effective design can foster self-directed learning and improve engagement with educational content. The study's significance lies in its potential to create empowering digital spaces for seniors, ultimately advocating for digital inclusion and educational equity. This study is significant as it explores the user interface challenges older adults face on social media. Understanding these experiences is essential for promoting digital inclusion and communication skills among seniors. As the global demographic shifts toward older populations, it is critical that technology accommodates their diverse needs to enhance social connectivity and emotional health. This research highlights barriers to engagement and supports the development of age-friendly digital environments.

2 Research Purposes and Questions

2 Research Questions comprises 1) How do UI elements affect informal learning among elderly users? and *2)* Which pedagogical strategies in digital interfaces best support older adults' digital literacy? Hence, research aims to 1) Assess how current UI designs affect elderly individuals' self-directed learning 2) Identify UI components that hinder effective engagement 3) Evaluate the effectiveness of various pedagogical approaches in digital interfaces and 4) Develop evidence-based design principles that improve educational experiences for elderly users.

3 Literature Review

3.1 Theoretical Frameworks in Educational Technology for Elderly Users

Three interrelated theoretical frameworks guide the design of educational technology for senior learners: andragogy, geragogy, and research on technology-enhanced learning. *1) Andragogy* [1] asserts that adult learners exhibit self-direction, intrinsic motivation, and leverage their life experiences when acquiring new knowledge. Consequently, effective adult education should promote autonomy, establish clear relevance, and link content to practical applications in the real world [2]. Additionally, *2) Geragogy* builds upon these concepts by focusing on the unique learning requirements of older individuals. Findsen and Formosa [3] stress that educational strategies for seniors must consider cognitive and physical transformations, such as reduced working memory and slower information processing speeds. Advocates for content simplification and reduction of cognitive load within interfaces, ensuring accessibility for individuals with visual and motor challenges [4] and *3) Elderly Learners and Technology-Enhanced Learning.* Research on Technology-Enhanced Learning for Older Users indicates significant variability in the technical competencies of older adults [5]. Hargittai's [6] notion of the "second digital divide" underscores how differences in technological proficiency influence digital participation among seniors. To effectively engage this demographic, digital learning platforms must offer clear guidance, practical applicability, social support, and adhere to high accessibility standards [7].

3.2 UI Design Elements and Cognitive Challenges

The design of the user interface plays a critical role in shaping user experience and enhancing task performance [8], especially for older adults who encounter unique age-related difficulties. These challenges encompass: *1) Visual impairments*: Diminished visual acuity hampers the ability to read small text or differentiate between low-contrast elements [5] 2) *Motor limitations*: A decline in dexterity affects the ability to interact precisely with touchscreens and small buttons and 3) *Cognitive changes*: Possible declines in working memory and slower processing speed can impede navigation through intricate interfaces [9]. Design principles grounded in research for older adults include larger font sizes (at least 16pt) and high-contrast imagery (minimum ratio of 4.5:1). Expanded, touch-friendly interactive components. Simplified navigation with explicit feedback mechanisms. Decreased cognitive load via intuitive and minimalist design. Elderly individuals also encounter specific cognitive obstacles when engaging with social media platforms, particularly in evaluating content validity and adjusting to complex, rapidly evolving interfaces. Concerns regarding privacy and security pose substantial emotional obstacles, with apprehensions about data misuse preventing full participation in digital spaces [10].

3.3 Pedagogical Strategies and Research Gaps

Robust educational methodologies tailored for older learners encompass task decomposition, multimodal content dissemination, and enhanced peer support networks [11]. The design of interfaces significantly influences pedagogical success, with evidence indicating that 68% of users aged 65 and above have disengaged from educational activities on platforms due to complex interface designs. Notable research deficiencies remain in this area: a scarcity of investigations into the impact of specific UI elements on the digital literacy of the elderly, a lack of application of andragogical and geragogical frameworks within digital contexts, insufficient accessibility criteria for older learners engaging with social media platforms, an underdeveloped comprehension of how interface design promotes social interaction and lifelong learning, and a limited number of evidence-based initiatives aimed at addressing the "second digital divide".

4 Research Methodology

This study employed a mixed methods approach, combining quantitative surveys and qualitative interviews for comprehensive insights into older adults' social media use. A diverse sample of 300 participants aged 65 to 80 was recruited through stratified random sampling based on various demographics. Data Collection Methods: Phase 1- Quantitative (Survey): Participants completed a digital survey with adapted questions.

assessing usability, digital literacy, and demographics. Phase 2- Qualitative (Interviews & Groups): Selected participants engaged in interviews, think-aloud sessions, and focus groups for deeper exploration of their experiences. Data Analysis: Quantitative data was analyzed statistically, while qualitative data underwent thematic analysis to discern common challenges and experiences. Ethical approval was secured, ensuring informed consent and confidentiality, with support provided during data collection. This mixed methods design enabled a comprehensive understanding of usability and barriers faced by older adults on social media.

5 Research Findings and Results

Results are organized according to the research questions: identifying the primary UI challenges confronting elderly learners, determining which interface adaptations most improve digital literacy and task performance, and elucidating user experiences and preferences.

5.1 Participant Demographics

The study involved 300 respondents with a mean age of 72.3 years and a standard deviation of 7.5 years. The data demonstrates a frequency distribution across four distinct senior age classifications. The age group 65–69 includes 60 participants. The following category, 70–74, has the highest representation at 100 participants. The 75–79 age category consists of 80 individuals. Lastly, the 80–84 age group contains 60 participants, mirroring the count of the 65–69 age range.

5.2 Inferential Statistics

The analysis revealed significant relationships between UI design elements and learning outcomes for elderly users. ANOVA results confirmed that font size substantially impacts usability ($F(2, 297) = 12.5$, $p < 0.001$, $\eta 2 = 0.08$). Participants using 16-point font reported significantly higher usability ratings ($M = 4.5$, $SD = 0.6$) compared to those using 12-point ($M = 3.8$, $SD = 0.7$) or 10-point fonts ($M = 3.2$, $SD = 0.8$).

Multiple regression analysis identified digital literacy ($\beta = 0.42$, $p < 0.001$) and navigation clarity ($\beta = 0.31$, $p < 0.001$) as the strongest predictors of educational performance, collectively explaining 62% of the variance in outcomes ($R^2 = 0.62$, $p < 0.001$).

Correlation analysis demonstrated strong positive relationships between larger fonts and clear labels with higher digital literacy scores ($r = 0.62$ and $r = 0.55$, $p < 0.01$ respectively). Additionally, a moderate positive correlation between digital literacy and preferred font size ($r = 0.35$, $p < 0.01$) was observed.

Factor analysis categorized UI elements into two primary components: visual clarity and navigational efficiency, with visual clarity explaining the largest portion of variance (eigenvalue = 2.9). Gender differences were noted in overall satisfaction ratings, with female participants reporting slightly higher satisfaction ($M = 4.3$, $SD = 0.7$) than males ($M = 4.1$, $SD = 0.8$); $t(298) = 2.1$, $p = 0.035$, $d = 0.25$.

5.3 Analysis of Variance (ANOVA)

To assess mean differences in usability, cognitive load, and educational outcomes across demographics, the following analysis was conducted. A One-Way ANOVA was performed on perceived usability within four age groups (60–65, 66–70, 71–75, 76–80).

The findings indicated a significant age effect on usability ($F(3, 296) = 8.21$, $p < 0.001$, $\eta 2 = 0.08$). Post hoc tests using Tukey's HSD revealed that the 60–65 age group ($M = 4.3$, $SD = 0.6$) had significantly better usability compared to the 76–80 group ($M = 3.3$, $SD = 0.8$). Furthermore, the 66–70 group ($M = 4.0$, $SD = 0.7$) also showed significantly better usability compared to the 76–80 cohort. No significant differences were found between the 60–65 and 66–70 groups, or between the 71–75 ($M = 3.7$, $SD = 0.7$) and 76–80 groups (Table 1).

Table 1. Differences in perceived usability, cognitive load, and educational outcomes

Age Group	N	Mean (M)	S.D	Significant Differences (Tukey's HSD)
60–65	75	4.3	0.6	Enhanced usability over 76–80
66–70	75	4	0.7	Enhanced usability over 76–80
71–75	75	3.7	0.7	None
76–80	75	3.3	0.8	Lower usability compared to 60–65, 66–70

5.4 Multiple Regression Analysis

Two multiple regression analyses was used to examine factors affecting educational outcomes and user satisfaction in digital learning environments for older adults.

Regression 1: Predicting Learning Outcomes
Our first analysis revealed that UI components and digital literacy significantly predicted learning outcomes, explaining 65% of the variance ($R2 = 0.65$, $p < 0.001$). Digital literacy emerged as the strongest predictor ($\beta = 0.40$, $p < 0.001$), followed by navigation clarity ($\beta = 0.30$, $p < 0.001$), font size ($\beta = 0.20$, $p < 0.001$), and information layout ($\beta = 0.15$, $p = 0.005$) (Table 2).

Table 2. Connections of Learning outcomes to user interface elements and digital literacy levels.

User interface components	Results	Learning outcomes
Font Size	$\beta = 0.20$, $p < 0.001$	An increase in font size correlates with improved learning outcomes)
Navigation Clarity	$\beta = 0.30$, $p < 0.001$	Enhanced clarity in navigation correlates with improved learning outcomes
Information Layout	$\beta = 0.15$, $p = 0.005$	A superior layout is correlated with improved learning outcomes
Digital Literacy	$\beta = 0.40$, $p < 0.001$	Elevated levels of digital literacy correlate with improved learning outcomes

Regression 2: Predicting User Satisfaction The analysis found factors impacting user satisfaction, with UI elements and digital literacy explaining 50% of variance ($R2 = 0.50$,

$p < 0.001$). Visual appeal had the greatest impact ($\beta = 0.40$, $p < 0.001$), followed by navigation clarity ($\beta = 0.20$, $p < 0.001$), digital literacy ($\beta = 0.15$, $p = 0.01$), and font size ($\beta = 0.10$, $p = 0.02$). These results underscore the significance of UI design and digital literacy in improving learning experiences for older adults in digital settings.

5.5 Correlation Analysis

Pearson correlation analysis was employed to investigate the relationships between user interface (UI) components and the digital literacy levels of participants. This analysis identified several significant associations: A moderate positive correlation was found between the preferred font size and digital literacy ($r = 0.42$, $p < 0.001$), indicating that individuals with enhanced digital skills are inclined to choose larger font styles. Clarity of navigation indicated a strong positive correlation with digital literacy ($r = 0.71$, $p < 0.001$), suggesting that participants with advanced digital capabilities viewed navigation systems as more user-friendly. The arrangement of information revealed no significant correlation with digital literacy ($r = 0.08$, $p = 0.20$), implying that organizational preferences were stable across varying levels of digital competence. Visual appeal showed a weak yet statistically significant positive correlation with digital literacy ($r = 0.20$, $p = 0.01$), demonstrating that digitally adept participants rated aesthetic features somewhat more favorably. These results underscore the diverse effects of digital literacy on the perception of UI elements, with the most substantial impact observed on the evaluation of navigation clarity and preferences for font size, while perceptions of information layout remain uniform across all levels of digital proficiency.

5.6 Factor Analysis

Eight pivotal variables associated with user interface design were established for reliable assessment: 1) Font Size: Quantified in points to enhance text visibility 2) Navigation Clarity: Assessed via user surveys regarding interface comprehension 3) Information Layout: Evaluated on its organization to facilitate improved accessibility 4) Visual Appeal: Measured through user feedback on aesthetic elements influencing engagement 5) Ease of Use: Investigated through surveys targeting learnability and intuitive interaction 6) Response Time: Recorded in milliseconds or ratings reflecting user experience timing 7) Accessibility: Scrutinized for the adaptation to elderly users 8) Clarity and Ease of Reading Information: Evaluated through surveys focusing on text understanding. Furthermore, the eight variables underwent meticulous evaluation concerning a digital learning interface tailored for seniors, establishing a robust framework for assessing usability and overall satisfaction. While a comprehensive factor analysis was performed on the eight variables to reveal underlying structures and condense dimensions while preserving critical design information. Then, the analysis revealed three primary latent factors from the eight components, streamlining data architecture and enhancing interpretability, with factor loadings presented in Table 3 elucidating variable interrelation.

Factor analysis was utilized to reduce the dimensionality of UI elements. Three main factors were identified: 'Usability', 'Visual Design', and 'Accessibility'. The factor loadings indicate that 'Usability' correlates strongly with navigation clarity, information

Table 3. Factors to each UI Element

UI Element	Factor 1: Usability	Factor 2: Visual Design	Factor 3: Accessibility
Font Size	0.1	0.2	0.8
Navigation Clarity	0.8	0.1	0.3
Information Layout	0.7	0.2	0.2
Visual Appeal	0.2	0.8	0.1
Ease of Use	0.9	0.3	0.4
Response Time	0.4	0.2	−0.1
Accessibility	0.3	0.1	0.9
Clarity and Ease of Reading Information	0.5	0.6	0.2

layout, and ease of use; 'Visual Design' is closely linked to visual appeal, clarity, and readability; and 'Accessibility' pertains to font size and overall accessibility. Together, these factors accounted for 70% of the total variance in UI elements.

5.7 Semi-structured Interviews

During phase 2, interviews were performed with a diverse group of 300 participants who chosen to capture various demographics and digital literacy levels. Interviews featured open-ended questions on UI experiences and strategies for overcoming challenges, recorded for analysis. Thematic analysis was applied to identify themes through coding and refinement, supported by participant quotes to assess how UI design affects elderly learners' engagement, revealing key predictors and challenges emphasizing the need for age-inclusive design to enhance digital literacy for older adults.

There are 4 Thematic Analysis Results. *Theme 1: Frustration and Cognitive Overload.* Participants expressed frustration and cognitive overload from complex interfaces, leading to anxiety and stress. "It induces a sense of inadequacy when I am unable to ascertain how to perform a task. I am apprehensive about committing errors." (72-year-old woman). *Theme 2: Social Disconnection Due to UI Barriers.* Participants describe how user interface challenges hinder their social interactions with family and friends, resulting in feelings of isolation. "I long to view my grandchildren's photographs on Facebook, yet the interface is overly complex. I perceive that I am missing valuable experiences." (75-year-old woman). *Theme 3: Strategies for Coping with Inaccessible Design.* UI challenges hinder social interactions, causing feelings of isolation among participants. "I consistently require my daughter to demonstrate how to perform tasks. I would be utterly lost in her absence." (70-year-old woman). *Theme 4: Desire for Simplified and Customizable Interfaces.* Customizable interfaces with features like larger fonts and voice control. "It would significantly enhance usability if I could simply articulate commands to it." (80-year-old man).

5.8 Think-Aloud Protocols

The think-aloud protocols identified significant cognitive and usability obstacles encountered by participants. *Theme-Navigation as a Cognitive* Bottleneck. Participants experienced difficulties with intricate menu structures, particularly in locating specific settings or features, leading to confusion and frustration, especially among those with lower digital literacy. "Where do I even go to change this? I thought it would be here, but now I'm completely lost." *Theme-Information Overload and Processing Challenges.* Participants frequently felt overwhelmed by the screen's information density, struggling to prioritize relevant content and retain what they had read, particularly due to small fonts and disorganized layouts. "There's just so much stuff here. I don't know where to look, and I can't remember what I just read."

5.9 Focus Group Analysis

In the qualitative phase, 42 elderly social media users were divided into six focus groups. This approach aimed to capture diverse experiences among older users addressing those with prior UI difficulties. Guided discussions explored participants' social media experiences and UI feedback. Sessions were recorded and transcribed to analyze group dynamics and emotional responses. Thematic analysis identified two main themes. The first theme revealed feelings of exclusion among older users due to social media design favoring younger individuals. The second theme illustrated the challenges elderly users faced in maintaining social connections due to UI barriers. Many reported that complex navigation hindered social media benefits, leading to feature avoidance. Combining think-aloud methods with focus group results provided insights into elderly users' experiences and navigation challenges. Information overload was identified as a key issue for low digital literacy users, highlighting its emotional effects.

6 Conclusion and Discussion

This research undertook an examination of the influence exerted by user interface design principles on the engagement levels of elderly learners with educational technology. The outcomes of investigation illuminate significant correlations between particular design features and engagement metrics, bearing crucial implications for the formulation of digital learning environments that are tailored to the needs of older individuals. The findings affirm that digital learning platforms possess the potential to markedly enhance the educational experiences of elderly learners when crafted with meticulous attention to age-related requirements. The pronounced feeling towards text legibility ($M = 4.67$, $SD = 0.48$) is congruent with the findings of Czaja and Lee [13] concerning age-related visual deterioration, while also expanding comprehension of the specific ways in which these alterations affect engagement with educational technology. The notable correlation between age and preferences for font size ($r = 0.73$, $p < 0.001$) offers empirical justification for the adoption of graduated design strategies as opposed to uniform "senior-friendly" guidelines. The insights related to the simplicity of navigation corroborate prior research conducted by Barnard et al. [12], while also yielding a significant contribution:

the pronounced preference for linear progression (78%) over hierarchical organization (22%) contests conventional design practices of educational platforms that typically utilize intricate hierarchical frameworks. The substantial enhancement in time-on-task metrics ($t(76) = 4.28$, $p < 0.001$) when employing linear navigation indicates that the simplification of interfaces constitutes not merely a matter of preference but a meaningful augmentation of learning efficacy. The qualitative findings regarding the apprehension of irreversible errors (identified by 87% of interviewees) expand the theoretical construct of technology anxiety in older adults as previously articulated by Vroman et al. [14]. Implementation of explicit error recovery mechanisms directly addresses this issue and furnishes concrete design recommendations that have been deficient in prior research. The documented increase in self-reported confidence (from 2.8 to 4.1 on a 5-point scale) illustrates that judicious interface design can alleviate psychological barriers to technology adoption among elderly learners. The notable enhancements in task completion rates (a 34% increase) and the duration spent engaging with educational content (from $M = 14.2$ to $M = 23.7$ min) present compelling evidence that suitable interface design is not merely an issue of accessibility, but rather a fundamental determinant of educational effectiveness for elderly demographics. These findings establish a connection between previously isolated research domains in geragogy [3] and interface design [15], thereby illustrating their critical interdependence within digital learning environments.

This study offers guidelines for educational tech developers targeting older adults. Adaptive text sizing is crucial, with minimum font sizes of 16pt for users over 75 and 14pt for those aged 65–74. Clear linear navigation pathways should be emphasized to lower cognitive load, resulting in improved navigation success. Effective error recovery mechanisms, including confirmations and reversible actions, are necessary to boost user confidence and alleviate technology anxiety. Ensuring a color contrast ratio of at least 7:1 is vital, significantly enhancing target identification speed. Simplifying terminology and providing context is essential, as many participants faced comprehension difficulties. As digital literacy is crucial for social interaction and education, findings address gaps in the literature and highlight the importance of interdisciplinary design.

Disclosure of Interests. The author declares that there are no competing interests or conflicts of interest related to the research presented in this paper. The research was conducted with adherence to ethical guidelines without any influence from external parties.

References

1. Knowles, M.S., Holton, E.F., Swanson, R.A.: The Adult Learner: The Definitive Classic in Adult Education and Human Resource Development. Routledge, New York (2015)
2. Merriam, S.B., Caffarella, R.S., Baumgartner, L.M.: Learning in Adulthood: A Comprehensive Guide. Jossey-Bass, San Francisco (2007)
3. Findsen, B., Formosa, M.: Lifelong Learning in Later Life: A Handbook on
4. Older Adult Learning. Sense Publishers, Rotterdam (2011)
5. Withnall, A.: Improving Learning in Later Life. Routledge, London (2010)
6. Fisk, A.D., Rogers, W.A., Charness, N., Czaja, S.J., Sharit, J.: Designing for Older Adults: Principles and Creative Human Factors Approaches. CRC Press, Boca Raton (2009)

7. Hargittai, E.: Second-level digital divide: differences in people's online skills. First Monday 7(4) (2002)
8. Czaja, S.J., et al.: Factors predicting the use of technology: findings from the center for research and education on aging and technology enhancement (CREATE). Psychol. Aging **21**(2), 333–352 (2006)
9. Stone, D., Jarrett, C., Woodroffe, M., Minocha, S.: User Interface Design and Evaluation. Morgan Kaufmann, San Francisco (2005)
10. Charness, N., Boot, W.R.: Aging and information technology use: potential and barriers. Curr. Dir. Psychol. Sci. **18**(5), 253–258 (2009)
11. Hargittai, E., Piper, A.M., Morris, M.R.: From internet access to internet skills: digital inequality among older adults. Univ. Access Inf. Soc. **18**(4), 881–890 (2018)
12. Nguyen, M.H., Gruber, J., Fuchs, J., Marler, W., Hunsaker, A., Hargittai, E.: Changes in digital communication during the COVID-19 global pandemic: Implications for digital inequality and future research. Soc. Media + Soc. 6(3) (2020)
13. Barnard, Y., Bradley, M.D., Hodgson, F., Lloyd, A.D.: Learning to use new technologies by older adults: perceived difficulties, experimentation behaviour and usability. Comput. Hum. Behav. **29**(4), 1715–1724 (2013)
14. Czaja, S.J., Lee, C.C.: The impact of aging on access to technology. Univ. Access Inf. Soc. **5**(4), 341–349 (2007)
15. Vroman, K.G., Arthanat, S., Lysack, C.: Who over 65 is online?" Older adults' dispositions toward information communication technology. Comput. Hum. Behav. **43**, 156–166 (2015)
16. Czaja, S.J., Sharit, J.: Designing Training and Instructional Programs for Older Adults. CRC Press, Boca Raton (2012)

VR/AR/MR/XR in Education

Evaluation of the Effectiveness of Integrating Virtual Reality with Goal-Based Scenario Learning Theory in Tree Risk Assessment

Bo-Yuan Cheng[1(✉)], Jan-Chang Chen[2], and Chia-Ching Lin[3]

[1] Languages Center, National Pingtung University of Science and Technology, Pingtung City, Taiwan
Oakley.cheng@mail.npust.edu.tw
[2] Department of Forestry, National Pingtung University of Science and Technology, Pingtung City, Taiwan
[3] Graduate Institute of Science Education and Environmental Education, National Kaohsiung Normal University, Kaohsiung City, Taiwan

Abstract. This study investigates integrating Virtual Reality (VR) technology with the Goal-Based Scenario (GBS) learning theory in tree risk assessment education. The aim was to enhance students' learning performance and understanding of Visual Tree Assessment (VTA) methods through a GBS-based SVVR Tree Risk Assessment Assisted Learning System (hereafter referred to as the SVVR-GBS system) that simulates real-world risk assessment scenarios. The research was conducted with forestry students at the University of Science and Technology, employing a quantitative approach to assess the SVVR-GBS system's impact on students' learning outcomes, cognitive load, and acceptance. Results showed that the SVVR-GBS system significantly improved students' learning performance while managing cognitive load effectively. Moreover, students demonstrated high acceptance of the SVVR-GBS system. The findings indicate that integrating VR and GBS in tree risk assessment education offers a promising approach to enhancing learning outcomes and engagement.

Keywords: Virtual Reality · Goal-Based Scenario · Tree Risk Assessment · Visual Tree Assessment · Cognitive Load · Learning Performance · Technology Acceptance

1 Introduction

Tree risk assessment is a fundamental component of arboricultural education [1]. However, traditional instructional methods are constrained by limited access to field scenarios, seasonal variability, and safety concerns, which hinder students' ability to engage in authentic and hands-on learning experiences. VR has emerged as a promising educational tool, offering immersive, interactive, and repeatable learning experiences that help overcome field-based instruction's spatial and temporal limitations. Prior research

W.-S. Wang et al. (Eds.): ICITL 2025, LNCS 15913, pp. 297–305, 2026.
https://doi.org/10.1007/978-3-031-98185-2_31

has demonstrated that VR can improve learners' comprehension, motivation, and overall learning outcomes by simulating authentic environments [2–4]. GBS learning, proposed initially by Schank [5], is a student-centered instructional framework emphasizing learning-by-doing through goal-driven tasks in realistic contexts. This approach has demonstrated positive outcomes across various disciplines [6–8]. While VR and GBS have shown promise in supporting active learning, their integration within forestry education, particularly in tree risk assessment, remains underexplored. To address this gap, this study proposes and evaluates the SVVR-GBS system, which integrates goal-based learning strategies within a virtual environment to simulate authentic tree risk scenarios. This research examines the SVVR-GBS system's effectiveness in improving students' learning performance, managing cognitive load, and promoting technology acceptance within a professional forestry education context. The objectives of this study are threefold:

1. To investigate the impact of the SVVR-GBS system on students' learning performance in the module.
2. To examine whether integrating the SVVR-GBS system into professional courses enhances students' willingness to use the SVVR-GBS system.
3. To analyze the effects of this learning system on students' cognitive load and further explore its moderating role in learning effectiveness.

2 Literature Review

2.1 Virtual Reality

Virtual Reality (VR) is a technology that creates a computer-generated three-dimensional environment, allowing users to immerse themselves in this space through VR headsets or displays and interact with virtual objects. Its key characteristics include immersion, interactivity, and imagination, which make VR a unique and powerful learning tool by enhancing user engagement and experiential learning [9]. Immersion refers to the sensation that users feel as if they are physically present in the virtual environment. This characteristic enhances learner engagement and motivation, making the learning experience more interactive and impactful [10]. Interactivity allows users to engage with objects within the virtual environment and enables real-time adjustments based on learner feedback. This dynamic interaction enhances the learning experience by providing personalized and adaptive learning opportunities [11]. Imagination refers to the ability of virtual environments to create scenarios that are impossible or difficult to achieve in the real world. This feature stimulates learners' creativity and enhances their problem-solving skills, allowing them to explore and experiment in novel and immersive contexts [12].

VR technology can concretize abstract concepts in education, helping students better understand and retain key knowledge points. By providing immersive and interactive experiences, VR enhances comprehension and facilitates deeper learning [13]. Additionally, VR technology can create safe, simulated environments, allowing students to conduct experiments and explore concepts without real-world risks. This capability is particularly beneficial for training in hazardous or complex scenarios, enabling experiential learning in a controlled setting [14]. Research has shown that this learning approach enhances learning interest, deepens understanding of the content, and improves adaptability in problem-solving situations.

2.2 Goal-Based Scenario Learning

Goal-Based Scenarios (GBSs) is a training methodology initially developed for human resource development to increase students' engagement in authentic scenarios and tasks. First proposed by Schank (1997) [5], GBSs emphasize goal-oriented instructional models designed using computer-based hypermedia. This approach follows a learning-by-doing framework, enabling learners to apply prior experiences to reason through and solve real-world problems. GBSs have been widely applied across various disciplines and skill domains. Educators can enhance student interest by incorporating GBSs into instruction and fostering an active learning environment. Three key features characterize the GBS framework:

a. Students have a clear goal to achieve.
b. A set of core skills requires repeated practice.
c. Learning occurs within a specific task environment.

According to Schank (1997), the design of GBSs consists of seven fundamental elements:1.)Learning goals; 2.)Learning tasks; 3.)Story scenarios; 4.)Roles; 5.)Scenario operations; 6.)Resources; 7.)Feedback. Numerous studies have demonstrated that GBSs increase student confidence [15] and enhance logical thinking skills [6].

2.3 Visual Tree Risk Assessment

Tree Risk Assessment (TRA) is a systematic process for identifying and analyzing tree-related risks to determine potential hazards before safety incidents occur. This process enables the early detection of risks and helps assess their location, extent, and potential impact on the surrounding environment [16]. Tree risk evaluation primarily focuses on the internal condition of branches and trunk structures and the distribution of root systems while also considering the risk targets associated with the tree [17].

Mattheck [1] introduced the Visual Tree Assessment (VTA) method to facilitate tree risk assessment, which integrates biological and mechanical principles. VTA is a comprehensive visual diagnostic approach that evaluates tree structure and growth conditions based on the anatomical composition, mechanical strength of wood, and biological theories. This method helps distinguish between unpredictable damage and foreseeable structural weaknesses, enabling a systematic tree stability assessment. According to Li [18], the VTA process consists of three key steps:

a. Visual Inspection: Diagnosing the tree's growth condition and structure, identifying signs of damage, decay, cavities, and other structural weaknesses that may indicate potential hazards.
b. Advanced Testing: If risk indicators are detected, diagnostic instruments are used to measure internal decay, cracks, and the overall structural integrity of the tree.

c. Risk Evaluation – Assessing and quantifying the degree of structural damage, then evaluating the tree's residual strength to determine necessary risk mitigation measures.

3 Research Methods

3.1 The SVVR-GBS System

This study integrates VR technology with the GBS learning approach to design a SVVR-GBS system. The SVVR-GBS system enables students to learn about tree morphology, degrees of structural damage, and assessment methods for different tree components within a virtual environment, providing a comprehensive understanding of VTA knowledge and techniques. A key feature of the SVVR-GBS system is the use of Unity3D, combined with 360-degree panoramic images and Meta Quest 2 VR headsets, to create an immersive learning environment that allows students to move around and view trees from different vantage points, enabling them to closely examine the overall structure and physical features of the tree from various positions (see Fig. 1 =a). The VTA assessment process is transformed into interactive learning tasks, and shows task items on UI guiding students through structured activities (see Fig. 1 =b). For example, Measuring tree height: Students use a virtual height-measuring device within the VR environment to practice tree height measurement, enhancing their understanding and application of tree risk assessment techniques. Identifying tree characteristics: Students can use the camera to recognize key tree features within the virtual environment (see Fig. 1 =c), applying their acquired knowledge in a simulated risk assessment scenario.

(a) Hotspot Navigation (b) Learning Tasks (c)Virtual Observation

Fig. 1. VR system operation screen: Demonstrates the interactive task interface for tree height measurement and characteristic identification in the SVVR-GBS system.

3.2 Experiment Participants

The participants of this study were forestry students from the Southern University of Science and Technology who had not previously taken a tree risk assessment course. A total of 20 participants were recruited, including 11 males and nine females. Among them, 9 were first-year undergraduate students, while 11 were second-year students. The experimental teaching activity was conducted during the first semester of the 113th academic year. The experimental procedure was divided into three main phases:

a. Pre-Experiment Phase: Before the experiment, each participant completed a pre-test (20 min) to assess learning motivation and learning performance.
b. Experimental Phase: Participants engaged in learning activities using the SVVR-GBS system for 60 min (see Fig. 2).
c. Post-Experiment Phase: Immediately after completing the learning activity, participants took a post-test (30 min) measuring learning motivation, cognitive load, and learning performance.

The collected data were analyzed to evaluate learning outcomes and determine the effectiveness of the experimental system in enhancing students' understanding of tree risk assessment.

Fig. 2. Students using VR equipment for learning.

3.3 Assessment Tools

(1) **Learning Achievement Test**

This study evaluates learning outcomes based on the VTA module from the Tree Health and Risk Assessment course in the University of Science and Technology's Forestry Department. Invite two experts from the University of Science and Technology Forestry Department to compile 50 questions. Each question is worth 2 points, with a total score of 100. A higher score indicates better learning performance. Sample questions include:

- "Which part of a tree is most commonly damaged during construction?"
- "Which of the following conditions increases the risk of tree failure?"

These questions assessed students' understanding of tree risk assessment principles and practical applications.

(2) **Cognitive Load Scale**

This study adopts the Cognitive Load Scale developed by Klepsch [19] to assess participants' perceived cognitive load after the experimental learning activity. The scale consists of three dimensions: intrinsic, extraneous, and germane cognitive load. The cognitive load scale includes eight items distributed as follows:

- Intrinsic cognitive load: 2 items
- Extraneous cognitive load: 3 items
- Germane cognitive load: 3 items

The Cronbach's alpha values for each dimension are 0.81, 0.86, and 0.67, respectively, indicating acceptable reliability. Responses are measured using a 7-point Likert scale, where 1 = strongly disagree and 7 = strongly agree. The total score is then summed for further analysis.

(3) **Technology Acceptance Model (TAM) Questionnaire**
This study adopts the TAM questionnaire, adapted from Hwang [20], to evaluate participants' acceptance of different assisted learning systems. The questionnaire consists of 13 items, categorized into two dimensions:

- Perceived usefulness of the learning system: 6 items
- Perceived ease of use of the learning system: 7 items

The Cronbach's alpha values for these dimensions are 0.95 and 0.94, respectively, indicating high reliability. Responses are measured using a 5-point Likert scale, where 1 = strongly disagree and 5 = strongly agree. The total scores are summed for further analysis.

4 Results and Discussion

4.1 Impact of the Learning System on Students' Learning Performance and Cognitive Load

This study employed the Wilcoxon signed-rank test to analyze the effects of the SVVR-GBS system on learning performance and cognitive load among 20 participants. The results are presented in Table 1. The findings indicate that post-test scores were significantly higher than pre-test scores regarding learning performance (Pre-test: M = 58.00, SD = 5.92; Post-test: M = 76.00, SD = 6.82). The difference reached statistical significance (W = 168.00, p < .001). These results suggest using the SVVR-GBS system to study tree risk assessment knowledge and skills can effectively enhance students' learning outcomes.

Table 1. Summary table of pre- and post-test learning performance.

	N	Pre-test		Post-test		W	effect size
		M	SD	M	SD		
learning performance	20	58.00	5.92	76.00	6.82	168.00^{***}	0.96

$^{*}p < .05$, $^{**}p < .01$, $^{***}p < .001$

To further examine the impact of the SVVR-GBS system on cognitive load, the results indicate that students experienced a moderate level of cognitive load during the learning process, suggesting that the SVVR-GBS system did not impose an excessive cognitive burden. A one-sample Wilcoxon signed-rank test against the neutral midpoint of 4 on a 7-point Likert scale was conducted to analyze each dimension of cognitive load. The findings are as follows:

- Germane Load ($M = 4.94$, $SD = 1.28$): Students perceived the SVVR-GBS system as highly effective in facilitating their understanding of tree health and risk assessment. The Wilcoxon signed-rank test revealed that germane load was significantly higher than the neutral midpoint ($W = 117.50$, $p = .011$), indicating that the learning content contributed meaningfully to knowledge construction and deeper comprehension.
- Intrinsic Load ($M = 3.61$, $SD = 0.97$): The instructional content (i.e., the structured modules on tree morphology and VTA risk indicators) and learning tasks presented an appropriate level of complexity. The test showed no significant difference from the neutral midpoint ($W = 17.50$, $p = .174$), suggesting that the SVVR-GBS system design was well-aligned with students' learning capabilities without causing excessive cognitive challenges.
- Extraneous Load ($M = 2.93$, $SD = 1.10$): The SVVR-GBS system interface and operations were intuitive and easy to use. The extraneous load was significantly lower than the neutral midpoint ($W = 9.00$, $p = .004$), indicating that unnecessary cognitive burden was effectively minimized, allowing students to concentrate on the learning content without distraction.

These findings suggest that the SVVR-GBS system effectively supports knowledge acquisition while maintaining an optimal cognitive load balance, ensuring an engaging and effective learning experience. The SVVR-GBS system design integrates the principles of Goal-Based Scenario (GBS) theory, incorporating a real-time feedback mechanism within the immersive learning environment. Key features include:

- Knowledge Integration and Self-Directed Exploration: Additional knowledge points are embedded in assessment tasks to encourage active learning and foster a deeper understanding of tree risk assessment.
- Testing Mechanism and Learning Feedback: The SVVR-GBS system includes a built-in assessment feature, enabling students to track their learning progress in real-time and enhancing learning outcomes.
- Application of Panoramic Imaging Technology: The use of 360-degree panoramic images provides realistic representations of trees, allowing students to concretely learn assessment methods and techniques while reducing extraneous cognitive load during the learning process.

These results demonstrate that integrating GBS theory into the SVVR-GBS system enhances students' learning performance and optimally manages cognitive load in immersive learning environments.

4.2 Questionnaire Results of the Learning System

The questionnaire results indicate that participants provided highly positive feedback regarding applying the SVVR-GBS system in tree risk assessment education.

Regarding the TAM, the SVVR-GBS system received a high overall score (M = 4.27). Specifically:

- Perceived Usefulness (M = 4.25, SD = 0.55): Students reported a positive user experience, indicating that the SVVR-GBS system effectively supported their learning of tree risk assessment knowledge. For example, The feedback mechanism embedded in the SVVR-GBS system allowed students to identify mistakes clearly and provide correct answers, enabling them to learn from errors.
- Perceived Ease of Use (M = 4.32, SD = 0.52): The SVVR-GBS system intuitive interface and consistent interaction design ensured that students could easily navigate and complete learning tasks. Once familiar with the operational process, students could independently complete their learning activities.

These findings suggest that the developed SVVR-GBS system was well-received by students, demonstrating both high usability and effectiveness in supporting tree risk assessment education.

5 Conclusion

This study provides empirical evidence supporting the effectiveness of VR in tree risk assessment learning and underscores the value of applying GBS strategies in immersive learning environments. The findings indicate that the SVVR-GBS system significantly improves students' learning performance while maintaining a manageable cognitive load. Students also reported high acceptance of the SVVR-GBS system, particularly appreciating its ease of use and perceived usefulness. Cognitive load analysis reveals a well-balanced instructional design that fosters effective learning without inducing cognitive overload.

Nevertheless, this study has certain limitations, including a small sample size and the need for system improvements such as enhanced image resolution and increased interactivity. Future research could examine how this GBS-based VR framework can be adapted to other domains, such as environmental science, civil engineering, or healthcare education, where risk evaluation, spatial reasoning, and safety procedures are essential learning goals.

Additionally, ethical considerations should be taken into account when simulating hazardous or high-risk environments to ensure learner well-being. Lastly, investigating how VR-based GBS instruction contributes to improved student learning performance—particularly in the development of practical skills and real-world knowledge application—represents a promising direction for further study.

References

1. Mattheck, C., Bethge, K., Erb, D.: Failure criteria for trees. Arboricult. J. **17**(2), 201–209 (1993). https://doi.org/10.1080/03071375.1993.9746963
2. Checa, D., Miguel-Alonso, I., Bustillo, A.: Immersive virtual-reality computer-assembly serious game to enhance autonomous learning. Virt. Real. **27**, 3301–3318 (2023). https://doi.org/10.1007/s10055-021-00607-1

3. Gorman, D., Hoermann, S., Lindeman, R.W., et al.: Using virtual reality to enhance food technology education. Int. J. Technol. Des. Educ. **32**, 1659–1677 (2022). https://doi.org/10.1007/s10798-021-09669-3
4. Parong, J., Mayer, R.E.: Learning science in immersive virtual reality. J. Educ. Psychol. **110**(6), 785–797 (2018). https://doi.org/10.1037/edu0000241
5. Schank, R.C.: Virtual Learning: A Revolutionary Approach to Building a Highly Skilled Workforce. McGraw-Hill (1997)
6. Kandin, E., Şendurur, E.: The effects of goal-based scenarios used for programming education of 5th graders. Interact. Learn. Environ. **31**(10), 6335–6355 (2022). https://doi.org/10.1080/10494820.2022.2036199
7. Foster, D.A.: FRA: Teaching financial accounting with a goal-based scenario. Intell. Syst. Account. Finan. Manag. **4**(3), 173–189 (1995). https://doi.org/10.1002/j.1099-1174.1995.tb00090.x
8. Schoenfeld-Tacher, R., Jones, L.L., Persichitte, K.A.: Differential effects of a multimedia goal-based scenario to teach introductory biochemistry—who benefits most? J. Sci. Educ. Technol. **10**(4), 305–317 (2001). https://doi.org/10.1023/A:1012291018178
9. Burdea, G.C., Coiffet, P.: Virtual Reality Technology. John Wiley & Sons, Hoboken (2003)
10. Witmer, B.G., Singer, M.J.: Measuring presence in virtual environments: a presence questionnaire. Pres. Teleoper. Virtual Environ. **7**(3), 225–240 (1998). https://doi.org/10.1162/105474698565686
11. Sherman, W.R., Craig, A.B.: Understanding Virtual Reality: Interface, Application, and Design. Morgan Kaufmann, Burlington (2018)
12. Herrera, G., Jordan, R., Vera, L.: Abstract concept and imagination teaching through Virtual Reality in people with Autism Spectrum Disorders. Technol. Disabil. **18**, 173–180 (2006). https://doi.org/10.3233/TAD-2006-18403
13. Wang, W.-S., Lee, H.-Y., Lin, C.-J., Li, P.-H., Huang, Y.-M., Wu, T.-T.: Enhancing students' learning outcomes in self-regulated virtual reality learning environment with learning aid mechanisms. Br. J. Edu. Technol. **56**, 366–387 (2025). https://doi.org/10.1111/bjet.13512
14. Singh, G., Mantri, A., Sharma, O., Kaur, R.: Virtual reality learning environment for enhancing electronics engineering laboratory experience. Comput. Appl. Eng. Educ. **29**(1), 229–243 (2021). https://doi.org/10.1002/cae.22333
15. Hsu, C.-Y.: Formative research on the goal based scenario model applied to computer delivery and simulation. J. Appl. Instruct. Des. (2011)
16. Smiley, E.T., Matheny, N., Lilly, S.: Tree risk assessment: a foundation. Arborist News **20**, 12–20 (2011)
17. Li, C., Weng, S., Lin, Y., Pang, R.: Advance on assessment of landscaping tree health and hazard. Guangdong Agric. Sci. **7**, 186–189 (2009)
18. Li, H., Zhang, X., Li, Z., Wen, J., Tan, X.: A review of research on tree risk assessment methods. Forests **13**(10), 1556 (2022). https://doi.org/10.3390/f13101556
19. Klepsch, M., Schmitz, F., Seufert, T.: Development and validation of two instruments measuring intrinsic, extraneous, and germane cognitive load. Front. Psychol. **8**, 1997 (2017). https://doi.org/10.3389/fpsyg.2017.01997
20. Hwang, G.-J., Yang, H., Wang, S.-Y.: A concept map-embedded educational computer game for improving students' learning performance in natural science courses. Comput. Educ. **69**, 121–130 (2013). https://doi.org/10.1016/j.compedu.2013.07.008

Implementation and Validation of the Innovative VR Distance Learning System with Simulated Physical Interaction Functions and Target Language Learning

Yingling Chen[1] and Chinlun Lai[2](✉)

[1] General Education Center, National Defense University, Taoyuan, Taiwan
[2] Asia Eastern University of Science and Technology, Taipei, Taiwan
fo001@mail.aeust.edu.tw

Abstract. This paper presents the implementation and validation of an innovative VR distance learning system designed to enhance remote education through simulated physical interaction and target language learning. The system leverages virtual reality technology to create an immersive educational environment that replicates the dynamics of a physical classroom or laboratory. It enables real-time interactions among learners and instructors, including face-to-face voice discussions in the target language, collaborative physical activities, virtual object manipulation, and cooperative equipment operation. By integrating these interactive elements, the system overcomes the limitations of traditional distance learning methods, providing a more engaging and effective learning experience. This approach facilitates authentic communication and hands-on training while bridging geographical barriers, ensuring that learners can fully participate in educational activities without being physically present. To evaluate the system's effectiveness, student surveys and user performance assessments were conducted, demonstrating positive feedback on its functionality, practicality, and impact on language learning. The findings validate the system's potential to enhance remote learning through immersive simulation and interactive engagement. This study lays the groundwork for future enhancements and broader applications of VR technology in distance education.

Keywords: Immersive simulation · Interactive virtual training · L2 · Simulated physical interaction · Virtual classroom · VR Distance learning

1 Introduction

The COVID-19 pandemic accelerated the shift to distance learning, making education more flexible and accessible through internet advancements. Virtual Reality (VR) has become a key tool, especially in language learning, by offering immersive, interactive environments that simulate real-world scenarios. VR allows learners to practice language skills with real-time feedback, while AI-driven tutors personalize instruction and enhance learning outcomes.

W.-S. Wang et al. (Eds.): ICITL 2025, LNCS 15913, pp. 306–316, 2026.
https://doi.org/10.1007/978-3-031-98185-2_32

VR distance learning systems combine interactive exercises, real-time speech recognition, and collaborative learning. AI analytics track student progress, while virtual environments provide immersive, real-world language practice. Studies such as those by Kebritchi et al. [1] emphasize the importance of well-structured learning environments, interactive content, and continuous feedback mechanisms, all of which are critical for language learners. Despite the advantages of online learning, traditional distance education has several limitations, including a lack of real-time interaction, limited hands-on practice, and reduced engagement. Research byDzemidzic Kristiansen et al. [2] suggests that face-to-face interaction enhances learning by fostering social connections between students and instructors. However, standard online courses often fail to provide the same level of engagement, leading to decreased motivation and learning effectiveness. Additionally, technical issues such as unstable internet connections, lack of dynamic interaction, and technology disparities can further hinder the learning experience.

VR-based simulated learning addresses these challenges by offering a more interactive and immersive environment. Unlike conventional online education, VR learning allows for real-time collaboration, hands-on practice, and multi-user engagement, overcoming limitations such as lack of physical presence and reduced interaction. Studies in simulated learning, such as those by McGaghie et al. [3] and Cook et al., [4] highlight the effectiveness of VR in improving knowledge retention, skill acquisition, and learner engagement. These studies emphasize that simulated learning uses VR, AR, and simulation-based training to create realistic, hands-on environments without physical resources. Widely used in fields like medicine, engineering, and aviation, it enhances practical skills and professional competence through safe, repeatable practice.

McGaghie et al. [3] introduced a comprehensive framework for simulated learning, offering evidence-based best practices for its design, implementation, and evaluation. The guide covers various simulation methods, including standardized patients, virtual reality, and high-fidelity models, and presents strategies to optimize student learning outcomes. Cook et al. [4] conducted a systematic literature review and meta-analysis on simulated learning in healthcare education, demonstrating significant improvements in knowledge acquisition, skill proficiency, and learner engagement. The study highlighted multiple applications of VR in medical training, such as surgical simulation, patient communication, and diagnostic procedures [5–7]. Other related studies [8–10] reinforce the significance of simulated learning in professional education and provide empirical validation of its effectiveness. Similar conclusions have been drawn in our recent related research [11, 12].

While online distance learning offers advantages such as accessibility, flexibility, and contact-free education, it also presents inherent challenges that traditional in-person instruction addresses more effectively. Research findings indicate several limitations of online learning, including:

- Lack of Face-to-Face Interaction: According to Bagheri & Mohamadi Zenouzagh (2021) [13] face-to-face interaction fosters social connections, improving student engagement. Online learning environments, however, often lack this element, leading to reduced student-to-student and student-to-teacher interactions.

- Technical Issues: Akmad & Abatayo (2024) [14] found that unstable internet connections, hardware malfunctions, and software-related disruptions negatively impact student participation and instructional continuity.
- Lack of Hands-On Opportunities: Dwivedi, Tosendra & Prajapati (2024) [15] identified that online learning struggles to provide practical experience, particularly in fields requiring hands-on training, such as laboratory sciences and technical skill development.
- Limited Dynamic Interaction: Picciano (2017) [16] noted that physical classrooms allow real-time adaptability to student needs, whereas online teaching restricts immediate pedagogical adjustments.
- Reduced Student Concentration: Aivaz (2022) [17] reported that students in online environments are more prone to distractions, reducing their focus and learning efficiency.
- Social Isolation: Pavin Ivanec (2020) [18] highlighted the emotional and social challenges students face due to the lack of in-person peer interactions in online education.
- Technology Disparities: Yu, Bekerian & Osback (2024) [19] pointed out that disparities in technological access and digital literacy can create barriers to effective online learning.

Online education often lacks real-time interaction, engagement, and hands-on training. To address this, the paper proposes a VR-based distance learning system that simulates physical interaction and supports target language learning. The system includes a multi-user virtual classroom where students and instructors can collaborate and manipulate virtual objects, providing realistic, hands-on practice beyond traditional online learning. The proposed system is particularly designed for English training and technical skill acquisition, utilizing immersive scenarios to facilitate task-based language learning while performing hands-on operations in a virtual environment. By simulating realistic and technical contexts, the system supports target language acquisition through interactive and experiential learning methodologies. A Proof of Concept (PoC) study showed that the system boosts motivation, engagement, and learning outcomes. Key benefits include: (a) hands-on practice with virtual equipment for skill mastery. (b) contextualized language learning within technical tasks. (c) real-time collaboration and feedback for interactive learning.

2 The Research Methodology

Descriptions of the research methodology include two aspects: namely the system implementation and the exploration of preliminary analysis of system functionality and achievement indicator validation, which are described as follows:

2.1 Constructing the Simulation Classroom System

To construct the instructional environment for the proposed VR-based distance learning system, we must first develop realistic 3D models of classroom environments and interactive objects to ensure an immersive and interactive experience. The 3D classroom scenes and instructional materials are initially created using Autodesk Maya, then imported into the Unity3D development platform for further adjustments, interaction scripting, and system integration. This process ensures that the virtual learning space accurately replicates real-world instructional instruments and materials, enabling students to engage in simulated physical interactions within a virtual classroom. The interactive teaching system is built on Unity3D, which serves as the primary development platform for scripting and executing interactive learning scenarios. Once the 3D models are finalized, the next step is to develop scripts that define interactive operations. These scripts are programmed in C# to simulate essential classroom functionalities, enabling multi-user real-time interaction, bidirectional operation of virtual equipment, and interactive language learning exercises. The proposed system features four key learning scenarios, each designed to validate the system's ability to enhance instructional effectiveness.

1. Multi-user Interactive Lecture Hall – Supports real-time participation with live video/audio communication, AI-powered virtual assistants for in-class support, multilingual translation, and interactive discussions. The virtual assistants offer personalized guidance, assist with navigation, provide contextual help, and support language learning by answering user queries during instruction.
2. Fiber Optic Communication Experiment – Allows students to manipulate virtual laboratory equipment, conducting hands-on experiments in a collaborative environment.
3. Indoor Firefighting Practice – Simulates emergency response scenarios where users apply theoretical knowledge in realistic, high-risk environments.
4. Interactive English and Mathematics Learning – Enhances language acquisition and STEM education through task-based, interactive exercises in VR, supported by real-time language translation features to enable learners from diverse linguistic backgrounds to engage with instructional content effectively.

A core differentiating feature of this system is the "submission and inheritance of personal objects" function. This capability allows instructors to introduce and share virtual devices (e.g., a teacher's oscilloscope) within the public virtual space, where students can inherit and manipulate these objects. This mechanism enables learners to practice operations on virtual equipment just as they would in a physical classroom, eliminating the limitations of one-way demonstrations in traditional online teaching.

2.2 Exploration of the Preliminary Analysis of System Functionality and Achievement Indicator Validation

To ensure effective validation of the system, the implementation and evaluation of the multiple functional aspects includes (a) real-time video/audio interaction: measuring latency, participant capacity, and multilingual communication support enhanced by AI-powered translation tools. (b) Simulated equipment interaction: Ensuring seamless transition from teacher demonstration to student hands-on practice. (c) Engagement and learning outcomes: Assessing student motivation, participation, and language proficiency improvement, particularly in response to real-time feedback from virtual AI assistants. Upon completion of the system, users will interact within the VR classroom environment using a VR headset and motion controllers, allowing for natural, intuitive engagement with the virtual world. This approach not only enhances target language learning through immersive experiences but also ensures a more effective, hands-on educational experience that surpasses traditional online learning limitations.

To assess the system's practicality and user experience, a questionnaire-based survey was conducted among students enrolled in an electronics laboratory course using the VR classroom system. The study explores students' subjective perceptions regarding learning motivation, user experience, course engagement, achievement of experimental learning objectives, and the impact of VR-enhanced interactive learning compared to conventional online education. The survey utilizes a 5-point Likert scale, ranging from 5 (Strongly Agree) to 1 (Strongly Disagree), to quantify student perceptions and engagement levels. All surveys were conducted online via Google Forms, ensuring anonymity so that students' responses would not affect their course performance. The survey consists of two key dimensions: a) Learning Effectiveness, Satisfaction, and Target Language Learning, and b) Learning Motivation, Interest, and System Practicality.

3 Experimental Results and Discussions

The proposed virtual classroom system is implemented on the Unity3D platform. The hardware architecture includes high-end laptops (equipped with an Intel Core i9 CPU, 16GB DDR RAM, and an NVIDIA GeForce GTX2070 graphics accelerator) and a VR headset (HTC VIVE Pro). In terms of teaching content, in addition to the designated assessment items in the communication technology verification test being implemented as practice exercises, additional features such as multi-user video and audio interaction, real-time language translation, and interactive English learning courses are included.

To enhance the innovative VR distance learning system with simulated physical interaction functions and target language learning, the system incorporates advanced haptic feedback and motion tracking to create a more immersive learning experience. Users can manipulate virtual objects with precise hand movements, allowing for realistic interaction with simulated equipment. These features are particularly beneficial in military English training, where students can engage in scenario-based exercises that mimic real-world operations. Additionally, AI-driven language learning modules adapt to each participant's proficiency level, providing real-time pronunciation evaluation, grammar correction, and context-based vocabulary recommendations. This personalized feedback mechanism ensures that learners actively improve their target language skills while participating in mission-oriented tasks.

Participants of the course are required to wear the headset and hold the controllers to enter the virtual classroom. They can choose whether to bring their personal belongings into the lobby and then freely select the course content they want to participate in and engage in practical exercises or interact with others, including conversations and collaborative assignments. To simulate realistic field operations, the system allows students to use virtual hand signals, voice commands, and interactive scenario-based dialogues, enhancing their ability to communicate effectively in English under mission-specific conditions. Personal belongings brought by individuals can be shared and inherited among participants in the lobby. For example, devices demonstrated by the instructor can be inherited by students, allowing them to immediately practice and learn relevant skills, similar to the scenario where a teacher hands over equipment to a student for practical exercises in a real classroom. This system greatly improves the limitations of existing online teaching systems that only allow one-way demonstrations, creating a realistic teaching environment with multi-directional online interaction. The related system architecture, operational processes, and examples can be referred to in Figs. 1, 2, 3 and 4.

In the process of validating the system's effectiveness, this study employed a combination of qualitative and quantitative analysis through questionnaire assessments. A total of 30 students from a four-year university program, who had prior experience with online courses including electronic laboratory sessions, were selected as participants. These students were invited to engage in the same course content within our developed virtual classroom, incorporating the distinctive online laboratory operation features of our system. The validation process specifically examined the impact of simulated physical interaction on learners' engagement, comprehension, and retention of technical English vocabulary. The system's ability to provide real-time interaction and immersive task-based learning was a key focus, aiming to bridge the gap between theoretical knowledge and practical application. Their valuable feedback was then collected to compare their subjective experiences using traditional online teaching platforms with our proposed virtual classroom system. Through meticulous analysis of the questionnaire results, we present the students' perspectives on utilizing the virtual classroom system for online learning, accompanied by insightful quantitative findings showcased in Table 1.

When observing the results presented in Table 1, it becomes evident that students who replaced the conventional online course system with the virtual classroom system rated its functional effectiveness in hands-on laboratory sessions at 4.3 (Row 1), 4.7 (Row 5), 4.1 (Row 7), and 4.2 (Row 8) respectively. Their satisfaction with the system's design and usability reached 4.6 (Row 3) and 4.2 (Row 4). However, when compared to the experience of physical classroom teaching, there is a lower rating of 3.8 (Row 2) and 3.9 (Row 6), potentially due to the limitations in simulation realism and the completeness of the functional structure in the course. Nonetheless, the overall recommendation for system usage still achieved a satisfactory rating of 4.1 (Row 9). Furthermore, if we consider the responses in the first two columns (Strongly Agree and Agree) as positive, it can be noted that 83% of users provided a positive response regarding the "system's functional effectiveness," while 80% of users expressed a positive response regarding the "system's satisfaction of use." On the other hand, in the subjective evaluation of the system's strengths and weaknesses, the main responses include:

3.1 Advantages of the System

a. Creates a safe, stress-free environment for skill practice without real-world risks.
b. Promotes global diverse collaboration through target language communication.
c. Removes time and location barriers with 24/7 access to training modules.
d. Enhances traditional online learning by introducing interactive virtual objects and real-time simulated interactions.
e. Supports autonomous learning with adjustable difficulty, personalized learning paths, and AI-driven feedback.

f. Enables unlimited practice using simulated equipment and realistic task scenarios.
g. Offers a more engaging experience through motion tracking, voice interaction, and real-time AI support.
h. Simulates physical interactions with tools and contextual language use in VR.
i. Enhances military English training with AI-based pronunciation evaluation, grammar correction, and real-time translation.

3.2 Disadvantages of the System

a. Lacks full haptic feedback, limiting realism in physical simulations.
b. Requires initial adaptation for users unfamiliar with VR.
c. Dependent on stable internet for real-time collaboration and voice interaction.
d. Some tasks may lack clarity and need additional guidance.
e. Virtual scenes may not fully match real-world richness.
f. Risk of motion sickness during extended use.
g. High-performance hardware is needed for smooth operation and AI features.

Survey feedback confirms that the system outperforms conventional online learning in interactivity, user satisfaction, and language acquisition. Key strengths include its immersive, hands-on approach and AI-assisted support for military English learning. Despite some technical and sensory limitations, students find it more enjoyable and flexible than traditional methods. The system is well-suited for practical, communication-intensive courses and has strong potential to supplement or replace current online teaching platforms. By merging VR with AI, it offers a powerful tool for improving both practical skills and target language proficiency.

Fig. 1. The implemented VR classroom with multi-users interaction test. (main hall).

Fig. 2. Demonstration of inherit function (the tools and instruments).

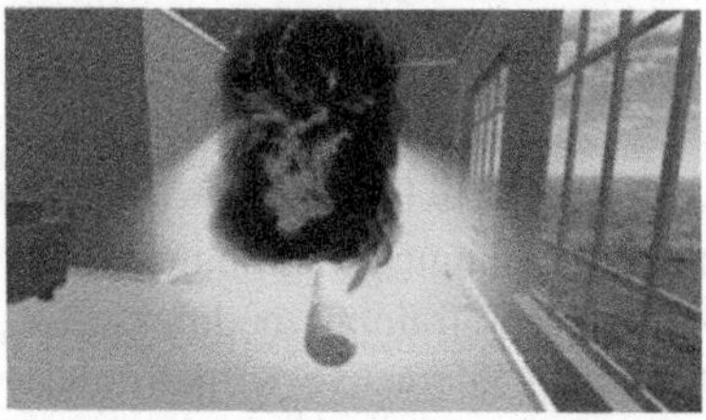

Fig. 3. Simulation learning scenario for English learning (fireman).

Fig. 4. Simulation learning scenario for English learning (mathematics).

Table 1. Summary of response to 9 survey questions using 5-point Likert Scale.

Survey Questions	Strongly Agree	Agree	Neutral	Disagree	Strongly Disagree	Mean Value
1.a This system allows me to interact fully with remote participants	16(53%)	9(30%)	4(13%)	1(3%)	0	4.3
1.b I can experience a similar feeling to real on-site teaching environments	12(40%)	7(23%)	6(20%)	3(10%)	2(7%)	3.8
1.c I feel more engaged in the course through this system	20(67%)	8(27%)	2(7%)	0	0	4.6
1.d I am satisfied with the various features of using this system	15(50%)	8(27%)	6(20%)	1(3%)	0	4.2
1.e I can practice the practical exercises demonstrated by the instructor firsthand	22(73%)	7(23%)	1(3%)	0	0	4.7
2.a This system creates an interactive teaching environment suitable for my needs	13(43%)	6(20%)	7(23%)	2(7%)	2(7%)	3.9
2.b It motivates and interests me in this online learning systems than before	14(47%)	8(27%)	5(17%)	2(7%)	1(3%)	4.1

(continued)

Table 1. (*continued*)

Survey Questions	Strongly Agree	Agree	Neutral	Disagree	Strongly Disagree	Mean Value
2.c *This system meets various interactive needs I have during online learning*	15(50%)	9(30%)	4(13%)	2(7%)	0	4.2
2.d *I would recommend others to use this virtual classroom for online learning*	14(47%)	7(23%)	8(27%)	1(3%)	0	4.1

4 Conclusions

This paper presents an innovative virtual reality-based online teaching system designed to overcome limitations in traditional online education. The system offers an immersive, interactive classroom environment with multi-user connectivity, voice/video communication, and real-time language translation. A key feature is object inheritance, allowing students to interact with virtual lab equipment, enhancing hands-on learning. It also includes AI-driven language tools and scenario-based training to support language acquisition.

To conclude the performance outcome of this work, first and foremost, it is noted that the primary contribution of this work lies in proposing and implementing an innovative distance online teaching system aimed at addressing the short-comings of current online teaching systems. Therefore, at this stage, we have only collected data through a single experimental course and a small number of specific skills training sessions to preliminarily validate the feasibility and potential applications of the system. Further analysis of the system's overall performance and student learning effectiveness will be the focus of future research. In the validation phase of the system, the questionnaire evaluation method is employed to gather and analyze feedback from students who have experienced both the existing online teaching system and the virtual classroom system for practical laboratory courses. The experimental results reveal that, except for the perceived lack of haptic realism, a significant percentage of users, specifically over 83% and 80% respectively, affirm the positive effects and express their satisfaction with the functionality of the virtual classroom system. Furthermore, due to the inherent characteristics of virtual reality technology, users also emphasize the advantages of a stress-free, flexible, and interactive learning environment that transcends the constraints of time and space, ultimately fostering greater motivation and interest in learning. These positive responses lay a solid foundation for future applications of the proposed system to a wider range of course types and exploration of its learning outcomes.

References

1. Kebritchi, M., et al.: Key elements of online learning environments for adult learners: an integrative review. Comput. Hum. Behav. **46**(1), 4–29 (2017)
2. Dzemidzic Kristiansen, S., Burner, T., Johnsen, B.H.: Face-to-face promotive interaction leading to successful cooperative learning: a review study. Cogent Educ. **6**(1), 1674067 (2019). https://doi.org/10.1080/2331186X.2019.1674067
3. McGaghie, W.C., et al.: Simulation in healthcare education: a best evidence practical guide. AMEE Guide No. 82. Med. Teach. **35**(10), 1511–1530 (2013)
4. Cook, D.A., et al.: Technology-enhanced simulation for health professions education: a systematic review and meta-analysis. J. Am. Med. Assoc. **306**(9), 978–988 (2011)
5. Gurusamy, K., et al.: Systematic review of randomized controlled trials on the effectiveness of virtual reality training for laparoscopic surgery. J. Brit. Surg. **95**(9), 1088–1097 (2008)
6. Lier, E.J., et al.: Effect modifiers of virtual reality in pain management: a systematic review and meta-regression analysis. PAIN **164**(8), 1658–1665 (2013). https://doi.org/10.1097/j.pain.000 0000000002883
7. Laspro, M., et al.: The use of virtual reality in surgical training: implications for education, patient safety, and global health equity. Surgeries **4**, 635–646 (2023). https://doi.org/10.3390/ surgeries4040061
8. Xie, B., et al.: A review on virtual reality skill training applications. Front. Virt. Real. **2**, 645153 (2021). https://doi.org/10.3389/frvir.2021.645153
9. Abidi, M.H., et al.: Assessment of virtual reality-based manufacturing assembly training system. Int. J. Adv. Manuf. Technol. **105**, 3743–3759 (2019). https://doi.org/10.1007/s00 170-019-03801-3
10. Akdere, M., Jiang, Y., Lobo, F.: Evaluation and assessment of virtual reality-based simulated training: exploring the human-technology. Front. Eur. J. Train. Dev. (2021). https://doi.org/ 10.15405/epsbs.2021.02.17
11. Lai, C.L.: A simulation learning in communication technique skill by virtual reality - certification of telecommunication line plant. In: Huang, Y.-M., Lai, C.-F., Rocha, T. (eds.) ICITL 2021. LNCS, vol. 13117, pp. 74–84. Springer, Cham (2021). https://doi.org/10.1007/978-3-030-91540-7_9
12. Chang, Y.M., Lai, C.L.. Exploring the experiences of nursing students in using immersive virtual reality to learn nursing skills. Nurse Educ. Today **97**, 104670 (2021). https://doi.org/ 10.1016/j.nedt.2020.104670
13. Bagheri, M., Mohamadi Zenouzagh, Z.: Comparative study of the effect of face-to-face and computer mediated conversation modalities on student engagement: speaking skill in focus. Asian. J. Second. Foreign. Lang. Educ. **6**(5) (2021). https://doi.org/10.1186/s40862-020-001 03-0
14. Akmad, A., Abatayo, A.V.: Caught in the slow lane: effects of unstable internet connectivity on accessing academic resources and collaborative learning. J. Interdisc. Perspect. **2**(9), 278–286 (2024). https://doi.org/10.69569/jip.2024.0370
15. Dwivedi, T., Prajapati, V.: Analyzing the benefits and drawbacks of online learning in higher education. Afr. J. Biol. Sci. **6**, 1115–1125 (2024)
16. Picciano, A.G.: Theories and frameworks for online education: seeking an integrated model. Online Learn. **21**(3), 166–190 (2017). https://doi.org/10.24059/olj.v21i3.1225
17. Aivaz, K.A., Teodorescu, D.: College students' distractions from learning caused by multitasking in online vs. face-to-face classes: a case study at a public university in Romania. Int. J. Environ. Res. Public Health **19**(18), 11188 (2022). https://doi.org/10.3390/ijerph191811188

18. Pavin, I.T.: The lack of academic social interactions and students' learning difficulties during COVID-19 faculty lockdowns in Croatia: the mediating role of the perceived sense of life disruption caused by the pandemic and the adjustment to online studying. Social Sci. **11**(2), 42 (2022). https://doi.org/10.3390/socsci11020042
19. Yu, J., Bekerian, D.A., Osback, C.: Navigating the digital landscape: challenges and barriers to effective information use on the internet. Encyclopedia **4**(4), 1665–1680 (2024). https://doi.org/10.3390/encyclopedia4040109

Influence of Red and Blue Virtual Environments During a Listening Evaluation: A Preliminary Study of Academic Performance and Subjective Self-Perception

Gabriel Ávila-Muñoz[1(✉)], Miguel A. López-Gordo[1,2(✉)], and Manuel Rodríguez-Álvarez[1,3]

[1] Neuroengineering and Computation Lab, Research Centre for Information and Communication Technologies (CITIC-UGR), University of Granada, 18014 Granada, Spain
{gabriavila,malg,manolo}@ugr.es

[2] Department of Signal Theory, Research Centre for Information and Communication Technologies (CITIC-UGR), Telematics and Communications, University of Granada, 18014 Granada, Spain

[3] Department of Computer Engineering, Automation and Robotics, Research Centre for Information and Communication Technologies (CITIC-UGR), University of Granada, 18014 Granada, Spain

Abstract. Color and lighting have been shown to influence human physiology and may affect cognitive performance. Some theories suggest that blue background colors promote relaxation and concentration, whereas red colors induce arousal and alertness. However, empirical evidence remains inconclusive due to variations in experimental designs and task types, making it unclear how color ultimately affects cognitive performance. The aim of this preliminary study is to compare performance and subjective self-perception throughout a listening evaluation and to determine whether red or blue colors yield differences in performance. We conducted a study in which university students completed five listening tests within a red or blue virtual environment and answered questions about their subjective self-perception at the beginning and end of the experiment. Our results showed that: i) students in an environment characterized by a blue color obtained higher median performance (6.8 vs. 6.0) as time progressed during the evaluation; ii) medium positive correlations were found in the blue group (0.36 and 0.36) between the performance-attention and performance-relaxation that exceeded that of the red group; iii) a medium negative correlation was discovered in the red group (-0.48) between the performance-mental effort that exceeded that of the blue group. The preliminary findings of this study could suggest that a blue environment may facilitate relaxation and attentional focus, which could enhance performance. Despite the modest sample size, these findings underscore the necessity for additional research to determine the true impact of color on academic performance, with potential implications for educational settings and academic institutions.

Keywords: Red · Blue · Listening evaluation · Academic performance · Virtual Reality (VR)

W.-S. Wang et al. (Eds.): ICITL 2025, LNCS 15913, pp. 317–323, 2026.
https://doi.org/10.1007/978-3-031-98185-2_33

1 Introduction

It is hypothesized that color influences cognitive processes. In our previous study [1], we analyzed brain signals using EEG and found that red and blue colors induced distinct patterns of cerebral activity. Additionally, Elliot et al. posits that red color engenders a state of alertness due to its association with blood, and its historical utilization in danger signals across various cultures. Conversely, both blue and green have been linked with positive emotions, such as peace and calm, due to their association with nature [2].

Several studies have reported divergent findings regarding color effects. For instance, red backgrounds have been linked to improvements in short-term memory compared to blue or white backgrounds [3], while other study have shown that blue color enhance performance in an attention task compared when compared to a white background [4], suggesting that color may exert differential effects relative to neutral color. Nevertheless, due to the diverse range of experiments carried out under varying conditions, there remains no consensus regarding the specific impact of each color [5].

Some research suggests that warm colors may be more effective for detail-oriented or simple cognitive tasks, whereas cold colors enhance performance in more complex or demanding tasks [6, 7]. For example, Liu et al. found that cold-colored walls were more effective for relaxation, but yellow walls yielded the highest performance scores on the Stroop task, mental arithmetic and reading, followed by red, green, blue, and white walls [8]. Conversely, Llinares et al. reported that cold hues improved auditory attention and memory tasks more effectively than warm colors [9], reinforcing the notion that task complexity and modality may mediate color effects on cognition.

The aim of this preliminary study is to extend our previous study by comparing performance and subjective self-perception throughout a listening comprehension task, designed to closely resemble an authentic academic setting requiring sustained attention, and to determine whether blue or red colors present differences.

2 Methods

2.1 Participants and Experimental Design

Fourteen students (four females and ten males; 20.4 ± 2.4 years) from the University of Granada participated in the study. After providing informed consent, the Ishihara test was administered to all the participants due to the color-based nature of the experiment. One participant was excluded for expressing discomfort during the test. The study was approved by the Research Ethics Committee of the University of Granada (3702/CEIH/2023) and conducted at the Research Centre for Information and Communication Technologies (CITIC-UGR).

Participants fitted with a virtual reality headset and initially immersed in a fully white environment. The experiment started with a subjective questionnaire designed to assess the participants' state, consisting of five items evaluating attention, stress, interest, mental effort, and relaxation on a scale from 1 to 5. Participants were assigned to a red or blue group, and the virtual environment was adjusted accordingly. After a 3-min relaxation in the colored environment, participants completed five C2 Spanish audio tests (six questions, two options each), followed by another relaxation period and subjective questionnaire. Further details are in our previous study [1].

2.2 Statistical Analysis

A dataset was constructed by combining the responses to the subjective questionnaires, listening tests, and the assigned color background to each participant.

Firstly, performance was analyzed using the median scores (scaled to 10) due to the small sample size, and median absolute deviation for uncertainty. Subsequently, cumulative performance, calculated individually for each participant before computing the median, was analyzed across the tests.

Secondly, subjective questionnaires were analyzed using the median for each group. Both absolute self-perception states (responses at the beginning and end) and relative self-perception states (difference between them) were examined. The relative state may differ slightly from the absolute difference due to individual calculation before computing the median.

Finally, the correlation between performance and self-perception relative state was assessed using Kendall's Tau correlation [10], suitable for non-Gaussian data and small samples. Only medium (0.3–0.49) and large (0.5–1) correlations, as defined by Cohen [11], were considered.

3 Results

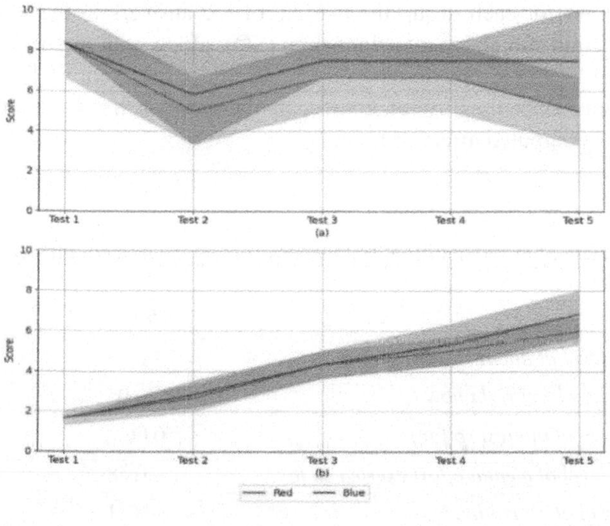

Fig. 1. Median performance (0–10 points) throughout the listening tests for each group. Red and blue represent the group's virtual environment color. Colored shadows represent the median absolute deviation. (a) Scores from each test (medians). (b) Weighted cumulative scores throughout the tests (median of the sum).

Figure 1 shows the median performance throughout all the listening tests for each group. Red and blue colors represent the median for the students within a red and blue virtual environment respectively. Colored shadows represent the median absolute deviation as an indicator of uncertainty for each group. Figure 1a represents the median scores from each test, scaled to 10; Fig. 1b represents the weighted median for each group of the cumulative scores from each participant. In other words, we first sum the scores for each participant and then the median is computed.

Table 1. Median of the answers to the first and second subjective questionnaires (SQ) and the difference between them for each group and question.

Question	*Red Median*			*Blue Median*		
	1st SQ	2nd SQ	Diff SQ	1st SQ	2nd SQ	Diff SQ
What has your level of attention been so far?	5	4	−1	5	5	0
What is your stress level right now?	2	3	1	1.5	2.5	0.5
What is your level of interest so far?	5	4	0	5	5	0
What has your level of mental effort exerted so far?	1	4	2	1	4	3
What is your level of relaxation?	3	2	−1	3.5	2.5	0

Table 1 shows for each group the median of the answers in the five questions of the first and second subjective questionnaires (SQ), along with the difference between them. The 'Diff SQ' columns do not correspond to the subtraction of '2nd SQ' minus '1st SQ' columns, since the difference was calculated for each subject individually, and the median was computed afterward.

Table 2. Kendall's Tau correlation coefficient between performance and subjective self-perception for each group and question. Bold values correspond to medium level correlations.

Questions	*Red*	*Blue*
What has your level of attention been so far?	−0.23	0.36
What is your stress level right now?	−0.05	0.08
What is your level of interest so far?	0.06	0.16
What has your level of mental effort exerted so far?	−0.48	−0.16
What is your level of relaxation?	−0.21	0.36

Table 2 shows the Kendall's Tau correlation coefficient between performance and the median difference of the responses to the subjective questionnaires for each group and question. Bold values correspond to medium level correlations.

4 Discussion

In this study we explored the influence of red and blue virtual environment on performance and subjective self-perception during a sustained auditory attention task, simulating a realistic academic context. Preliminary results would suggest that a blue environment may facilitate relaxation and attentional focus, which could enhance performance.

Figure 1.a shows a trend in which the blue group begins to outperform the red group from the second test onward, maintaining a relatively stable performance level until the end of the experiment. In contrast, the red group exhibits a final decline in performance. This final divergence (Test 5) is echoed in the cumulative analysis (Fig. 1.b), where the shaded regions representing the median absolute deviation reveal that the blue group's variability band still overlaps the red group's median, whereas the red group's band does not extend into the blue group's median range. This asymmetry suggests a potential divergence in performance trajectories between the groups. While these patterns may indicate a performance advantage in blue environments, the degree of statistical uncertainty prevents any definitive conclusion. Therefore, the results should be interpreted as preliminary and hypothesis-generating rather than confirmatory regarding the effects of red or blue color on sustained cognitive performance.

Table 1 shows that both groups experienced increased stress and reduced relaxation; however, the blue group reported more favorable absolute values in both dimensions. These findings suggest that participants perceived themselves to be in a more relaxed state when immersed in a blue environment, consistent with prior studies indicating that blue color generated a more relaxed state [2, 4, 5, 8]. In fact, in our previous study [1] where brain signals were analyzed, participants in the blue condition exhibited higher alpha power levels (an electrophysiological marker traditionally linked to relaxed mental states) at the end of the session. This convergence between neurophysiological signals and self-reported measures supports the interpretation that blue environments may facilitate relaxation.

Table 2 shows a positive medium correlation for attention and relaxation in the blue group, suggesting that the enhanced attention and relaxation fostered by the blue environment may have improved performance. In contrast, a negative medium correlation for mental effort was found in the red group, indicating that reduced mental effort may have facilitated better performance. This correlation in the red group could reflect differences in academic level among participants, which were not present in the blue group.

5 Conclusions and Future Work

This study has several limitations. First, the small sample size (seven in the red group and six in the blue group) led to large error margins and necessitated using the median as the central tendency measure. Second, while we measured performance and subjective states like relaxation and mental effort through listening tests, we did not assess participants' cognitive capacity, which is closely linked to performance.

Although the present results are not conclusive, they offer preliminary insights that justify further investigation. The trends identified suggest that environmental color, particularly blue, may influence self-perceived cognitive states and sustained performance during attention-demanding tasks. However, the findings should be interpreted with caution and regarded as hypothesis-generating rather than confirmatory. Replication of this study with a larger and more diverse sample is essential to validate these patterns. While incorporating cognitive capacity measures could help control participant heterogeneity, a sufficiently large sample may itself dilute the effect of outliers and allow for more reliable group-level inferences.

Additionally, it may be valuable to include other color conditions, such as green or yellow, and to combine behavioral analysis with complementary methods (e.g., EEG) to better understand the mechanisms underlying color-related cognitive effects.

Acknowledgements. This work was supported by grant PID2021-128529OAI00, MCIN/AEI/https://doi.org/10.13039/501100011033, and by ERDF A way of making Europe; grant PROYEXCEL 00084, P21 00084, Projects for Excellence Research, funded by the Council for Economic Transformation, Industry, Knowledge and Universities, Junta de Andalucía 2021.

References

1. Ávila-Muñoz, G., López-Gordo, M.A., Rodríguez-Álvarez, M.: Influence of color on academic performance: a studio with auditory sustained attention within a virtual scenario. In: Vicente, J.M.F., Calvo, M.V., Adeli, H. (eds.) Artificial Intelligence for Neuroscience and Emotional Systems: 10th International Work-Conference on the Interplay Between Natural and Artificial Computation, IWINAC 2024, Olhâo, Portugal, June 4–7, 2024, Proceedings, Part I, pp. 528–538. Springer, Cham (2024). https://doi.org/10.1007/978-3-031-61140-7_50
2. Elliot, A.J., Maier, M.A.: Color psychology: effects of perceiving color on psychological functioning in humans. Ann. Rev. Psychol. **65**, 95–120 (2014). https://doi.org/10.1146/annurev-psych-010213-115035
3. Jadhao, A., Bagade, A., Taware, G., Bhonde, M.: Effect of background color perception on attention span and short-term memory in normal students. Natl. J. Physiol. Pharm. Pharmacol. **10**, 981–984 (2020). https://doi.org/10.5455/njppp.2020.10.06162202017072020
4. Soltanzadeh, S., Chitsaz, S., Kazemi, R.: Color and brightness at work: shedding some light on mind wandering. Brain Behav. **14**, e70020 (2024). https://doi.org/10.1002/brb3.70020
5. Llorens-Gámez, M., Higuera-Trujillo, J.L., Omarrementeria, C.S., Llinares, C.: The impact of the design of learning spaces on attention and memory from a neuroarchitectural approach: a systematic review. Front. Archit. Res. **11**, 542–560 (2022). https://doi.org/10.1016/j.foar.2021.12.002
6. Mehta, R., Zhu, R.: Blue or red? Exploring the effect of color on cognitive performance. ACR North Am. Adv. (2009)
7. Xia, T., Song, L., Wang, T.T., Tan, L., Mo, L.: Exploring the effect of red and blue on cognitive task performances. Front. Psychol. **7** (2016). https://doi.org/10.3389/fpsyg.2016.00784
8. Liu, C., Zhang, Y., Sun, L., Gao, W., Zang, Q., Li, J.: The effect of classroom wall color on learning performance: a virtual reality experiment. Build. Simul. **15**, 2019–2030 (2022). https://doi.org/10.1007/s12273-022-0923-y
9. Llinares, C., Higuera-Trujillo, J.L., Serra, J.: Cold and warm coloured classrooms: effects on students' attention and memory measured through psychological and neurophysiological responses. Build. Environ. **196**, 107726 (2021). https://doi.org/10.1016/j.buildenv.2021.107726

10. Kendall, M.G.: A new measure of rank correlation. Biometrika **30**, 81–93 (1938). https://doi.org/10.1093/biomet/30.1-2.81
11. Cohen, J.: Statistical Power Analysis for the behavioral Sciences. L. Erlbaum Associates, Hillsdale (1988)

Non-Immersive Virtual Learning Environments (VLEs) with XR Elements in Nursing Education: Learning Interaction and Clinical Competence

Satu-Maarit Korte[1(✉)], Heli Ruokamo[1], Loru Reinikka[2], Tuulikki Keskitalo[2], and Katja Saukkoriipi[2]

[1] Media Education Hub, Faculty of Education, University of Lapland, Rovaniemi, Finland
{satu-maarit.korte,heli.ruokamo}@ulapland.fi
[2] Lapland University of Applied Sciences, Rovaniemi, Finland
{loru.reinikka,tuulikki.keskitalo,katja.saukkoriipi}@lapinamk.fi

Abstract. The way nursing students acquire clinical competence and patient safety awareness has changed as a result of the adoption of virtual learning environments (VLEs) in healthcare education. Non-immersive VLEs that display virtual scenarios offer secure learning experiences. Easily accessible and reasonably priced non-immersive VLEs can safely enhance learning clinical procedures. To the best of our knowledge, there is no earlier research on non-immersive VLEs with extended reality (XR) elements in nursing education, and this research fills that gap.

This study investigates nursing students' expectations and experiences of using non-immersive VLEs with XR elements to learn interaction and clinical competence, such as infusion pump operations. It also explores the strengths, weaknesses, opportunities, and threats related to the use of non-immersive VLEs with XR elements in this context. Fifteen first-year nursing students engaged in two non-immersive learning scenarios. The learning process was structured using a seven-phase simulation pedagogy. The data were collected using pre- and post-questionnaires; group discussions; and strengths, weaknesses, opportunities, and threats (SWOT) analysis. The data were analyzed using both qualitative and quantitative methods.

The findings highlight the potential of non-immersive VLEs with XR elements to enhance engagement, confidence, and competence acquisition in nursing students while complementing traditional hands-on training. The study highlights the importance of blended learning strategies that integrate technical and scenario-based approaches, as well as simulation pedagogy, to optimize knowledge retention and clinical competency development. As digital technologies continue to shape healthcare education, non-immersive VLEs with XR elements are valuable in bridging the gap between theory and practice, ultimately contributing to patient safety and improved healthcare outcomes.

Keywords: Non-immersive virtual learning environments (VLEs) · extended reality (XR) · simulation pedagogy · nursing education · interaction competence · clinical competence

W.-S. Wang et al. (Eds.): ICITL 2025, LNCS 15913, pp. 324–334, 2026.
https://doi.org/10.1007/978-3-031-98185-2_34

1 Introduction

The use of immersive and non-immersive virtual learning environments (VLEs) has become increasingly critical in fields such as healthcare education, where practical training is exceptionally important so that medical mistakes can be avoided. In a non-immersive system, such as certain implementations of extended reality (XR), augmented reality, or mixed reality, digital content is presented on standard screens or through semi-transparent overlays while users remain aware of their physical surroundings. The displays allow interaction via keyboard, mouse, joystick, or remote controller. Unlike fully immersive virtual reality (VR), which isolates users within a completely digital environment, these non-immersive systems often rely on devices such as smartphones, tablets, or heads-up displays. Interaction is typically limited to traditional input methods, such as touchscreens, controllers, or voice commands, rather than the full-body engagement characteristic of immersive VR systems [9]. Conversely, an immersive VR system—often comprising modern head-mounted displays or cave automatic virtual environment (CAVE) systems—envelops the user in a three-dimensional computer-generated space, enabling natural sensory–motor interaction using their own body [6]. Particularly in nursing education, virtual simulations provide a safe and controlled setting for students to practice complex procedures without endangering patients [3, 5, 10, 14]. This approach is particularly important when training involves high-risk equipment, such as infusion pumps, which are widely used in clinical settings but are also associated with a significant proportion of nursing errors [8]. Research has highlighted that infusion pump errors constitute one of the most common and potentially fatal mistakes in nursing practice, often stemming from inadequate training and human errors [1, 8]. By incorporating virtual training tools, educators can mitigate these risks while offering students a realistic and interactive platform to build their competencies.

Prior studies on VLEs indicate that students typically appreciate the learning experience provided by VLEs, as they offer an engaging and immersive approach to education [e.g., 2]. While immersive VLEs offer a more comprehensive sense of presence, they do not necessarily lead to better learning outcomes compared to non-immersive VLEs [12]. Therefore, it is important to develop and test accessible and affordable VLEs to complement the training possibilities of healthcare students. This study investigated the use of non-immersive VLEs with some XR elements in nursing education through two structured scenarios involving 15 first-year nursing students. This paper examines the students' experiences and asks the following questions:

1) *What kinds of expectations and experiences do nursing students have using non-immersive VLEs with XR elements in learning interaction and clinical competences?* and 2) *What are the strengths, weaknesses, opportunities, and threats of using non-immersive VLEs with XR elements for learning interaction competence and clinical competence according to nursing students?*

2 Background

Technological advancements have created new opportunities in the education of healthcare students and professionals. Currently, there is a proliferation of XR applications, and research in this area is growing. Various technological applications offer multiple benefits within the healthcare sector. They offer a secure, active, and experiential learning environment for both the practice and maintenance of interaction and clinical competences among both students and professionals. Interaction and communication competence in nursing refers to the ability to convey information clearly and effectively using a shared professional language, enabling consistent understanding and collaboration among healthcare and social service professionals to support high-quality care [15]. At the same time, clinical competence can be defined as the integrated combination of knowledge, skills, attitudes, and abilities that enables nurses to provide safe, effective, and independent patient care [15]. VLEs are vital for the development of both technical or clinical and non-technical competences that, while infrequently utilized, are essential for the effective management of life-threatening situations.

Consequently, students demonstrate appreciation for the opportunity to learn through more engaging and immersive learning methods, which also affects motivation [12]. However, research results on the educational outcomes of various XR applications are inconsistent [12]. The evaluation of learning outcomes presents challenges because XR applications are seldom employed in isolation within higher education; they are typically integrated with other technological tools and pedagogical methods to enhance participants' learning experiences [cf. 11]. Therefore, the impact of VLE alone is difficult to ascertain.

Teaching methods have an important effect on student learning [11]. Previous studies have developed pedagogical models that can be used for planning, implementing, and evaluating education and students' learning with VLEs [2, 7] but also to describe and understand learning with them [11]. In this study, earlier models [7] helped script the learning process to support students' learning with VLEs with XR elements. The learning process was divided into seven distinct phases based on a previous study with VLEs [7]. The first phase included (1) *pre-activities*, during which students familiarized themselves with the topic to be able to practice with the case scenario simulated through the VLE. In this phase, educators are usually responsible for the organization of the learning process. The second phase is often a formal face-to-face (2) *introduction*, in which students become acquainted with the topic and the general rules for the learning process. The (3) *technology* and (4) *scenario briefing* phases consist of familiarizing learners with the technology as well as providing general knowledge of the case scenario's roles and tasks. Familiarity with technology is viewed as vital when using VLEs, particularly for people with limited expertise or no gaming history. The (5) *VLE scenario* phase focuses on actual training with the VLE, either alone or in a group. The last phase is (6) *debriefing*, during which participants can reflect on the learning experience and exchange feedback. Constructive feedback and dialog during debriefing can elucidate misconceptions and shortcomings in learners' competencies, thus enhancing learning. Lastly, (7) *post-activities* provide learners with an opportunity to apply newly acquired knowledge in practice or in a more comprehensive full-scale simulation [7].

3 Research Methodology

3.1 Research Context and Participants

The participants of this study are 15 first-year nursing students. This group was chosen because they had not covered the topics of the scenarios of the workshop and because they were the daytime study group available to join the workshop and research. The data collection was conducted during a workshop day that included two different virtual scenarios: learning 1) interaction competence (sending a patient home) and 2) clinical competence (in the case of infusion pump operations) (Fig. 1).

Fig. 1. Technology briefing (3) for Scenario 1 with a virtual patient (sending patient home) at Virtual Production Studio

Before the workshop day, the pre-activities involved preparing for the workshop and giving students some information about the workshop. The beginning of the two scenarios was organized in the Virtual Production Studio of the University Lapland, which has a 3 m × 7.5 m light-emitting diode (LED) screen. The LED panels were ROE's Black Pearl 2V2 model, and the used LED processor was Megapixel Helios Jr. The screen was used to brief the students about immersive and non-immersive learning environments and, subsequently, to provide an introduction briefing to the topics of the scenarios and the platforms' functions that they were to use for learning for 30 min. The first scenario theme was Interaction Competence (Fig. 2.) in the context of sending a patient home after a hospital stay. Subsequently, the students were first introduced to using the "Interaction Competence" interactive platform with a moving patient and voice recognition, which constituted the XR element in this scenario.

Fig. 2. Scenario 1 with a virtual patient and speech recognition, which constitute the XR elements in the non-immersive VLE

Fig. 3. Scenario 2 with a virtual infusion pump with XR elements

Fig. 4. Infusion pump for practical exercise

The exercise used in the first scenario was originally developed as a VR-based training tool and was in this research project adapted for use on any display screen without a VR headset. Initially designed for nurses learning Finnish as a second language, the exercise aimed to provide a safe environment in which users could practice their Finnish language skills with virtual patients. The training tool was built using the Unreal Engine 5 game engine, featuring a realistic hospital environment and lifelike virtual patients who engaged in conversations with the player. The exercise functions by prompting the user to ask the virtual patient a health-related question to which the patient responds. The conversation continues until the exercise is successfully completed. The exercise is designed with a single predefined outcome: guiding the user toward its completion. Speech recognition was implemented using artificial intelligence (AI), which was trained to understand various ways of expressing the required phrases in Finnish. The study participants were native Finnish speakers, yet they were still able to practice patient interactions and conversations in a controlled, interactive setting. After the introduction, the students moved to a nearby classroom to work peacefully in pairs or triads, with the non-immersive VLE already installed on the laptop computers. Here, they had 60 min for hands-on work on the simulation scenario, enough for all students to personally use the non-immersive VLE and interact with the virtual patient. After this practical part of the scenario, the students were gathered together to facilitate debriefing group discussion on their learning experience.

After a 15-min break, the workshop continued with the second scenario, which again started with *briefing* in the Virtual Production Studio. The second scenario focused on *Clinical Competence*—in this case, infusion pump operation (Fig. 3)—and followed a similar structure as the first scenario. A 30-min introductory session included an explanation of virtual infusion pump functionality and its application. The virtual infusion pump exercise is a web-based training tool with XR elements designed to teach the operation of the *Braun Infusomat Space* infusion pump (Fig. 4).

The exercise focuses on the correct tubing setup and parameter adjustment of the device. Users can complete the exercise either with the assistance of a tutorial or independently. The tutorial provides step-by-step virtual guidance, allowing users to practice tubing and parameter adjustments with on-screen instructions and directional arrows indicating the correct actions. The exercise operates by having users click on interactive on-screen elements to perform the necessary tasks. Once the tubing and settings have been correctly configured, users have the opportunity to assemble the pump from memory without tutorial assistance. After the virtual practice, the use of medical devices and device safety in nursing were discussed with the students. First-year students do not yet have experience using an infusion pump and will be taught it next semester, along with device safety and device management. Hence, this was the first experience of the participants with an infusion pump. Following the discussion, the students practiced operating the virtual pump in groups of two or three, followed by a 15-min hands-on session for each student with a real infusion pump. Both scenarios concluded with a facilitated group debriefing and discussions, a strengths, weaknesses, opportunities, and threats (SWOT) analysis, and a final feedback survey.

3.2 Research Instruments

Data collection in this study included pre- and post-scenario surveys to address research question 1, and recorded group debriefing discussions and SWOT analysis outcomes to address research question 2. For the SWOT analysis, 26 post-it notes were received after the first scenario and 29 after the second. Group debriefing discussions were held after both scenarios, allowing the students to reflect on their learning and discuss their experiences with the VLE. The discussions for the first scenario lasted 18 min and 25 min for the second scenario. After the group discussion, the students wrote their views on post-it notes regarding the SWOT of VLEs with XR elements to bring together the biggest takeaways from the group *debriefing*. This was followed by a survey of their perceptions about the VLE and their learning, which, at the same time, served as a place for *post-activity* and *self-reflection* on their learning. In this study, based on the recorded debriefing discussions and SWOT post-it notes, we highlight only the main points when answering the research question 2.

The surveys were developed by merging two models, the scale of expected interactivity (EI) [13] and the technology acceptance model (TAM) [4], to obtain holistic data from a small number of participants. The EI scale [13] measures EI across three dimensions—sensory (visual and sensory engagement), semantic (meaningful communication or personalization), and behavioral (user agency, control, and customization)—each including items designed to capture users' expectations regarding interactive experiences. TAM [4] focuses on user perceptions of ease of use and usefulness, which are crucial for evaluating VLEs. TAM's simplicity and focus make it a good fit for small-group evaluations. All survey questions were made with a 7-point Likert scale, and the results were analyzed quantitatively, with the lowest value being 1 (strongly disagree) and the highest being 7 (strongly agree). The key objectives of the survey included evaluating user expectations and experiences of non-immersive VLEs with XR elements, assessing their impact on learning and interactivity, and exploring their potential to enhance nursing competencies.

4 Results

The first research question asks what kinds of expectations and experiences do nursing students have using non-immersive VLEs with XR elements in learning interaction and clinical competence. To answer this question, the pre- and post-scenario surveys were analyzed, and the main points from the group debriefings were highlighted.

In the first scenario, the students exercised interaction with a virtual patient in the context of sending a patient home after a hospital stay. From the pre-activity and post-activity surveys, it appears that the participants generally expected an engaging and interactive experience, and while some aspects aligned with these expectations, others fell short. Regarding engagement and visual appeal, both before and after the activity, the participants rated the visual and stimulating aspects of the non-immersive VLEs with XR elements highly. However, the post-activity average score for this dimension (mean = 4.8; SD = 1.7) indicates room for improvement in meeting expectations (mean = 5.1; SD = 1.7). Regarding interactivity and personalization, while initial expectations for personalization (mean = 3.9; SD = 1.7) and interactivity (mean = 4.1; SD = 1.9) were moderate to high, the post-activity scores revealed that their expectations were met with scores for both personalization (mean = 4.0; SD = 1.7) and interactivity (mean = 5.2; SD = 1.4). The expectations of communication were quite high (mean = 5.2; SD = 1.5), and the experience of communication on the platform scored only a little lower (mean = 5.0; SD = 1.5). These findings suggest that the participants desired more dynamic and interactive scenarios rather than predictable or guided interactions. The participants rated the ease of use of the VLE as quite high (mean = 5.5; SD = 1.6), indicating that the platform was user friendly even after their high expectations (mean = 5.6; SD = 1.5). They also expected the VLE to motivate them to engage in learning activities (mean = 5.5; SD = 1.2). However, the perceived motivation (mean = 4.6; SD = 1.7) and learning effectiveness (mean = 4.4; SD = 1.0) were somewhat moderate, showing that while the platform was accessible, it could improve in fostering motivation and deeper learning outcomes to meet the participants' expectations (mean = 5.0; SD = 1.7). In the debriefing group discussions, the students' suggestions for improvement included incorporating more diverse and challenging scenarios to sustain interest and offer more actionable feedback. Several participants emphasized the need for some improvements such that the exercises adapt dynamically based on user input toward more challenging scenarios. They also wished for more complex patient responses that deviated from predefined scripts. They also hoped for improved communication AI with enhanced natural language capabilities for patient interactions.

In the second scenario, the students exercised the use of an infusion pump. In the initial assessment, the respondents had high expectations for the non-immersive VLE with XR elements to be visually stimulating and easy to use, with a score of 5.9 for both (SD = 1.4 and SD = 1.3, respectively). The final assessment showed that these expectations were met in terms of visual appeal (mean = 5.9; SD = 1.0), with a slightly lower score for ease of use (mean = 5.6; SD = 1.4). The learning efficiency fell only slightly short of the students' high expectations (mean = 6.1; SD = 1.0) compared to their experience (mean = 5.9; SD = 1.0). However, other aspects, such as expectations of personalization (mean = 4.3; SD = 1.4) and communication (mean = 5.1; SD = 1.3), did not meet the expectations of the students; personalization scored only 4.1 (SD =

1.4), and communication with the pump scored only 3.3 (SD = 1.0). The expectations of interactivity were only 3.5 (SD = 1.7), but interactivity received a higher score of 4.7 (SD = 1.8) after the experience. The students' expectations of the effectiveness of the learning activity were high (mean = 6.1; SD = 1.0). While the participants initially anticipated and experienced interactive learning experiences, communication mechanisms were a weak point in the final assessment. This indicates that the virtual tool succeeded in maintaining engagement. The participants consistently found the tool easy to use, with high scores (mean = 5.9; initially SD = 1.3, mean = 5.6; SD = 1.4 finally) for usability and user friendliness. In the debriefing group discussions, the students' suggestions for improvement included a wider range of medications and mistakes. It is noteworthy that the present lecturers of nursing at the workshop saw a significant improvement in the students' abilities to handle the actual infusion pump compared to earlier years, when the students did not exercise with the virtual pump.

The second research question asked what are the strengths, weaknesses, opportunities, and threats of using non-immersive VLEs with XR elements for learning interaction competence and clinical competence according to nursing students. For this question, the students' recorded debriefing discussions and SWOT results were investigated within the themes of the SWOT: strengths, weaknesses, opportunities, and threats. Regarding the first scenario, the negative perspectives of threats and weaknesses, students mentioned that the monotonic, emotionless speech of the virtual patient did not feel realistic but sometimes nearly rude, and the virtual element did not feel to have a connection with reality. The students also mentioned that even if they learned something from any exercise, this did not give room for any changing variables. There were too many positive responses that did not lead to any further action. Speech recognition also needs to be improved to understand dialects and accents. However, at the same time, as opportunities and strengths, the students felt that the non-immersive VLE with XR elements provided them with a safe place to learn and make mistakes. They were pleased that they had a place to exercise and develop competencies without pressure.

The second scenario's SWOT analysis revealed that the students felt as weakness and threat the need to have more details in the non-immersive VLE with XR elements so that it was more realistic and forced them to think more carefully. They also wanted more feedback on mistakes and that the VLE should not let you continue if you have made a mistake so that you do not learn wrong. However, the students felt as an opportunity and strength that the exercise in a VLE helped them catch on the use of the actual infusion pump very quickly, as the buttons were very realistic. The students were pleased with the real working life connection of the infusion pump and the fact that it enabled repetitive learning without risks.

5 Discussion, Limitations, and Conclusion

The findings highlight a clear interest in more sophisticated and adaptive VLEs. While the XR-enhanced tools used in this study were visually engaging and user-friendly, participants called for greater interactivity, personalization, and dynamic feedback. Requests for more complex and variable scenarios align with the broader goal of preparing students for real-world clinical challenges. These expectations versus actual experiences speak directly to RQ1, showing that while learners valued the overall approach, certain instructional and technological features did not fully meet their initial hopes. A novelty effect may have contributed to positive motivation scores, as few participants had prior VR experience. However, reduced ratings for interactivity and personal impact suggest a gap between expectation and experience, which future design efforts should address. In terms of RQ2, the recorded debriefing discussions and SWOT analysis offered valuable insight into how students perceive the pedagogical utility of non-immersive VLEs for interaction and clinical competence. Strengths included accessibility, safety, and usability, while weaknesses focused on limited feedback and a lack of adaptive interaction. Opportunities included the expansion of content to support increasingly complex clinical scenarios, while threats included reduced realism and the potential for over-reliance on simplified simulations. These findings suggest that although the platform was positively received, pedagogical refinement is still needed to fully support complex nursing competencies.

These results are significant for nursing education. Non-immersive VLEs with XR elements offer safe, scalable, and cost-effective platforms for practicing high-risk procedures and sensitive interactions, particularly benefiting students in rural or resource-limited areas. Policymakers and educators can use these findings to inform curriculum development and investment in digital learning tools that enhance clinical preparedness and patient safety. The results also contribute to a key debate in educational technology: more immersion does not necessarily yield better learning outcomes. While immersive VR offers stronger presence, it can also introduce cognitive overload, simulator sickness, and logistical challenges [16, 17]. In contrast, the non-immersive solutions tested here were cognitively manageable, motivating, and accessible.

The study supports the view that instructional design, task relevance, and learner readiness are more influential than immersion level alone [17]. The phased model—combining pre-activities, structured simulation, and debriefing—aligns well with experiential learning and scaffolding principles, offering pedagogical strength without high-tech demands. Ultimately, immersive and non-immersive systems serve different educational purposes. Non-immersive XR-enhanced VLEs offer greater inclusivity and scalability, making them ideal for contexts where technological or financial barriers exist. Future research should expand on these findings by comparing immersion levels using matched content and learner groups to refine the alignment between technology and learning objectives.

This study has certain limitations, most notably the small sample size, which restricts the generalizability of findings. Additionally, while the surveys used were relatively simple, this design ensured that they were not overly burdensome for participants and allowed for easy adaptation in future studies. Moving forward, it would be beneficial to conduct research with larger and more diverse participant groups, ideally incorporating control groups, or side-by-side comparisons of immersive and non-immersive environments. Further studies should also examine the pedagogical impact of such tools in preparing nursing students for real-life clinical scenarios, particularly those involving high-risk equipment and procedures, where patient safety is paramount.

Acknowledgments. The article is based on a collaboration between the Lapland University of Applied Sciences' Frost Bit Software Lab and the University of Lapland in the Virtual Production

Studio Technologies project (2023–2025), which is coordinated by the Lapland University of Applied Sciences and financed by the European Regional Development Fund.

Disclosure of Interests. The authors report that there are no competing interests to declare.

References

1. Beaudart, C., Witjes, M., Rood, P., Hiligsmann, M.: Medication administration errors in the domain of infusion therapy in intensive care units: a survey study among nurses. Arch. Public Health **81**, 23 (2023). https://doi.org/10.1186/s13690-023-01041-2
2. Birkheim, S.L., Calogiuri, G., Martinsen, R.: Advancing immersive virtual reality-based simulation practices: developing an evidence-based and theory-driven pedagogical framework for VR-based simulations of non-technical skills among healthcare professionals. Interact. Learn. Environ. **32**(7), 3579–3591 (2024). https://doi.org/10.1080/10494820.2023.2186896
3. Chang, C.Y., Sung, H.Y., Guo, J.L., Chang, B.Y., Kuo, F.R.: Effects of spherical video-based virtual reality on nursing students' learning performance in childbirth education training. Interact. Learn. Environ. **30**(3), 400–416 (2022). https://doi.org/10.1080/10494820.2019.1661854
4. Davis, F.D., Bagozzi, R.P., Warshaw, P.R.: Technology acceptance model. J. Manag. Sci. **35**(8), 982–1003 (1989)
5. Dieckmann, P.: Simulation setting for learning in acute medical care. In: Dieckmann, P. (ed.) Using Simulations for Education, Training and Research, pp. 40–138. Pabst Science Publishers, Lengerich (2009)
6. Fusco, A., Tieri, G.: Challenges and perspectives for clinical applications of immersive and non-immersive virtual reality. J. Clin. Med. **11**(15), 4540 (2022). https://doi.org/10.3390/jcm11154540
7. Keskitalo, T., Saukkoriipi, K.: Co-designing a pedagogical model for immersive virtual environments in healthcare education. Interact. Learn. Environ. 1–11 (2025). https://doi.org/10.1080/10494820.2025.2450643
8. Kirkendall, E.S., Timmons, K., Huth, H., Walsh, K., Melton, K.: Human-based errors involving smart infusion pumps: a catalog of error types and prevention strategies. Drug Saf. **43**, 1073–1087 (2020). https://doi.org/10.1007/s40264-020-00986-5
9. Korte, S. M., Väätäjä, J.: A semi-systematic literature review of holoportation in education: the potential of immersive technology. In: Y. M. Huang, S.C. Cheng, J. Barroso, & F.E. Sadnes. (Eds.), Innovative Technologies and Learning. ICITL 2022. Lecture Notes in Computer Science, vol. 13449, pp. 68–78.Springer, Cham (2022). https://doi.org/10.1007/978-3-031-15273-3_8
10. Lavoie, P., et al.: Immersive and nonimmersive virtual reality: a quasi-experimental study in undergraduate nursing education. Clin. Simul. Nurs. **99**, 101682 (2025). https://doi.org/10.1016/j.ecns.2024.101682
11. Makransky, G., Petersen, G.B.: The cognitive affective model of immersive learning (CAMIL): a theoretical research-based model of learning in immersive virtual reality. Educ. Psychol. Rev. **33**(3), 937–958 (2021). https://doi.org/10.1007/s10648-020-09586-2
12. Poupard, M., Larrue, F., Sauzéon, H., Tricot, A.: A systematic review of immersive technologies for education: Learning performance, cognitive load and intrinsic motivation. Br. J. Edu. Technol. **56**(1), 5–41 (2025). https://doi.org/10.1111/bjet.13503
13. Sohn, D., Choi, S.M.: Measuring expected interactivity: scale development and validation. New Media Soc. **16**(5), 856–870 (2014)

14. Vogelsang, L., et al.: Exploring the use of immersive virtual reality in nursing education: a scoping review. Clin. Simul. Nurs. **97**, 10 (2024). https://doi.org/10.1016/j.ecns.2024.101648
15. Schrimmer, K., Williams, N., Mercado, S., Pitts, J., Polancich, S.: Workforce competencies for healthcare quality professionals: leading quality-driven healthcare. J. Healthcare Qual. (JHQ) **41**(4), 259–265 (2019)
16. Makransky, G., Lilleholt, L.: A structural equation modeling investigation of the emotional value of immersive virtual reality in education. Educ. Tech. Res. Dev. **66**(5), 1141–1164 (2018). https://doi.org/10.1007/s11423-018-9581-2
17. Radianti, J., Majchrzak, T.A., Fromm, J., Wohlgenannt, I.: A systematic review of immersive virtual reality applications for higher education: design elements, lessons learned, and research agenda. Comput. Educ. **147**, 103778 (2020). https://doi.org/10.1016/j.compedu.2019.103778

A Virtual Reality-Based Co-creation Approach to Developing Narrative Competence and Empathy in EFL Nursing Education

Tuyuan Cheng(✉)

General Education Center, National Tainan Junior College of Nursing, Tainan, Taiwan R.O.C.
TYCheng@ntin.edu.tw, 2010tuyuan@gmail.com

Abstract. This study investigates the use of virtual reality (VR) as a pedagogical tool to foster English narrative competence and empathy among nursing students in an English as a Foreign Language (EFL) context. Through a 16-week course-integrated intervention, 98 third-year nursing students in a five-year associate degree program at a junior nursing college participated in a co-creation project using CoSpaces Edu to collaboratively design immersive, first-person 3D narratives based on an end-of-life care scenario. The project aimed to develop students' linguistic skills while promoting humanistic understanding through perspective-taking. Employing a mixed-methods design, the study incorporated pre- and post-intervention vocabulary tests, oral narrative evaluations, student reflections, and interviews. Results demonstrated significant gains in English vocabulary and narrative expression, increased oral confidence, and evidence of enhanced empathy as students adopted diverse character roles in their digital stories. The findings underscore the pedagogical affordances of VR-based co-creation in EFL instruction for healthcare students, revealing how immersive storytelling can bridge language learning with humanistic nursing education. Implications for XR-enhanced language education and interdisciplinary curriculum design are discussed.

Keywords: Virtual Reality · EFL · Nursing Education · Immersive Learning · Digital Storytelling · Empathy

1 Introduction

In today's globalized healthcare environments, nursing professionals must demonstrate strong English communication skills. Yet, many EFL nursing students—especially in Taiwan—struggle with low proficiency and lack confidence using English [1, 2]. Prior research shows that students often translate literally from their first language, producing Chinglish expressions, and tend to view English as an exam subject rather than a professional tool. This disconnect between language instruction and practical communication needs limits both academic development and readiness for international clinical contexts. At the same time, empathy and humanistic care are essential competencies in nursing. Educational approaches like narrative-based learning have been shown to enhance students' ability to understand others and deliver patient-centered care. The

W.-S. Wang et al. (Eds.): ICITL 2025, LNCS 15913, pp. 335–344, 2026.
https://doi.org/10.1007/978-3-031-98185-2_35

challenge for educators is to design experiences that build both language proficiency and empathic capacity.

Extended reality (XR) technologies, particularly virtual reality (VR), offer immersive environments where students can engage in meaningful, contextualized learning. VR allows for creative, interactive, and collaborative tasks that reduce anxiety and promote motivation. These open-ended experiences align with communicative language learning principles and ecological models that emphasize authentic language use in real-world contexts. Unlike fixed vocabulary drills, VR storytelling tasks allow students to construct narratives based on personal or professional experiences, enhancing engagement and ownership.

Beyond language development, VR's immersive storytelling can foster empathy by enabling students to virtually step into others' perspectives. In nursing education, narrative reflection helps students develop a compassionate outlook. VR enhances this by offering experiential simulations that mirror real-life patient care scenarios.

This study brings together these elements—second language learning, narrative-based pedagogy, and VR technology—through a project titled *Virtual Co-Creation for EFL Nursing Students' English Narrative Skills and Empathy Competence*. Implemented in a 16-week English course, the project used CoSpaces Edu to help associate-degree nursing students create and share interactive, medically themed 3D stories. Students took on character roles, scripted in English, and designed scenes via block-based coding. Prior research shows such co-creation tasks promote learner agency and creativity [3]. Our aim was to explore how this immersive narrative approach supports both English language growth and empathy development.

2 Purpose and Research Questions

Building on these considerations, our study aimed to investigate how an immersive VR-based storytelling project would impact EFL nursing students' English narrative abilities and their empathy development. In particular, we sought to examine: (1) whether students' English language skills (especially narrative writing and speaking) improved after participating in the VR story co-creation project; (2) how the use of VR as a storytelling medium influenced students' engagement, anxiety, and willingness to communicate in English; (3) whether and in what ways the activity fostered empathy or perspective-taking related to nursing care; and (4) what affordances and challenges were observed in using an immersive co-creation tool (CoSpaces) in an EFL classroom. By addressing these questions, we aim to contribute knowledge on the pedagogical value of XR in education, specifically how VR can be harnessed to integrate language learning with essential soft skills like empathy in a vocational context.

3 Literature Review

This study draws on three interrelated strands of literature: XR in second language learning, narrative pedagogy and empathy in nursing education, and immersive storytelling tools and student agency.

XR for Language Learning and Narrative Competence. Virtual Reality-Assisted Language Learning (VRALL) has gained momentum as XR technologies—VR, AR, and MR—offer immersive, interactive learning environments. Research shows that VR can lower speaking anxiety, enhance motivation, and improve learner confidence [4]. Its simulation-based nature enables context-rich interactions beyond traditional textbook drills. Learners can engage in real-time communication, receive immediate feedback, and repeat practice in less judgmental settings. However, gains in measurable fluency or accuracy are not guaranteed. Technical complexity and cognitive load may offset VR's benefits without proper support and integration [5]. Crucially, VR supports holistic language use, making it a suitable tool for tasks like storytelling, which engages multiple skills simultaneously. Storytelling promotes coherence, vocabulary expansion, and fluency. Godwin-Jones (2023) highlights XR's capacity for "learner co-design," enabling students to actively shape content in ways aligned with communicative and task-based learning approaches [6]. Instead of responding to scripted interactions, learners create and enact original scenarios, supporting deeper engagement and more authentic language output. Few studies have explored students as *creators* of VR narratives rather than users. An exception is ChanLin and Chou (2022), who found that Taiwanese EFL students designing 3D stories with CoSpaces developed digital, narrative, and linguistic competencies. Students reported increased enjoyment and ownership, as well as strategic decision-making to realize their narrative vision [3]. These findings indicate that immersive co-creation tasks, though demanding, can empower students and stretch their language capabilities.

Narrative Pedagogy and Empathy in Nursing. Narrative education is a well-established strategy in nursing to foster empathy and reflective thinking. Writing and analyzing patient stories helps learners connect medical knowledge with human experiences. Huang et al. (2023) demonstrated that narrative education significantly improved students' empathy and humanistic awareness, as reflected in both quantitative gains and qualitative themes in student reflections [7]. This builds on Diekelmann's (2001) assertion that storytelling fosters connection, ethical insight, and care [8]. In our project, narrative thinking was central. Students engaged with a life-and-death scenario—terminal illness and family care decisions—through role-based storytelling. By crafting stories from various viewpoints (patient, nurse, family), learners had to consider the emotions and motivations of each stakeholder. The shift from third-person narrative in scripts to first-person perspective in VR scenes simulated lived experience, reinforcing perspective-taking. Research suggests that such immersive narrative work can deepen empathic understanding, even in non-clinical settings. Though conducted in an English course, the activity's alignment with nursing values added authenticity and relevance.

Immersive Storytelling Tools and Student Agency. CoSpaces Edu and similar platforms allow non-programmers to create 3D stories using drag-and-drop tools and block coding. Studies highlight their pedagogical affordances: multimodal expression, teamwork, problem-solving, and learner agency. Martin (2024) observed that elementary students designing VR scenes became more invested in their writing and contributed actively to a "community of learners." Visualization of written content helped improve both creativity and literacy [9]. However, challenges exist. Open-ended tasks can overwhelm learners unfamiliar with tech tools, especially in language classrooms. ChanLin and Chou (2022) noted that students struggled with story logic and time management, leading some to scale back their ideas [3]. Similarly, in our study, students cited technical difficulties and the steep learning curve of CoSpaces as barriers. Some described the digital workload as dominating the English course, and we had to mitigate this by offering tutorials, group work, and setting a clear timeline due to platform trial limits. Despite these challenges, immersive storytelling provided meaningful contexts for language use, heightened engagement, and fostered learner ownership. It also supported interdisciplinary aims by combining language, empathy, and digital literacy.

Summary and Rationale. This review shows that VR can enhance communicative competence and student motivation, narrative pedagogy builds empathy in nursing, and immersive co-creation tasks foster deeper learning and engagement. Our study brings these strands together through a VR-based narrative project for EFL nursing students, aiming to develop both English proficiency and empathy through role-based virtual storytelling. This fills a gap in existing research by exploring the learner as VR content creator in a healthcare-themed language classroom.

4 Methodology

4.1 Participants and Context

This study was conducted at a public five-year junior nursing college in Taiwan during the 2022–2023 academic year. The participants were 98 third-year nursing students (approximately 19–20 years old), equivalent in age to college sophomores. All students had completed at least three years of formal English instruction in high school and were familiar with basic English medical terminology from prior coursework. As part of their regular curriculum, they were enrolled in an English course with weekly instruction. Informed consent was obtained from all participants, and anonymity was maintained throughout in accordance with ethical and double-blind research standards.

At baseline, students completed the EF Standard English Test (EF SET), an online adaptive proficiency test aligned with CEFR levels. Results showed most students were at the lower-intermediate level (A2–B1), confirming the instructor's observations of limited proficiency. A 40-item vocabulary pre-test targeting general and nursing-specific English terms (e.g., related to healthcare and end-of-life care) was also administered. The average scores indicated low familiarity with many target words (detailed in Results).

The English course was theme-based, centered around "life issues and humanistic care." Students read and discussed the English text *The Last Day*, which depicted an elderly patient's end-of-life decisions. Through guided class discussion, students identified eight narrative perspectives—including the patient, family members, a nurse, doctor, and others. They were divided into 16 groups (5–6 students each), with each group assigned one perspective to develop into a collaborative narrative. This structure laid the foundation for the subsequent VR storytelling project.

4.2 Design of the Virtual Co-creation Project

This study followed a one-group pretest–posttest design with qualitative inquiry, centered on a VR storytelling project using CoSpaces Edu. The project spanned a 16-week English course.

Weeks 1–3: Preparation. Students completed baseline assessments (EF SET, vocabulary pre-test), read *The Last Day*, and explored its themes. Eight narrative roles were defined, and students grouped by interest. A brief CoSpaces orientation was provided.

Weeks 4–6: Script Writing. Groups drafted English narratives from their chosen character's perspective, incorporating narrative elements and first-person voice to foster empathy and authentic expression.

Week 8: Midterm. Students completed comprehension and vocabulary questions, along with a short reflective essay on character viewpoints.

Weeks 9–12: VR Creation. Groups transformed their scripts into CoSpaces VR scenes using dialogues and voice-overs.

Week 13: Peer Feedback. Groups presented drafts and revised based on peer suggestions.

Week 15: Final Showcase. Students publicly shared their VR stories in a gallery-style event, interacting with peers from other departments in English.

Week 16: Post-Assessment. A vocabulary post-test, oral narrative task, and student survey were administered to measure learning outcomes and perceptions. This design enabled triangulated data collection (quantitative and qualitative) and was ethically approved by the institution. The structure balanced language development with creative collaboration, supporting both cognitive and affective learning goals.

4.3 Measures and Analysis

We adopted a one-group pretest–posttest quasi-experimental design with mixed methods. Quantitative data included the EF SET (baseline only), a 40-item vocabulary pre/post-test (analyzed using paired-samples t-tests, $\alpha = 0.05$), and a final oral narrative scored by two raters (max = 15; inter-rater $r = 0.88$). Correlations were calculated between oral scores, vocabulary gains, and EF SET results. A 10-item Likert-scale survey assessed perceived learning, anxiety reduction, and engagement; open-ended responses were coded thematically. Twelve student interviews and instructor journals were also analyzed for emergent themes (e.g., empathy, confidence). VR artifacts were reviewed for narrative quality and perspective use, supplemented by comparisons to poster texts. All quantitative analyses were conducted in SPSS; qualitative data were narratively integrated.

5 Results

5.1 English Language Outcomes

Vocabulary Gain and Narrative Performance. The VR storytelling project led to significant gains in students' vocabulary and improvements in narrative performance. Pre-test vocabulary scores averaged $M = 23.5$ out of 40 (58.8%), rising to $M = 30.1$ (75.3%) post-project—a 16.5% increase ($t = 9.42$, $p < .001$). Gains were most evident for terms relevant to the narrative (e.g., hospice, terminal, compassion), suggesting that contextual use reinforced retention.

Oral narrative scores averaged 11.2 out of 15 (~75%). Students, who previously struggled with extended speech, delivered coherent 2-min summaries by project end. While some persistent errors were noted (e.g., dropped "-s"), overall fluency improved. Vocabulary gain positively correlated with oral scores ($r = 0.45$, $p < .001$), while baseline EF SET proficiency did not ($r = 0.20$, $p = .06$), suggesting the project benefitted students regardless of prior level.

In the survey, 84% agreed that creating and presenting the VR story improved their speaking ability. Students described feeling less nervous and more expressive during the final showcase. Writing also improved: final scripts demonstrated clearer narrative structure and greater emotional depth. For example, "The patient did not want to continue treatment" evolved into, "I don't want any more treatments. I just want peace." This shift to personal tone reflected deeper engagement and perspective-taking.

5.2 Empathy and Perspective-Taking Outcomes

The project's multi-perspective design fostered empathy. Although no formal empathy scale was used, student reflections and interviews revealed emotional insight. One student shared: "At first, I disagreed with the mother's decision in the story. But after speaking as her, I understood her pain." All 12 interviewees stated the role-play shifted their understanding—of patients, doctors, and families alike.

After seeing peer presentations, students noted the dilemma was more complex than they first thought, with no simple "right" answer. One student said, "Now I understand why nurses feel stuck when families argue. I felt that in my role." The instructor noted that the VR context simulated a "clinical" situation, prompting authentic emotional engagement. One student recounted, "When I saw our patient avatar in bed, and I had to say goodbye as her daughter, I almost cried." Though cartoon-like, the 3D environment created a real emotional impact.

5.3 Student Engagement and Agency

Student engagement remained high throughout the project. Survey data showed that 92% viewed the project as valuable, 89% found it enjoyable, 76% felt more confident in English, and 73% said it reduced their speaking anxiety. However, only 65% felt technical support was sufficient, and 30% reported tech-related difficulties. Several students suggested simplifying the project or adding in-class time. One said, "Maybe we could have just made one scene instead of a whole story." Another noted, "It would help if we had a technical assistant."

Despite challenges, students expressed pride in creating a lasting, interactive artifact—"our story world"—which they found motivating. The experience also boosted student agency: many took initiative in scripting, designing, and coordinating tasks. The project's multimodal nature allowed diverse strengths to emerge, enabling all students—regardless of English level—to contribute meaningfully.

Table 1 summarizes key student feedback, highlighting both the benefits and drawbacks of the immersive storytelling experience.

Table 1. Student Feedback Summary (Qualitative Themes)

Perceived Benefits	Challenges/Drawbacks
Novelty & Enjoyment: Students described the experience as "fun" and "special." Many appreciated the creative format and the chance to "see our story come alive in VR."	*High Time Investment:* Most groups found the workload heavy, especially outside class. "It took too much time," was a common remark
Skill Development: Students learned new tech skills like scene design, voiceovers, and basic coding—skills not typically part of English class	*Technical Issues:* Some faced crashes, lagging, or device access problems. Others noted the need for clearer technical guidance
English Communication: Students felt more capable expressing ideas in English, both in writing and speaking	*Learning Curve:* Some struggled with CoSpaces functions and wished for more practice or tutorials
Collaboration & Creativity: Teams enjoyed building stories together. One group even added a creative "ghost" twist beyond the original plot	*Role of Technology in English Class:* A few felt that too much tech might *overshadow* language learning, suggesting better integration with English instruction

Student feedback revealed that although the immersive VR project was demanding, its benefits were widely acknowledged. Many appreciated the creativity, teamwork, and novelty of digital storytelling. Common suggestions included extending the timeline or simplifying the task—for example, creating one scene instead of a full narrative. Despite the workload, students expressed pride in their accomplishments. One noted, "We made a thing that stayed—our story world—and that feels rewarding." This reflects the motivational power of creating tangible products. From the instructor's perspective, the project fostered agency: students took initiative, shared tasks, and used diverse skills in writing, design, and coding. Even quieter learners engaged meaningfully, highlighting how multimodal projects promote inclusive participation and empower students through collaborative language learning.

Summary of Key Findings

This study addressed four key research questions.

RQ1 (Language Improvement): Students demonstrated significant gains in vocabulary ($p < .001$), narrative fluency, and perspective-taking in both speaking and writing, indicating that immersive storytelling supports English language development.
RQ2 (Speaking Anxiety and Communication): The VR environment reduced speaking anxiety by providing visual and contextual scaffolding. Most students reported greater confidence and willingness to communicate in English.
RQ3 (Empathy and Humanistic Outcomes): Although not formally measured, qualitative reflections revealed increased emotional insight and understanding. Role-play in caregiving roles helped students engage with humanistic aspects of nursing education.
RQ4 (Affordances and Challenges): The CoSpaces platform enabled creative, collaborative learning that integrated language use with digital literacy. However, technical difficulties and time pressure posed challenges. Students recommended more in-class support and a simplified project scope.

Overall, immersive VR storytelling fostered language growth, communicative confidence, and empathy when aligned with clear pedagogical goals.

6 Discussion

This study demonstrates that immersive VR co-creation is a promising pedagogical strategy for English language development in specialized EFL contexts, such as nursing education. Students showed significant vocabulary gains and improved narrative fluency, including a 16.5% increase in test performance ($t = 9.42$, $p < .001$) on key vocabulary related to the story context. These results affirm the value of embedding language instruction in meaningful, emotionally resonant tasks. When students co-construct stories rooted in authentic human dilemmas, they become more motivated to use English purposefully and accurately.

Importantly, the VR environment supported reductions in speaking anxiety. Students reported feeling more confident due to the presence of a visual narrative scaffold, group rehearsal, and the ability to "speak through" their characters. These findings are consistent with the idea that immersive contexts and emotionally engaging content help lower affective filters and encourage communication, particularly among anxious EFL learners.

The empathy development observed is a critical outcome. Rooted in a story about terminal illness and ethical decision-making, the project required students to assume roles such as patient, nurse, or family caregiver. Through role-play and first-person scripting, students began to internalize their characters' struggles and emotional perspectives. Reflections revealed that this process shifted their understanding of complex patient-care dynamics. This mutually reinforcing relationship between language learning and humanistic development illustrates the potential of narrative-based, affectively grounded instruction.

Theoretically, the project aligns with both task-based language learning (TBLT) and content-based instruction (CBI). Following Skehan's (1998) task framework [10], the project provided a cognitively engaging, outcome-driven task with real-world relevance. Students collaborated to produce a tangible product (VR story), engaged in perspective-taking, and practiced sustained English output across writing and speaking. Moreover, the humanistic content—empathy in end-of-life care—deepened cognitive and emotional involvement, aligning with CBI's principle of integrated content and language learning.

Our findings also resonate with Godwin-Jones' (2023) argument that extended reality (XR) fits well with holistic SLA theories when used for meaningful simulation and learner co-design [6]. Students in our study acted as co-creators of their learning environment, and we observed increased motivation, agency, and sustained interaction in the target language. As in other VRALL research, some challenges emerged—namely, technical hurdles and occasional cognitive overload—but these can be mitigated as platforms improve and educators gain experience structuring XR projects.

From the lens of nursing education, the empathy development aligns with Benner's (1984) novice-to-expert model [11]. Benner theorized that novice nurses advance toward expertise through experiential learning and reflective practice, gradually moving from rule-based reasoning to intuitive, contextual understanding. While our students were at the novice stage, the immersive storytelling experience simulated care dilemmas that required them to grapple with conflicting values and ethical ambiguity. By stepping into the emotional realities of a patient or nurse, they engaged in perspective-taking akin to reflective clinical experience. Although not a substitute for patient care, the narrative immersion provided a valuable simulation of the human side of healthcare, reinforcing the early development of ethical and empathic reasoning.

In sum, this study illustrates that immersive storytelling using VR can bridge linguistic, cognitive, and affective domains of learning. Language tasks (speaking and writing) became vehicles for building empathy, while the emotionally charged narrative context deepened students' motivation to communicate authentically. The result is a synergistic learning environment that supports both communicative competence and personal growth—especially relevant for nursing students preparing for emotionally complex professional roles.

7 Conclusion

This study demonstrates that virtual reality–facilitated co-creation can serve as an effective pedagogical approach in EFL nursing education. By engaging students as both English users and narrative creators, the VR storytelling project fostered not only language development—evidenced by gains in vocabulary, writing coherence, and oral fluency—but also higher-order learning outcomes such as empathy and perspective-taking.

Through immersive role-play, students explored ethically complex scenarios, aligning with the goals of holistic and humanistic education. The project functioned as a microcosm of real-world communication, requiring students to consider what to say, how to express it in English, and why it matters in a caregiving context.

Crucially, this initiative illustrates a successful integration of technology and pedagogy. VR was not used for novelty, but as a purposeful medium for expression, collaboration, and reflection. While challenges such as workload and technical limitations were noted, thoughtful scaffolding helped maximize learning outcomes.

In sum, the "Virtual Co-creation" project empowered nursing students to become active authors of their own learning. The combination of immersive technology and narrative pedagogy supported both linguistic and affective growth. As XR becomes more accessible, such integrative projects hold strong potential for enriching CALL and interdisciplinary education when grounded in pedagogical intent.

Acknowledgments. This study was funded by grants from the Ministry of Education (MOE) 111-Year Teaching Practice Research Program, Taiwan, R.O.C. 2022/08/01~2023/07/31 (PHA1110316).

Disclosure of Interests. The author has no competing interests to declare that are relevant to the content of this article.

References

1. Yang, C.L.: The necessity for nursing staff to strengthen English communication ability under international medical trends. J. Nurs. **58**(1), 97–101 (2011)
2. You, S.Y., Jhang, R.H., Su, S.M.: The nursing register-specific vocabulary – medical terminology: a qualitative and quantitative exploration. J. Chang Gung Inst. Technol. **3**, 291–301 (2004)
3. ChanLin, L.J., Chou, T.L.: Storytelling with block coding among college students at a university in Northern Taiwan. Creat. Educ. **13**(2), 347–365 (2022)
4. Yudintseva, A.: Virtual reality affordances for oral communication in English as a second language classroom: a literature review. Comput. Educ. X Real. **2**, 100018 (2023)
5. Koushik, S., Guinness, R., Kane, L.: StoryBlocks: a tangible programming game to create VR experiences. In: Proceedings of ACM CHI Conference on Human Factors in Computing Systems, pp. 1–12. ACM, New York (2019)
6. Godwin-Jones, R.: Presence and agency in real and virtual spaces: the promise of extended reality for language learning. Lang. Learn. Technol. **27**(3), 6–26 (2023)
7. Huang, Q., et al.: Role of narrative education in cultivating humanistic care and empathy in nursing students. Research Square preprint (2023). https://doi.org/10.21203/rs.3.rs-3284130/v1
8. Diekelmann, N.: Narrative pedagogy: heideggerian hermeneutical analyses of lived experiences of students, teachers, and clinicians. Adv. Nurs. Sci. **23**(3), 53–71 (2001)
9. Martin, T.L.: Learning in 3D: Creating Virtual Reality Environments. Doctoral dissertation, University of North Carolina at Greensboro (2024)
10. Skehan, P.: A Cognitive Approach to Language Learning. Oxford University Press, Oxford (1998)
11. Benner, P.: From Novice to Expert: Excellence and Power in Clinical Nursing Practice. Addison-Wesley, Menlo Park (1984)

The Impact of Virtual Art Exhibitions on Achievement Motivation and Technology Acceptance: A Case Study of Upper-Grade Elementary Students in Rural Areas

Yu-Hsuan Lin(✉) and Yu-Ying Hsu

Department of Digital Media and Education Industry, National Taitung University, Taitung, Taiwan
y.hsuan0307@gmail.com

Abstract. In rural areas, gifted art classes often face limitations in organizing traditional exhibitions due to constraints of time and location, which may hinder student participation and dampen their motivation and sense of achievement. To address these issues, this study examines how virtual reality (VR) art exhibitions influence the achievement experience and technology acceptance among upper-grade elementary school students. A total of 42 students from a rural elementary school in Taitung County participated in this study. Pre- and post-intervention questionnaires were used to evaluate changes in students' perceived achievement and their acceptance of the VR-based exhibition. The results revealed that the VR exhibition contributed positively to students' sense of achievement. Most students showed a favorable attitude toward the technology, particularly in terms of perceived usefulness. However, students' perceptions varied in areas such as enjoyment and ease of use, with some reporting challenges related to navigation and interface design. Technical factors like device stability and operational fluency also affected the overall experience. These findings offer practical implications for the development and implementation of VR art exhibitions, especially in resource-limited educational settings. Future research may explore applications across different age groups and focus on enhancing interactivity, engagement, and usability to support student learning and acceptance.

Keywords: Virtual Reality Exhibition · Rural Students · Achievement Motivation · Technology Acceptance · Digital Art Exhibition

1 Introduction

In rural gifted art programs, traditional physical exhibitions often face challenges due to time and location constraints, limiting students' opportunities to present their artworks. These limitations not only restrict exposure but also negatively impact students' motivation, confidence, and willingness to continue engaging in creative endeavors. The lack of educational resources and diverse exhibition formats in remote areas may further reduce students' enthusiasm for artistic expression and hinder their overall development.

W.-S. Wang et al. (Eds.): ICITL 2025, LNCS 15913, pp. 345–353, 2026.
https://doi.org/10.1007/978-3-031-98185-2_36

In recent years, the rise of digital art and virtual reality (VR) exhibitions has provided new possibilities for overcoming the spatial and temporal barriers of traditional displays [1, 2]. VR eliminates physical and economic limitations by offering flexible access to immersive exhibition experiences. Students can now present their work in interactive 3D environments, enhancing both visibility and engagement. For example, VR allows users to "enter" a virtual gallery, navigate freely, and explore artworks in depth—features that go beyond the limitations of 2D platforms [3]. These immersive experiences have been shown to increase viewers' motivation and sense of participation [1], especially for students in remote areas who may otherwise lack opportunities to share their work on a broader stage.

Digital exhibitions also introduce practical advantages over traditional exhibitions, such as greater flexibility, reduced long-term costs, and enhanced multimedia interactivity [4]. Unlike in-person displays that require physical attendance and venue logistics, digital exhibitions can be accessed anytime, allowing wider participation. Though the initial setup cost for VR exhibitions may be high, the long-term benefits—such as reusability, reduced transportation needs, and ease of content updates—make them a valuable educational tool. Moreover, VR exhibitions can integrate audio guides, 3D models, AR/VR technologies, and hyperlinks to create rich, interactive experiences. However, it is worth noting that they may not fully replicate the tactile or sensory depth of traditional exhibitions [5].

For students in rural areas, who often face logistical and resource barriers to participating in exhibitions [6], VR serves as an inclusive and equitable alternative. It not only enables broader presentation opportunities but also fosters cross-regional exchange and cultural diversity in art education [1]. As digital technologies continue to advance, VR is becoming increasingly integrated into educational settings. Its immersive and interactive nature transforms both teaching and learning by offering engaging environments that promote participation and improve learning outcomes [7].

In the context of art education, VR expands the creative space, allowing students to explore, create, and exhibit in new ways. Accordingly, integrating VR into art instruction has become a critical topic in educational research. This study aims to examine whether VR art exhibitions can enhance elementary school students' sense of achievement and their acceptance of technology. By evaluating the effectiveness of VR learning environments, this research seeks to provide empirical support for the future integration of immersive technologies in art education—especially in under-resourced and rural settings. The research questions of this study are as follows:

The research topics this study aims to explore are as follows:

(1) Can VR art exhibitions enhance the sense of achievement among upper-grade elementary school students?
(2) How do upper-grade elementary students perceive the usefulness of VR art exhibitions?
(3) How do they perceive the ease of use of VR art exhibitions?
(4) How do they perceive the enjoyment of VR art exhibitions?
(5) What is the overall level of technology acceptance among upper-grade elementary school students regarding VR art exhibitions?

2 Literature Review

2.1 Online Exhibitions

Online exhibitions integrate digital content and images through web-based technologies, allowing audiences to access exhibitions remotely. Over time, these platforms have evolved from static displays to incorporating multimedia elements such as audio, video, gamified experiences, guided tours, and interactive virtual galleries, offering more engaging and flexible user experiences. Tseng [8] highlighted that digital technologies have blurred the boundaries between physical and virtual exhibition spaces, encouraging curators and artists to explore innovative spatial and display strategies. More recently, Li et al. [9] reported that during the COVID-19 pandemic, about 90% of physical exhibitions were suspended worldwide, while digital activities increased by 5.6%, and 6.5% of museums began actively developing online exhibitions as part of their digital transformation efforts. This shift demonstrates the growing significance of online exhibitions in overcoming physical limitations and reaching broader audiences.

In summary, online exhibitions have transitioned from basic presentations to immersive and interactive experiences. While they have expanded access and enhanced engagement, most still rely on 2D interfaces, which limits immersion. Therefore, researchers are increasingly exploring more immersive exhibition formats—such as VR—to improve viewer interaction and educational outcomes.

2.2 VR in Exhibitions

With the rapid advancement of virtual reality (VR) technology, digital exhibitions have moved beyond traditional 2D displays. Viewers can now explore immersive 3D environments, freely navigating spatial layouts and engaging with exhibition details [1]. VR combines visual, auditory, and interactive elements to simulate realistic exhibition spaces, enhancing users' sense of presence and learning experiences. For example, the National Museum of Natural Science in Taiwan applied VR in its 2017 exhibition Dunhuang Revisited, reconstructing the Mogao Caves with detailed 3D visuals and a 720° panoramic tour. This immersive setup allowed users to virtually navigate the exhibition, breaking through spatial and temporal limitations. Li et al. [9] found that VR's interactivity and immersion significantly influenced users' perceptions of presence and authenticity, which positively impacted their engagement. In the educational field, Zhou and Li [10] reported that students involved in VR/AR-based exhibitions achieved greater aesthetic appreciation, emotional connection, and cognitive depth than those in traditional settings. These findings suggest that immersive technologies can effectively boost learning motivation and provide enriched educational experiences.

In conclusion, VR exhibitions offer audiences interactive and immersive engagement with content. While VR is increasingly used in cultural contexts, its potential in education—particularly in enhancing students' sense of achievement and technology acceptance—deserves further exploration. This study investigates how VR art exhibitions influence these factors in upper-grade elementary students to inform future applications in art education.

2.3 Achievement Goal Theory

Achievement goal theory, centered on the concept of ability [11], explores how students' motivational orientations impact learning and performance. Originally proposed in the 1980s, it has since been widely applied in both educational and work-related contexts [12]. The theory has evolved from a two-dimensional model (mastery vs. performance goals) to a more nuanced framework. Elliot and Harackiewicz [13] introduced the distinction between performance-approach and performance-avoidance goals, leading to a three-dimensional model. Later, Elliot [14] further refined the model by distinguishing between mastery-approach and mastery-avoidance goals, forming the four-dimensional framework. To address different evaluative standards, Elliot [15] proposed the 3×2 achievement goal model, incorporating task-based, self-based, and other-based goals with both approach and avoidance orientations. Achievement goals are also closely linked to academic engagement. For example, Ndyareeba et al. [16] found that mastery-oriented goals enhanced engagement among Ugandan adolescents, while performance goals were more likely to result in strategic, pressure-driven learning.

In this study, the four-dimensional achievement goal framework is adopted to examine how VR art exhibitions may influence upper-grade elementary students' sense of achievement.

2.4 Technology Acceptance Model

The Technology Acceptance Model (TAM), developed by Davis [17], explains users' adoption of new technologies by emphasizing two key beliefs: perceived usefulness and perceived ease of use. These beliefs influence users' attitudes and behavioral intentions, ultimately affecting actual usage. External factors can also shape these perceptions. Later, Moon and Kim [18] expanded TAM by introducing perceived enjoyment as another factor influencing users' attitudes. When users find a technology useful, easy to use, and enjoyable, they are more likely to adopt it [19]. Recent studies, such as Musa et al. [20], have confirmed TAM's broad applicability across fields, especially in predicting behavioral intention. For instance, Ma et al. [21] demonstrated that higher acceptance of technology significantly improves users' behavioral intention and actual usage. These findings support TAM as a reliable framework for evaluating technology use.

In this study, TAM is applied to investigate elementary students' acceptance of VR art exhibitions, focusing on three key factors: perceived usefulness, ease of use, and enjoyment.

3 Research Methods

3.1 VR Art Exhibition

The online exhibition developed for this study was created using the MAKAR platform. The students' artwork was digitized and transformed into a virtual art exhibition, which was then experienced through VR headsets. Figure 1 shows the VR art exhibition designed using the MAKAR platform. The VR exhibition allowed students to freely navigate a 3D gallery space, view their artworks from different angles, and zoom in on details. Additionally, students could click on individual artworks to access guided introductions, providing further explanations about each piece.

Fig. 1. VR art exhibition screen

3.2 Participants

This study involved 42 upper-grade elementary school students from a primary school located in eastern Taiwan.

3.3 Experimental Process

The aim of this study was to examine the impact of a VR art exhibition on upper-grade elementary students' sense of achievement and their level of technology acceptance. Each participant was equipped with a VR headset (HTC VIVE Focus), and due to space limitations in the classroom, only two students could participate in the VR experience at a time. The procedure consisted of a pre-test questionnaire (approximately 8 min), followed by a brief instructional session (around 2 min) to introduce the use of the VR headset. Students then engaged with the VR art exhibition for about 20 min. After the experience, they completed a post-test questionnaire, which took approximately 10 min. Figure 2 illustrates students participating in the VR exhibition.

Fig. 2. Students participating in the VR art exhibition

3.4 Research Tool

(1) Achievement Scale:

The achievement scale used in this study was adapted from the questionnaire developed by Tzoh and Lu [22]. It was designed to explore whether the VR art exhibition could enhance the achievement sense of upper-grade elementary school students. The original questionnaire contained 16 items, but items 6, 8, and 10 were removed due to inadequate reliability. After the removal, the Cronbach's alpha increased to 0.717, indicating improved internal consistency and greater reliability in measuring achievement. A five-point Likert scale was used, with scores ranging from 1 to 5, representing "strongly disagree," "disagree," "neutral," "agree," and "strongly agree." Higher scores indicated a higher level of perceived achievement. The questionnaire was administered as both a pre-test and a post-test, completed before and after the VR art exhibition experience.

(2) Technology Acceptance Scale:

The technology acceptance scale used in this study was adapted from the questionnaire developed by Hwang et al. [23] to assess upper-grade elementary students' acceptance of the VR art exhibition. The Cronbach's alpha for this scale was 0.711. The questionnaire included 8 items and adopted a five-point Likert scale, with scores ranging from 1 to 5, representing "strongly disagree," "disagree," "neutral," "agree," and "strongly agree." Higher scores reflected a higher level of technology acceptance.

4 Results

4.1 Achievement Evaluation

This section explores the impact of the VR art exhibition on the sense of achievement among upper-grade elementary school students. As shown in Table 1, the study examined whether students' sense of achievement improved after experiencing the VR art exhibition. The results revealed that the overall pre-test mean score was 3.40 (SD = 0.360), while the post-test mean score was 3.47 (SD = 0.364). The higher post-test mean indicates an overall improvement in students' achievement scores. The p-value was 0.013, suggesting a statistically significant difference between the pre- and post-test scores. The effect size was d = 0.400, indicating a moderate effect, which suggests that the VR art exhibition had a positive impact on students' sense of achievement.

Table 1. Paired Sample t-Test of Pre-test and Post-test Scores (N = 42)

Dimension	Mean (SD)		df	t	p	d
	Pre-test	Post-test				
Achievement	3.4908 (0.481)	3.6088 (0.463)	41	−2.592	0.013	0.400

4.2 Technology Acceptance Evaluation

This study investigates the overall technology acceptance of upper-grade elementary school students toward a VR art exhibition. The technology acceptance is divided into three dimensions: perceived enjoyment, perceived usefulness, and perceived ease of use. As shown in Table 2, the average score for overall technology acceptance is 3.40

(SD = 0.714), indicating a high level of acceptance among students toward the VR art exhibition. Among the three dimensions, perceived usefulness received the highest score, suggesting that students generally believe the VR exhibition is helpful for learning. The scores for perceived enjoyment and perceived ease of use are similar, but with relatively higher standard deviations, indicating greater variability in students' opinions regarding the fun and ease of using the VR exhibition.

Table 2. Descriptive Statistics for Technology Acceptance

	N	Min	Max	Mean	SD
Perceived Enjoyment	42	1	5	3.23	1.190
Perceived Usefulness	42	1.67	5	3.74	0.819
Perceived Ease of Use	42	1.67	5	3.23	0.865
Overall Scale	42	1	5	3.40	0.714

4.3 Qualitative Analysis Results

This study explored students' experiences of achievement in a VR art exhibition through thematic analysis of open-ended questionnaire responses. Among the 16 items, students most frequently responded to Q3 ("I hope my artwork in the exhibition can showcase my abilities to others") and Q14 ("I hope to learn broader and deeper artistic knowledge and drawing skills"), highlighting two key sources of achievement: external recognition and internal skill improvement.

(1) Family Recognition

Fourteen students indicated that they wanted their families and friends to see and acknowledge their work, as they often receive little attention in daily life. The exhibition provided a platform for their abilities to be seen and appreciated. S1 said, "With this VR art exhibition, my parents and aunt can see my work, and that makes me very happy". S5 shared, "My friend said he didn't expect me to be so good at drawing, which gave me a strong sense of achievement". These comments underscore the importance of external validation in boosting students' confidence and pride in their work.

(2) Skill Development

Thirteen students expressed a desire to improve their artistic knowledge and skills. They noted that viewing their work in a VR setting helped them observe details more clearly and explore new techniques. S9 noted, "When I saw my work enlarged in VR, I could observe the details more carefully, and I realized how much I've improved". S11 said, "In VR, my painting looked more three-dimensional, which made me feel more skilled". In summary, the VR art exhibition enhanced students' sense of achievement by offering external recognition and opportunities for self-improvement. The immersive experience helped students feel acknowledged while encouraging deeper reflection on their artistic growth.

5 Conclusion

This study integrates a traditional art exhibition with virtual reality technology to create a virtual exhibition that overcomes limitations of time and space. It explores the impact of this VR experience on upper-grade elementary students' sense of achievement and technology acceptance.

The results show that the VR art exhibition positively influenced students' sense of achievement, consistent with Serna-Mendiburu & Guerra-Tamez [24], who noted that immersive VR environments enhance students' control, satisfaction, and learning confidence. Students reported feeling more recognized and motivated through the immersive experience. Additionally, students showed generally high acceptance of the VR exhibition, highlighting its potential for art education.

In terms of technology acceptance, most students found the VR experience educational and helpful for observing artwork details, aligning with the Technology Acceptance Model (TAM), which emphasizes perceived usefulness and ease of use [17]. However, perceptions of enjoyment varied. Some students found the VR content engaging, while others reported low interest or technical challenges, such as internet instability or unfamiliar interfaces—factors that may impact perceived ease of use and behavioral intention [18].

Although no power analysis was conducted, the sample size of 42 participants is acceptable for this exploratory study. Future research could expand to different age groups, include qualitative methods for deeper insights, and incorporate a control group to compare VR with traditional exhibitions. This would allow for a more comprehensive understanding of VR's educational value and limitations.

Acknowledgments. This study would like to express gratitude for the support provided by the National Science and Technology Council, with the project number NSTC 113-2410-H-143 -014.

References

1. Lee, L.H., et al.: When creators meet the metaverse: a survey on computational arts. arXiv preprint arXiv:2111.13486 (2021)
2. Chung, S.J., Kim, S.Y., Kim, K.H.: Comparison of visitor experiences of virtual reality exhibitions by spatial environment. Int. J. Hum. Comput. Stud. **181**, 103145 (2024)
3. Kuo, Y.T., Garcia Bravo, E., Whittinghill, D.M., Kuo, Y.C.: Walking into a modern painting: the impacts of using virtual reality on student learning performance and experiences in art appreciation. Int. J. Hum.-Comput. Interact. **40**(23), 8180–8201 (2024)
4. Chen, S.-C.: Applications and practices of digital curating in libraries. In: Workshop on Public Library Management and Innovation (2021)
5. Chen, S.-C.: Introduction to online curatorial methodology. Training Program for Library Professionals, Interlibrary Cooperation Association of Taiwan (2022)
6. Liu, C.L.: The potential of visual arts education to address educational challenges in remote areas. Bamboo Dragonfly: Children's Lit. Cult. **2**, 115–153 (2024)
7. Fitrianto, I., Saif, A.: The role of virtual reality in enhancing experiential learning: a comparative study of traditional and immersive learning environments. Int. J. Post Axial: Futuristic Teach. Learn. 97–110 (2024)

8. Tseng, C.-Y.: From online to offline: a hybrid imagination of exhibition experience. J. Mod. Art Stud. (2019)
9. Li, J., Zheng, X., Watanabe, I., Ochiai, Y.: A systematic review of digital transformation technologies in museum exhibition. Comput. Hum. Behav. **161**, 108407 (2024)
10. Zhou, C., Li, J.: The development of aesthetic experience through virtual and augmented reality. Sci. Rep. **14**(1), 4290 (2024)
11. Elliot, A.J.: A conceptual history of the achievement goal construct. In: Elliot, A.J., Dweck, C.S. (eds.) Handbook of Competence and Motivation, pp. 52–72. Guilford Press, New York (2005)
12. Butera, F., Dompnier, B., Darnon, C.: Achievement goals: a social influence cycle. Annu. Rev. Psychol. **75**(1), 527–554 (2024)
13. Elliot, A.J., Harackiewicz, J.M.: Approach and avoidance achievement goals and intrinsic motivation: a mediational analysis. J. Pers. Soc. Psychol. **70**, 461–475 (1996)
14. Elliot, A.J.: Approach and avoidance motivation and achievement goals. Educ. Psychol. **34**(3), 169–189 (1999)
15. Elliot, A.J., Murayama, K., Pekrun, R.: A 3×2 achievement goal model. J. Educ. Psychol. **103**(3), 632–648 (2011)
16. Ndyareeba, E., Biirah, J., Kibedi, H.K.: Achievement of goal orientation and academic engagement among adolescents in southwestern Uganda. East Afr. J. Educ. Stud. **7**(2), 1–18 (2024)
17. Davis, F.: Perceived usefulness, perceived ease of use, and user acceptance of information technology. MIS Q. **13**, 319–340 (1989)
18. Moon, J.W., Kim, Y.G.: Extending the TAM for a world-wide-web context. Inf. Manage. **38**, 217–230 (2001)
19. Huang, Y.-C., Hao, T.-Y.: A study on the impact of digital teaching platforms' quality, technology acceptance model, and perceived enjoyment on university students' usage intention: a case study of Shih Hsin University. J. Chin. Print. Technol. Annu. Conf. (2014)
20. Musa, H.G., Fatmawati, I., Nuryakin, N., Suyanto, M.: Marketing research trends using technology acceptance model (TAM): a comprehensive review of researches (2002–2022). Cogent Bus. Manage. **11**(1), 2329375 (2024)
21. Ma, J., Wang, P., Li, B., Wang, T., Pang, X.S., Wang, D.: Exploring user adoption of ChatGPT: A technology acceptance model perspective. Int. J. Hum.–Comput. Interact. **41**(2), 1431–1445 (2025)
22. Tzoh, K.-H., Lu, C.-H.: Construct validity study of the children's version of the 2×2 achievement goal scale in sports contexts. J. Phys. Educ. **41**(1), 37–50 (2008)
23. Hwang, G.J., Yang, L.H., Wang, S.Y.: A concept map-embedded educational computer game for improving students' learning performance in natural science courses. Comput. Educ. **69**, 121–130 (2013)
24. Serna-Mendiburu, G.M., Guerra-Tamez, C.R.: Shaping the future of creative education: the transformative power of VR in art and design learning. Front. Educ. **9**, 1388483 (2024)

From Peer Educators to Digital Change Agents: Rethinking Health Education Through VR-Enhanced Peer Learning

Yngve Røe[1(✉)], Truls Sveløkken Johansen[1,2], and Else Britt Bruset[1]

[1] OsloMet – Oslo Metropolitan University, St. Olavs Plass, P.O. Box 4, 0130 Oslo, Norway
yngveroe@oslomet.no

[2] Sunnaas Rehabilitation Hospital, Bjørnemyrveien 11, 1453 Bjørnemyr, Norway

Abstract. The rapid digital transformation of healthcare necessitates new educational models that foster digital competence, innovation capacity, and student empowerment. This study explores the intersection of virtual reality (VR) and peer-assisted learning (PAL) in health professions education, presenting the development of the VR-PAL Innovation Model—a conceptual framework that integrates immersive simulation with student-led pedagogical leadership. Drawing on reflexive thematic analysis of focus group interviews with three cohorts of peer assistants (N = 10), the study identifies three interconnected components: a pedagogical foundation rooted in sociocultural learning theory, a structured train-the-trainer program cycle, and a set of innovation enablers, including inclusive design, co-creation, and the cultivation of a digital mindset. The findings highlight how peer educators, through their dual roles as learners and facilitators, emerge as digital change agents capable of driving innovation from within the learning environment. The model extends existing PAL frameworks by positioning students not only as knowledge sharers but also as agents of educational technology integration. While grounded in occupational therapy education, the VR-PAL model offers a transferable approach for institutions aiming to scale student-centered digital innovation. Implications for implementation, scalability, and future research are discussed.

Keywords: Virtual Reality in Education · Peer-Assisted Learning (PAL) · Digital Change Agents

1 Introduction

Digital transformation is reshaping healthcare delivery, demanding not only new technologies but also new competencies among future health professionals. As a result, higher education institutions face increasing pressure to prepare students who are not only clinically skilled but also digitally competent, innovative, and adaptive in the face of rapidly evolving systems. Within this realm, health professions education must move beyond traditional pedagogical structures, exploring new ways to embed technology meaningfully in both teaching and learning practices.

W.-S. Wang et al. (Eds.): ICITL 2025, LNCS 15913, pp. 354–362, 2026.
https://doi.org/10.1007/978-3-031-98185-2_37

In recent years, immersive technologies such as virtual reality (VR) have gained prominence in educational research and practice, particularly in fields where experiential learning is essential. VR enables learners to engage in simulated environments that replicate clinical complexity, foster decision-making, and enhance motivation. However, the successful integration of immersive technologies in education depends not only on access to tools but also on the pedagogical models that support their use.

Parallel to this, peer-assisted learning (PAL) has emerged as a transformative pedagogical strategy that fosters collaborative knowledge-building, leadership, and reflection. While PAL is well established in clinical training, its potential as a mechanism for digital transformation, particularly when combined with VR, remains underexplored. This paper addresses that gap by presenting a peer-led, VR-enhanced learning model that positions students as active contributors to educational innovation.

Since 2021, a VR-integrated module has been implemented within a Norwegian occupational therapy program, utilizing a "train-the-trainer" model where selected students take on the role of peer educators. These students, often with unconventional digital or gaming backgrounds, are trained to lead immersive, simulation-based learning sessions for their peers. The approach emphasizes student agency, inclusivity, and leadership development, aligning with broader aims of fostering digital competence and a digital mindset among future healthcare professionals.

Based on qualitative data collected across three cohorts of peer assistants, the study presented here extends previously published research by developing the VR-PAL Innovation Model, a conceptual framework highlighting the educational design, implementation logic, and enabling conditions of this peer-led, tech-enhanced model. This framework is intended to support scalability, institutional replication, and interdisciplinary transfer across higher education settings.

The paper contributes to conference themes on innovative learning environments, immersive technology, digital competence, and learner empowerment. It offers a concrete example of how higher education institutions can co-create smart learning ecosystems by empowering students as digital change agents, that is, students who actively champion and drive the adoption of new digital tools and practices in their learning environments.

2 Background and Related Work

The digital transformation of education has been accelerated by both technological advances and institutional policies. The European Commission's Digital Education Action Plan [1] and national frameworks in countries like Norway [2] emphasize the need for integrating digital competence across disciplines. In health professions education, digital tools such as electronic records, telemedicine, and simulation technologies have already transformed clinical practice, requiring new skillsets among future practitioners.

Virtual reality (VR) has become increasingly relevant as a pedagogical tool, particularly in health and rehabilitation education, where it provides realistic, safe, and interactive simulations [3]. However, the challenge lies not only in access to immersive tools but also in developing pedagogical strategies that support sustained use, learner engagement, and reflective practice [4].

Peer-assisted learning (PAL) is a well-established method that promotes leadership, collaboration, and metacognitive growth [5]. Traditionally used in clinical skills training, PAL is now being revisited as a potential driver for pedagogical innovation and technology integration. Studies have shown that PAL can improve students' confidence and foster horizontal, non-hierarchical learning cultures [6, 7].

This study builds on a previously published qualitative research project [8] conducted at a university in Norway, where a VR-based peer teaching program has been integrated into the occupational therapy curriculum since 2021. Unlike the initial study [8], which reported on early experiences with the VR peer-teaching program and its impact on digital competence, the present work develops a conceptual framework (the VR-PAL Innovation Model). This framework synthesizes insights across three student cohorts, offering new methodological and theoretical contributions beyond the prior findings.

To our knowledge, few studies have combined PAL with immersive technologies like VR, and none have formalized a model to do so. By presenting the VR-PAL Innovation Model, this paper fills that gap, offering a transferable blueprint for peer-led digital innovation in education. To develop this model, we conducted a qualitative study using focus group interviews with peer educators, as described below.

3 Methodology

3.1 Design

A reflexive thematic analysis approach [9] was used to analyse focus group data from three cohorts of student peer assistants. We followed Braun and Clarke's six-phase reflexive thematic analysis process [9] to ensure a systematic yet flexible analysis. After transcription and familiarization with the data, two researchers independently coded the focus group transcripts line-by-line, generating initial codes inductively. We then met to discuss and refine these codes, engaging in reflexive dialogue about how our own perspectives might influence interpretation (acknowledging researcher reflexivity as per Braun & Clarke's approach [9]). Through iterative reviewing and clustering of codes, we developed candidate themes that captured patterned responses across participants. These themes were reviewed against the dataset to ensure they authentically represented participants' voices and were refined and defined through consensus among the research team. Throughout this process, we maintained an audit trail and memo notes to track analytic decisions, consistent with a reflexive thematic analysis ethos.

The study adhered to the COREQ guidelines for qualitative research reporting, thus ensuring rigor of the analysis and credibility of the findings [10].

3.2 Participants

Ten peer assistants (six male, four female) participated in three focus group interviews. Participants had varied experience levels, including those newly trained and those who had completed the program. Participants were recruited through purposive sampling. All student peer assistants who had served in the VR program between 2021 and 2023 (three cohorts) were invited via email to participate in a focus group. This included both newly trained peer assistants and those who had completed the program, to capture a range of experience levels. The recruitment aimed for diversity in gender and experience; notably, many invitees had unconventional digital or gaming backgrounds (as was characteristic of the peer assistant role). While this meant participants were likely enthusiastic about technology, it also helped ensure the focus groups included those most immersed in the VR-PAL experience.

3.3 Data Collection

Each focus group followed a semi-structured interview guide and were conducted by one researcher (Y.R.). We began with broad, open-ended questions (e.g., 'Can you describe your experience acting as a VR peer educator?') to let participants narrate their overall experience. This was followed by probing questions targeting key areas like skill development ('How did this experience influence your digital skills or confidence?'), role challenges ('What difficulties did you face in teaching peers with VR?'), and perceptions of impact ('In what ways do you feel your role contributed to innovation or change in the program?'). The focus groups lasted approximately 60–90 min. Focus groups were held in person, or via Zoom. Sessions were audio-recorded (with consent) and later transcribed verbatim for analysis.

3.4 Ethics

Ethical approval was obtained from the Norwegian Agency for Shared Services in Education and Research (Sikt), ref. 620228.

4 Findings and Model Development

The analysis generated three overarching themes, which form the foundation of the VR-PAL Innovation Model (Fig. 1). The model outlines how peer-led immersive learning can be sustainably embedded in higher education.

The generated themes from the analysis, sub-themes and examples of student quotes, are displayed in the paragraphs below.

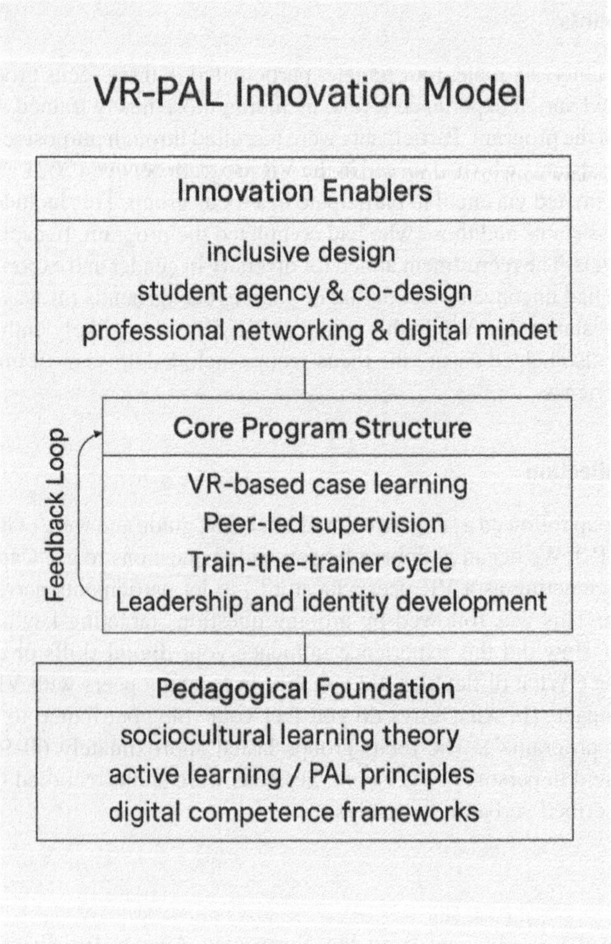

Fig. 1. The VR-PAL Innovation Model: A conceptual framework illustrating the pedagogical foundation, core program structure, and innovation enablers in peer-assisted, VR-enhanced learning.

4.1 Pedagogical Foundation

The program is grounded in sociocultural learning theory [11], where learning occurs through interaction, scaffolding, and situated experience. It also builds on active learning and PAL principles [5], promoting student autonomy and responsibility.

"I would say we actually learned a lot more than the others in class, considering how much more we worked with the cases and everything. Even though we were teaching, we definitely had an advantage, we got to practice and reflect a lot more". Student 5, focus group 2.

This reflects the reciprocal learning and metacognitive depth typical of PAL frameworks, where teaching reinforces content mastery.

4.2 Core Program Structure

At the center of the model is the train-the-trainer cycle. Peer assistants undergo a structured process:

- Initial recruitment and onboarding
- Mentored training in VR tools and case facilitation
- Independent supervision of peer learners
- Transition into training new peer assistants
- This sequence develops both technical and pedagogical competence and promotes identity formation as future professionals.

4.3 Innovation Enablers

Several factors enable the success of this model:

- Inclusive design: Gender-sensitive recruitment and support
- Student agency and co-design: Peer assistants help shape learning content

"I felt like we had a lot of influence. They asked us for input on what we thought might work best. [...] We would always take that feedback back to Else Britt and Truls and discuss what we could do differently. There were actually several things we changed for the next skills training session". Student 4, focus group 2.

This illustrates how peer assistants not only delivered the training but actively participated in its iterative refinement, demonstrating a sense of ownership and authentic partnership in the educational design process.

- Professional networking and digital mindset: The experience not only enhances career orientation but also fosters confidence in working with technology, both of which contribute to a developing digital mindset.

"I was a bit nervous at first ... thinking, what if I can't answer everything ... but I realized I was actually capable of more than I thought. And it really wasn't such a big deal to lead fellow students – it was reassuring to feel that". Student 6, focus group 1.

The quote exemplifies how the peer educators' confidence grew over time, reflecting a developing digital mindset marked by self-efficacy, resilience, and comfort in leadership roles involving educational technology.

Collectively, these themes portray the peer assistants as digital change agents within their community – students who not only adopt an educational innovation (VR) but actively drive it forward by instructing others, refining the practice, and fostering an environment receptive to technological change. The three interconnected themes form the basis of the VR-PAL Innovation Model. We next discuss how this model contributes to understanding peer-led technology integration, and how it compares to existing educational frameworks.

5 Discussion

Our findings illustrate that a peer-led approach to VR integration can cultivate student educators as digital change agents, capable of bridging pedagogy and technology in health education. By taking on dual identities as learners and teachers, the peer assistants in our study were uniquely positioned to mediate between technological innovation and educational practice. The pedagogical foundation we identified aligns with sociocultural learning theory and supports previous findings of how Peer-assisted learning can foster horizontal, non-hierarchical learning cultures in [6, 7].

Our data provide empirical grounding for the notion of digital change agents. We saw peer educators take initiative in various ways: some coached hesitant classmates through their first VR experience, others suggested improvements to the VR activities that were later adopted by faculty, and a few even became advocates of the approach in informal settings (like student forums or meet-ups). These actions go beyond their formal role and illustrate students driving change in attitudes and practices around technology. This confirms that given the opportunity and support, students can become genuine agents of digital transformation in education.

This finding also resonates with broader movements advocating for student partnership in innovation [12]. Our contribution is one of the first to empirically demonstrate this in the context of VR-enhanced learning, thereby expanding the discussion of student change agency into the realm of immersive technology integration.

The structured yet student-driven nature of the model supports educational resilience and adaptability. By embedding leadership, reflection, and tech literacy into peer teaching roles, the model aligns well with future-oriented competence frameworks in healthcare and education [13]. This student-driven model extends the traditional notions of peer-assisted learning. In classic PAL frameworks [5], peers mainly support each other's content learning in a given subject. By contrast, in VR-PAL, peer educators are not only tutors but also innovators—they introduce and normalize a new technology among their cohort. In doing so, they fulfil a role akin to 'change agents' in educational innovation. This goes beyond the scope of typical PAL, aligning more closely with the concept of students as partners in curriculum design and technology adoption.

Unlike top-down technology integration models (where faculty or administrators drive adoption of tools), our bottom-up approach empowers students to lead the innovation. This peer-driven strategy may overcome some barriers noted in previous tech-integration studies – for instance, issues of faculty resistance or lack of contextual relevance can be mitigated when students tailor the innovation for their peers.

A key contribution of this study is the articulation of peer educators as digital change agents. While the term 'change agent' is often used in organizational studies or faculty development, we apply it here to students, grounded in our empirical data. The peer assistants didn't just implement a given curriculum; they actively shaped and sometimes challenged the learning process through their use of VR. They became advocates for the technology, mentors to other students, and even consultants to faculty on what worked or didn't. This student-led change dynamic is a novel insight, suggesting that empowering students in this way can accelerate digital transformation in education from the ground up.

Future research should examine how peer-led VR learning impacts the learners (the students being taught by the peer assistants) in terms of skill acquisition and engagement. It would also be valuable to test the VR-PAL model in different disciplines, for example, having student 'digital tutors' in fields like business or engineering, to see if similar enablers and outcomes emerge. Such studies will help determine which components of our model are core and which are context specific.

6 Limitations

Building on the peer educators' experiences, the VR-PAL model illustrates a new approach to tech integration. However, implementing such a model poses several challenges, which we acknowledge below. First, it was conducted in a single institution, within an occupational therapy program in Norway. The unique context (e.g., institutional support for VR, the specific healthcare discipline, and Norwegian educational culture) may limit direct generalizability of the VR-PAL model to other settings. Additionally, our participant pool, being volunteer peer educators, likely represented students with higher interest in technology and education, which could bias the findings (as discussed above). We did not directly measure outcomes for the peer learners in this study, so the model's impact on those receiving instruction remains an area for further research. While the model is empirically grounded in peer educators' experiences, it has not yet been empirically tested for learning outcomes among their peers or applied in other disciplinary contexts.

Despite these limitations, we believe the principles of the VR-PAL model have broader relevance. The core idea of training students to lead technological innovation in learning can be adapted to other disciplines (for example, nursing simulation labs or engineering design projects using AR) and other institutions, provided there is support for student-led initiatives. We encourage careful piloting of the model in new contexts to identify any necessary modifications. For instance, what worked in an occupational therapy program may need tailoring for larger class sizes or different cultural settings. By openly sharing our framework, we aim to provide a foundation that others can build upon rather than a one-size-fits-all solution.

7 Conclusions

This paper presents the VR-PAL Innovation Model as a scalable, peer-led strategy for integrating immersive technology in health professions education. By combining virtual reality with structured peer-assisted learning, students not only gain digital competence but also develop leadership, professional identity, and a mindset for innovation. While our experience is grounded in a specific context, it opens the door to reimagining students' roles in digital transformation. By viewing students as capable change agents in their own education, educators and institutions can tap into an often underutilised resource for innovation. As higher education navigates rapid technological shifts, empowering students as digital change agents offers a promising pathway toward inclusive and transformative learning environments.

Disclosure of Interests. The authors have no competing interests to declare that are relevant to the content of this article.

References

1. European Commission. https://ec.europa.eu/education/education-in-the-eu/digital-education-action-plan_en. Accessed 23 Oct 2024
2. Action Plan for Digitalisation in Higher Education and Research. https://hkdir.no/hoyere-utdanning-og-forskning/digital-omstilling/handlingsplan-for-digital-omstilling-i-hoyere-utdanning-og-forskning. Accessed 10 May 2025
3. Rutkowski, S., et al.: Use of virtual reality-based training in different fields of rehabilitation: a systematic review and meta-analysis. J Rehabil Med **52**(11), 1–16 (2020)
4. Liaw, S.Y., Ooi, S.L., Mildon, R., Ang, E.N.K., Lau, T.C., Chua, W.L.: Translation of an evidence-based virtual reality simulation-based interprofessional education into health education curriculums: an implementation science method. Nurse Educ. Today **110**, 105262 (2022)
5. Topping, K., Ehly, S.: Peer-Assisted Learning. Routledge, London (1998)
6. Aljahany, M., Malaekah, H., Alzahrani, H., Alhamadah, F., Dator, W.L.: Simulation-based peer-assisted learning: perceptions of health science students. Adv. Med. Educ. Pract. 731–737 (2021)
7. Brierley, C., Ellis, L., Reid, E.R.: Peer-assisted learning in medical education: a systematic review and meta-analysis. Med. Educ. **56**, 365–373 (2022)
8. Røe, Y., Johansen, T.S., Bruset, E.B.: Empowering digital competence through peer-assisted learning and virtual reality in health professions education. Front. Educ. **10**, 1550396 (2025)
9. Braun, V., Clarke, V.: Reflecting on reflexive thematic analysis. Qual. Res. Sport Exerc. Health **11**, 589–597 (2019)
10. Booth, A., Hannes, K., Harden, A., Noyes, J., Harris, J., Tong, A.: COREQ (consolidated criteria for reporting qualitative studies). Guidelines for Reporting Health Research: A User's Manual, pp. 214–226 (2014)
11. Vygotsky, L.S.: Mind in society: the development of higher psychological processes. Harvard University Press, London (1978)
12. Brown, N.: Partnership in learning: how staff-student collaboration can innovate teaching. Eur. J. Teach. Educ. **42**, 608–620 (2019)
13. Vuorikari, R., Kluzer, S., Punie, Y.: DigComp 2.2: the digital competence framework for citizens - with new examples of knowledge, skills and attitudes. EUR 31006 EN, Publications Office of the European Union, Luxembourg (2022)

Personalized Feedback in VR Hands-On Learning: Tiered Support Based on Adaptive Learning Mechanisms

Chang Zhi Chen and Yueh-Min Huang(✉)

Department of Engineering Science, National Cheng Kung University, Tainan City, Taiwan
N98131512@gs.ncku.edu.tw, huang@mail.ncku.edu.tw

Abstract. Virtual Reality technology is increasingly applied in education, providing unique opportunities for hands-on learning. However, existing VR learning environments often rely on static, one-way instruction, causing frustration when students face difficulties. Incorporating effective feedback mechanisms is essential, yet current VR systems lack adaptability for diverse student proficiency levels. This study explores the impact of personalized feedback within VR environments on learning outcomes. A quasi-experimental design involved 23 undergraduates, randomly assigned to an experimental group (N = 12) receiving personalised feedback based on their real-time learning status (high, medium, or low achievement), and a control group (N = 11) receiving static, uniform feedback. Participants completed a three-unit VR embedded systems course.Quantitative analyses, including Levene's test and a t-test, assessed post-test score differences between groups. Results showed a statistically significant improvement ($p < .05$) in the experimental group, indicating personalized feedback positively influences learning.This research uniquely integrates personalized feedback into VR education, offering new insights for future educational VR applications.

Keywords: Virtual reality · Personalized feedback · Hands-on tasks · Feedback mechanisms · Ability grouping · Differentiated instruction

1 Introduction

Virtual Reality technology has been widely applied in the field of education, particularly in courses that emphasize hands-on practice and application-oriented learning, where its value is even more pronounced [1]. Take Internet of Things courses as an example: students are required not only to master theoretical knowledge but also to develop practical skills. VR can provide a safe, cost-effective, and efficient simulated learning environment, allowing students to repeatedly practice without the need for expensive equipment, thereby helping them accumulate practical experience more effectively [2, 3]. In addition, VR-based learning has been shown to not only enhance students' knowledge construction and practical performance, but also boost their motivation and sense of engagement [1].

W.-S. Wang et al. (Eds.): ICITL 2025, LNCS 15913, pp. 363–372, 2026.
https://doi.org/10.1007/978-3-031-98185-2_38

However, current VR learning environments are mostly designed around one-way instructional materials, and students often have to rely on self-exploration within the VR space. Due to the lack of peer or teacher support, they are more likely to feel frustrated or even give up when encountering errors or difficulties [4, 5]. Therefore, providing timely hints and feedback when students feel helpless or frustrated is crucial. Existing studies have shown that feedback mechanisms can effectively improve students' learning motivation and self-regulation abilities [6–8]. Nevertheless, current feedback systems in VR environments still lack personalization—for example, they do not adapt based on individual differences or performance, making it difficult to fully meet students' personalized learning support needs.

On the other hand, personalized feedback has been widely explored in educational environments. Through adaptive systems, feedback can be tailored to students' real-time performance and needs, effectively enhancing their motivation and academic achievement [9, 10]. Therefore, integrating personalized feedback mechanisms into VR-based hands-on courses has the potential to fill the current gap in VR education environments and further promote students' practical skills and knowledge construction.

2 Literature Review

2.1 Application of Virtual Reality in Practical Tasks

According to constructivist learning theory, students actively construct their understanding and knowledge of the world through direct experiences [11]. Three-dimensional virtual environments offer opportunities for active exploration, which can foster student engagement and strengthen the connection between learned knowledge and practical application in an intuitive and vivid context. Research has shown that integrating VR into instructional design can effectively enhance students' problem-solving abilities and learning motivation, particularly in practice-intensive courses. VR provides learning experiences that closely resemble real-life environments, enabling students to acquire complex practical skills more effectively [3].

2.2 Feedback Mechanisms in VR

While VR offers many benefits in education, it also presents challenges. Students often lack immediate support from teachers or peers and must navigate learning independently. This can lead to confusion, repeated mistakes, and reduced self-efficacy, especially when learning goals feel out of reach—potentially causing anxiety and lowering motivation [12]. To address these issues, providing appropriate feedback in VR has proven effective. Feedback can boost motivation and encourage active knowledge exploration [5, 13]. For example, [7] showed that integrating real-time static feedback into VR enhances self-efficacy and facilitates knowledge transfer to real-world contexts.

2.3 Personalized Feedback

However, current VR feedback mechanisms often overlook learners' individual competence levels, providing uniform feedback regardless of student needs. This one-size-fits-all approach can limit high-achieving students, who typically possess strong self-regulation and problem-solving skills, and may benefit more from reduced intervention to foster deeper learning and motivation [14]. Conversely, low-achieving students often need more structured and personalized support. Tailoring feedback to individual differences has been shown to enhance learning outcomes [15]. Thus, the absence of adaptive, personalized feedback remains a key limitation in VR-based learning.

2.4 Research Purpose

In summary, while the application of VR in practical digital learning environments shows great potential, there is still a lack of well-developed and flexible personalized feedback mechanisms. This study aims to integrate personalized feed-back mechanisms into VR hands-on learning environments, with a focus on courses that emphasize practical skills, such as embedded systems. By dynamically detecting students' learning performance and providing real-time, personalized feedback, this study seeks to explore the impact on students' academic achievement and practical abilities.Accordingly, this study proposes the following research question:

RQ: Does incorporating personalized feedback in VR environments improve students' learning performance more effectively than fixed, non-personalised feedback mechanisms?

3 Method

3.1 Participants and Experimental Design

This study collected data from 23 undergraduate students (N = 23) from the Department of Engineering Science (from first to third year). A quasi-experimental design was adopted, with participants randomly assigned to the experimental group (n = 12) and the control group (n = 11). The experimental group used a VR learning environment with personalized feedback, while the control group experienced a VR environment with static feedback. The feedback for the experimental group was determined based on participants' proficiency and dynamic data collected during the learning process. In contrast, the control group adopted the static feedback mechanism integrated into VR as referenced in Wang et al. (2024). This study aims to explore the impact of personalized feedback mechanisms in VR on learning performance and practical skills. The complete experimental procedure is shown in Fig. 1.

First, in the pre-test phase, students' initial learning abilities were measured through a pre-test. According to the grading system of a university in southern Taiwan, students were classified into different achievement levels: scores above 80 were considered Grade A (high-achieving), scores between 70–79 were Grade B (medium-achieving), and scores below 69 were classified as Grade C and F (low-achieving). Second, during the experiment phase, participants were randomly assigned to either the experimental group or the control group. After completing questionnaires assessing prior knowledge and demographic information, a course teaching assistant gave a brief introduction to the course and instructions on using VR. The experiment then began. Both groups wore VR head-mounted displays and engaged in learning activities as shown in Fig. 2. Participants carried out hands-on tasks from an embedded systems course within the VR environment, completing three learning units in sequence. To account for visual load, each learning unit was limited to 25 min and delivered over three weeks. After each unit, participants were required to complete a task in VR related to the unit. The experimental group received personalized feedback throughout the learning and task processes, while the control group received static feedback prompts. Static feedback was defined as generalized feedback that provides the same information regardless of the learner's individual behavior and lacks adaptivity [16]. Finally, in the post-test phase, a post-test was administered after completing the tasks to assess the knowledge levels of both groups.

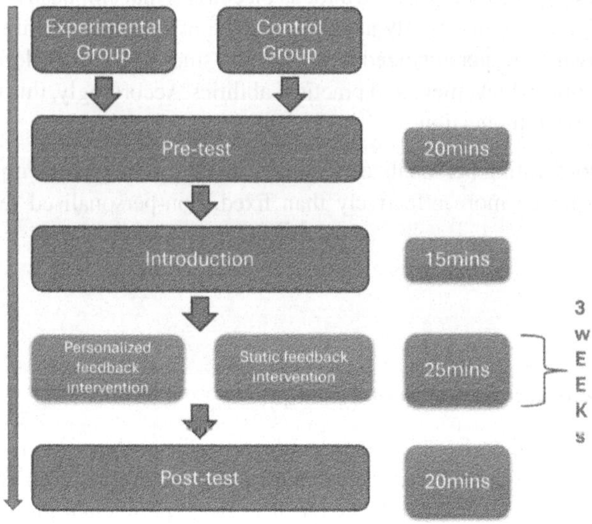

Fig. 1. Experimental Procedure

3.2 Learning Environment

The learning domain of this study involves an Internet of Things course. The instructional materials cover topics such as the fundamentals of embedded hardware, GPIO circuit design, and Python programming. Based on Bloom's Taxonomy [17] and with reference to the research of [7], the learning tasks were designed and divided into three units, as shown in Table 1.

The first unit introduces fundamental concepts related to IoT and the principles of GPIO circuit wiring. The second unit focuses on the relationship between code and circuitry; for example, if a sensor's pin is defined as Pin 12 in the code, the circuit must be wired accordingly. Learners are expected to understand the connection between the two. The final unit explains how to integrate programming with sensors to realize logical code operations in practical IoT applications.

Fig. 2. Experiment

Table 1. VR learning environment

Classification	Task and Course
Remember	Introducing knowledge related to the Internet of Things (IoT), including various sensors such as ultrasonic sensors, basic GPIO circuit connections, resistors, and other related concepts, followed by the completion of corresponding tasks
Understand	In this stage, learners are required to study the logic of Python programming, including the use of loops, as well as the relationship between hardware configuration and circuit wiring, and complete the corresponding tasks
Apply	Explaining how to control hardware operation through programming, learners will subsequently practice writing their own code logic in the tasks to implement IoT applications

3.3 Personalized Feedback

The personalized feedback mechanism proposed in this study is based on real-time monitoring of students' learning behaviors and states within the VR environment. These include factors such as the student's current task progress, the performance rating of the previous task, inactivity status, and more. By combining these observations with students' pre-classified achievement levels, the system delivers feedback tailored to each learner's current context and capability (as shown in Table 2). The content of the feedback is dynamically adjusted based on several dimensions (as illustrated in Table 3).

Table 2. Student Grouping and Feedback Types

Student Achievement Level	Feedback Type
High-achieving Students	Primarily facilitative feedback, encouraging independent exploration and avoiding excessive intervention
Mid-achieving Students	Mainly facilitative feedback, with occasional directive feedback based on student status (e.g., excessive errors or prolonged inactivity) to provide timely guidance
Low-achieving Students	Primarily clear and directive feedback to provide real-time guidance, reduce frustration, and alleviate anxiety

Based on the feedback mechanisms described in Table 1 and Table 2, as well as the learner's current learning status and predefined achievement level, students will receive corresponding feedback when encountering difficulties, as illustrated in Fig. 3. Each student receives a different type of feedback according to their current state and proficiency level (see Table 2). For high-achieving students, feedback is primarily facilitative; for mid-achieving students, facilitative feedback is supplemented with directive feedback; and for low-achieving students, feedback is mainly directive. Examples are provided in Table 3.

Fig. 3. Real-Time Feedback in VR

Table 3. Feedback Design

Achievement Level	Error Type	Feedback Approach	Example
High-achieving	Operational/Conceptual/Inactivity	Facilitative	"Double-check the correctness of your wiring pins" "This part is the key to solving the problem—keep going and give it a try!"
Mid-achieving	Operational/Conceptual/Inactivity	Directive/Facilitative	"Your pin is connected incorrectly—Pin 12 should be connected to the red wire" "Try to recall the task from the beginning—start by verifying the correctness of the GPIO pin positions"
Low-achieving	Operational/ Conceptual/Inactivity	Directive	"The red wire needs to be connected to Pin 12. Try following this step-by-step" "The correctly connected pin will light up, providing a visual cue to guide learners in the right direction"

3.4 Data Analysis Method

This study primarily adopted quantitative analysis to examine the research question. To ensure that the initial knowledge levels were comparable, a Levene's test was conducted. A t-test was then used to analyze the differences in post-test scores between the experimental and control groups. The purpose of this analysis was to determine whether the personalized feedback intervention had a statistically significant positive effect on learning outcomes.

3.5 Pre-test and Post-test

To assess changes in students' knowledge levels before and after the instructional intervention, this study developed pre-test and post-test instruments. The tests covered three dimensions: descriptive knowledge, conceptual understanding, and application ability—each aligned with the learning objectives of the instructional activities. The test items were co-developed and reviewed by three domain experts to ensure content validity. The assessment consisted of 7 multiple-choice questions and 5 short-answer questions, with a total score of 100 points.

4 Results

4.1 Pre-test Difference Analysis

To ensure comparable initial knowledge levels between groups, a Levene's test was conducted. The results indicated that the assumption of homogeneity of variances was not violated (Pre-test Knowledge Level: $F = 1.39$, $p = .25$), suggesting no significant difference in score variance between the two groups. An independent samples t-test was then performed on the pre-test scores, revealing no significant difference between the experimental and control groups, $t(21) = .16$, $p = .48$. This indicates that the students in both groups had no statistically significant differences in their initial knowledge levels prior to the instructional intervention, thereby providing suitable conditions for further comparison of post-test performance.

4.2 Post-test Performance Analysis

To investigate the effect of personalized feedback ($N = 12$) versus static feedback ($N = 11$) on learning outcomes, an independent samples t-test was conducted on the post-test scores of both groups. The results showed that the experimental group had a higher average post-test score ($M = 84.42$, $SD = 8.84$) compared to the control group ($M = 74.64$, $SD = 6.23$), and this difference was statistically significant. These findings support the research hypothesis, indicating that students who received personalized feedback in the VR learning environment performed significantly better than those who received static feedback as shown in Table 4.

To further understand the practical effectiveness of the personalized feedback intervention, this study also calculated Cohen's d. The result showed that Cohen's $d = 1.27$, indicating a large effect size. This suggests that the personalized feedback mechanism in a VR hands-on learning environment has meaningful educational implications. In other words, the intervention not only achieved statistically significant differences but also demonstrated considerable practical advantages.

Table 4. T-test Results of Post-test Scores

	Group	N	M	SD	t	p
Post-test Scores	Experimental Group	12	84.42	8.84	3.040	.006**
	Control Group	11	74.64	6.23		

Note: **indicate p < .05

5 Conclusion and Research Limitations

This study implemented a real-time, ability-tiered personalized feedback mechanism to provide appropriate support to students of different achievement levels (high, medium, low), and confirmed its effectiveness in enhancing learning performance. After confirming no significant difference in pre-test scores between the experimental and control groups, results showed that the experimental group receiving personalized feedback achieved significantly higher post-test scores ($p = .006$) with a large effect size (Cohen's $d = 1.27$), supporting the research hypothesis. The findings suggest that differentiated real-time feedback based on learner profiles is more effective than uniform static feedback.

Additionally, the results highlight the role of personalized feedback in promoting equity within VR-based hands-on learning. By avoiding one-size-fits-all feedback that may disadvantage lower-achieving students, the tiered approach ensures that all learners receive support aligned with their actual needs. Nevertheless, this study has limitations, including a relatively small sample size ($N = 23$) and an exclusive focus on knowledge-based quantitative assessment. Future research should expand the sample and incorporate diverse assessment methods, including qualitative interviews, to comprehensively evaluate the impact of personalized feedback.

In conclusion, this study contributes initial empirical evidence supporting adaptive feedback in immersive VR learning, offering practical insights and paving the way for optimizing personalized strategies to foster knowledge construction and educational equity.

References

1. Lai, Y.H., Chen, S.Y., Lai, C.F., Chang, Y.C., Su, Y.S.: Study on enhancing AIoT computational thinking skills by plot image-based VR. Interact. Learn. Environ. **29**, 482–495 (2021)
2. Tsirulnikov, D., Suart, C., Abdullah, R., Vulcu, F., Mullarkey, C.E.: Game on: immersive virtual laboratory simulation improves student learning outcomes & motivation. FEBS Open Bio **13**, 396–407 (2023)
3. Wang, W.S., Cheng, Y.P., Lee, H.Y., Lin, C.J., Huang, Y.M.: Impact of anxiety and confidence in virtual reality-mediated learning transferred to hands-on tasks. J. Comput. Assist. Learn. (2023)
4. Araiza-Alba, P., Keane, T., Chen, W.S., Kaufman, J.: Immersive virtual reality as a tool to learn problem-solving skills. Comput. Educ. **164** (2021)

5. Radianti, J., Majchrzak, T.A., Fromm, J., Wohlgenannt, I.: A systematic review of immersive virtual reality applications for higher education: design elements, lessons learned, and research agenda. Comput. Educ. **147**, 103778 (2020)
6. Theobald, M., Bellhaeuser, H.: How am I going and where to next? Elaborated online feedback improves university students' self-regulated learning and performance. Internet High. Educ. **55** (2022)
7. Wang, W.S., Pedaste, M., Lin, C.J., Lee, H.Y., Huang, Y.M., Wu, T.T.: Signaling feedback mechanisms to promoting self-regulated learning and motivation in virtual reality transferred to real-world hands-on tasks. Interact. Learn. Environ. **32**, 7661–7676 (2024)
8. Lin, C.-J., Pedaste, M., Huang, Y.-M.: Insights into precision education through multi-modal learning analytics in STEM education. In: International Conference on Innovative Technologies and Learning, pp. 57–63. Springer (2024)
9. Wu, T.-T., Lee, H.-Y., Wang, W.-S., Lin, C.-J., Huang, Y.-M.: Leveraging computer vision for adaptive learning in STEM education: effect of engagement and self-efficacy. Int. J. Educ. Technol. High. Educ. **20**, 53 (2023)
10. Lee, H.-Y., Huang, Y.-M.: Bridging STEM education and ubiquitous learning: a case study on developing a LINE chatbot with Google's gemini for virtual peer collaboration. In: International Conference on Innovative Technologies and Learning, pp. 237–246. Springer (2024)
11. Pan, S.H., Hafez, B., Iskandar, A., Ming, Z.: Integrating constructivist principles in an adaptive hybrid learning system for developing social entrepreneurship education among college students. Learn. Motivat. **87** (2024)
12. Panadero, E., Lipnevich, A.A.: A review of feedback models and typologies: Towards an integrative model of feedback elements. Educ. Res. Rev. **35** (2022)
13. Lin, C.J., Wang, W.S., Lee, H.Y., Huang, Y.M., Wu, T.T.: Recognitions of image and speech to improve learning diagnosis on STEM collaborative activity for precision education. Educ. Inf. Technol. **29**, 13859–13884 (2024)
14. Zimmerman, B.J.: Investigating self-regulation and motivation: historical background, methodological developments, and future prospects. Am. Educ. Res. J. **45**, 166–183 (2008)
15. Lee, H.-Y., Lin, C.-J., Wang, W.-S., Chang, W.-C., Huang, Y.-M.: Precision education via timely intervention in K-12 computer programming course to enhance programming skill and affective-domain learning objectives. Int. J. STEM Educ. **10**, 52 (2023)
16. Sailer, M., et al.: Adaptive feedback from artificial neural networks facilitates pre-service teachers' diagnostic reasoning in simulation-based learning. Learn. Instruct. **83** (2023)
17. Krathwohl, D.R.: A revision of Bloom's taxonomy: an overview. Theory Pract. **41**, 212 (2002)

Enhancing Higher-Order Thinking and Hands-On Performance in VR Learning Environments Through CTML-Based Feedback Design

Wei-Sheng Wang[1], Margus Pedaste[2], and Yueh-Min Huang[1](✉)

[1] Department of Engineering Science, National Cheng Kung University, Tainan, Taiwan
huang@mail.ncku.edu.tw

[2] Institute of Education of the University of Tartu, Tartu, Estonia

Abstract. This study investigates the impact of feedback mechanisms, grounded in the Signaling Principle of the Cognitive Theory of Multimedia Learning (CTML), on learners' higher-order thinking skills and hands-on performance in a virtual reality (VR) learning environment. A pilot randomized controlled trial (RCT) was conducted with 12 university students, divided into an experimental group that received signaling-based feedback and a control group that did not. The VR course, focused on electronic circuits and programming, incorporated interactive tasks and real-time feedback designed to guide learners through complex problem-solving and practical application. Results showed that participants who received CTML-informed feedback demonstrated significantly higher performance in both critical thinking domains and practical tasks. These findings highlight the importance of integrating instructional feedback into immersive environments to promote deeper cognitive engagement and procedural competence. Future research should extend this approach across diverse subject areas, consider long-term learning outcomes, and explore the integration of Generative AI tools such as GPT to enable adaptive, personalized support in VR-based education.

Keywords: Virtual reality · HOTS · Electronic circuits · Multimedia cognitive learning theory

1 Introduction

With the advancement of technology, Virtual Reality (VR) has emerged as a powerful tool in STEM education, offering immersive, interactive, and safe environments for hands-on learning [1–3]. VR enables learners to actively engage with complex concepts and conduct virtual experiments, thereby enhancing their motivation and learning outcomes. VR-based learning also aligns with the principles of self-regulated learning (SRL), allowing learners to explore content at their own pace and develop autonomy, problem-solving skills, and practical abilities [4]. However, without timely guidance or peer interaction, learners may become disoriented or demotivated in VR environments, leading to ineffective learning [5]. The Cognitive Theory of Multimedia Learning (CTML) provides

W.-S. Wang et al. (Eds.): ICITL 2025, LNCS 15913, pp. 373–381, 2026.
https://doi.org/10.1007/978-3-031-98185-2_39

a foundation for designing effective learning experiences in multimedia-rich environments. In immersive VR settings, where learners are exposed to high sensory input, CTML's signaling principle can help direct learners' attention to key content and reduce cognitive overload [6]. Incorporating well-designed feedback signals within VR can enhance learner focus, engagement, and comprehension [6]. Feedback also plays a critical role in supporting SRL by increasing motivation, clarifying goals, and guiding learners through their learning process [7]. While prior studies have explored feedback in traditional settings, limited research has examined how CTML-based feedback mechanisms in VR environments impact learners' higher-order thinking and hands-on performance. Therefore, this study investigates the integration of CTML-informed feedback mechanisms into a VR-based hands-on learning environment. By embedding signaling-based feedback during practical tasks, we aim to enhance learners' cognitive engagement and applied skills. To guide this investigation, we propose the following research questions:

1. Can CTML-based feedback mechanisms in a VR environment effectively improve learners' hands-on performance?
2. Can CTML-based feedback mechanisms in a VR environment effectively enhance learners' higher-order thinking skills?

2 Related Work

2.1 Learning Feedback

In immersive learning environments such as Virtual Reality (VR), learners are often required to navigate complex tasks independently. While this autonomy can foster engagement and self-regulation, it can also lead to confusion and frustration when appropriate support is lacking. In particular, the absence of timely and targeted feedback can leave learners uncertain about their progress, especially when they make mistakes or deviate from the intended learning path [8, 9]. Without corrective input, learners may fall into repetitive trial and error cycles, wasting cognitive resources and reinforcing misconceptions rather than developing accurate understanding [10]. This is especially problematic in VR, where immersive elements may intensify the feeling of disorientation, making it more difficult for learners to recover from failure or adjust their learning strategies effectively. As such, the design of effective feedback mechanisms is critical for optimizing learning in VR environments. Feedback serves not only as a means of error correction, but also as a scaffold that guides learners toward deeper understanding and better decision-making. In VR-based learning, well-designed feedback can help direct attention, clarify learning goals, and maintain learner motivation by providing a sense of progress and achievement. Furthermore, incorporating interactive or signaling-based feedback—such as visual highlights, audio cues, or contextual hints—can enhance learners' situational awareness and support their cognitive processing of tasks in real time. Therefore, feedback is not a peripheral element in VR learning design; rather, it is a core instructional component essential for fostering meaningful engagement, preventing cognitive overload, and promoting learning success.

2.2 Higher Order Thinking

Higher-order thinking (HOT) refers to advanced cognitive processes that go beyond basic recall or comprehension of information. These include skills such as analysis, evaluation, synthesis, and creation, as described in Bloom's revised taxonomy [11]. HOT is essential for learners to make connections between concepts, solve complex problems, and apply knowledge in unfamiliar contexts [12]. In various learning environments—whether traditional classrooms, online platforms, or technology-enhanced settings—cultivating higher-order thinking has been emphasized as a critical goal of modern education [13]. Moreover, HOT is not limited to advanced or high-performing students; it is a universal competency that all learners must develop to become effective problem-solvers and critical thinkers in real-world settings. Importantly, higher-order thinking is closely linked to learners' hands-on performance. Engaging in tasks that require planning, decision-making, hypothesis testing, and iterative refinement necessitates the use of HOT skills. In engineering, programming, science experimentation, and design-based learning, students must analyze problems, evaluate alternative solutions, and synthesize knowledge to complete practical tasks successfully. Without sufficient cognitive engagement, learners may merely follow procedural steps without truly understanding the underlying concepts. In contrast, HOT enables learners to internalize processes, transfer knowledge to new contexts, and improve their performance in authentic, hands-on tasks [14]. Despite the increasing use of Virtual Reality (VR) in education, most existing VR learning environments have focused primarily on providing immersive experiences, enhancing engagement, and delivering visual representations of content [15]. While these features offer benefits for motivation and conceptual visualization, few VR applications are explicitly designed to support or assess higher-order thinking skills. Many VR systems still emphasize content delivery and surface-level interaction, lacking mechanisms to prompt learners to analyze, reflect, or critically evaluate information. This gap suggests a missed opportunity to harness VR's immersive and interactive affordances to engage learners in deeper cognitive processes. Therefore, integrating instructional strategies that foster HOT within VR environments remains an underexplored but vital direction for research and development.

2.3 Cognitive Theory of Multimedia Learning

The Cognitive Theory of Multimedia Learning (CTML) has become a foundational framework in the learning sciences. Originally proposed by [16], CTML focuses on how multimedia content should be organized and presented to enhance meaningful learning. According to the theory, learners engage in three core cognitive processes during learning—selecting, organizing, and integrating information. Based on this structure, CTML offers several design principles, one of which is the signaling principle. The signaling principle posits that learning can be improved by highlighting essential information to direct learners' attention, thereby reducing cognitive overload and enhancing learning outcomes [17]. This principle is especially relevant in Virtual Reality (VR) learning environments, where the combination of visual, auditory, and spatial stimuli creates an immersive experience. However, this multisensory richness also increases the risk of distraction and cognitive overload, particularly during tasks that demand deep cognitive engagement or precise procedural execution [18].

In such contexts, the signaling principle provides a valuable instructional approach. Feedback designed with signaling cues—such as visual highlights or auditory prompts—can be delivered at critical moments during task completion to focus learners' attention on key information. For instance, in hands-on tasks like circuit building or programming, signaling-based feedback can help learners detect errors and correct them in real-time, thereby enhancing procedural accuracy and hands-on performance. Furthermore, signaling-based feedback also holds potential for fostering higher-order thinking skills. When designed effectively, such feedback can prompt learners to reflect on their problem-solving process, challenge their assumptions, or engage in multiple perspectives, all of which contribute to the development of analytical, evaluative, and creative thinking [19]. In this way, the application of CTML principles in VR does more than mitigate cognitive load; it actively supports deep thinking and reflective practice. Although some recent studies have successfully applied CTML in VR learning environments and demonstrated its positive effects on attention and learning outcomes, very few have explored how signaling-based feedback grounded in CTML could specifically enhance learners' higher-order thinking and hands-on performance. Most existing research has concentrated on basic knowledge acquisition or general engagement, without addressing the cognitive and procedural depth required for advanced learning outcomes. This highlights a critical research gap. Future work that leverages CTML to design feedback mechanisms tailored to complex cognitive and procedural tasks in VR could offer valuable insights into optimizing immersive learning environments. Such efforts may significantly improve learners' ability to transfer knowledge and skills from VR contexts to real-world applications, especially in fields where both conceptual understanding and practical ability are essential.

3 Method

3.1 Experimental Process

This pilot study adopted a Randomized Controlled Trial (RCT) approach, involving a total of 12 university students from a university in southern Taiwan. Participants were randomly assigned to either the control group ($n = 5$) or the experimental group ($n = 7$). Prior to the experiment, a preliminary survey revealed that the majority of students had no prior exposure to VR devices, nor had they taken courses related to electronic circuits or programming. As illustrated in Fig. 1, the experimental procedure began with a brief orientation session conducted by a teaching assistant. During this session, students were guided on how to properly wear and adjust the Head-Mounted Display (HMD) and were introduced to basic interactions within the VR learning environment. Once participants were comfortable with the system, they proceeded with the VR-based instructional activities.The entire learning session lasted around 2 h, segmented into six modules, each approximately 20 min in duration. The instructional content covered fundamental concepts of electronic circuits, operational procedures, and introductory programming techniques. Upon completing the VR course, participants were asked to complete a questionnaire designed to assess their higher-order thinking skills and hands-on performance, which served as key variables for analysis in this study.

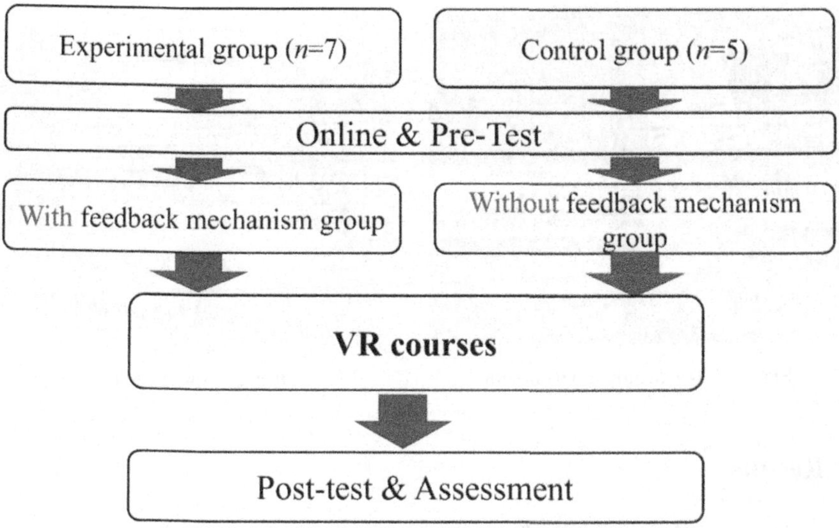

Fig. 1. Experiment procedure.

3.2 Experimental Design

The purpose of this study is to explore how feedback mechanisms integrated into a VR-based learning environment for electronic circuits and programming can support learners' development of higher-order thinking skills and hands-on performance. As illustrated in Fig. 2, the VR environment consists of a series of structured learning tasks and quiz activities related to circuit design and programming. Learners are required to complete these modules in a linear sequence. During the learning process, participants in the experimental group receive feedback generated by the system based on their interactions. For example, as shown in Fig. 3, if a learner makes an error—whether in executing a task or answering a quiz question—the system immediately provides feedback indicating whether the action was correct or incorrect.

In addition, learners can continuously track their progress through a real-time progress chart displayed within the VR interface. This visual progress tracker enables learners to monitor their advancement through the tasks, thereby supporting more effective engagement in learning and encouraging them to reflect on their actions—both of which are essential for fostering higher-order cognitive processing and practical competence.

The course structure is designed to guide learners step-by-step through each task. Upon successful completion of a task, a clear success notification appears, and the progress chart is updated accordingly. If an incorrect component is connected to an inappropriate port, the system will display a noticeable error prompt. Once the learner completes all tasks in a given scene, a completion message is shown on-screen, prompting them to move forward to the next learning area and continue with additional modules.

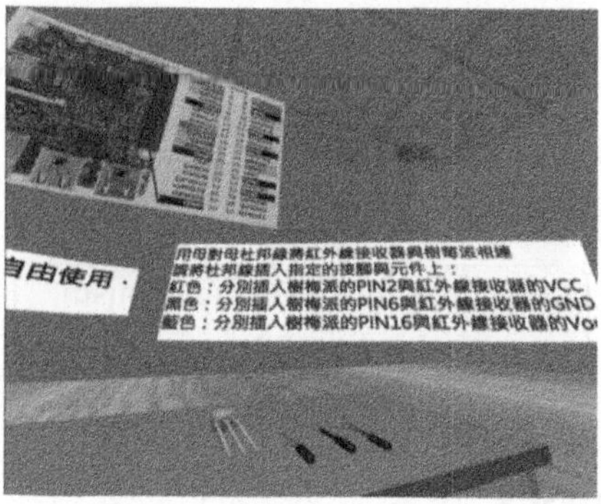

Fig. 2. VR learning environment.

Fig. 3. VR feedback.

4 Results

4.1 HOTs and Hands-On Performance

All participants were asked to complete an online questionnaire. To assess both their initial knowledge and the learning outcomes after the intervention, we administered open-ended pretest and posttest questions. These items were adapted from the work of [3], originally developed for embedded systems education focusing on electronic components and programming concepts.

In parallel, the hands-on task performance—including both hardware assembly and basic programming tasks—was evaluated by the same two experts. The evaluation criteria covered task completeness, time required to complete each task, and functional accuracy. Each of the two tasks was scored out of 50, yielding a maximum possible score of 100. The inter-rater correlation coefficient for this evaluation was $r = 0.89$, confirming strong scoring consistency between the two evaluators.

To assess participants' higher-order thinking abilities, we adapted a validated instrument from [20]. The scale encompassed 11 items across three domains: problem-solving, critical thinking, and creativity. The Cronbach's alpha coefficients for internal consistency across the three subscales were 0.733 for problem-solving, 0.709 for creativity, and 0.764 for critical thinking, indicating acceptable reliability for research use (Table 1).

Table 1. Descriptive of HOTs and performance

Measurement items	Groups	*M*	*SD*	*t*	*d*
HOTs	Experimental group	30.11	2.04	-4.89^{***}	−1.04
	Control group	22.8	1.81		
hands-on performance	Experimental group	27.1	2.81	-9.22^{***}	−2.02
	Control group	19.2	2.44		

Note. $^{*}p < .05$, $^{**}p < .01$, $^{***}p < .001$

5 Conclusion

In this study, we investigated the effectiveness of feedback mechanisms in a VR learning environment designed for electronic circuits and programming, with a particular focus on enhancing learners' higher-order thinking skills and hands-on performance. By employing an experimental approach grounded in the Signaling Principle from the Cognitive Theory of Multimedia Learning (CTML), the findings revealed that structured, real-time feedback significantly improved learners' ability to think critically, solve problems, and complete practical tasks effectively. These results highlight the importance of incorporating instructional feedback into VR-based environments—not only to foster deeper cognitive engagement, but also to strengthen learners' practical application of knowledge in complex, real-world scenarios. Despite these promising outcomes, several limitations should be acknowledged. First, the relatively small sample size may restrict the generalizability of the findings. Second, the current study was limited to the domain of electronics and programming; additional research is needed to determine whether similar benefits of feedback mechanisms can be observed in other subject areas. Third, the study primarily assessed short-term learning outcomes, and future research should examine the long-term impact of VR-based feedback on sustained higher-order thinking and practical competence. Looking ahead, future studies should aim to expand the participant pool and extend the research scope to include diverse academic disciplines and longer learning durations. Moreover, with the rapid evolution of educational technology, Generative AI (GAI) tools such as GPT offer new opportunities for adaptive, personalized feedback in immersive environments [21]. Integrating GAI could enable dynamic guidance, automated error correction, and conversational support that responds to learners' unique cognitive and procedural needs in real time. Additionally, future work should explore how individual differences—such as prior knowledge, learning preferences, and cognitive profiles—interact with VR and GAI-supported feedback to create more personalized and effective learning experiences. Overall, this study underscores the critical role of well-designed feedback in VR learning environments for promoting advanced thinking and practical skills. With continued exploration and technological integration, VR combined with intelligent feedback systems holds great promise for transforming the way learners engage in complex, hands-on learning tasks in the digital age.

References

1. Wang, W.-S., Lee, H.-Y., Lin, C.-J., Li, P.-H., Huang, Y.-M., Wu, T.-T.: Enhancing students' learning outcomes in self-regulated virtual reality learning environment with learning aid mechanisms. Br. J. Edu. Technol. **56**, 366–387 (2025)
2. Wang, W.-S., Cheng, Y.-P., Lee, H.-Y., Lin, C.-J., Huang, Y.-M.: Impact of anxiety and confidence in virtual reality-mediated learning transferred to hands-on tasks. J. Comput. Assist. Learn. **39**, 1368–1381 (2023)
3. Wang, W.-S., Chia-Ju, L., Hsin-Yu, L., Ting-Ting, W., Huang, Y.-M.: Feedback mechanism in immersive virtual reality influences physical hands-on task performance and cognitive load. Int. J. Hum.-Comput. Interact. **40**, 4103–4115 (2024)
4. Wang, W.-S., Margus, P., Chia-Ju, L., Hsin-Yu, L., Yueh-Min, H., Wu, T.-T.: Signaling feedback mechanisms to promoting self-regulated learning and motivation in virtual reality transferred to real-world hands-on tasks. Interact. Learn. Environ. **32**, 7661–7676 (2024)
5. Huang, Y.-M., Wang, W.-S., Lee, H.-Y., Lin, C.-J., Wu, T.-T.: Empowering virtual reality with feedback and reflection in hands-on learning: Effect of learning engagement and higher-order thinking. J. Comput. Assist. Learn. **40**, 1413–1427 (2024)
6. Fiorella, L., Mayer, R.E.: Role of expectations and explanations in learning by teaching. Contemp. Educ. Psychol. **39**, 75–85 (2014)
7. Shute, V.J.: Focus on formative feedback. Rev. Educ. Res. **78**, 153–189 (2008)
8. Lin, C.-J., Wang, W.-S., Lee, H.-Y., Huang, Y.-M., Wu, T.-T.: Recognitions of image and speech to improve learning diagnosis on STEM collaborative activity for precision education. Educ. Inf. Technol. **29**, 13859–13884 (2024)
9. Lin, C.-J., Lee, H.-Y., Wang, W.-S., Huang, Y.-M., Wu, T.-T.: Enhancing reflective thinking in STEM education through experiential learning: the role of generative AI as a learning aid. Educ. Inf. Technol. (2024)
10. Anderson, L.W., Krathwohl, D.R.: A Taxonomy for Learning, Teaching, and Assessing: A Revision of Bloom's Taxonomy of Educational Objectives: Complete Edition. Addison Wesley Longman, Inc. (2001)
11. Zohar, A., Dori, Y.J.: Higher order thinking skills and low-achieving students: are they mutually exclusive? J. Learn. Sci. **12**, 145–181 (2003)
12. Retnawati, H., Djidu, H., Apino, E., Anazifa, R.D.: Teachers' knowledge about higher-order thinking skills and its learning strategy. Probl. Educ. 21st Cent. **76**, 215–230 (2018)
13. Huang, B., Hew, K.F., Lo, C.K.: Investigating the effects of gamification-enhanced flipped learning on undergraduate students' behavioral and cognitive engagement. Interact. Learn. Environ. **27**, 1106–1126 (2019)
14. Poupard, M., Larrue, F., Sauzéon, H., Tricot, A.: A systematic review of immersive technologies for education: effects of cognitive load and curiosity state on learning performance. Br. J. Educ. Technol. **56**, 5–41 (2025)
15. Mayer, R.E.: The Cambridge Handbook of Multimedia Learning. Cambridge University Press (2005)
16. Mayer, R.E., Fiorella, L.: 12 principles for reducing extraneous processing in multimedia learning: coherence, signaling, redundancy, spatial contiguity, and temporal contiguity principles. In: The Cambridge Handbook of Multimedia Learning, vol. 279, pp. 279–315. Cambridge University Press, New York (2014)
17. Parong, J., Mayer, R.E.: Learning science in immersive virtual reality. J. Educ. Psychol. **110**, 785 (2018)
18. Makransky, G., Mayer, R.E.: Benefits of taking a virtual field trip in immersive virtual reality: evidence for the immersion principle in multimedia learning. Educ. Psychol. Rev. **34**, 1771–1798 (2022)

19. Hwang, G.-J., Lai, C.-L., Liang, J.-C., Chu, H.-C., Tsai, C.-C.: A long-term experiment to investigate the relationships between high school students' perceptions of mobile learning and peer interaction and higher-order thinking tendencies. Educ. Tech. Res. Dev. **66**, 75–93 (2018)
20. Wang, W.-S., Chia-Ju, L., Hsin-Yu, L., Yueh-Min, H., Wu, T.-T.: Integrating feedback mechanisms and ChatGPT for VR-based experiential learning: impacts on reflective thinking and AIoT physical hands-on tasks. Interact. Learn. Environ. 1–18 (2025)
21. Lin, C.-J., Lee, H.-Y., Wang, W.-S., Huang, Y.-M., Wu, T.-T.: Enhancing STEM collaboration through reflective strategies in the 6E learning model: insights from voice recognition analysis. Educ. Inf. Technol. **30**, 4251–4276 (2025)

Author Index

W.-S. Wang et al. (Eds.): ICITL 2025, LNCS 15913, pp. 383–385, 2026.
https://doi.org/10.1007/978-3-031-98185-2

The manufacturer's authorised representative in the EU is Springer Nature Customer Service Centre GmbH, Europaplatz 3, 69115 Heidelberg, Germany. If you have any concerns regarding our products, please contact ProductSafety@springernature.com

Printed and bound by CPI Group (UK) Ltd, Croydon, CR0 4YY
30/09/2026
02225566-0015